PAINTING PEOPLE and PLACES

CAPTURING EVERYDAY LIFE IN OILS

Adebanji Alade

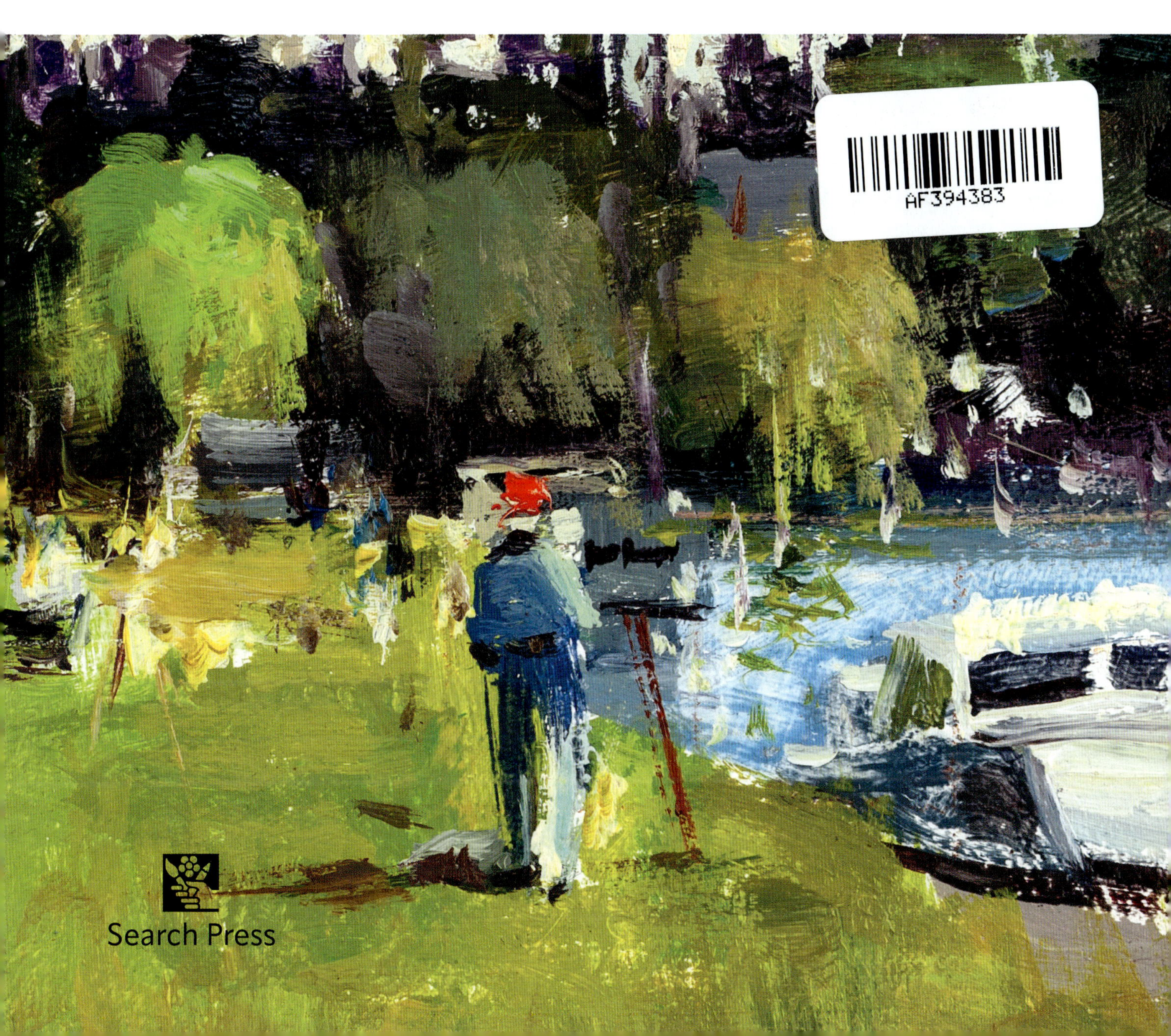

Search Press

First published in 2024

Search Press Limited
Wellwood, North Farm Road,
Tunbridge Wells, Kent TN2 3DR

Text copyright © Adebanji Alade, 2024
Photographs by Mark Davison at Search Press
Studios, except for pages 15, 56–57, 72–73, and
88–89, by Roddy Paine Photographic Studios.

Photographs and design copyright ©
Search Press Ltd. 2024

ISBN: 978-1-80092-032-3
ebook ISBN: 978-1-80093-025-4

The Publishers and author can accept no
responsibility for any consequences arising
from the information, advice or instructions
given in this publication.

Readers are permitted to reproduce any of
the artwork in this book for their personal
use, or for the purpose of selling for charity,
free of charge and without the prior
permission of the Publishers. Any use of
the artwork for commercial purposes is not
permitted without the prior permission of
the Publishers.

Suppliers

For details of suppliers, please visit the
Search Press website: **www.searchpress.com**

For further ideas and inspiration and to join
Bookmarked, our free online community,
please visit: **www.bookmarkedhub.com**

Publisher's note

All the step-by-step photographs in this
book feature the author, Adebanji Alade,
demonstrating painting with oils.
No models have been used.

DEDICATION

This book is dedicated to the Almighty God, who has given me this
wonderful gift to enjoy and explore great possibilities, all at the price of
labour. He has given me good health, good eyesight and a very curious
and creative mind, which keeps me constantly tuned to all the beauty
in the world.

Also I would love to dedicate this book to all the great artists who have
gone before and even those who are living now, whose works make
me hunger and long for another opportunity to walk in their steps or
beside them.

Finally I dedicate this book to my darling wife, Ruth – she is the one
who never stopped believing in me against all odds as I tried to juggle
art and living in the early stages of my career. We all need someone like
her to keep us from giving up when things get tough as they often do at
the very beginning of creative journeys.

ACKNOWLEDGEMENTS

I would like to express my deepest gratitude to Edward Ralph, my
editor. Without him, I don't ever think I would have ventured into
the realm of writing books as he would know from working with me
that I am the most disorganized when it comes to writing or meeting
deadlines, but he has the patience and the magic touch to turn my
chaos into an orderly beauty.

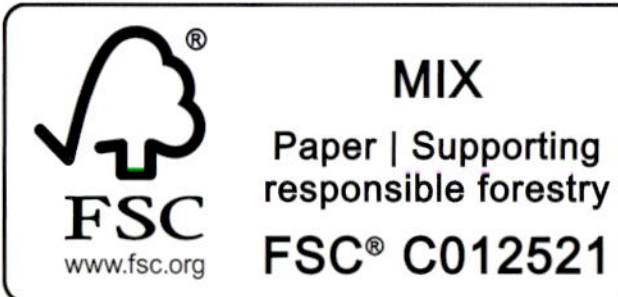

Contents

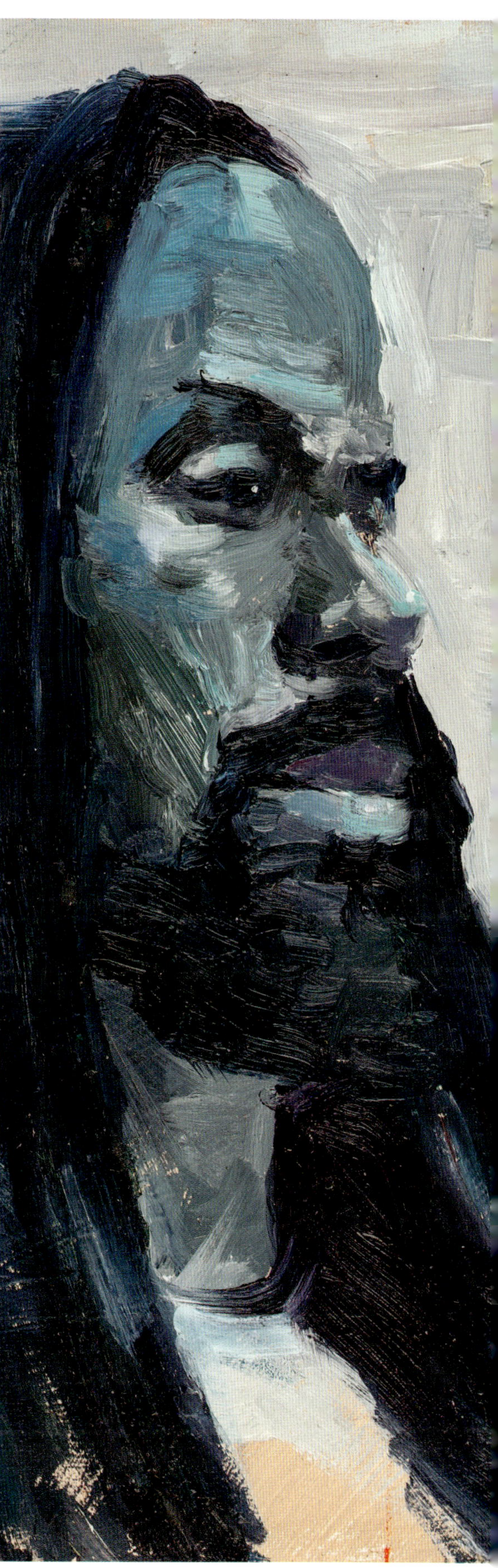

Introduction

WELCOME TO MY WORLD OF PAINTING! My previous books, *The Addictive Sketcher and Addictive: An Artist's Sketchbook,* focused on sketching, only touching on my oil painting. While it's undeniable that sketching every day has made me a better painter, in this book I want to show the fruits of my sketching habit: the techniques, approach and attitude I bring to my oil painting.

I studied Fine Art in Nigeria at Yaba College of Technology, and that's where my eyes were really opened to the possibilities and beauty of oil painting. Later I did a Diploma in Portraiture at Heatherley's School of Fine Art and it was during this course that I truly fell in love with painting people.

After my art studies I jumped into the world of art, craving and munching through any and every art instruction I could lay my hands on – books, magazines and instructional videos. My goal was to improve my ability to paint excellently with oils. I discovered so much on my journey to become better at painting – and what I learned is shared with you in this book.

My aim is to show you how much I love people and places, how I go about painting these subjects in oil, and how you can tap into this knowledge to infuse your paintings with colour, passion, vibrancy and energy!

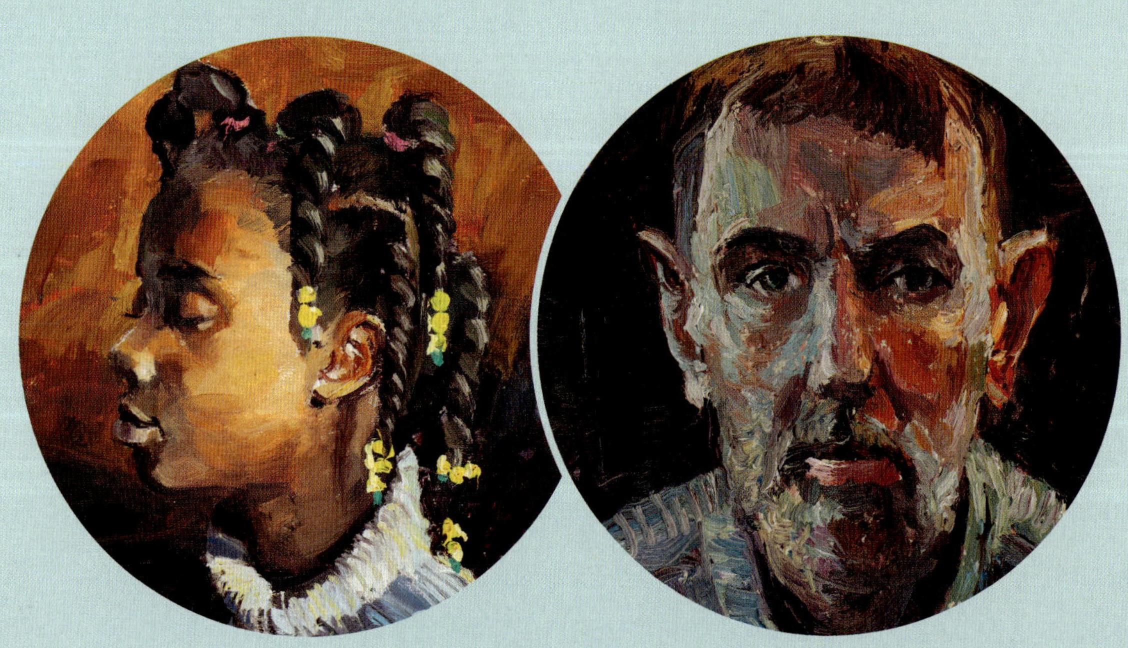

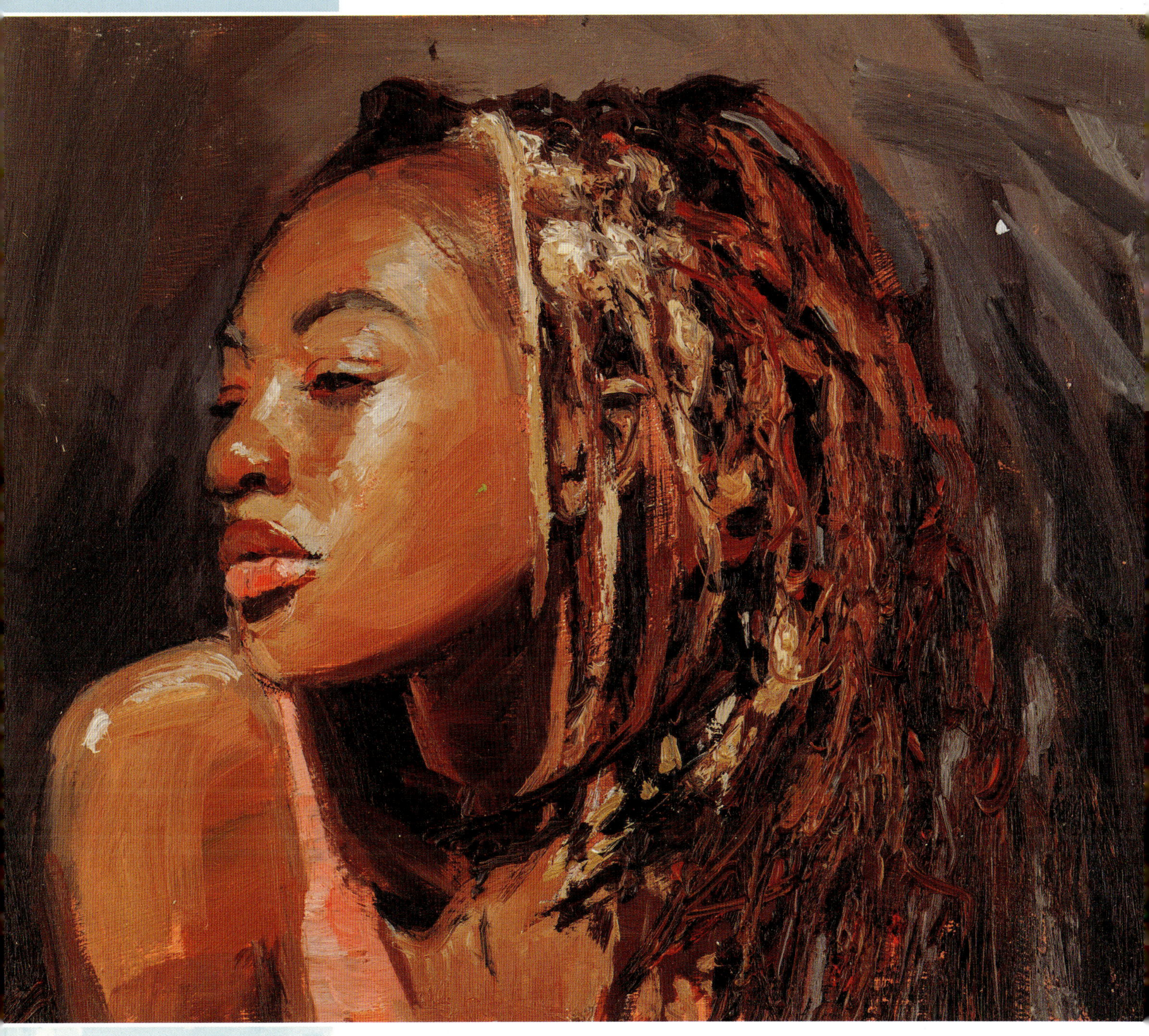

PAINTING PEOPLE and PLACES

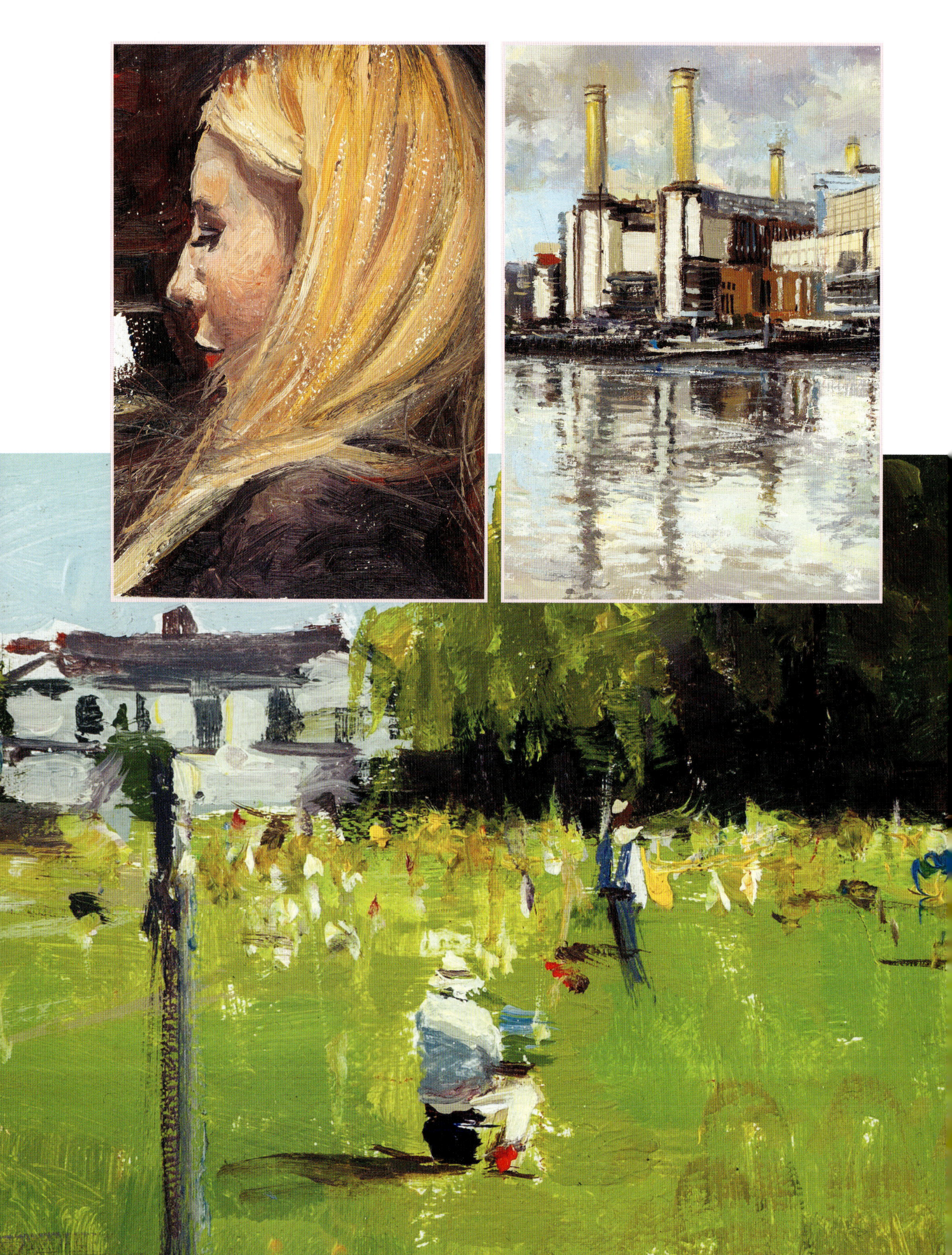

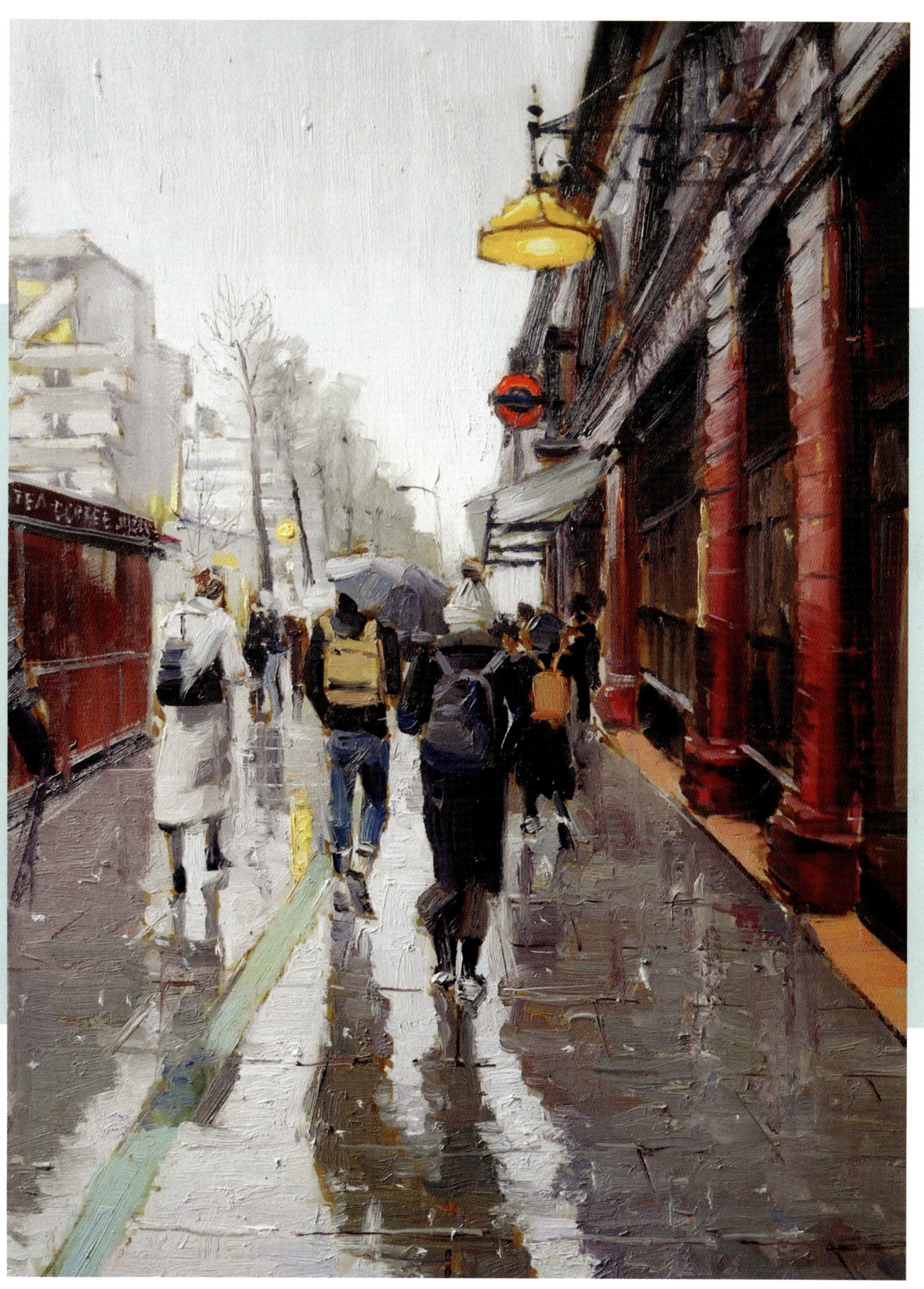

Grey Rainy Day, Russell Square 30 × 40cm (12 × 16in)

On my journey to become better at painting with oil, I developed an interest
in the Royal Institute of Oil Painters (ROI). They exhibit every year at the
Mall Galleries; I started exhibiting with them in 2007 and went on to become
a provisional member in 2009. I later became an associate member in 2013,
then finally I got elected as a full member in 2015 and in 2017, I became
the Vice President of the Institute. Finally, as of 2023, I am serving as the
President of the Royal Institute of Oil Painters.

Being a member of this Institute has exposed me to some of the most
amazing painters using the medium of oil paints, and I have learned so much
from working alongside them and seeing how they approach their paintings.
It has been a joy and a revelation.

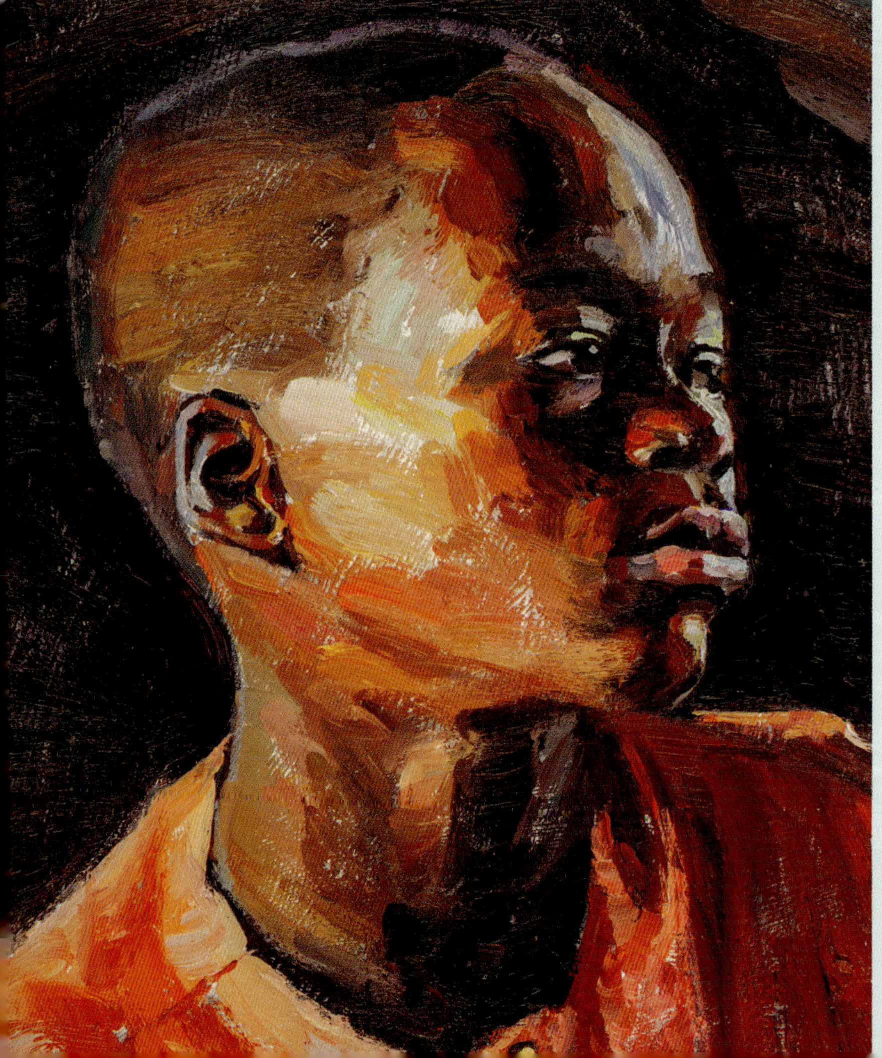

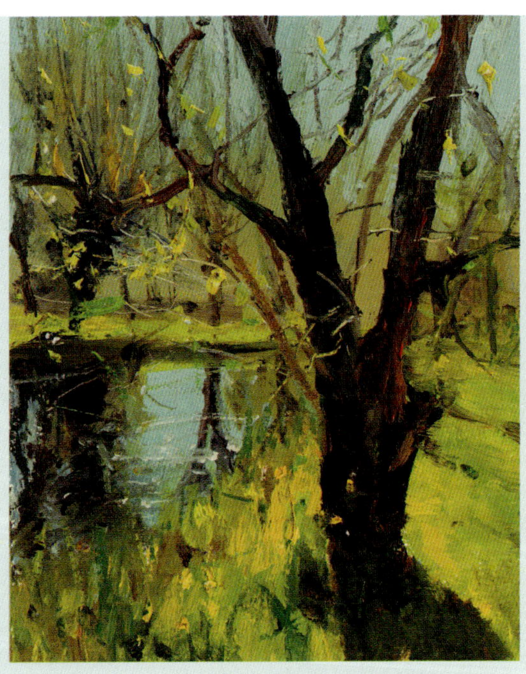

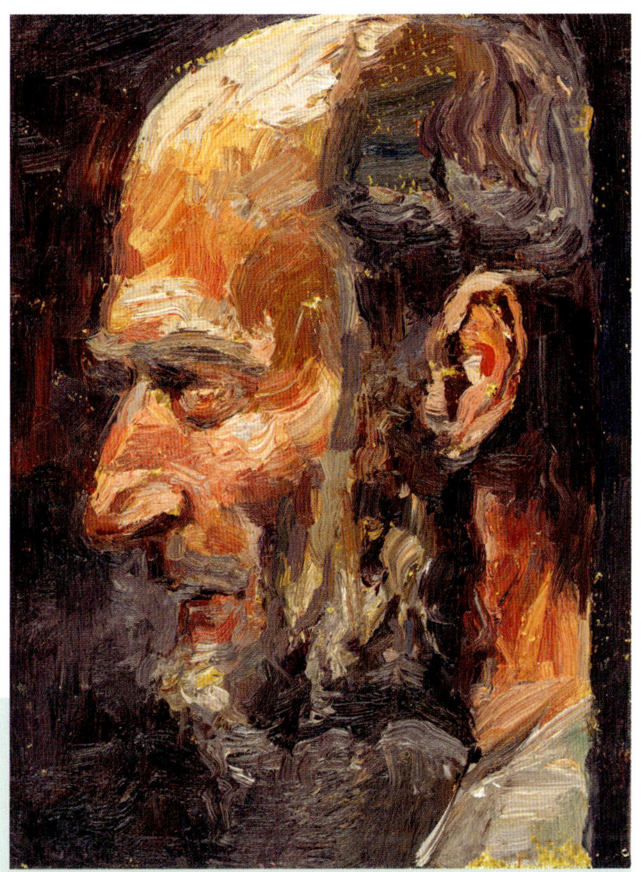

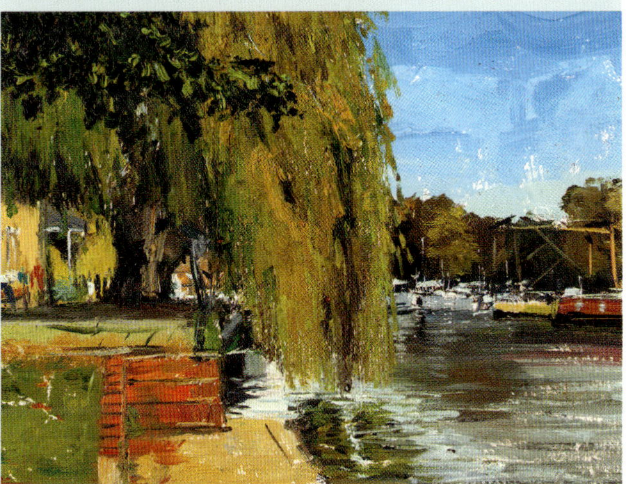

Every artist has a trademark style which has become their signature way of working. You too will have paintings and artists that you adore, and that inspire you to paint. Let this love drive you to improve the way you paint, by allowing their methods and techniques to guide you.

This book will give you an insight into the working methods of an artist who loves oil painting. We'll look at the whole process from the very beginning; you'll discover why I choose my subjects, how I make a start and everything I consider as I go along, from mixing the colours to applying the strokes, to adding the final details to complete each piece.

I don't want you to remain the same after reading this book!

My sincere wish is that you'll be inspired and motivated; that learning my approach will infuse you with something similar, and set a spark to your creative process any time you decide to paint in oil – or even just each time you see a person or place.

I want you to see a subject and say, 'Adebanji interpreted this person or place the way he did – how can I interpret this person or place in my own way?' Consider this my invitation: use my methods as a springboard to let you latch on to your own interests and desires in oils.

Oil paints and supporting materials

Oil paint is an amazing medium. As it is pressed out of the tube, the smell of the paints is so enticing – I simply can't resist working with oils. Very flexible to work with, it's been the favourite for many artists over the years as it can be used both thickly and thinly, allowing for a variety of styles and approaches. I particularly love oils because of their ability to give work texture and structure that's as close as paint can get to relief sculptural qualities.

These pages cover the basic materials you'll need and how to use them. I've tried to simplify it as best I can, and explain why I use these materials in particular.

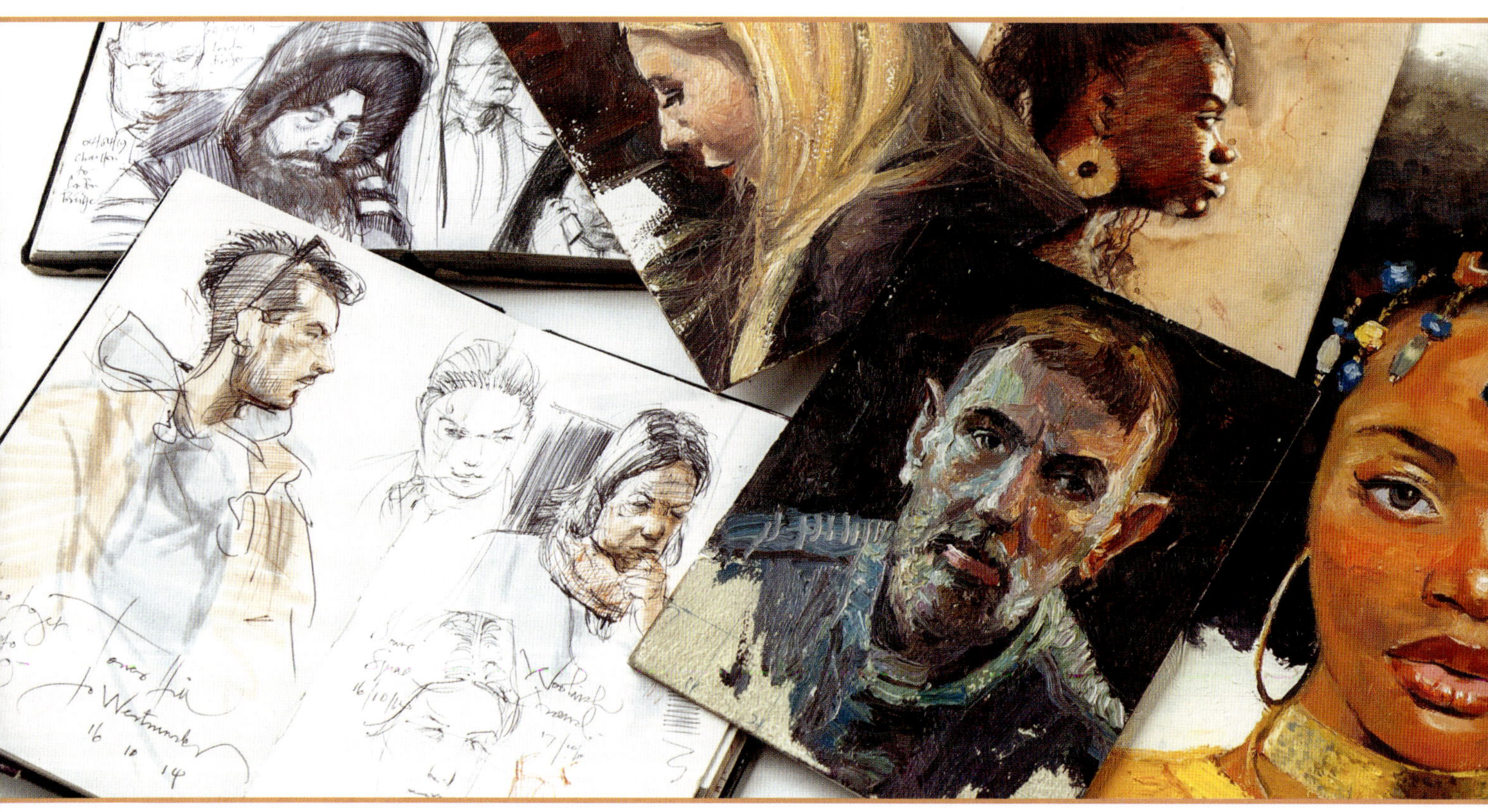

Sketching tools

A sketchbook is priceless. I can't emphasize enough the importance of owning one and using it to explore the world around you. We'll look in more detail later on at how important sketching is to oil painting; for now let's just look at what you need to sketch.

Sketchbooks Any sketchbook that has quality acid-free paper is good. The other thing to look out for is how the paper reacts with the pencils or pens you use. I love sketchbooks from Moleskine, Stillman & Birn and Daler-Rowney – any sketchbook from these brands would do the trick!

Pencils For sketching, I prefer coloured pencils and traditional graphite pencils to any of the more unusual pencils or tools out there. Having said that, when I really need to do some solid preparatory sketching I use a 2B or 3B pencil for the lines, and swap to a chunky graphite stick for tones.

Pens I'm in love with all kinds of pens but my favourite is the humble ballpoint pen for its simplicity and because it makes great clean lines. I combine these with various markers which are perfect for quickly adding tone to sketches. Tombow dual brush pens are worth a special mention – these markers have two tips: one fine and one like a small brush, making them particularly versatile.

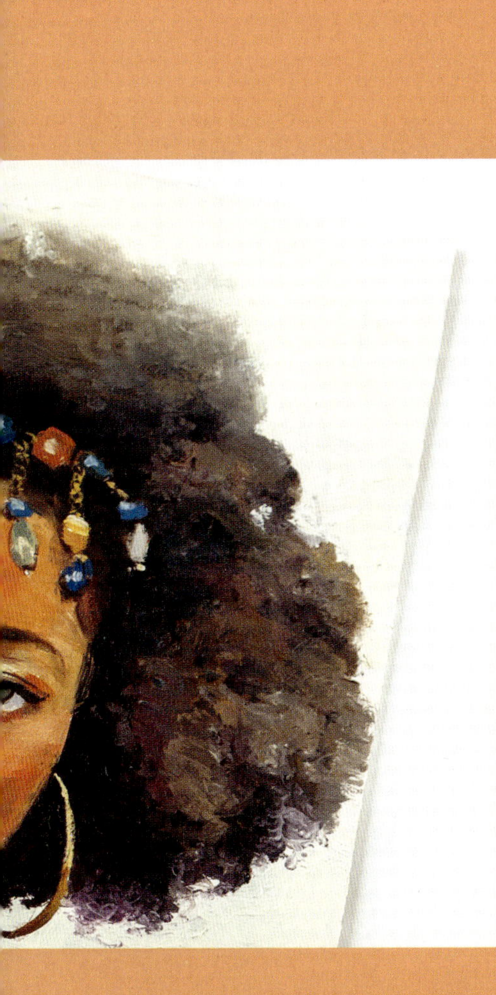

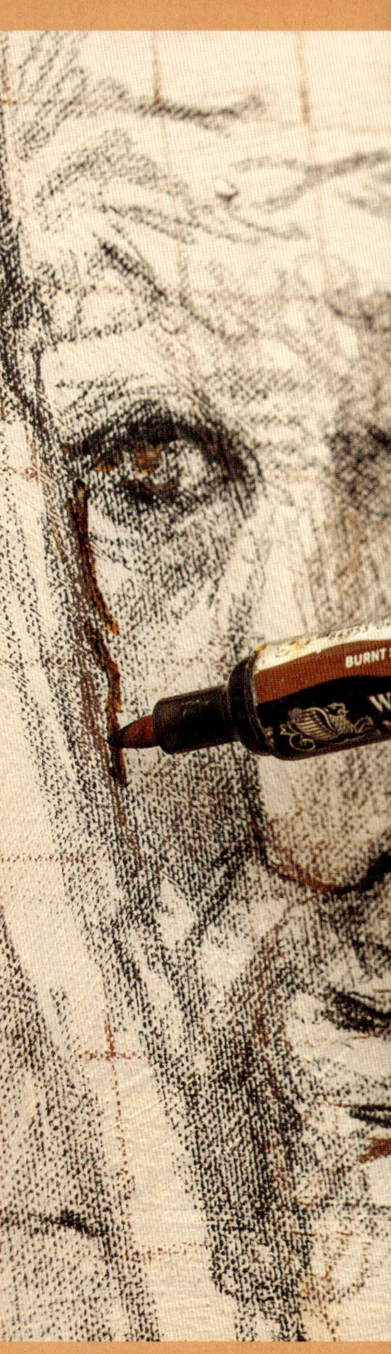

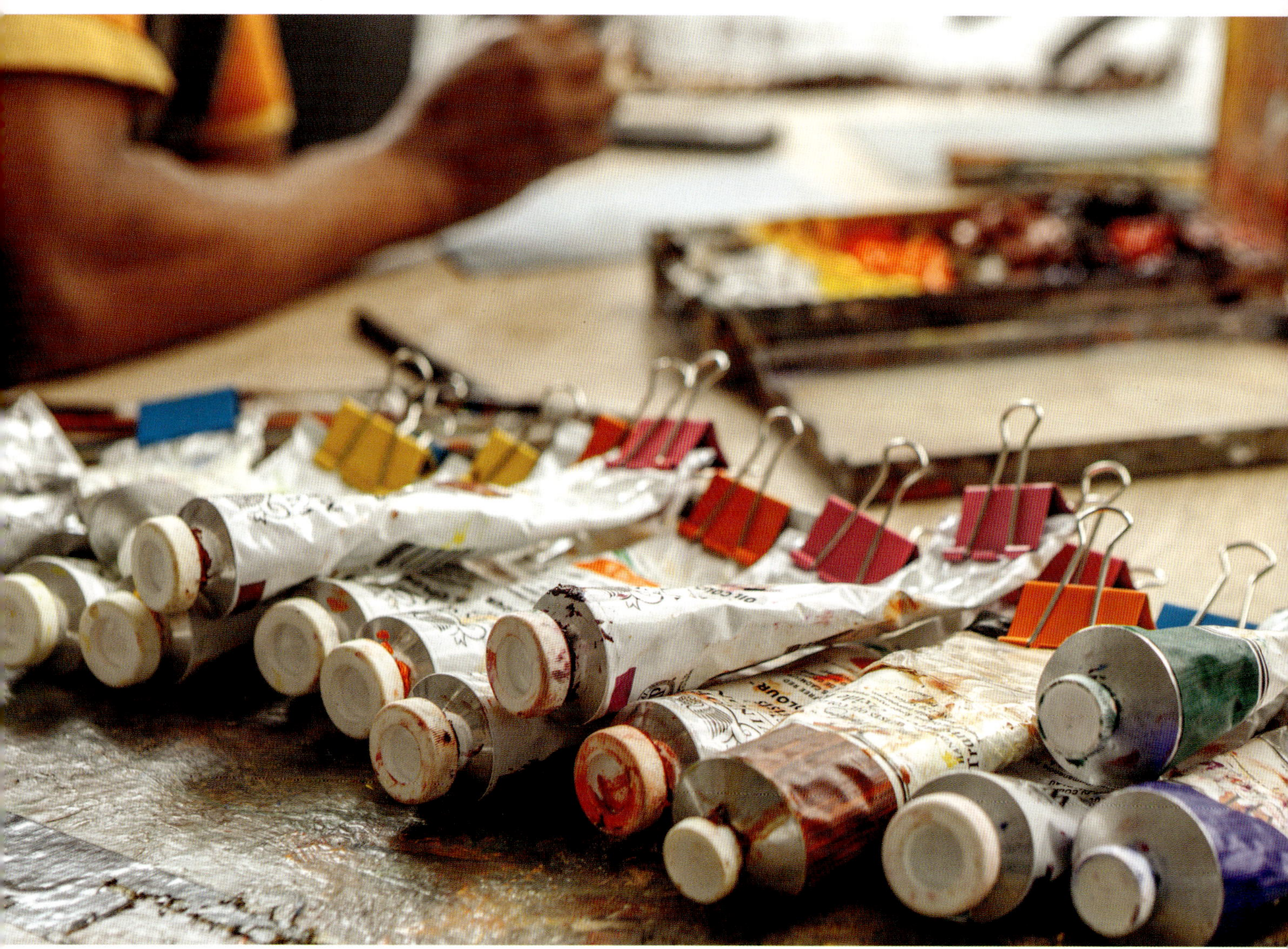

Oil paints

Oil paint is basically powdered pigment that is mixed with linseed oil.
To get the pigment and oil mixed in the tubes, binders are added to
the mixture.

Oil paints are widely available online or from any art store. The brands
I love the best are Michael Harding and Winsor & Newton, and always opt
for the artists' quality range which are of professional quality, rather than
the cheaper students' paints, which have lower-quality pigments and a
greater proportion of binder. I use plenty of colour when I paint, so I buy
the big tubes.

When you're using artists' quality oil and
you're using it undiluted, it'll give you the best
high-chroma results.

Brushes

Shapes Brushes are available in different shapes. The square-ended ones, known as flats, make the brushstroke too descriptively rigid for my taste – I like a little bit of flexibility with the strokes. The brushes I favour are filberts, which are similar to flats but with slightly rounded corners. This means that they can easily produce both soft and hard marks, and also razor-like marks when you use the tip, or blade, of the brush. I also love sable rounds for details and more refined passages in the work. I occasionally use other shapes, too, such as fan or egbert brushes.

Hair type Contrary to the advice in most conventional books on oil painting, I prefer brushes with softer synthetic hairs to stiff bristles, because I like the paint to be scooped with a delicate touch. Bristles are a bit too stiff and don't pick up the colours in a way that allows the brushstroke to simply sit on the surface.

Hair length Brush hairs also come in different lengths: I choose long-haired filberts, as the short ones are too stiff for the very flexible manner in which I like to work. I love the tip of the brush to hardly touch the surface or scratch it – that's for the paint itself to do.

Rosemary & Co. and Pro Arte are the brands that I favour, as they have brushes that meet the qualities I've mentioned above.

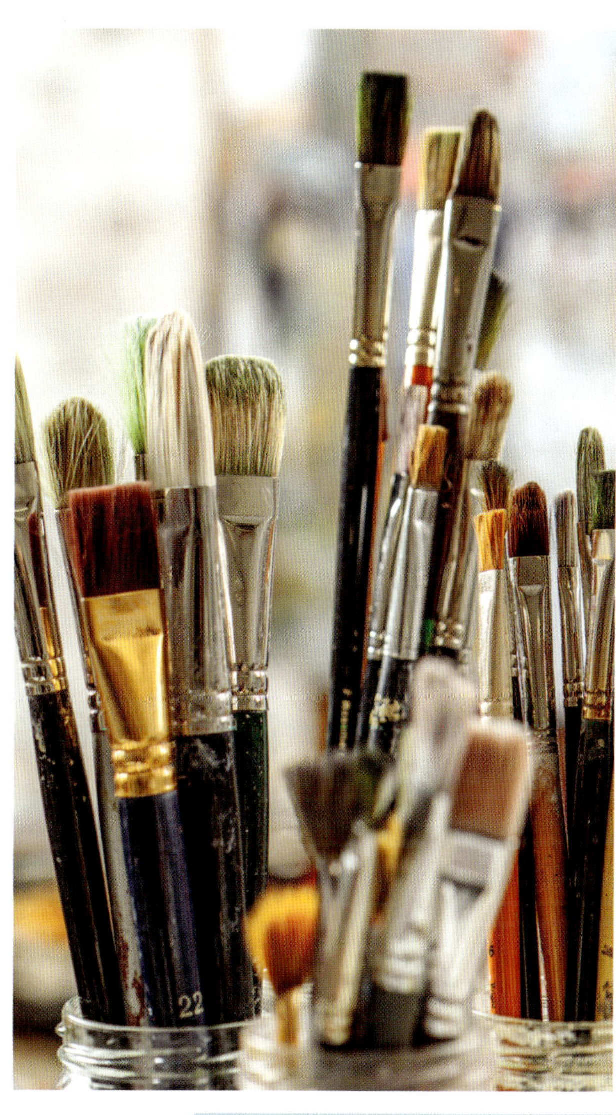

Thinning out the brush

Brushes rarely come just the way I want them, and so I often use a knife to cut into the hair and thin it down a little, as shown.

This makes stiffer hog bristle brushes much more flexible, which means the brush is more responsive when placing paint.

Just be careful not to trim too much away!

Solvents and mediums

These are the liquids that aid the use of oil paint. Being fat-based, oils can't be thinned with water. Instead the thinners, or solvents, help to dilute the paint and clean them, while the mediums I use help the paint to flow with a richer feel and more body.

Generally speaking, I prefer to use the colours directly from the tube without thinning or adding medium – but they're very useful to have to hand for particular purposes.

Thinner or solvent This is what you'll need to wash your brushes or thin your paint if you are painting lean (see page 27) at the beginning of a painting. Some artists also use it to create a very thin neutral base colour to cover the surface before they start to paint.

I use Bob Ross Odourless Thinner for washing my brushes and to dilute the paint for an oil sketch, but I hardly use it during my main painting technique.

Medium There are lots of different mediums available that affect the qualities of the paint – speeding up or slowing down drying time, for example, or making the paint stiffer or looser in consistency. The two I use most are Liquin, a fast-drying medium that helps the paint to flow a bit more freely; and Maroger, which gives the paint a buttery consistency, allowing it to be applied in a juicy, thick manner that suits my impasto style of painting.

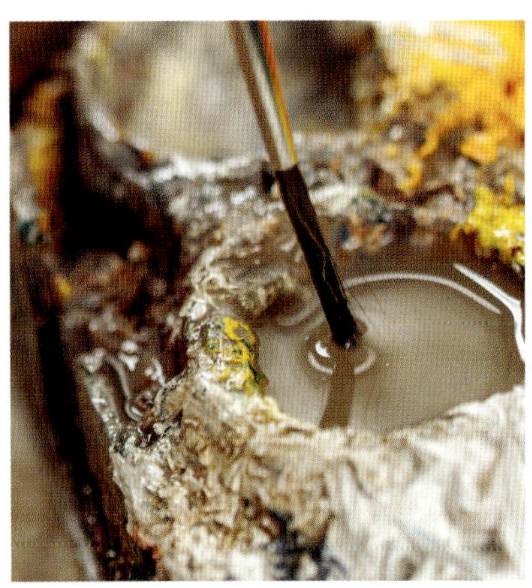

Thinner

Thinners, as the name suggests, make the paint behave more like water. I store it in a little pot that clips to my palette, where it is used to clean my brushes.

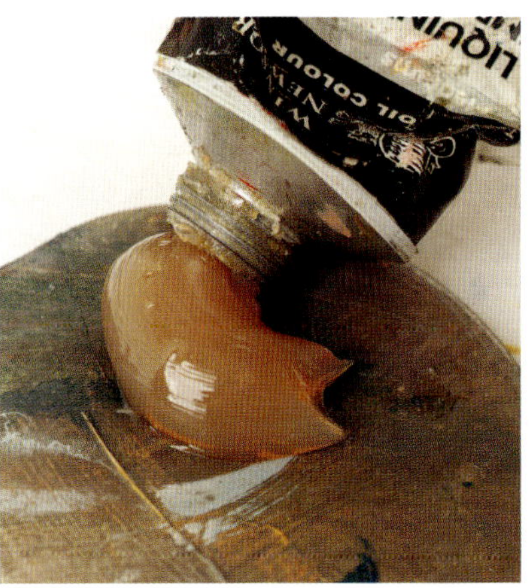

Liquin

I love Liquin – apart from the smell. It is great to use at the start of paintings to help the first few applications to dry more quickly. The pictured tube is Liquin Impasto, which I tend to mix with Maroger.

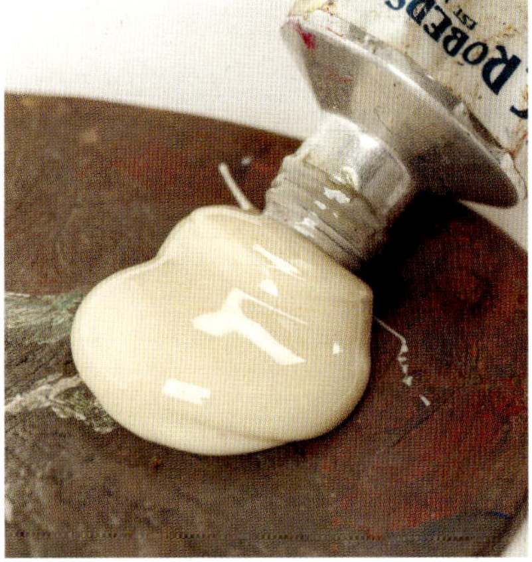

Maroger

I learnt about this medium from reading books by the great American Representational painter David Leffel; he said it was used by the Old Masters. The brand I prefer is made by Robersons.

Surfaces: board and canvas

The surface you paint on is also called a ground or support. When it comes to choosing the right support I usually use canvas or board as I prefer a smooth surface that doesn't have too much texture. This is because I like the paint, rather than the surface, to create the texture and give the work body.

Some artists prefer to prepare their own surfaces before painting. I do that with my boards. I use MDF (medium-density fibreboard) which I prepare with an MDF sealant, after which I prime it as explained on page 22. When it comes to canvases, I prefer to get them made for me or buy ready-made block canvases. I do, however, always prime the ones I buy from the shops with my own coats of gesso – just to be sure.

Other materials

Palette Ready-made palettes are available in art stores or online, but they can be made yourself from any non-absorbent material, if you prefer. The main goal is to have a big or wide enough surface on which you can mix your colours. It's preferable for the palette to be neutral in colour so you can judge your mixes easily.

Rags or kitchen paper You'll always need to clean your brushes after dipping them into paint or after mixing colours.

Containers When you need to clean your brushes more thoroughly than just wiping them on a rag, rinse them in a tin or glass container holding thinners. In between painting sessions, these containers can be emptied and used for storing brushes.

Palette knife Most artists use the palette knife both to mix colours and to apply paint, but as I prefer to use a brush for mixing, I only really use them for the techniques explained on pages 19 and 26. They can also be used for correcting errors by gently scraping the paint from the surface.

Eraser An eraser is useful to have to hand. I use one for taking out highlights in sketches, rather than to rub out mistakes.

Craft knife I use a knife rather than a pencil sharpener to keep my pencil sharp when sketching. This is also used for scratching out (see page 86) or thinning a brush (see page 13).

Retouchable varnish Just a few touches of varnish can help an in-progress painting, which has gone dull or dry, to look fresh again. Varnish can be applied to the painting either in brush-on liquid form, or from a spray can. Personally, I prefer the spray version for ease of use.

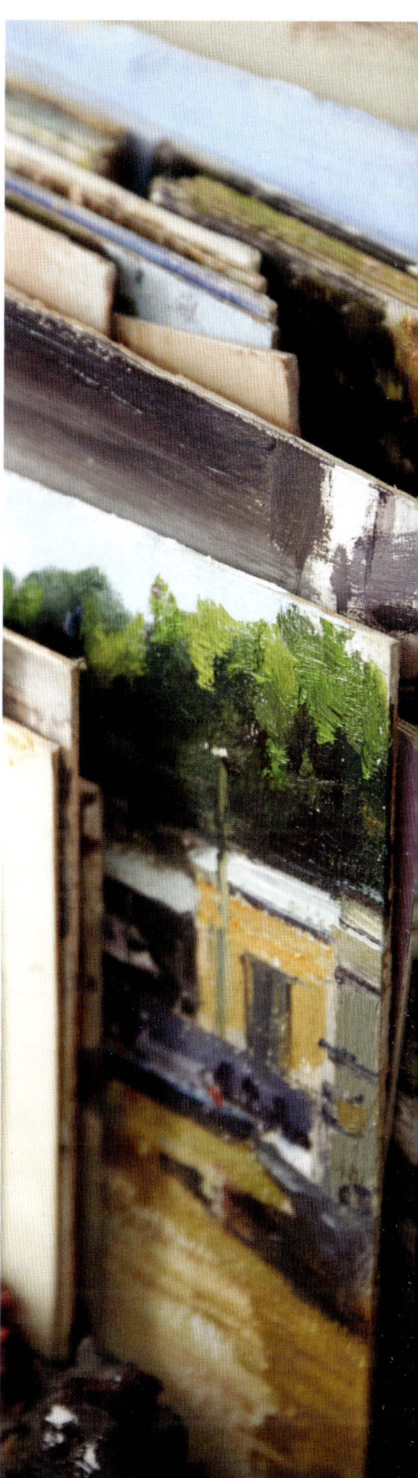

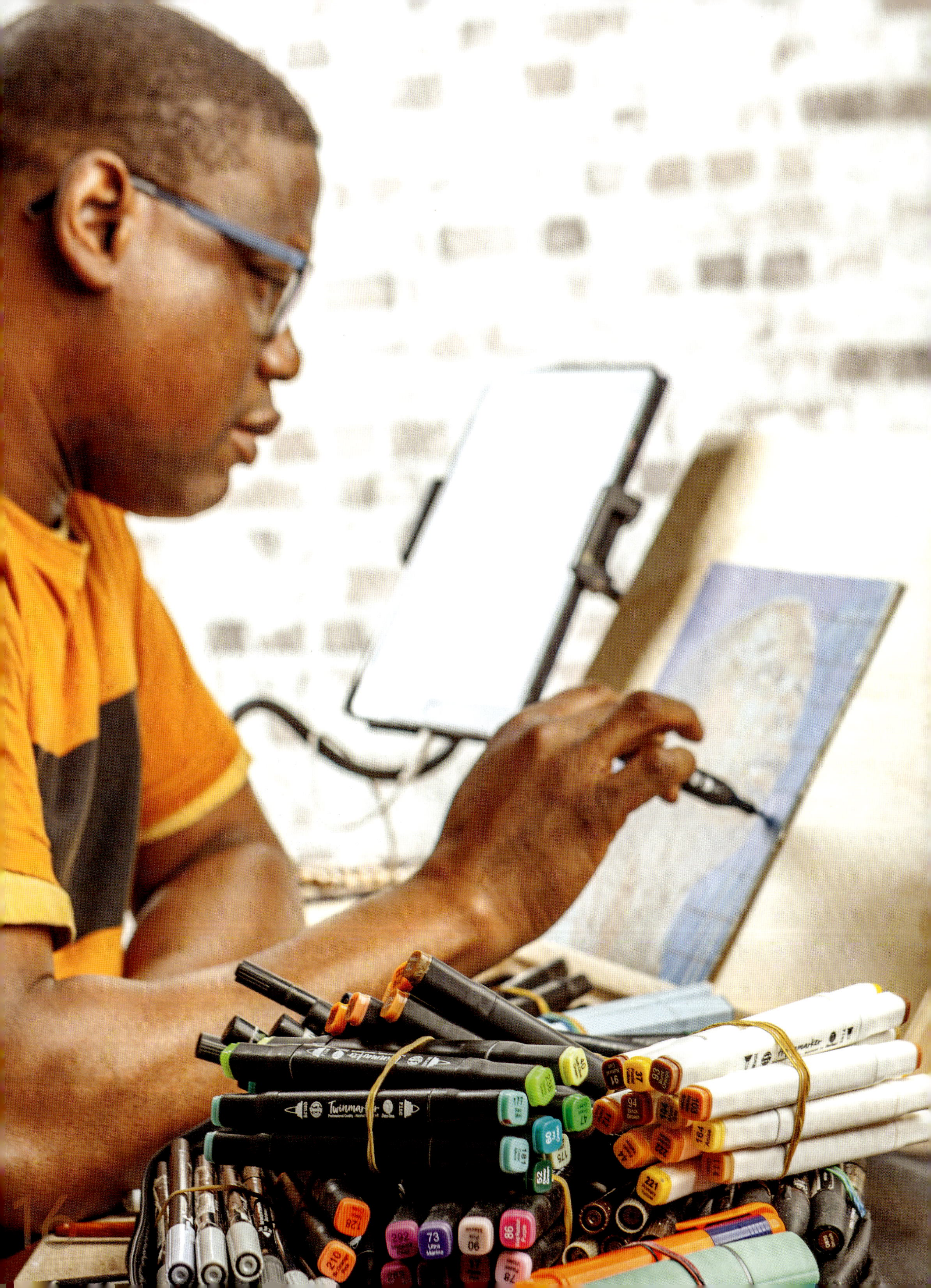

Setting strong foundations

FOR ME, PAINTING IS LIKE SCULPTURE in two dimensions. I want to feel the texture and build up multiple layers – and that means I don't go straight in with oil paints from the start. Instead, I build up with pencils, brush markers and sometimes other media to ensure I have everything just right before I commit to the oils.

As a professional artist, I feel strongly that the ability to sketch effectively will make one's paintings better. Sketching is the foundation upon which you build your painting. If that foundation is faulty – that is, you have a faulty drawing – then no matter how beautiful your painting is, it's not going to look right. Every painting in this book is built on solid drawing or sketching.

Before we start our paintings, there are important things to bear in mind – including where and how to set up, how to get good reference for your painting, and how to prepare your surface. In this chapter I'll also walk you through my different approaches to tackling a painting, and how to stay motivated.

Setting up

Before you start painting, make sure you are comfortable. Here's how I ensure my painting time is successful:

Use a pochade box These are portable boxes that combine an easel with storage space. A pochade box gives you somewhere to prop your board or canvas, mixing space and also a place to store your wet paintings, once done. Having everything in one box makes it easy to set up and start the painting process.

Good light I cannot over-emphasize the importance of light – good, clear light – while you are working. The same amount of light should be falling on your palette and what you are painting. If you can't get pure daylight, very strong daylight bulbs or daylight fluorescent tube lights will give you the best substitute.

Seated or standing? I'm a bit of a lazy one when it comes to the painting exercise. Creative work is hard enough. I don't want to add to it by straining myself – I want to be comfortable to paint for as long as I can, so most of the time, I prefer to sit.

Space for reference You need to have enough space for your tablet or photograph, as this must be easy to view and in alignment with your working hand.

Space for palette This is vital. As you work, you need enough room to create new fresh-looking mixes without them interfering with your initial colour mixtures. As noted above, the palette itself should be positioned where it receives sufficient light, so you can clearly judge your mixtures.

Lay out your colours I always lay out my colours in the same way, so that my brain can operate on 'auto-mode' when it comes to dabbing my brush into the colours. Starting with titanium white, I arrange them from light to dark and from warm to cool. I usually press out fresh colours for each painting, but another advantage of a pochade box is that it minimizes the paint's exposure to the air. Keeping it closed and in the fridge between painting sessions will help to keep the oils fresh and usable.

Separate mediums Keep your thinners, Maroger and any other additives separate from your paint, but nearby.

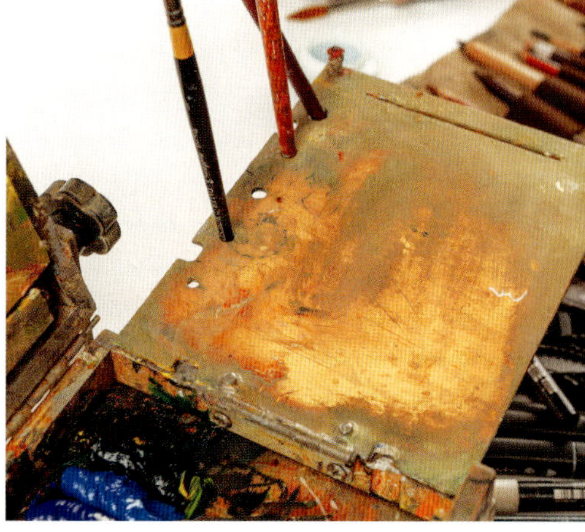

Mixing space

You should always have sufficient space on your palette to mix your colours. If you continue to mix when there's no space for fresh mixtures, your painting will quickly start to look like mud.

Once the space becomes full and there are no fresh areas to mix pure colours, scrape off the remaining paint and clean the palette. I do this with a palette knife, thinner and then finally with antibacterial wet wipes.

Some artists use tear-off disposable palettes – a good alternative approach to maintaining a clean surface for your mixing.

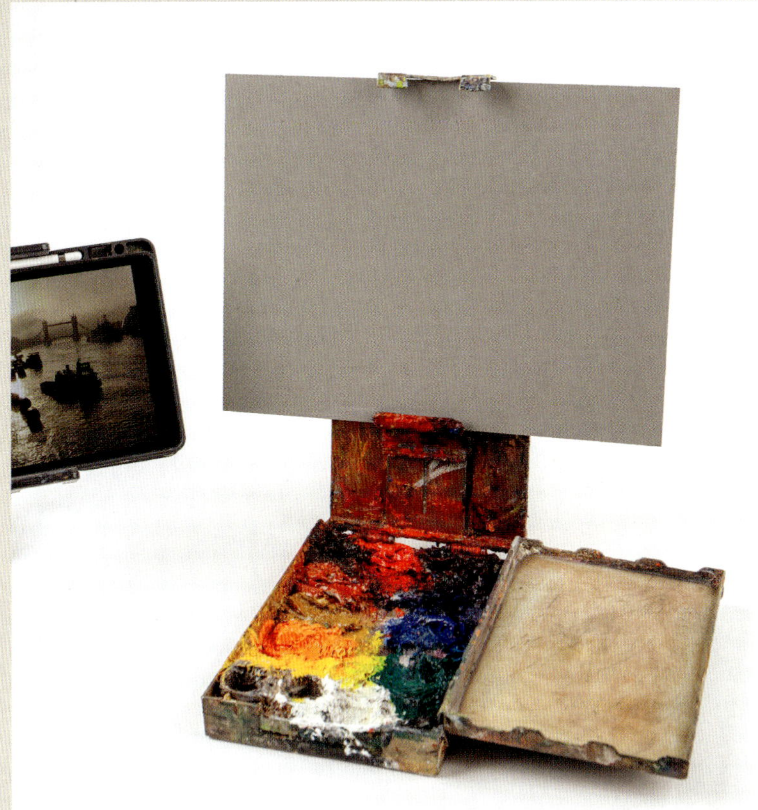

My set-up

The canvas board is primed and ready, secured in the pochade box. The paints, thinner and Maroger are laid out (the latter two in separate pots to keep them clean and accessible); a clean space is ready for mixing; and my reference – in this case on a tablet computer – is as close as possible to the canvas.

This pochade box is a Strada Mini. Designed by Bryan Mark Taylor, it's lightweight, sturdy and compact – which is why it suits me for both indoors and outdoors work.

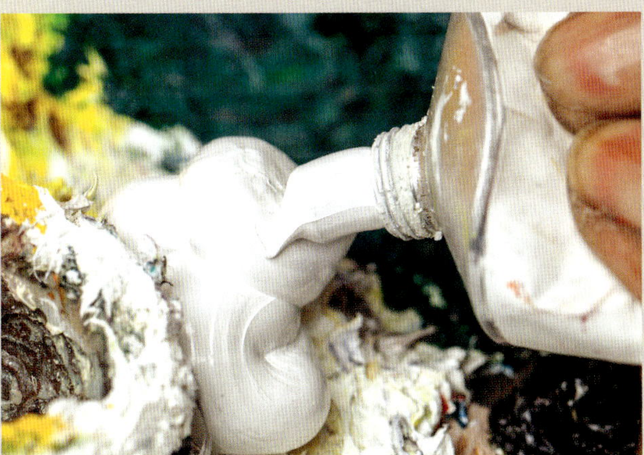

How much paint to use

When you're laying out all your paints, be generous with yourself. Put out more than you need. It's not blood. It's not gold. It's just paint. Put out enough that you don't need to keep putting more out. Don't be stingy, or you'll spoil your enjoyment of the process.

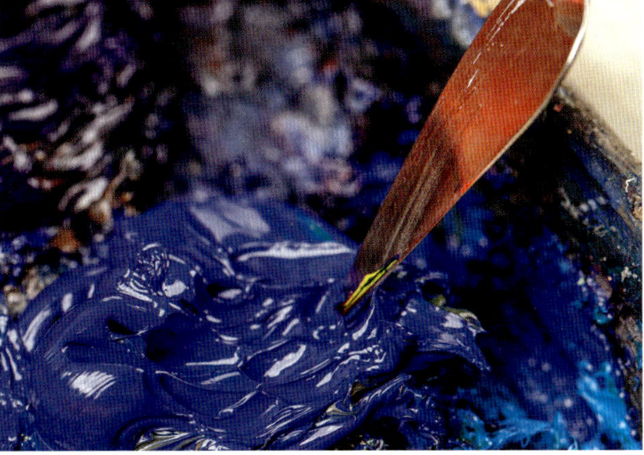

'Weeding' after a session

At the end of a session, spend some time using a palette knife to weed out any stray bits of paint that have got into other colours. This will keep your paints – and your paintings – clean and fresh.

Composition

Once I have an idea of what I want to paint, the next thing on my mind is how to portray that scene or subject, so that I can say what I want to say in the most interesting and effective way. At root, this is all composition is.

When painting from photographs, most of the composition is done when I am taking the shots – and I will take hundreds of photographs in search of the perfect one. I love using 'pleasant accidentals' – photographs that don't have to be altered at all because it says everything I want in the most effective way! I rely partly on instinct to recognize these perfect shots, but it mostly comes down to having a clear idea of what the painting is going to be about.

When arranging or deciding what will work, make sure that you have a main actor and supporting actors. In more formal terms, the main actor is the centre of interest – what the painting is really about – while the supporting actors are every other thing that helps that centre of interest to be a delight to behold, not simply existing in isolation. The main actor could be a certain colour, shape, object, person, segment of the surface or even a bit of light or shadow. It could be anything, but it must have other things around it to keep the picture in balance.

Getting good reference

This all starts from making sure you choose a scene that really depicts what you are trying to say. After that, ensure all the things you include in the painting work in supporting the main thing you want to say.

It's always good to take your own pictures where possible, because it means you have started the thought process of what you want to show even before you start painting. When you get into this habit and you are walking along a path, in the forest, at the market, in the pub – wherever you are – you will start seeing possibilities for painting ideas in everything around you. You'll keep composing with your eyes and mind even before you choose which picture will serve you the best.

Shown here are some thumbnails of the same scene, along with notes on I why I settled for the one I painted. Here, the main actor is the effect of reflections on wet London pavements.

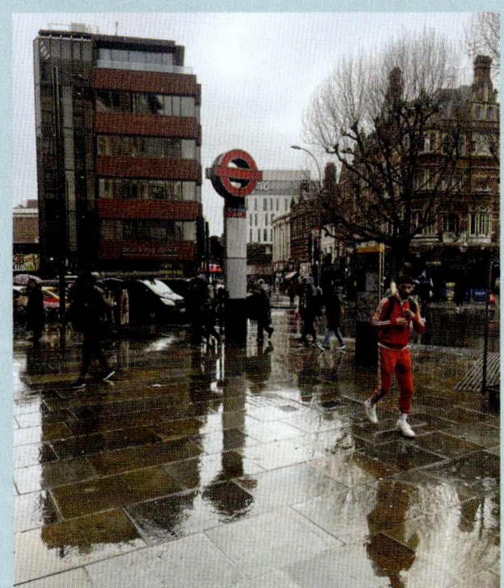

Even though the reflections on this rainy day were great, I didn't like the position of the figure in red (a supporting actor) as he was leading viewers out of the painting.

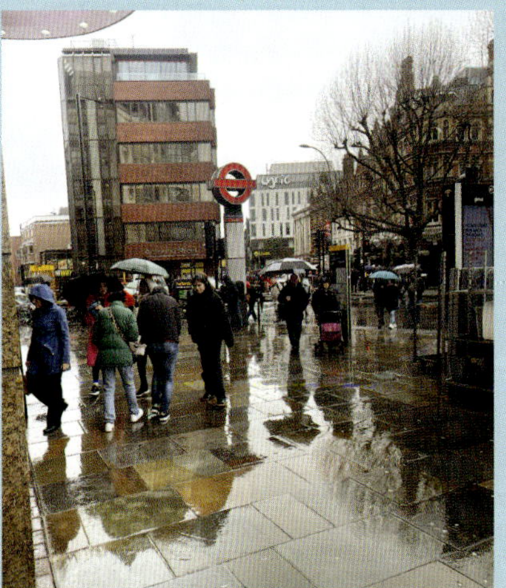

I didn't choose this shot because the supporting actors all drew near-equal attention. I wanted a stronger effect for my supporting actor.

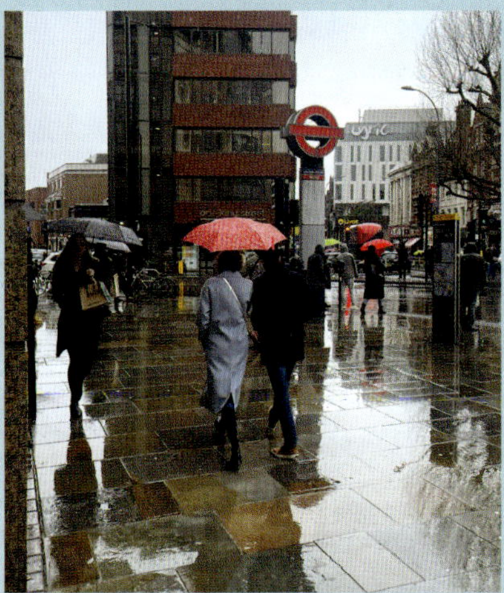

This was the best choice. The various figures act as good supporting actors, and all the elements combine to bring about a successful composition, in which the reflections are key.

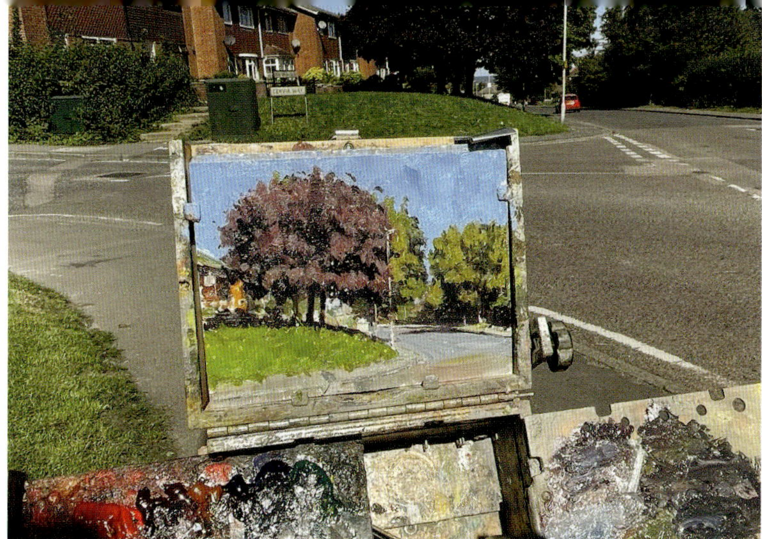

Reference: to compose from life or from photographs?

Some people think that because the style of a painting is loose, it means it was painted quickly and from life – but that's seldom the case. I've seen painters who painted the loosest pictures from screens and photographs, and I've seen painters who painted in a very detailed way from life.

What is most important is to develop a brush-writing language, or manner, of painting that remains the same whether you paint from a still reference or from life. This will only come through mileage: you must paint loads to improve loads. This way you will be flexible and able to adapt to all kinds of situations and scenarios that life throws at you. Working outside will help your working inside and working inside will help your working outside. Together, the two methods will make you a better artist.

Even though I personally don't need all the detail in the world because I am more of an impressionist, still I believe the more detail you can see, the easier it is to edit the detail into simpler shapes and tiles of colour.

Painting from life This approach forces you to make all your decisions right there on the spot. You must be able to work fast, because the light changes quite quickly and moving things never remain in the same position. It is also the best way to develop a good language of painting (or sketching). Working from life will teach you how to compensate for all the lies that the camera tells – like everything being in sharp focus, or the tendency for shadows to appear much darker, to mention just two.

Painting from photographs Painting from photographs makes the painting experience enjoyable but it is never a substitute for working from life – both of my first two books focus on sketching from life, because I believe it is fundamental. It is worth noting that painting from a digital photograph on a screen is totally different from painting from a print photograph. With the screen you can zoom in and see a little bit more detail. It also makes it easier to add a grid, as explained on page 24.

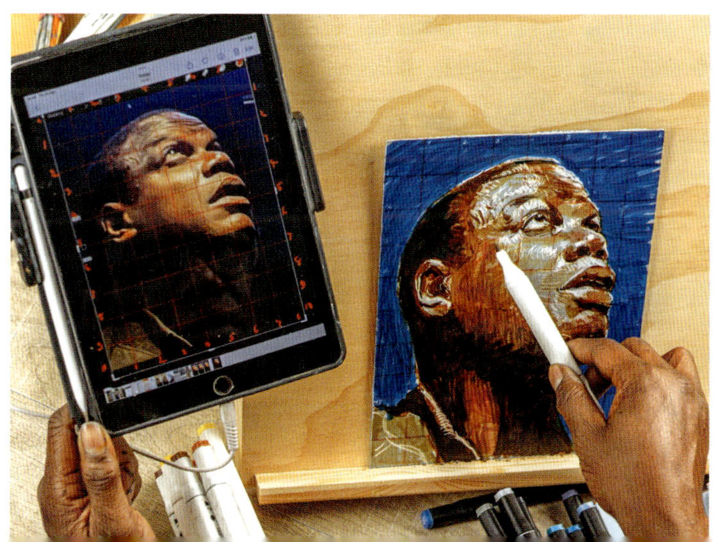

Priming boards

If you paint directly onto a board, the oil will soak into the board surface, meaning the results will be flattened or muted. The colours will also be affected by the underlying colour of the board. To prevent this, we need to prime the board. This was traditionally done with size (a sort of animal-skin glue) and gesso, and that's pretty much what we still do.

Historically, most gessos were slightly absorbent, so when you painted, it still drew a little oil out of the paint. The primer I recommend you use is Michael Harding's Non-Absorbent Acrylic Primer. This (as the name suggests) is non-absorbent, which helps to keep the results fresh because it keeps all the oil in the paint, where it belongs.

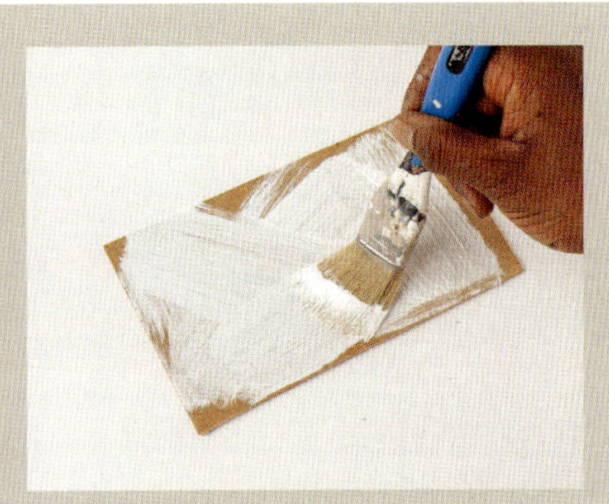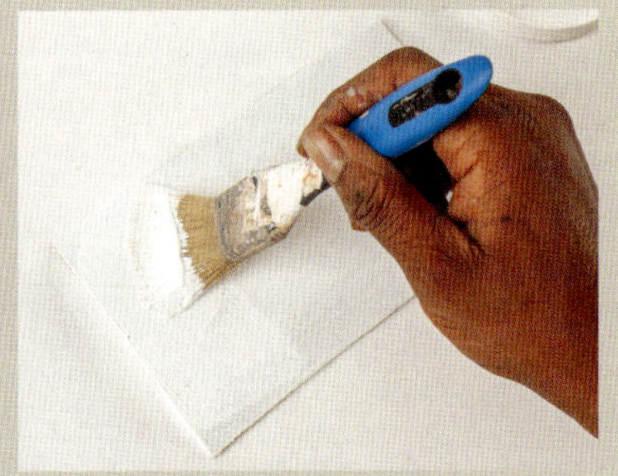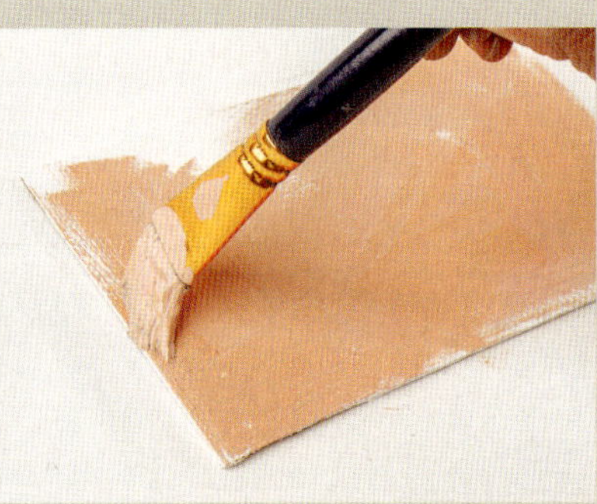

1 Cut the board to size and (optionally) brush on a sealant such as MDF sealer or size. Once dry, use a large household brush to paint on the primer. Cover the surface and allow to dry. You can use a hairdryer to speed up the process.

2 Once touch-dry, repeat the process three or four times until you have a completely clean, bright white surface.

3 You can now paint on the surface, but I usually add an acrylic underpainting. Here I'm using a peachy mix of titanium white, yellow ochre and a little cadmium red.

What colour underpainting?

The underpainting needs to cover the surface in one consistent colour. We use one because occasional gaps appear when painting. If the surface is pure white, they're really obvious and distracting. If you instead have a soft colour underpainting, any gaps will be less obvious.

A neutral grey is a good choice for an underpainting, as it'll blend in with anything on top. However, you can also use a colour that helps the surface colours to sing. By using an underpainting that's a complementary colour to the dominant surface colour, you ensure that any little glimpses of it will make the surface colours appear richer and more vibrant by contrast.

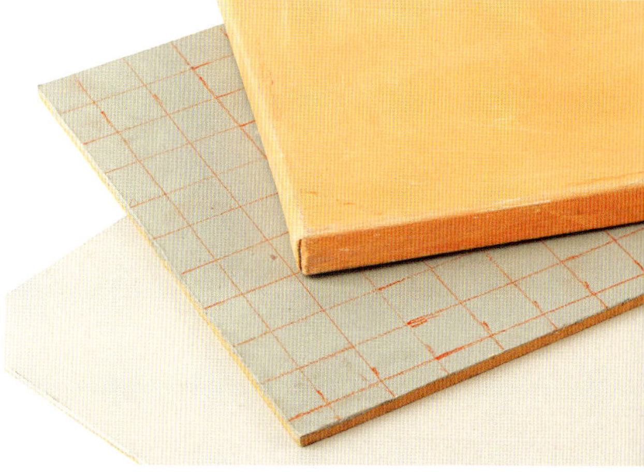

A good grey underpainting mix, as in the lower two boards, is titanium white, ultramarine blue and burnt sienna. I occasionally add a little yellow ochre to the mix for variety, too – as with the box canvas here.

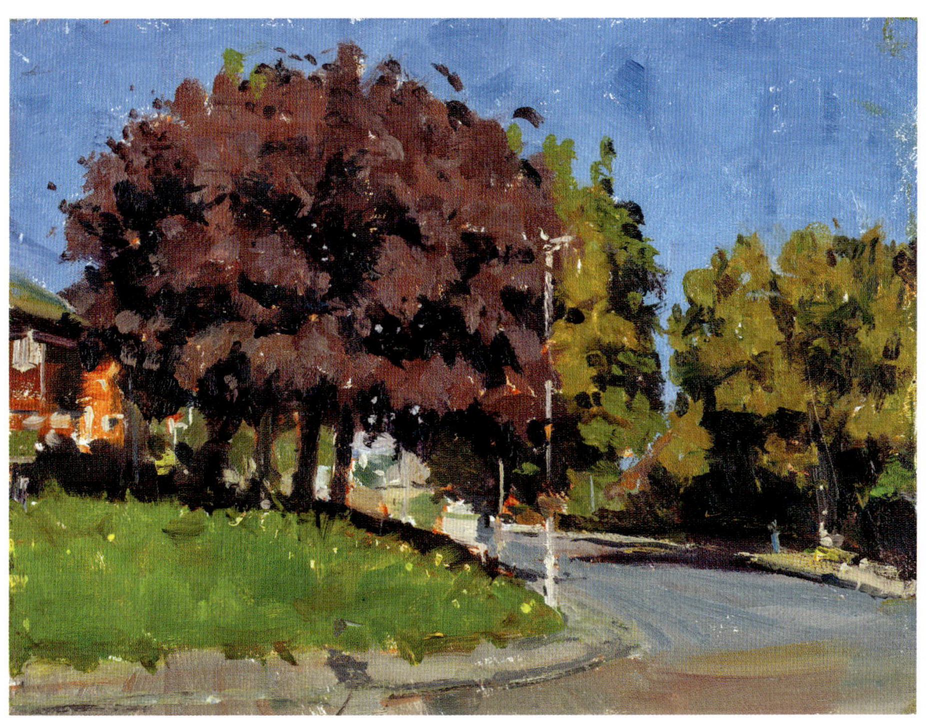

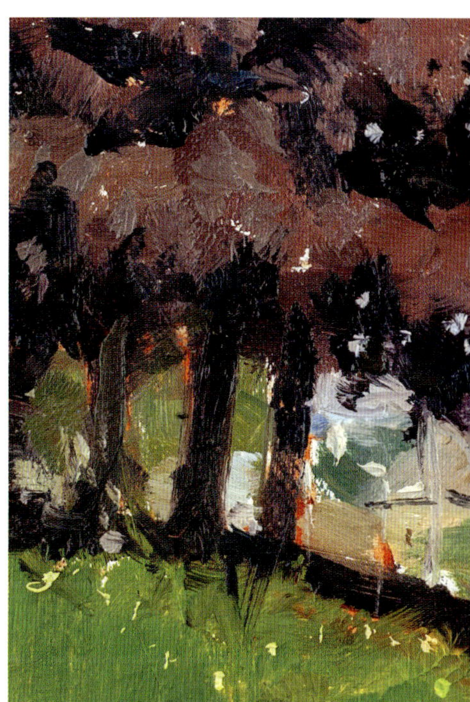

The peachy colour of this underpainting is a warm, red-based colour. It's perfect for green landscapes or urban landscapes where there are lots of trees. The detail to the right shows how areas of underpainting visible in the finished artwork just look like the soft glow of sunlight.

Getting an image onto the surface

I bring my love of sketching into every aspect of my painting – in fact, I don't make any distinction between the two. The work flows naturally from pencil and pen to paint, and each stage is important. With my reference close to hand, I will usually use coloured pencils to get the shapes in place and in proportion, and then switch over to using brush markers.

I don't want to have to consider tone or line once I'm painting: that's when I want to concentrate on colour. The underlying tonal drawing therefore needs to be just right – essentially, it's a textureless painting. If you get this stage right, the painting is enjoyable and the process will flow smoothly.

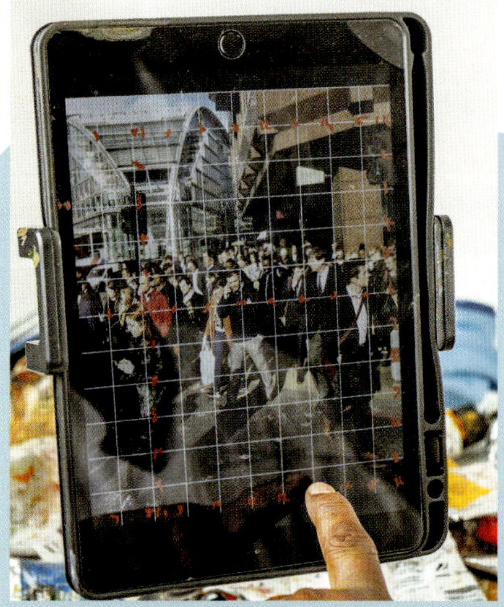

Adding a grid

With a printed photograph, you can draw a grid freehand with a ruler and pencil. If you're working from a screen, there are lots of free apps or websites that will let you add a grid, such as:

https://yomotherboard.com/add-grid-to-image/

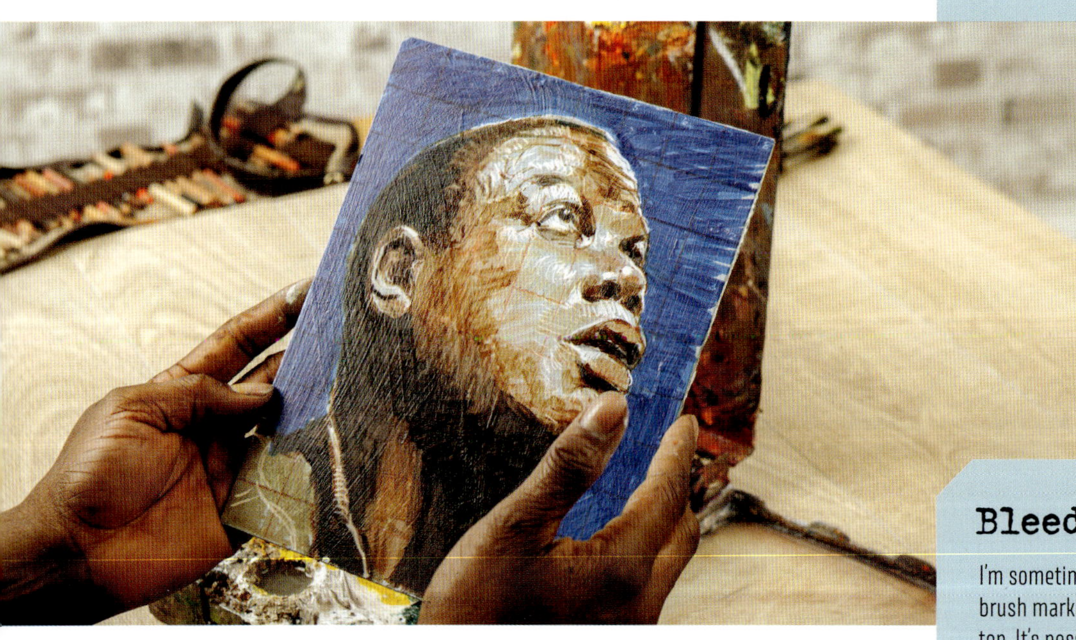

An ideal sketch, made with pencils and pens, is like a complete painting in its own right – all the shapes and values firmly in place. From this solid starting point, the oils can build on top, and you'll find the process rewarding, relaxing and enjoyable.

Bleed-through

I'm sometimes asked if the alcohol-based brush markers will bleed through the oil on top. It's possible they can, if you work with thin layers, but I love rich, thick, luscious impasto-style painting, so I've never found it to happen.

Using a grid

Drawing a grid on both the photograph and the surface will break the image up into small 'tiles'. Each tile can then be numbered and treated like a mini-painting, making the whole image easier to understand and approach. It's important that the proportions of your surface match the photograph, or you'll distort things.

Generally, a 3:4 ratio is what I prefer – though this is simply because the screen on the smartphone that I use is in that proportion. You can easily adjust the grid to use any proportion you want as long as both reference and surface match. Most smartphones will allow images to be quickly and easily cropped to various common ratios. Mine, for example, offers square (1:1), 9:16, 4:5, 5:7, 3:4, 3:5 and 2:3 ratios.

Triangular tiles

Instead of a simple square grid, you can use diagonal, vertical and horizontal lines to break the image into trianglular shapes. I discovered this style of gridding in a sculpture class while at Yaba College of Technology; there we used it to make relief sculpture from pictures, using clay as the base. The process is simple:

1 Start by drawing a line from one corner of the picture to the other.

2 Next, draw a vertical and horizontal line to cut through the diagonals.

3 Repeat this process to the four sections of the surface until you have enough grids to help you portray the image accurately from the picture to the surface you are painting on.

4 Number the horizontal and vertical lines on both the reference and the surface, and you're ready to go.

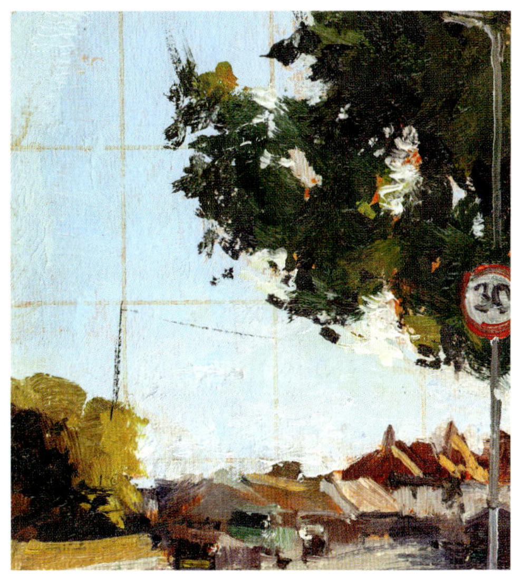

This close-up shows that the underlying grid of squares is still visible in this finished painting.

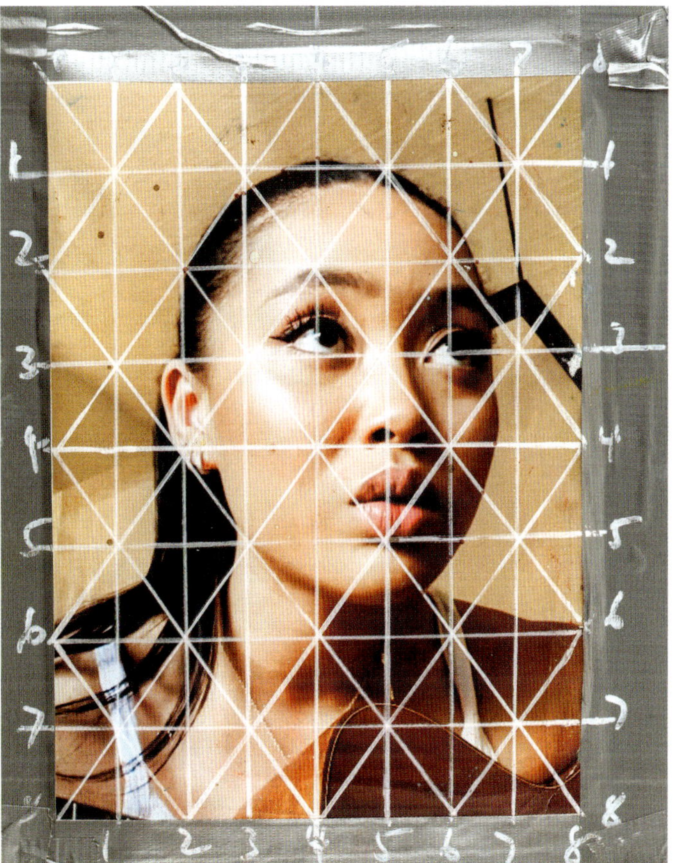

An example of a portrait broken up into triangular tiles, which further divides the squares and makes things easier to work through.

Paints ready for purpose

Pure paint

You can use the paints straight from the tube – you don't have to do anything to them to get nice, rich results. In their fresh state, oils are smooth, buttery and naturally beautiful to use.

Straight from the tube, oil paint it can look too good, too perfect – and this can make you feel like you don't want to use it. Break this psychological barrier by stirring the paint with a palette knife. This also serves the purpose of ensuring the oils, pigments and binders that make up the paint are all well-combined, evenly distributed and ready to paint with.

A palette knife is useful to mix particularly big blobs of colour for very large surfaces, or for mixing paint with a medium, but generally I prefer mixing with the brush – it just feels more natural that way. I see the mixing as part of the painting process and wouldn't want to interfere with that by 'changing gears' with different tools. Using the brush means the processes of mixing and application remain in perfect synchronization.

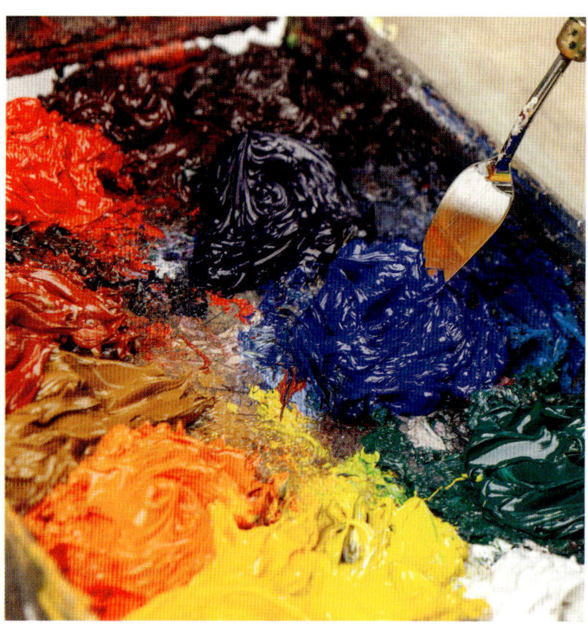

After squeezing out the paint, I whip it up into 'pastries' with the tip of a clean palette knife to get it ready to use.

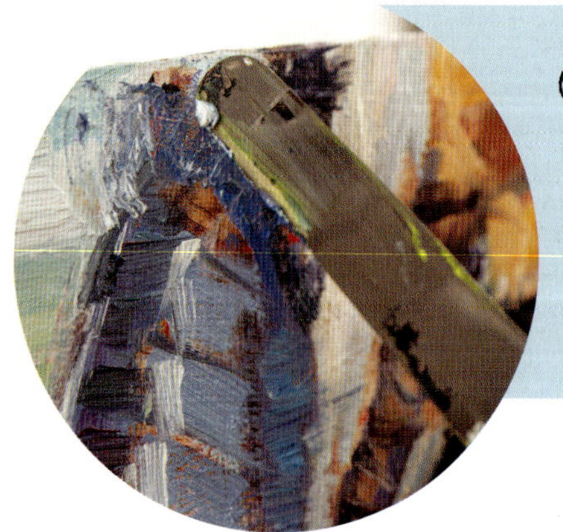

Correcting errors

Oils can be gently scraped off the surface with a palette knife, if you need to fix a mistake.

Adapting the paint for different effects

You may want to adjust how the paint behaves for particular purposes. For this, we need to add mediums. Adding thinner, for example, will make the paint 'lean', increasing the flow but losing the texture.

Impasto style Maroger is a perfect additive if you enjoy textural effects. Squeeze out the Maroger onto the surface of your palette (I tend to keep it to one side), then scoop it up on your palette knife, and combine it with your paint. There's no magic proportion. More Maroger will simply make the paint increasingly thick and sticky.

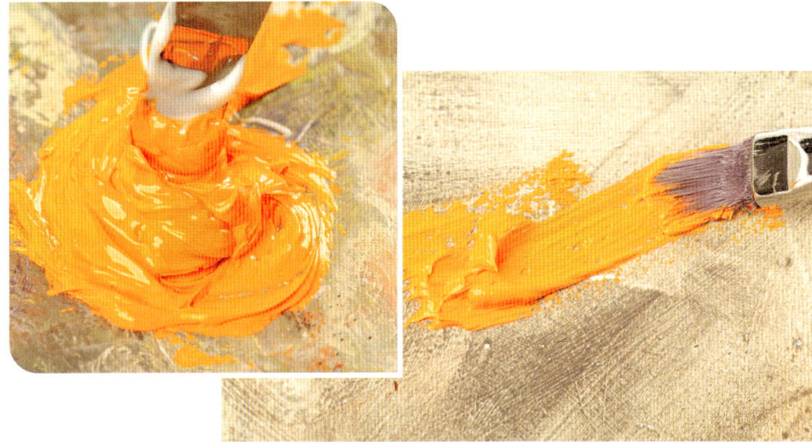

Speeding drying Liquin Impasto speeds the drying time of the paint. It also increases the flow and flexibility – when used directly from the tube, paints can sometimes be too thick to work into large areas for the initial block-in stage. Liquin also helps here, allowing the paint to flow without thinning it.

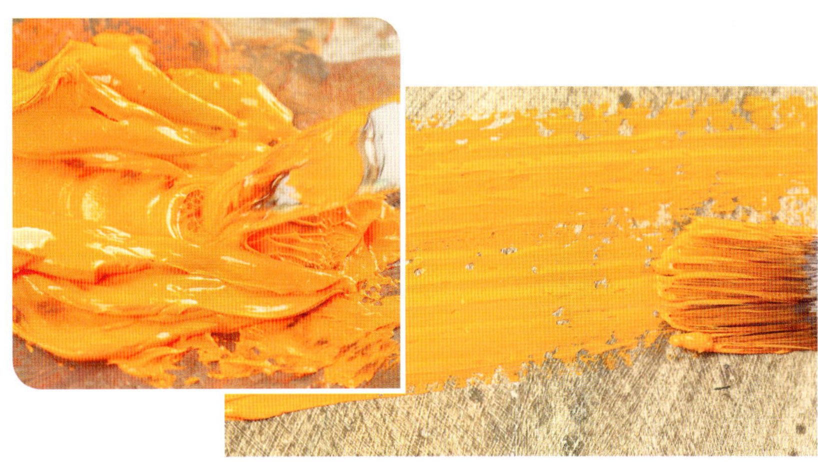

Flow and glazes I rarely thin my paints, preferring heavy texture, but if you want to work with oils in thin glazes like watercolours, then you can add a thinner. You'll need a little pot to hold it. Use the brush to transfer the thinner to your paint, and stir it in with the brush.

This approach is useful if you're painting underpaintings (see page 23), which need to be lean.

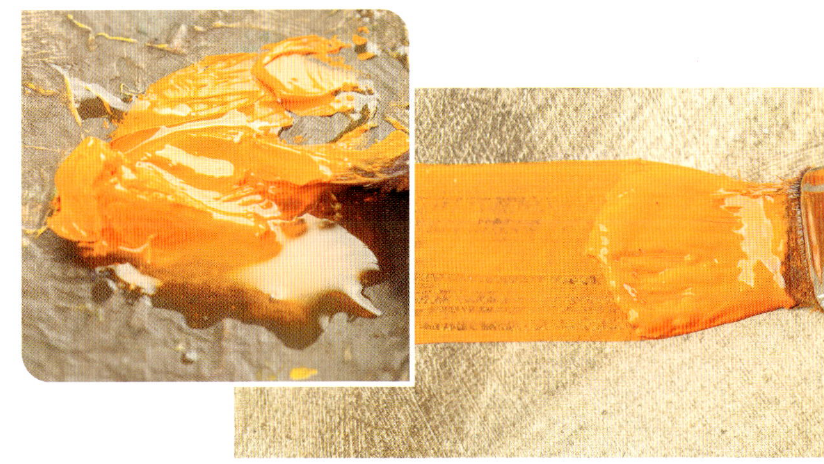

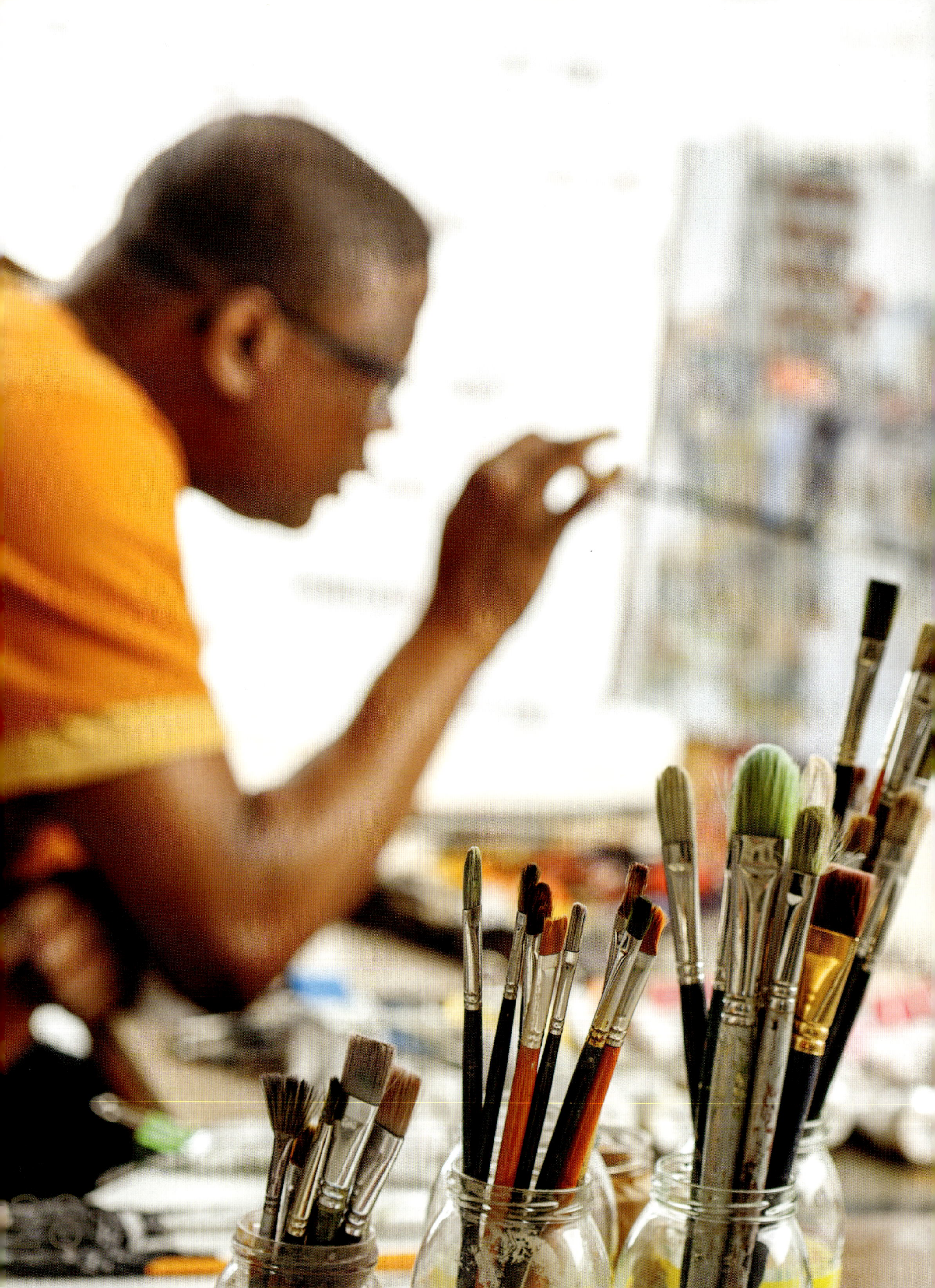

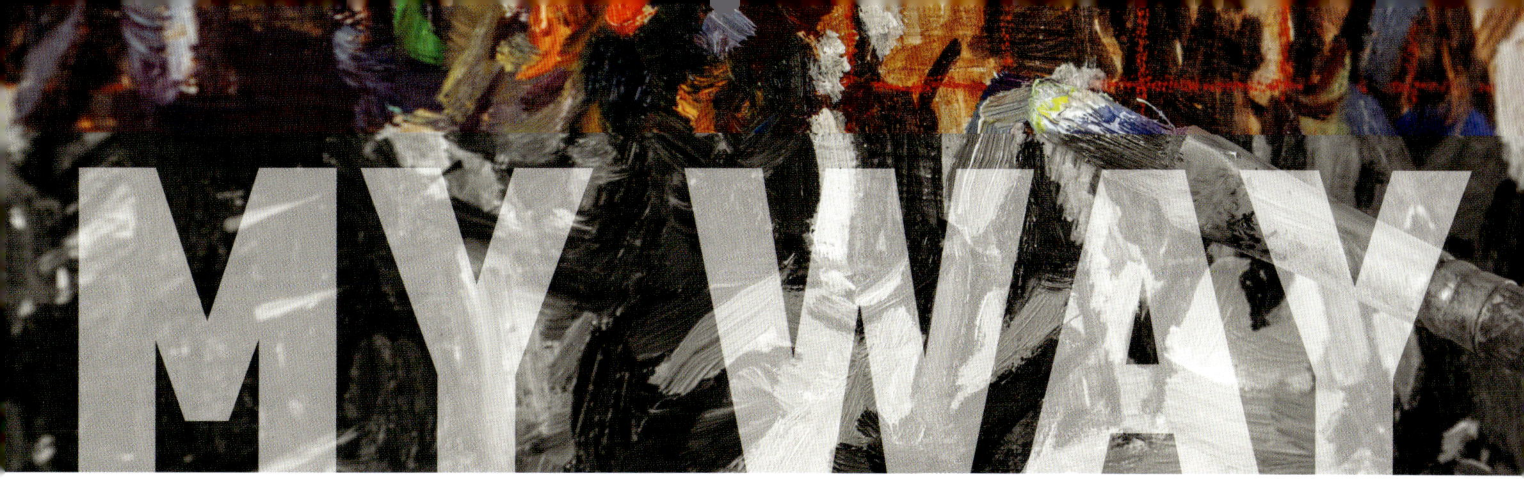

I CONSIDER MYSELF AN IMPRESSIONIST, because it is the effects of light that interest me. My work also tends towards naturalism, however, because I try my best to paint exactly what I see. Perhaps I'll say I am a 'natural impressionist', if there's any such thing.

Now you've read about my sketching practice and the basics of the tools and materials are out of the way, in this chapter I want to take a little time to consider a few important general aspects of oil painting before we dive into the different subjects.

How I paint with oils

When sketching, my method is immediate and spontaneous: I think only of drawing and tone. This makes my sketching more rapid than my painting, where I am more thoughtful and consider many additional factors. These include the mixing of colours, colour temperature, the value of the colour, what kind of strokes to use to depict what I am trying to portray, and the act of drawing with the brush.

Different approaches

I usually approach any subject in one of two ways: either working outside-in or inside-out. When working outside-in, I block in all the major shapes around the piece, covering the whole surface, then gradually return to the details and refine the painting as a whole.

When working inside-out, I pick a spot within the painting and work it up to completion, then gradually expand outwards from this point: the painting is completed area by area until the canvas surface is covered.

The method I choose depends on how much painting time I have at my disposal and how complicated the scene might be. If the scene is simple and I have little time (or if I am painting outdoors), I'll definitely use the outside-in technique. When I have a complicated scene to paint and the luxury of time in my studio, I tend to prefer using the inside-out technique because it helps to keeps me interested and excited about the piece.

Other approaches

Another approach I use in very rare situations is to use the oil paints to sketch with the paints heavily diluted with thinner – almost like watercolour. Everything is loose, there's hardly any heavy body colour and everything is lean (see page 27). There's no harm in experimenting like this – in fact, it'll help push you on.

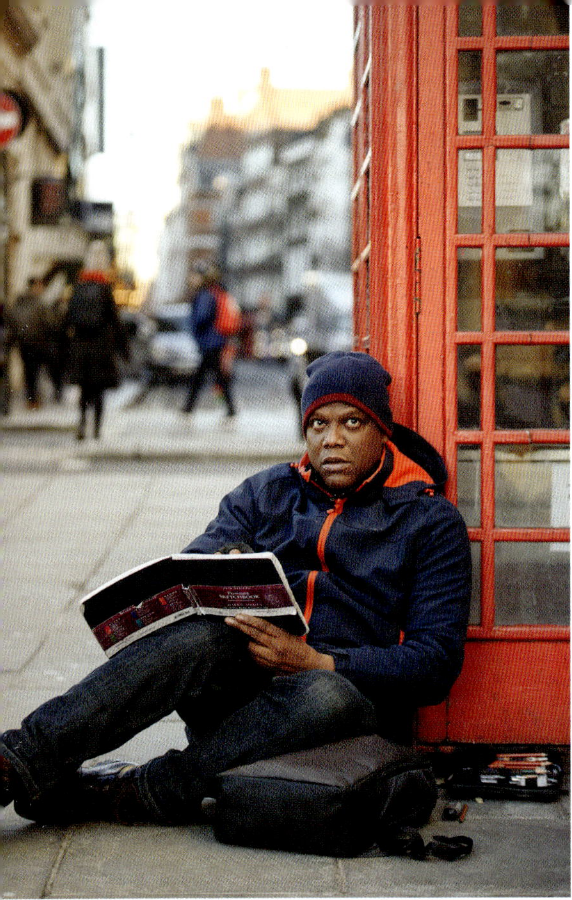

I think of myself as a sketcher, even when painting. Sketching is my comfort zone, and it's the sketcher in me that means I use drawing materials as the basis for all of my paintings, even when working outside.

Working outside

Whether to work indoors or outdoors, *en plein air*, is a big question, and one that causes a lot of debate among artists. I am a big fan of both.

I think working outside is the best way to refine your skills and improve your observational powers. While working outside, most of your decisions are being made right there and then as you don't have the luxury of time to stop and think. This helps to create spontaneity and energy in your work.

Whether it has been painted indoors or outside, I aim for my work to have the same energy. To achieve this, I bring my years of experience of painting outside into the studio, and paint indoors in the same way, in the same style and for the same duration as if I was painting outdoors. Use your own experience to inform your approach so that your style remains the same, wherever you are painting.

What equipment to use

When working outdoors; minimize what you take with you. You are like a hunter ready to 'pounce' on a scene that captures your attention: you must be ready to seize the moment. Moving around with less is a blessing. A pochade box (see page 18) is perfect for working outdoors, lightweight and quick to set up.

I also advise working on relatively small panels, as this will make it easier to finish the works in an hour and a half or so, before the light changes.

Small paintings

Small paintings simply changed my life. I read *Fill your Oil Paintings with Light and Color* by Kevin Macpherson, in which he championed painting small on a regular basis. The same idea was echoed in Trevor Chamberlain's *Oil Painting, Pure and Simple*, and these master artists aren't wrong. Indeed, I can't over-emphasize how the simple change to using smaller boards helped me to improve my painting skills.

Try starting a series of landscape or portrait paintings on 12.5 × 18cm (5 x 7in) boards. Aim for each to take between ninety minutes and three hours. Once you're happy with the series, try again with a series on 15 x 20cm (6 x 8in) boards, then 20 x 25.5cm (8 x 10in) – though I suggest you don't go any larger. Master the possibilities on these small surfaces and you'll be amazed at your progress.

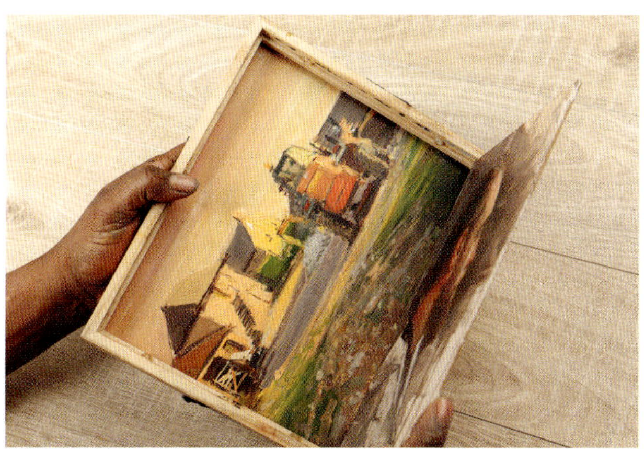

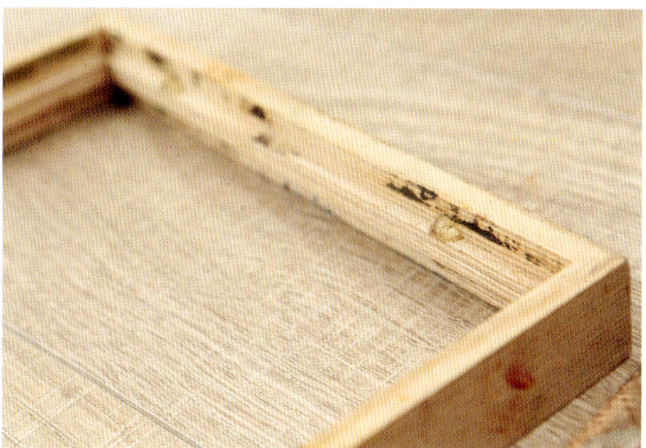

Transporting wet oil paintings

Oils dry slowly, so if you paint outdoors, you need some way of carrying wet oils. This requires a little preparation and equipment, but there are many ways to transport them. I use the panel carriers shown above, which allow a pair of panels to face each other without touching. These can then be secured with a little tape until you can get them home.

Once you can get over the pain of carrying wet oil paintings, you will discover a new joy and excitement in being ready to paint – and the whole world will become your studio.

Panel carriers

These frame-style panel carriers are like picture frames, into which the panel slots, face-inwards. A ridge in the centre prevents the painting touching the panel on the other side, and small bumps on the edge (see above right) mean that only a tiny part of the wet painting is in contact.

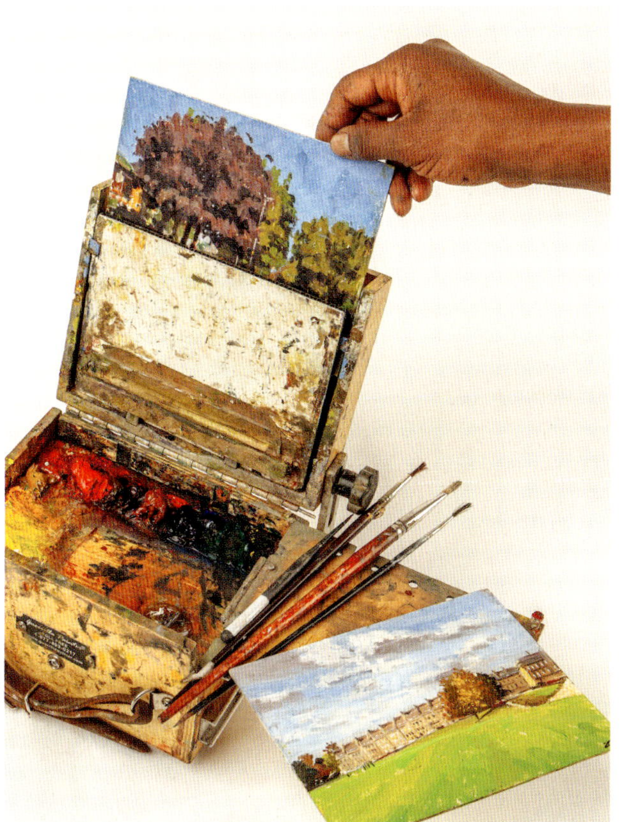

Pochade boxes and wet paintings

There are so many different pochade boxes available out there. Some, like this Guerrilla Painter ThumBox pochade box, include areas that will carry wet panels safely.

I love this box – it has enough storage space under the palette for small tubes of paint and brushes, and will carry two 20 × 15cm (8 × 6in) panels in the slots at the back, as shown. As it's compact and light, I find it great for on-the-go paintings. Look for these qualities in your choice of pochade box.

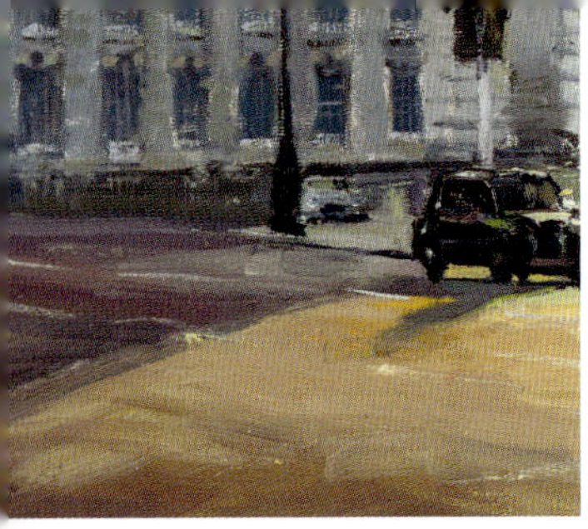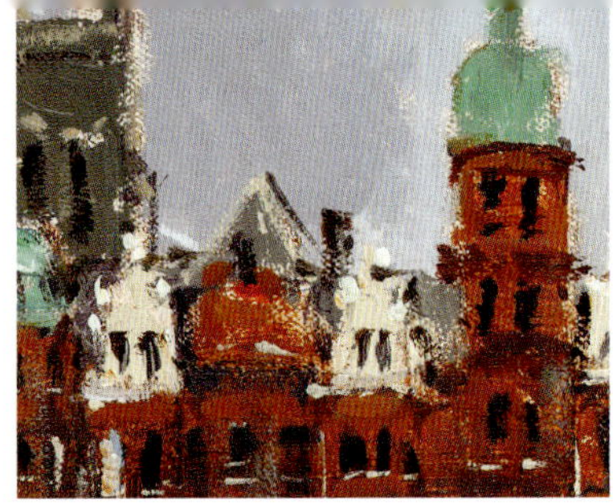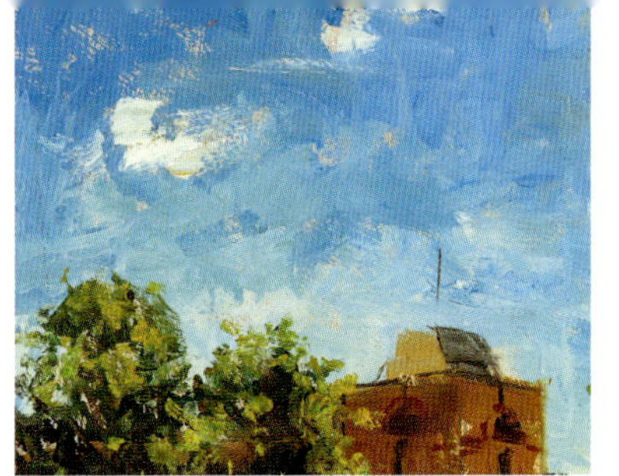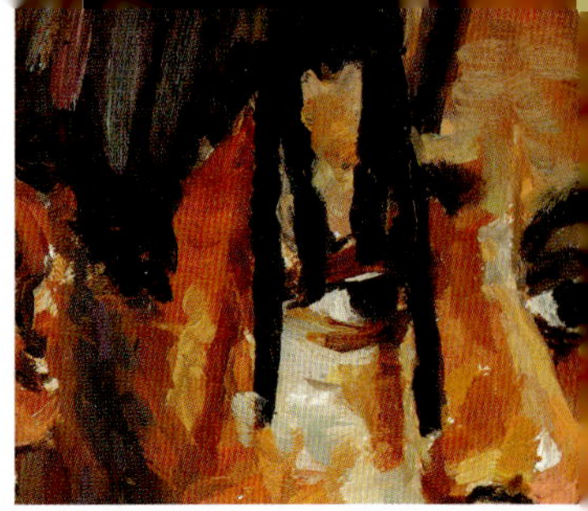

Retaining energy: staying motivated

The whole process and act of painting is a marathon. To be good at your craft you must paint, paint, paint. It's for this reason that staying motivated is so important. I set little challenges for myself: perhaps to paint the same subject in a series of different paintings; or paint ten or so small paintings over the course of a week; or create a target of doing three paintings in a day. The purpose of challenges like these is to keep yourself motivated to paint.

Another approach is to 'paint for the bin' – that is, painting knowing that there's a clear possibility that the painting isn't going to turn out right. Without the false pressure that your work has to be perfect or a masterpiece every time, you are free. By the time you have done three to four 'paint for the bin' paintings you will be back in your flow and ready to keep going.

In terms of my own motivation, for me nothing beats watching the art videos, reading articles or books written by my favourite artists or looking at paintings done by artists I admire. These get me fuelled and ready to go. Beware, however, what I call 'the social media slump' – where you get so immersed in what other artists are doing, you never get down to doing your thing because you feel you can never be good enough. If this happens to you, simply remember this: There are 10,000 artists out that there that you are far better than, and 10,000 artists out there that are far better than you. The first group will reassure you that your plight is not that bad; the second group will keep you humble.

The key thing here is self-confidence. I have seen some artists develop a powerful belief in what they do, and how they do it, and these are the artists that make the most progress in the shortest time. Self-confidence only comes through constant and consistent working plans. So, find a way to keep painting, stick to it and enjoy the process.

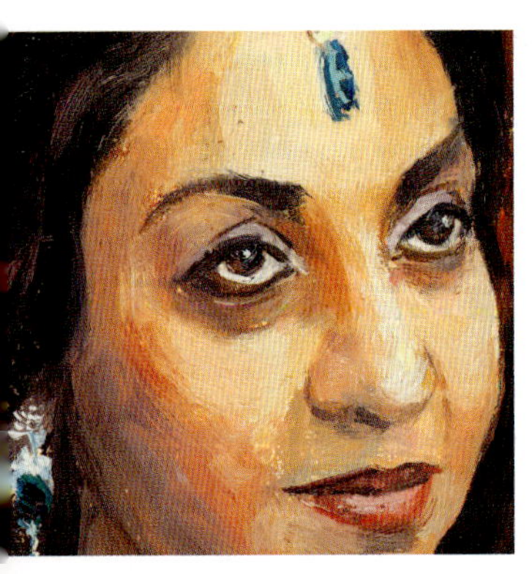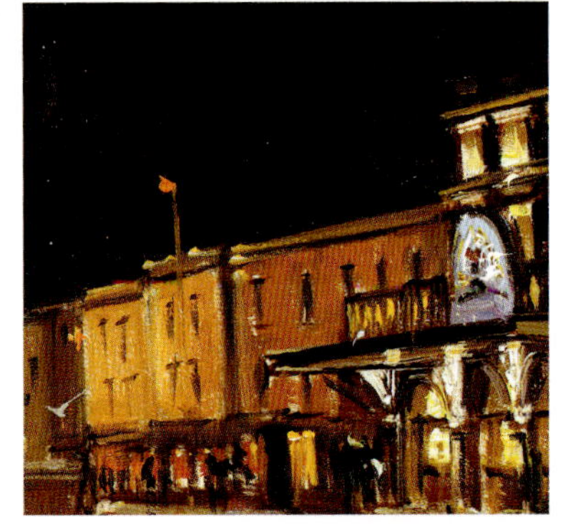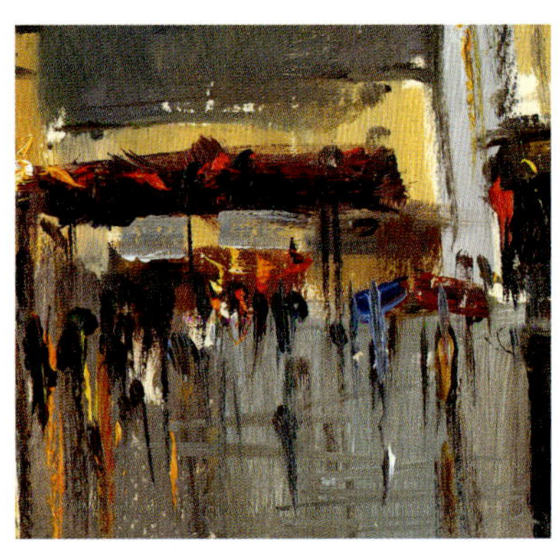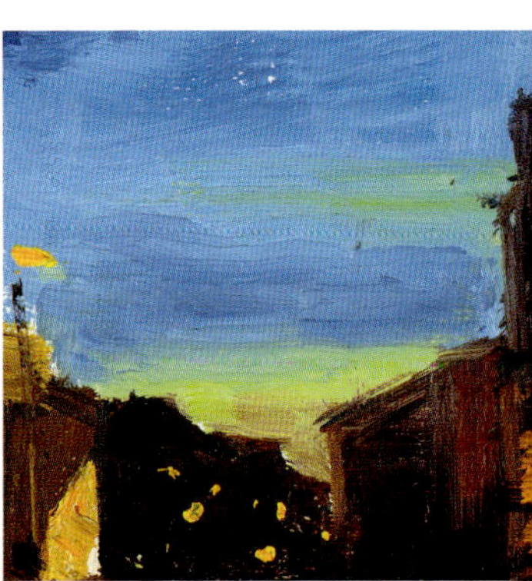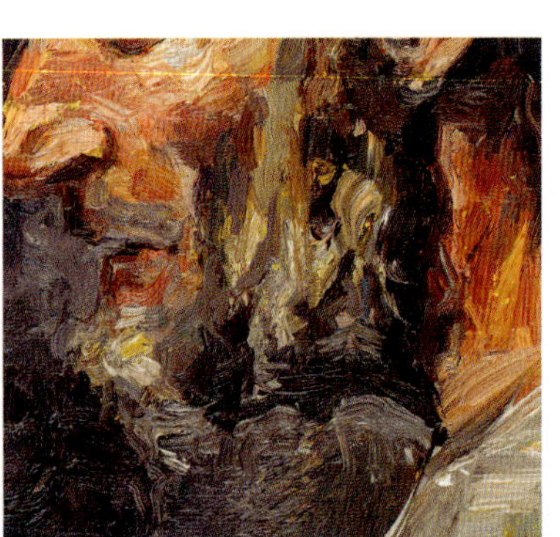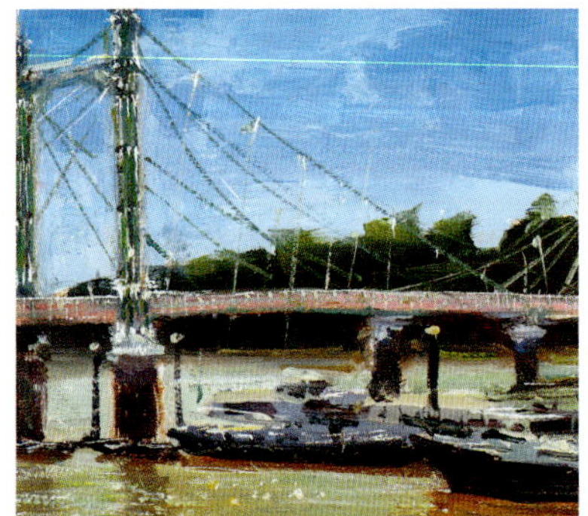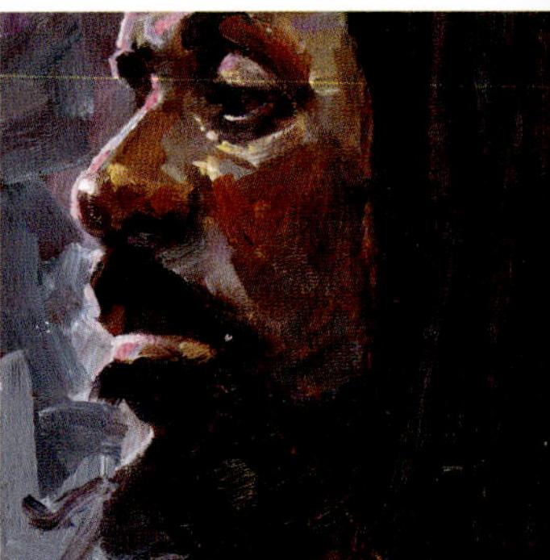

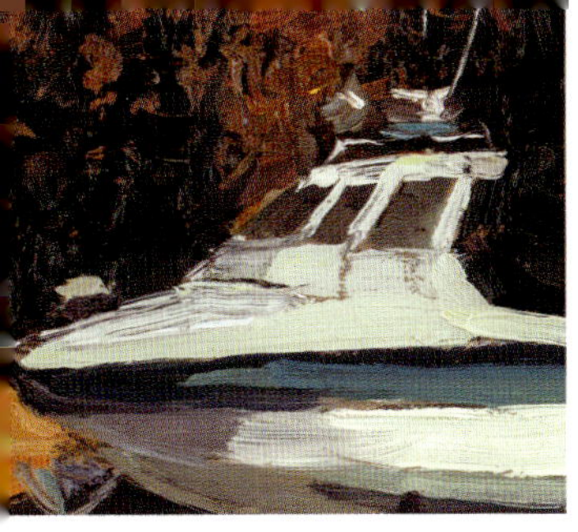
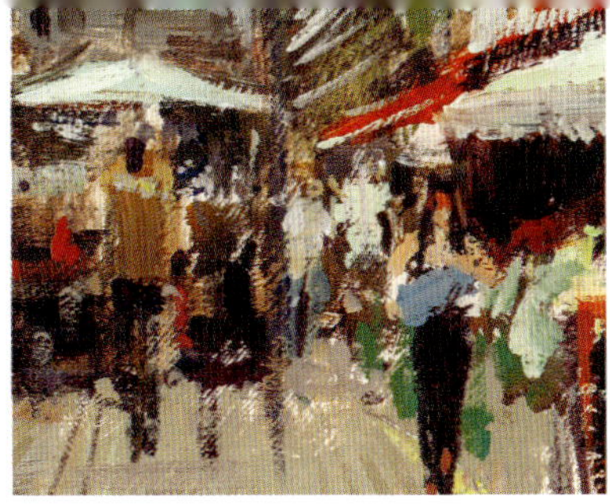
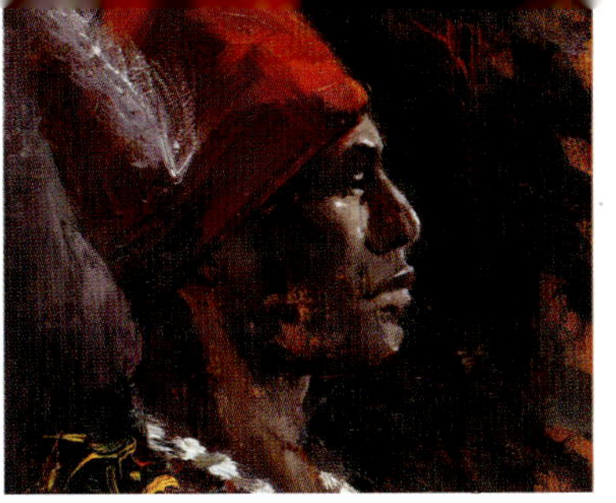
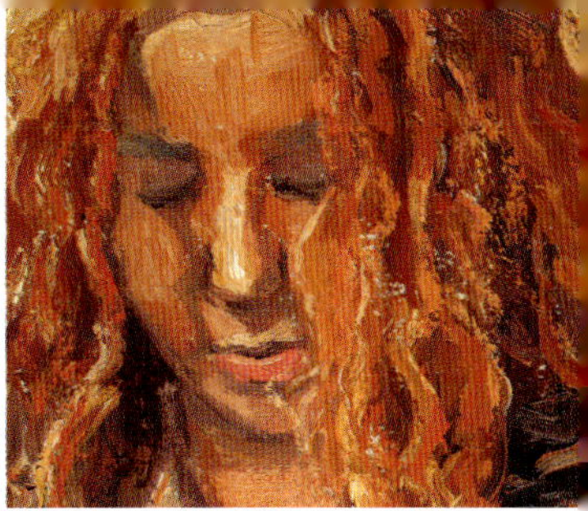

Mileage

Mileage is the god of progress in painting improvement. You can't tell me you are not getting any better at your painting skills with only thirty or fifty paintings – that number is way too small to be able to judge your true capability. You've got to put in the effort, and that's why motivation is key!

Start with the aim to complete 100 paintings, perhaps one a day, or all in a month. Such a process is powerful – you never remain the same after that – and when you compare the first to the last, you'll see how much you have improved.

While thinking about mileage, I'll never forget what I did to improve my standard of *plein air* painting in 2010. I had hit a plateau, and decided it was time to raise my game. I set myself the challenge of completing 200 paintings in four months, all worked in the open air of the city of Bath, UK. Some of the paintings were good, some bad, some ugly – but by the time that project was over I wasn't the same person. I had learnt so much in those four months of concerted effort that I could never have learnt if I was stopping and starting. Even though most people say, 'quantity doesn't matter, only quality', I believe quantity plays a massive role in your development: just do it!

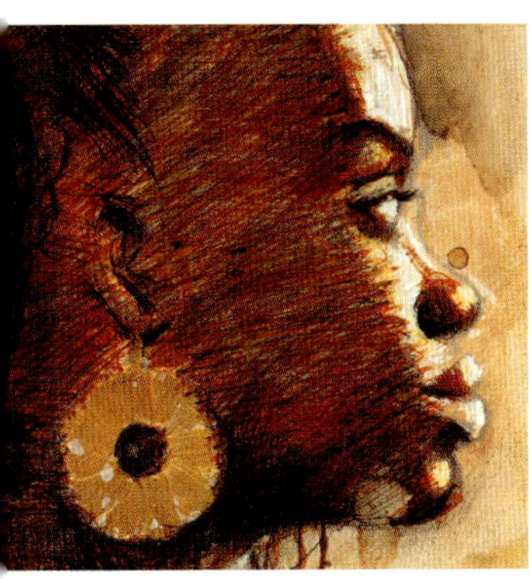
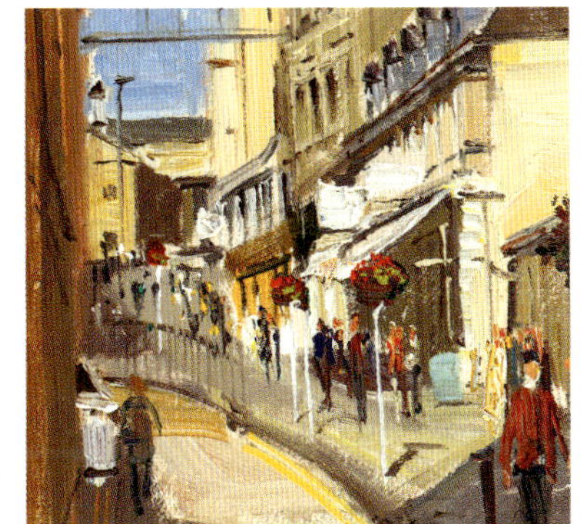
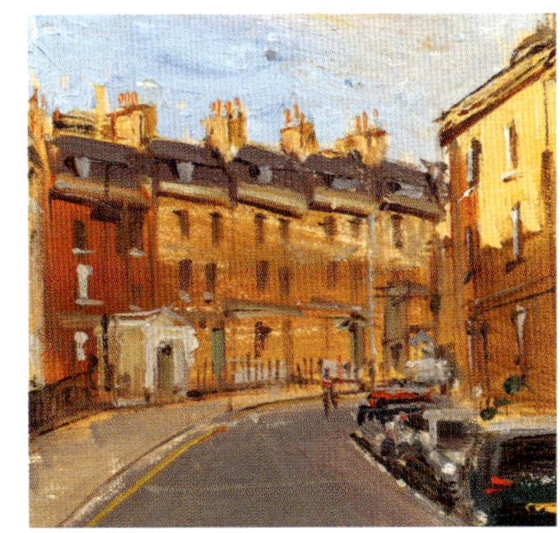

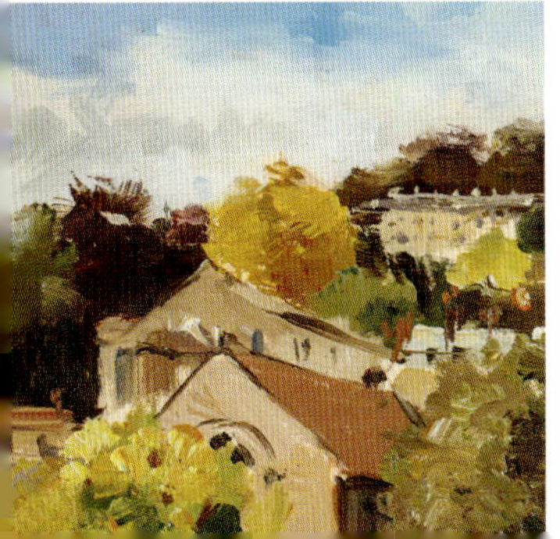
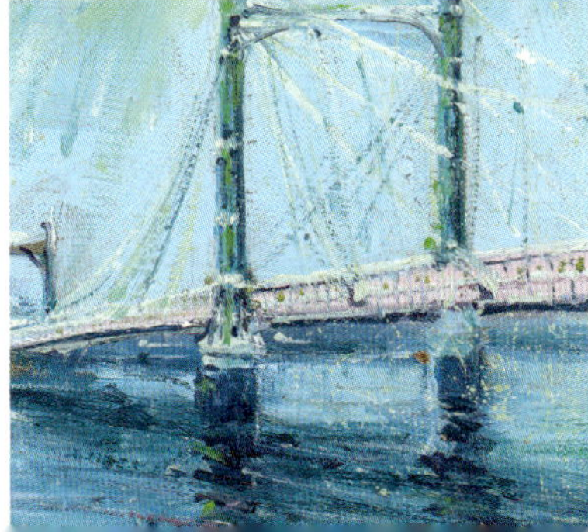
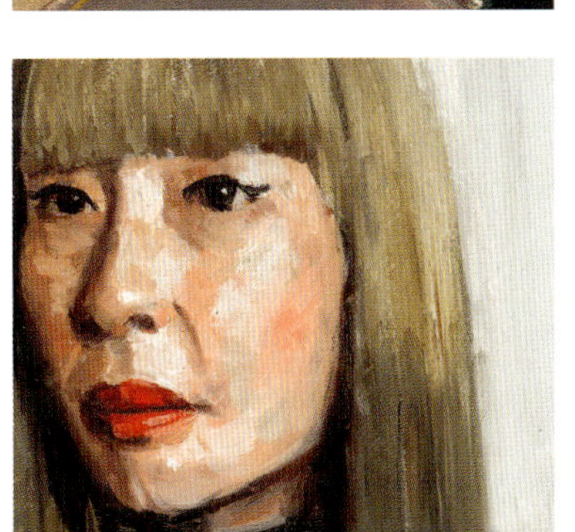
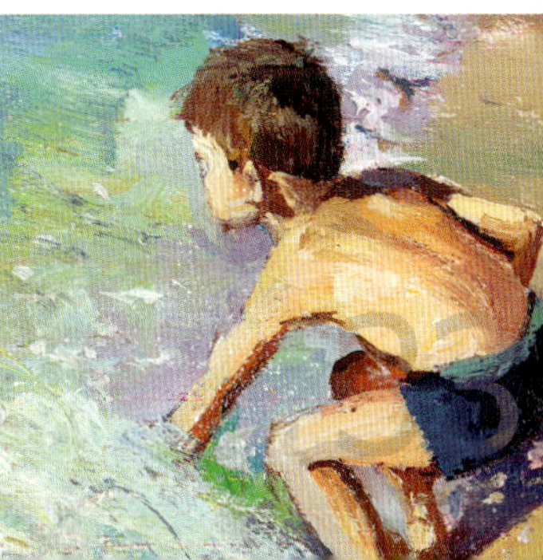

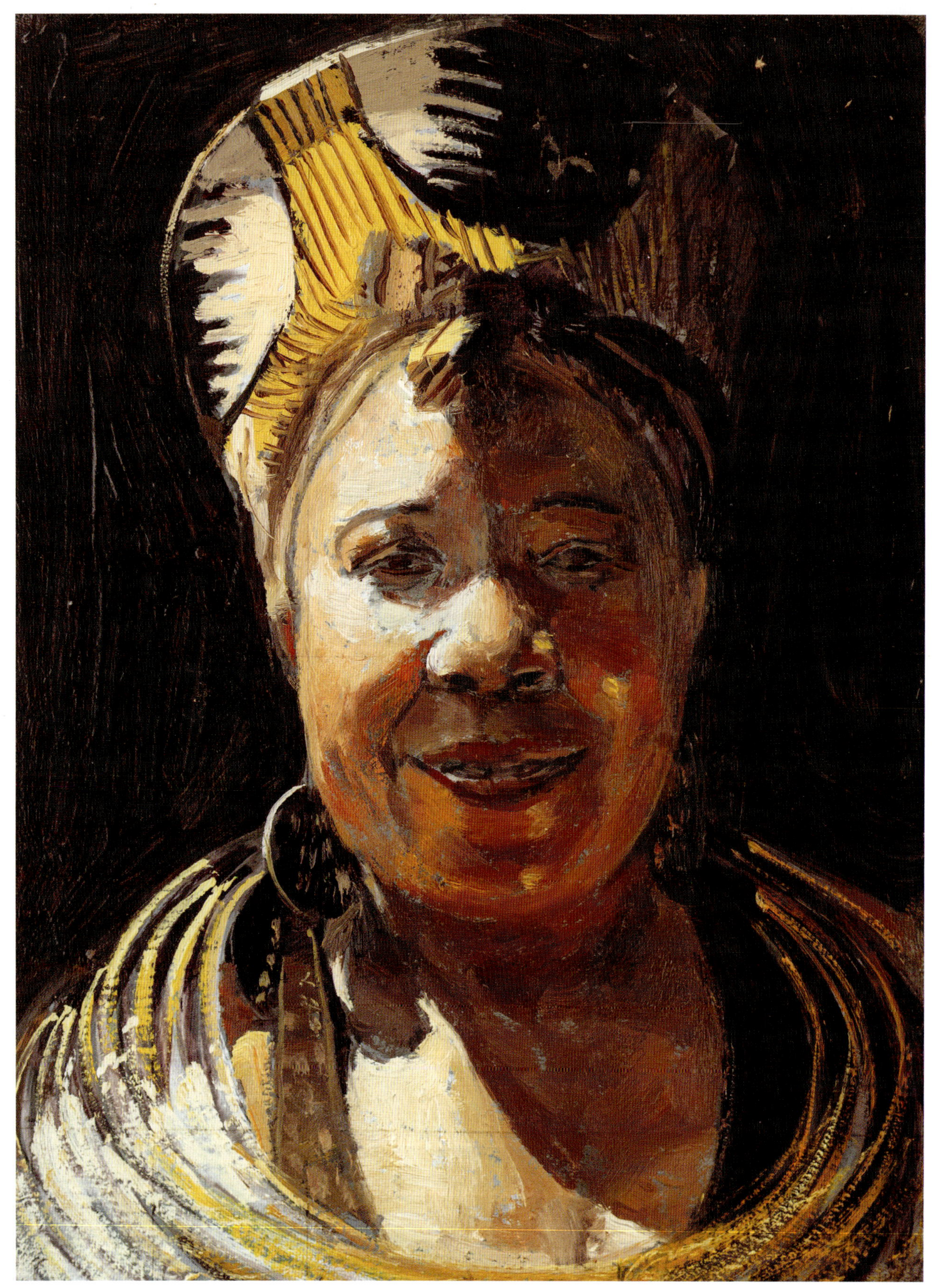

Queen Zambezi   15 × 20cm (6 × 8in)

Edges

Edges are an element of the composition that rarely get the focus that tone and shape are given in teaching, but edges are the bones of a painting. Without an understanding of them, you'll find yourself in trouble.

There are lost edges, where the transition between shapes is lost entirely; hard edges, where transitions are obvious; and soft edges, where you can see the transition, but it's subtle and gradual.

Portraits are very good to demonstrate edges because the human face, with all its complexities, has so many planes where one shape transitions into another or one tone merges into another. Whenever either of these happen, an edge of one form or another is produced. The painting opposite is a good example of this, and I have picked out some details of places where particular types of edge occur – take a few minutes to see if you can identify some more.

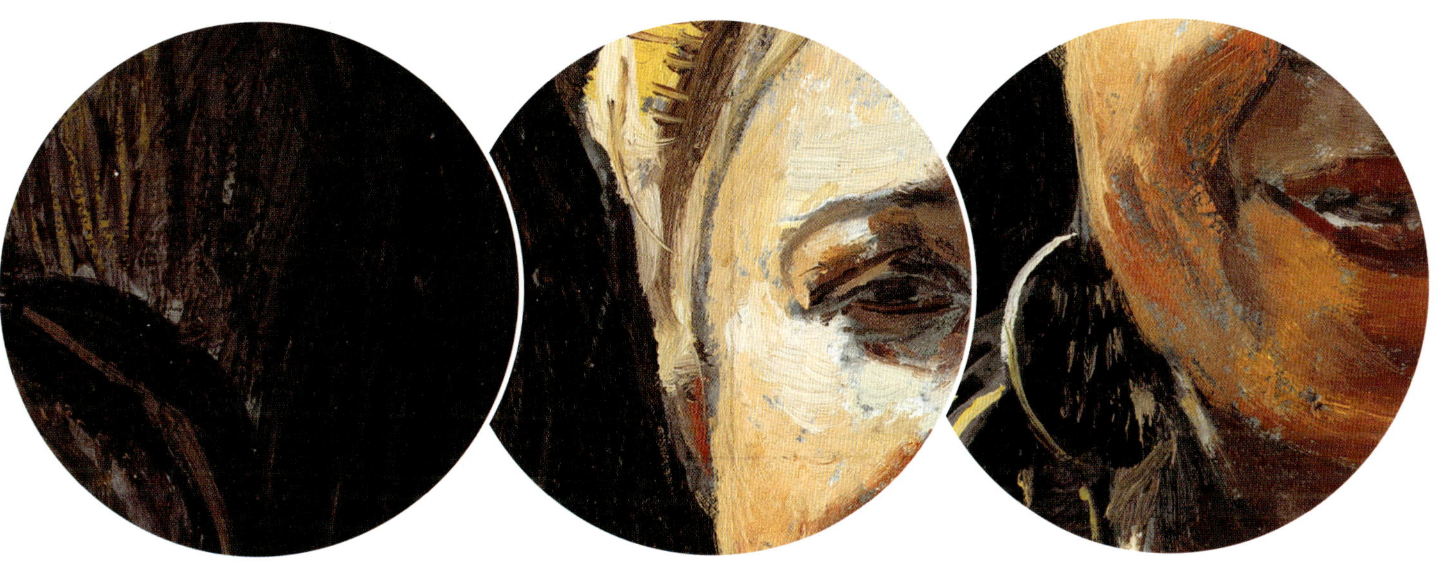

Lost edge
The side of the hat in shadow is lost against the dark background.

Hard edge
Here, the break between face and background is obvious.

Soft edge
The bottom of the subject's face includes a number of soft edges, where the edge is indistinct but nevertheless present.

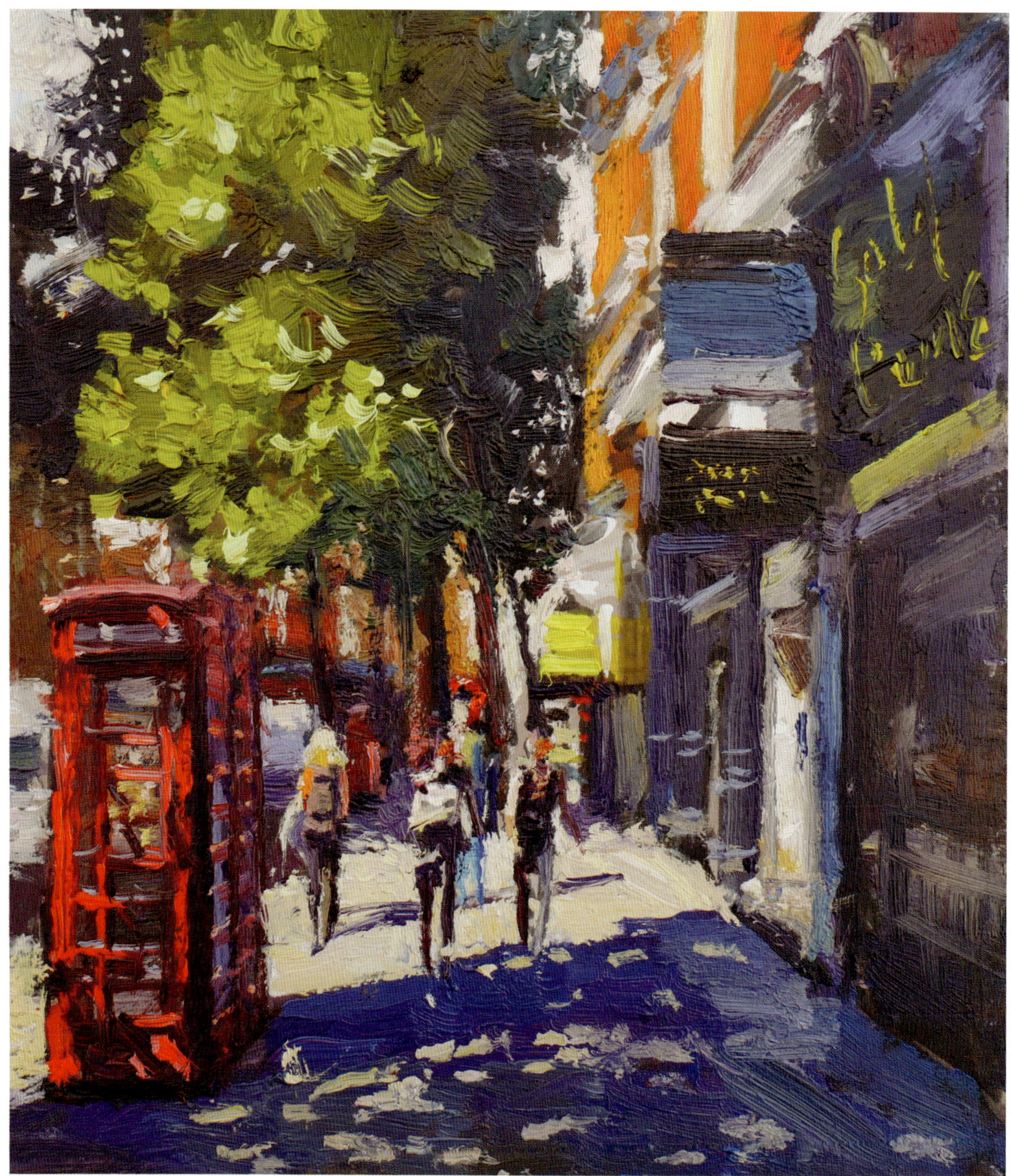

Blaze and Shade II, London Streets
15 × 17.5cm (6 × 7in)

Key

One way to help create a mood in a painting is to choose a high or low key – that is, to have more of either light or dark values. A low-key painting, with a preponderance of dark values, will appear moodier; while a high-key painting with an emphasis on light values, will appear fresher and livelier.

Value

Value, or tone, is simply how light or dark an area in the painting is.
A successful painting will almost always include the whole tonal range,
from very dark to light. This is one of the most important aspects of
picture making. If your paintings don't have clear tones they will look flat,
with little or no three-dimensional quality and depth.

Compare the image in black and white below with the full colour
painting opposite, to see how important value is. Even without the
colours, the composition still works well, because the values are very
clear and distinct.

Mostly I simply stick to three major tones: light, medium and dark. In
this painting, the sunlit path is the lightest tone, the tree is mainly in the
middle tone and the shadow in the foreground is the darkest tone.

If you can instinctively see things in terms of how light or how dark they
are, and you can depict that in your painting in a successful manner, you
are way ahead of lots of others, who may struggle with this kind of seeing.
If not, you can practise by simplifying the tones in your painting and
building up from three, to five or even nine tones over time.

Personally, I love to paint as I go along, but you may find pre-mixing your
colours helps you to balance your tones – that's perfectly okay: I know a lot
of painters who do this.

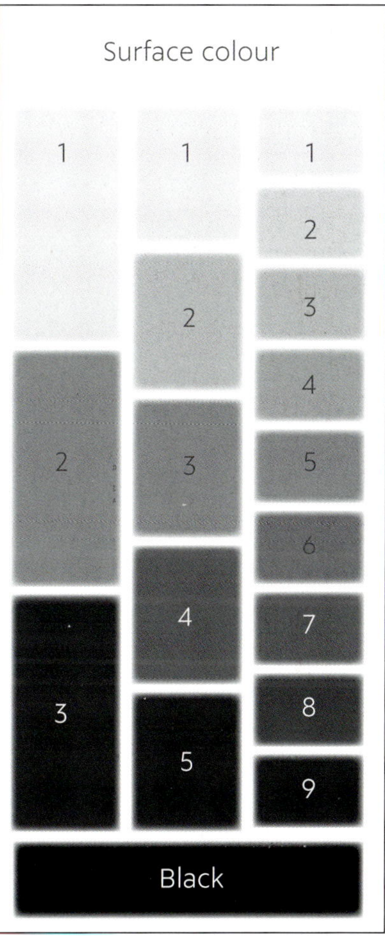

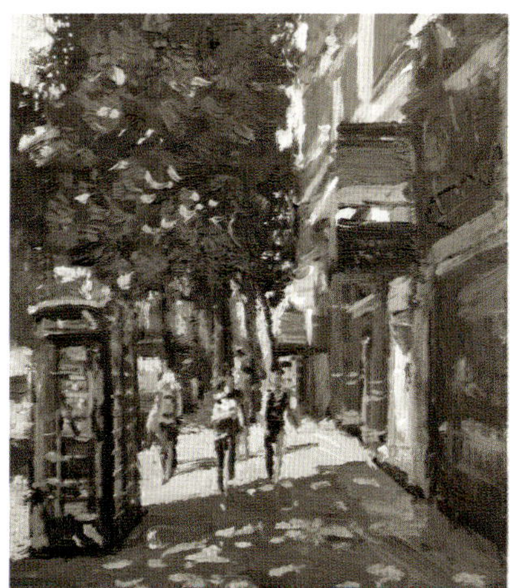

Strip out the colour

Squinting at your reference picture will
help to reduce the complexity and make
it easier to identify the key areas of light,
dark and midtone.

A black and white filter, or desaturation
tool on your phone, tablet or computer
can also help.

Counterchange

Contrast draws the eye, so for maximum
impact, consider composing your work
so the lightest tints are directly next
to the darkest shades, as here with the
shadows on the paving.

The value scale

Identifying three tones – light, mid
and dark – makes things simpler, but as
shown above, you can break down the
tones in front of you further, into five,
nine or more depending on your ability,
and what you want to achieve with
the painting.

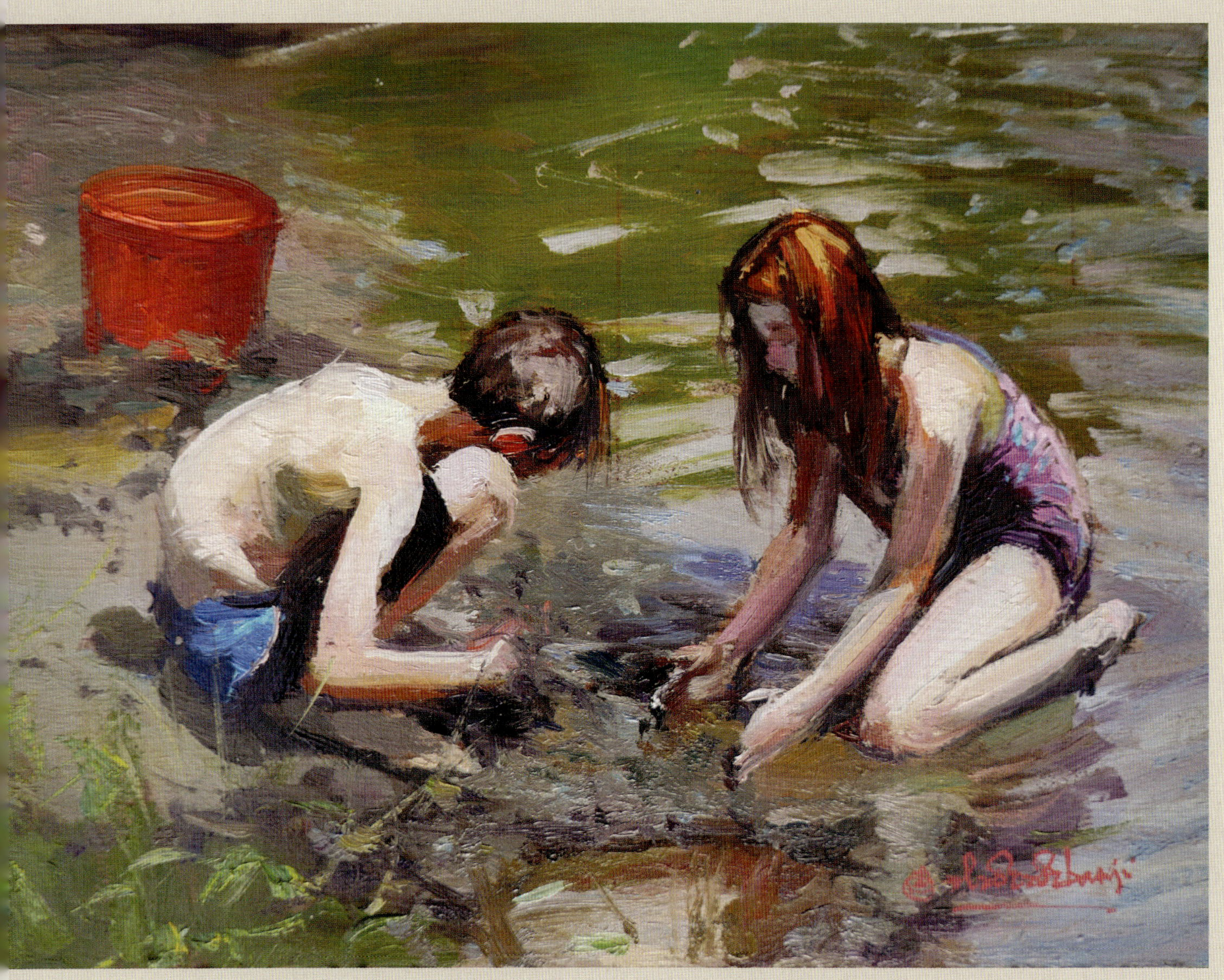

Summer Memories I   20 × 15cm (8 × 6in)

Colour temperature

I remember having a pure 'Eureka!' moment when colour temperature all made sense to me. It was a concept that I never really learnt while at Yaba College of Technology, but it was really expanded upon at The Heatherley School of Fine Art, and I was able to understand what it meant when people said certain colours were 'warm' and other colours were 'cool'.

We were given six colours to paint with: lemon yellow – green-tinged and cool; cadmium yellow, orange-tinged and warm; cadmium red, orange-tinged and warm; alizarin crimson, blue-tinged and cool; cobalt blue, green-tinged and cool; and ultramarine blue, red-tinged and warm. Working with these basic primary pairs was the simple way I was taught to understand colour temperature – the warm colours attracted my eye, while my gaze drifted over cool colours. Just as contrasts in tone made for interesting paintings, so did contrast in colour temperature.

At its most basic, understanding colour temperature is simply about being able to identify how warm or cool the colours you are using and going to be mixing are. You can use warm colours and high contrasts in temperature in your painting where you want to draw attention; and likewise use cool colours for less important areas, and the distance.

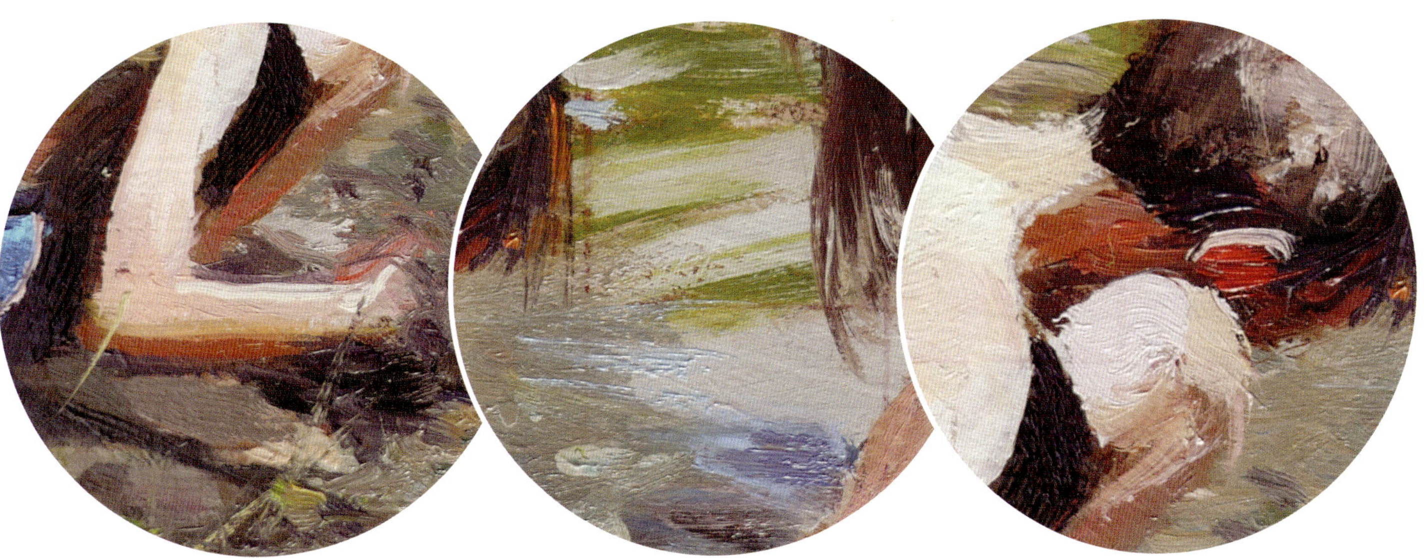

Warmth in shadows

Shadows are not black, but instead contrast both in tone and temperature. The light in the painting is cool hence the warmer shadows under his arm.

Paint what you see

The water in this painting is hardly blue or clear, there are colours to observe, analyse and respond to. The water has some warm parts in the greenish background and some cool parts in the foreground reflection part of the painting.

Details

Little bits and pieces of detail painted in the right temperature can really bring a piece to life. Here, the boy's ear is completely warm red because the light at the edge of his hair is cool. This contrast gives the area extra impact.

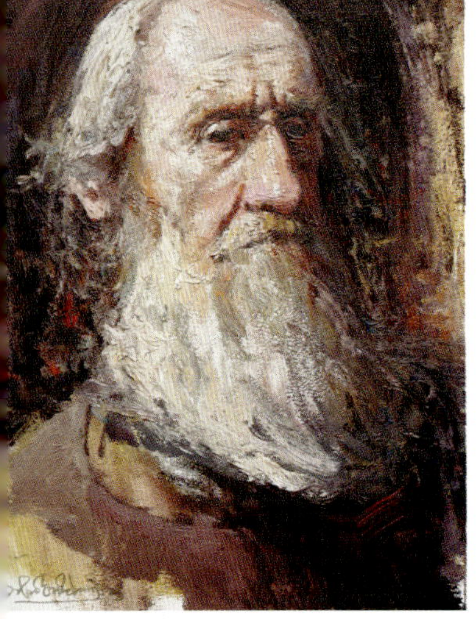

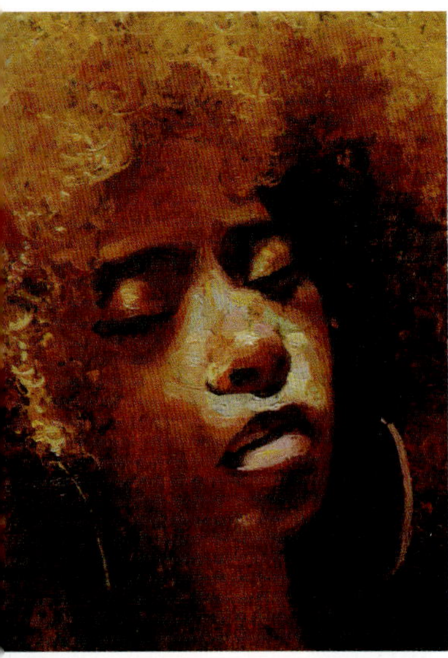

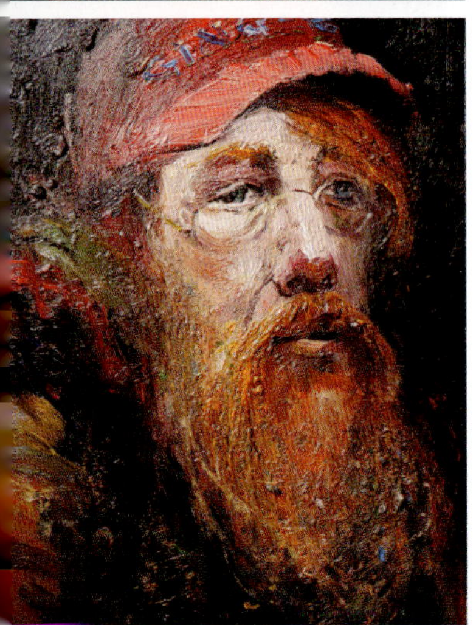

In a bid to improve my portraits, I once set myself the task of painting 250 portraits in 250 days – this is another good example of the value of mileage (see page 33). While this time I didn't finish, I got a good way through the challenge, and remember clearly what it taught me: a clear sense of the essentials of successful portrait painting.

Firstly, accurate drawing. Whether you intend to approach the portrait with an inside-out or an outside-in technique (see page 29), you must have a drawing that is positioned properly and with the right proportions. Inaccurate proportions can kill a portrait, so grid your work if you are working from photographs or the screen, or, when working directly from life, use a pencil or brush stretched at arm's length from your eyes to measure and relate distances from one part of the face to the other, constantly comparing and looking for relationships. Until this process of getting the drawing is right, I never start painting, because it would be a futile exercise to paint on a faulty drawing or sketch.

PORTRAITS

The other crucial thing for portraiture is a clear understanding of value and edges. I suggest you identify and mix three distinct tones – light, medium and dark – on your palette before you start painting (see page 37). These overall tones will help in anchoring your decision-making. Once the basic tones are in place and correct, work on refining the edges. With this procedure a portrait will seldom go wrong.

If you can master drawing, value and edges, you'll be on your way to conquering the act of portrait painting. Note that I don't mention colour, which some might think is so essential, but colour can only become successful if it is grounded on a solid understanding of tone. Even colour temperature is a bonus, rather than an essential.

Practice, practice, practice. It is the only way anyone can get better at portraiture, as it is the most demanding of all forms of painting in terms of attention, concentration and accuracy.

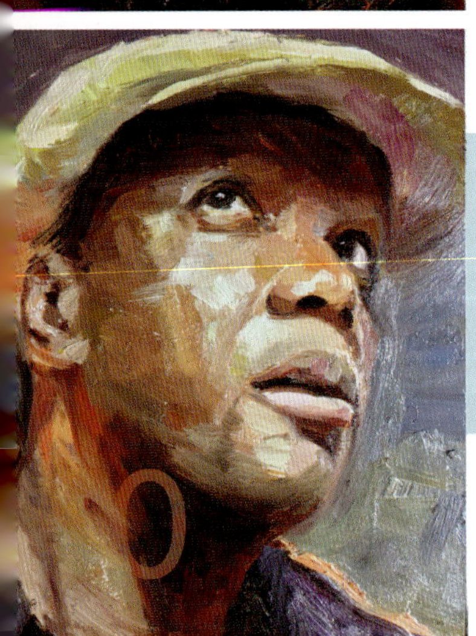

Small is beautiful

Most of the portraits shown on these pages are small: around 15 × 20cm (6 × 8in) or so. It's a good idea to keep your paintings small as you develop your style – they are quicker to finish and they will give you so much confidence to take on bigger pieces with ease.

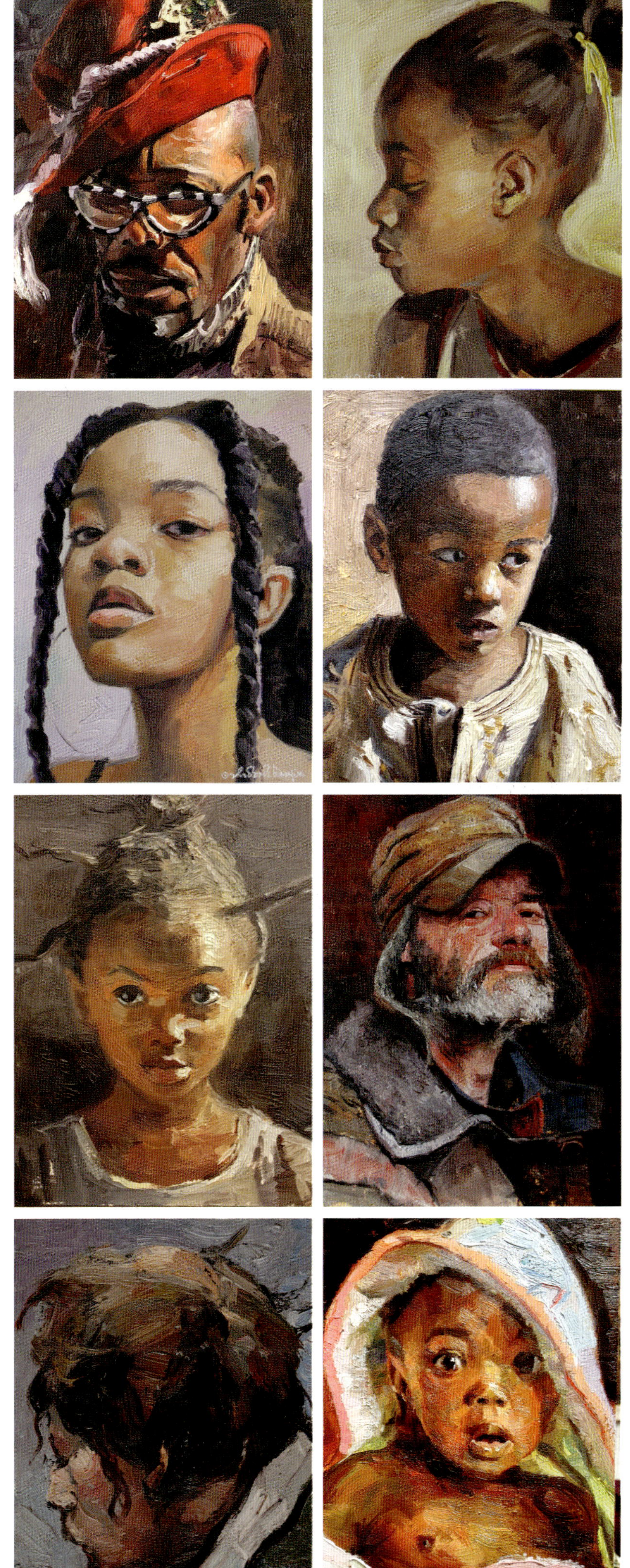

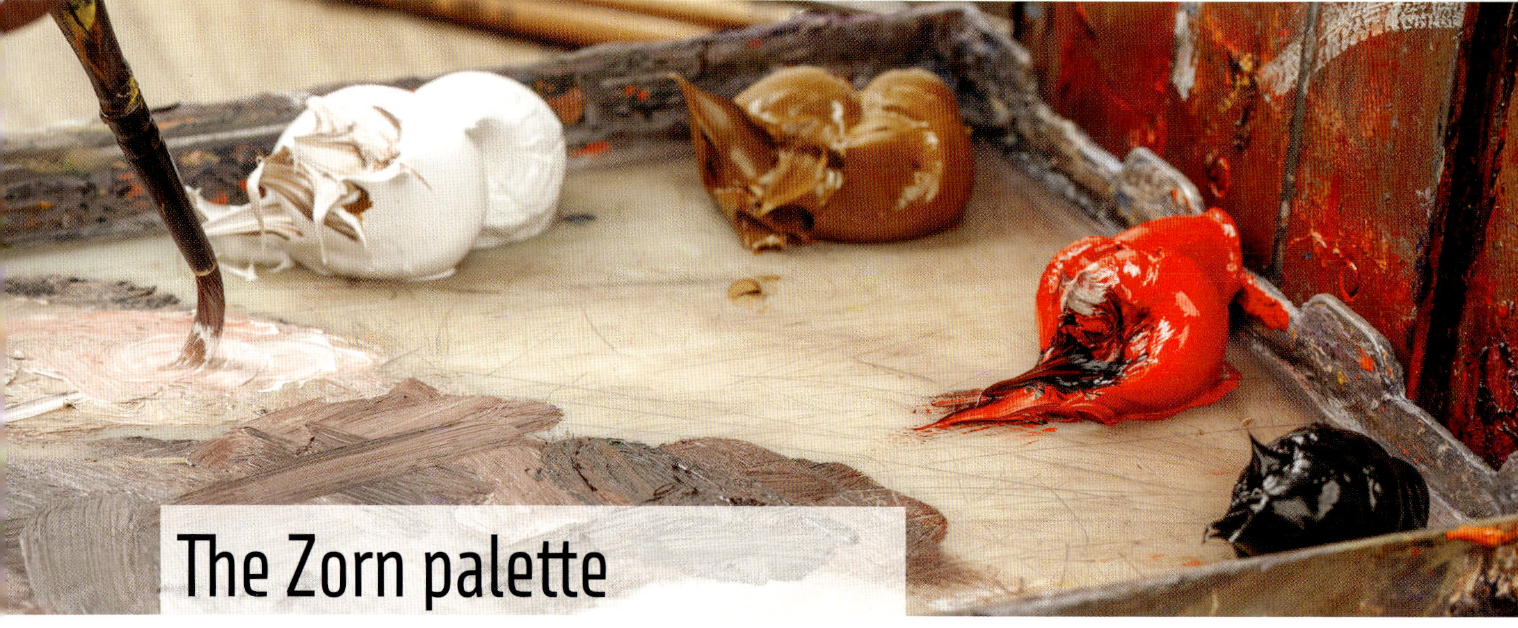

The Zorn palette

You'll learn more from a limited palette, as it forces you to adapt, mix and find routes rather than just diving into premixed paint.

I love the following limited palette, derived from the legendary Swedish artist, Anders Zorn. It consists of just four colours: titanium white, yellow ochre, cadmium red and ivory black.

You can get very close to human skin with this palette, and it'll look as rich as a full palette.

The paints

The magic of the Zorn palette is that the colours act like a hidden set of three primaries: red, yellow and blue; with the black working as a blue.

Titanium white Titanium white is the slowest-drying oil in my palette, so I often supplement my titanium white with alkyd white or Michael Harding titanium white 3, which have fast-drying qualities. This gives a midway speed of drying: the best of both worlds.

Yellow ochre This is a sweet, greyish yellow, a bit like sand in colour. It can give you the most enchanting warm and cool mixtures depending on whether you use it with the black or red.

Cadmium red A powerful, bright and vibrant colour which can produce the sweetest cool dark browns when mixed with ivory black and the sweetest warm browns when mixed with yellow ochre.

Ivory black A very powerful black, this takes the place of blue in your mixtures. It really helps with all the dark mixtures needed while painting and can give you the most muted greens when mixed with yellow ochre.

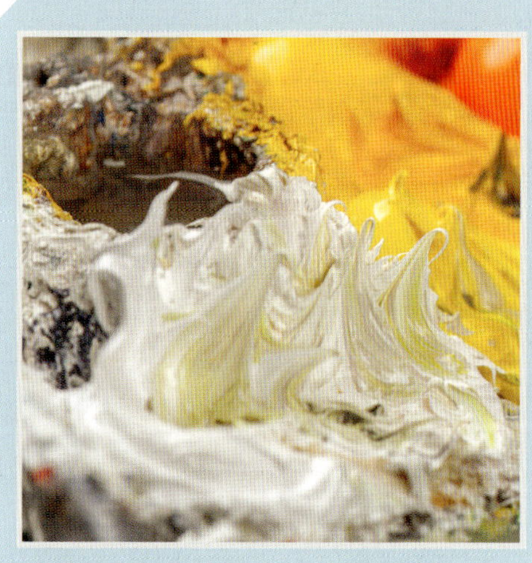

Preparing white

To combine standard titanium white with a fast-drying white, mix them together on the palette using a palette knife.

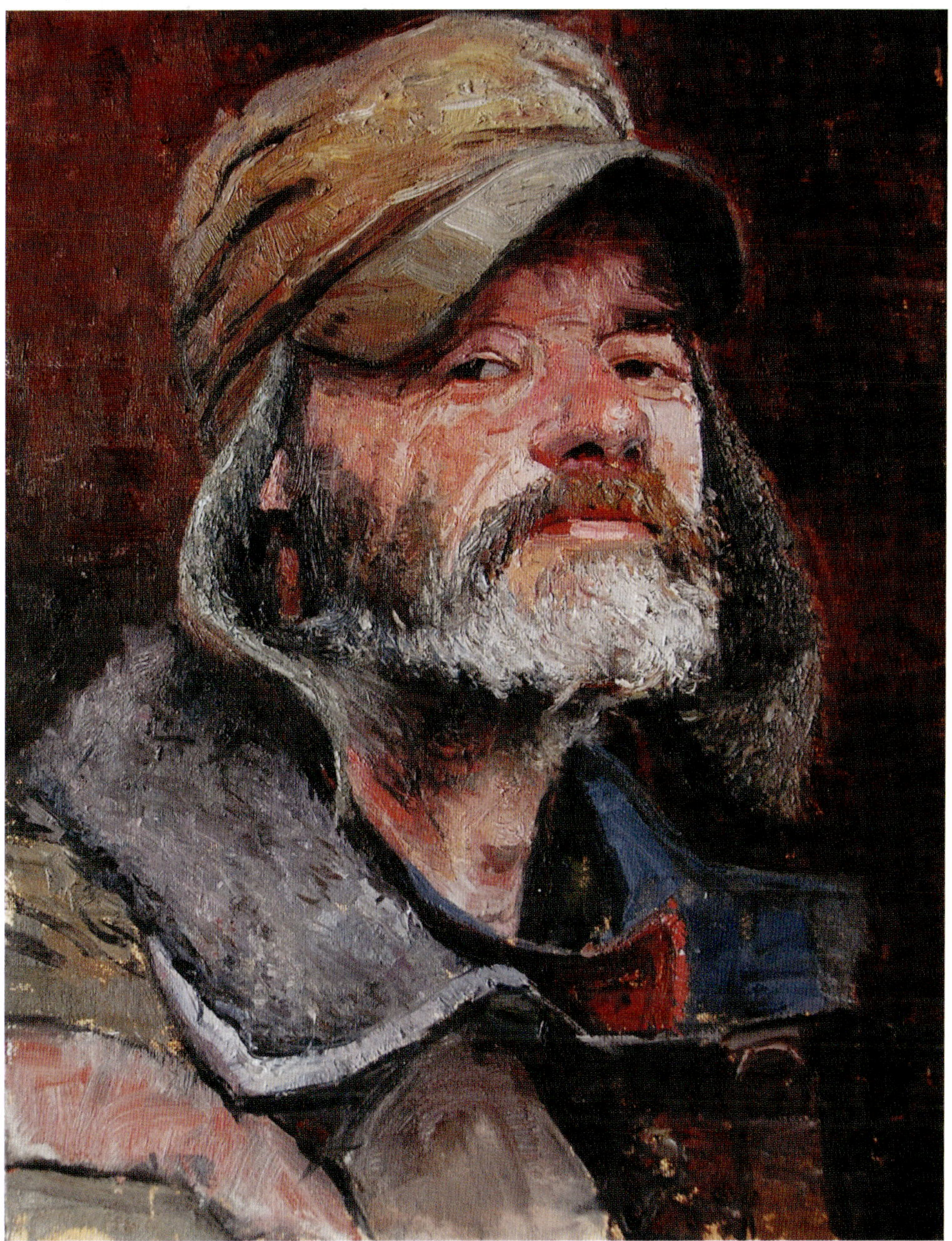

The Face of Homelessness – Earl's Court   30 × 40cm (12 × 16in)

This portrait, made with the Zorn palette, is of a guy I met very briefly at Earl's Court. His skin tones were mainly painted with combinations of yellow ochre, cadmium red and titanium white, while the shadows were mixtures of ivory black and cadmium red or ivory black and yellow ochre, depending on the area.

His jacket had touches of all the colours and that lovely bit of blue was derived by mixing ivory black with titanium white and a bit of yellow ochre. This palette is definitely worth exploring!

Paint: **After the Storm**

The Face of Homelessness

I never want to paint a picture that's flat: and what I mean by that is
that there are too many midtones. You need a mix of all three tones:
light, mid and dark; with a slight emphasis on either very strong
lights, or very strong darks. The choice of picture is essential, so avoid
anything where the midtones are dominant. This picture, where the
darks are dominant, is ideal for showing how to build up from darks
through to light.

The tones reflect the story of the picture. Being homeless is a dark
period in a person's life, so this should be shown. This is a face, but
as an artist, you need to communicate something else as well. The
sculptural quality of this man's skin and features means you can
treat it almost like a landscape, getting involved in the deep, craggy
features – just be careful not to lose sight of his humanity. Paint what
you want the viewer to see.

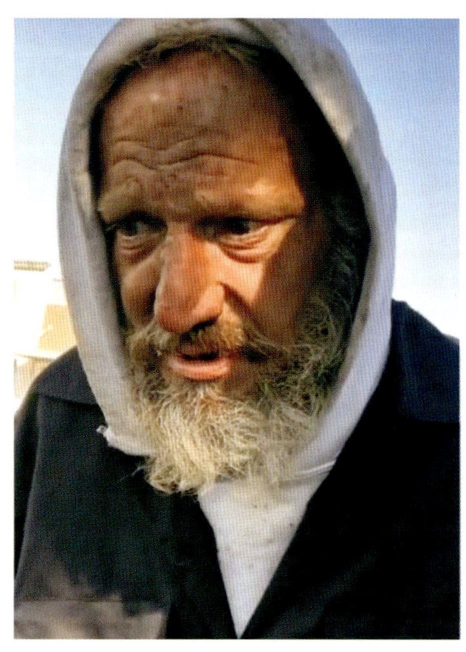

Source photograph.

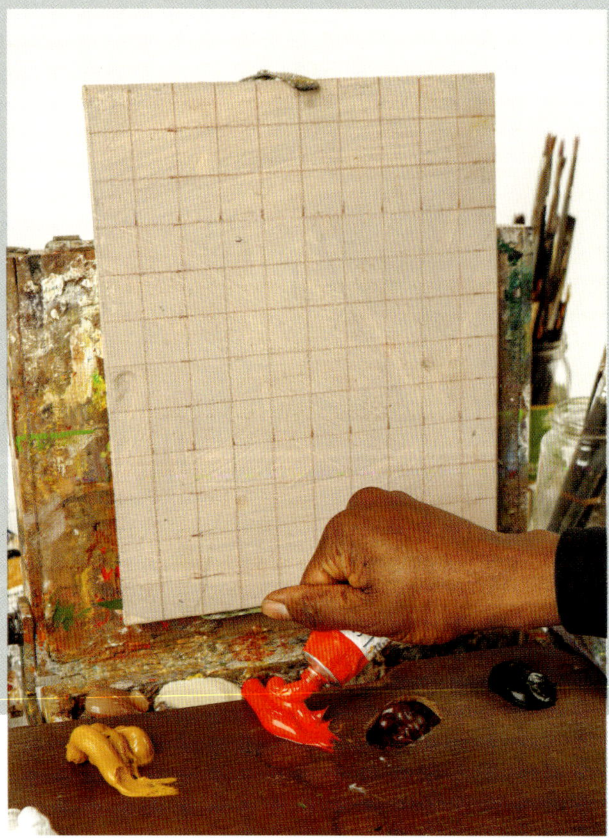

The original photograph is in 5:7 proportion. I overlaid
a grid on a copy of the photograph, which gave me ten
squares across and fourteen vertically (10:14 or 5:7). To
make the conversion to a 25.5 × 30.5cm board – that is,
10 × 12in – easier, I simply covered up the bottom row of
squares, making it ten across and only twelve down – a
ratio of 5:6.

I've numbered the squares with white Posca pen to ensure
that they stand out – and the numbering helps me to
quickly refer back and forth – a bit like a GPS system!

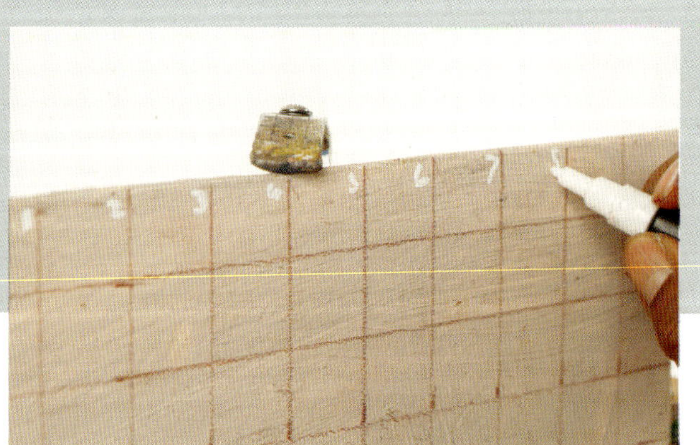

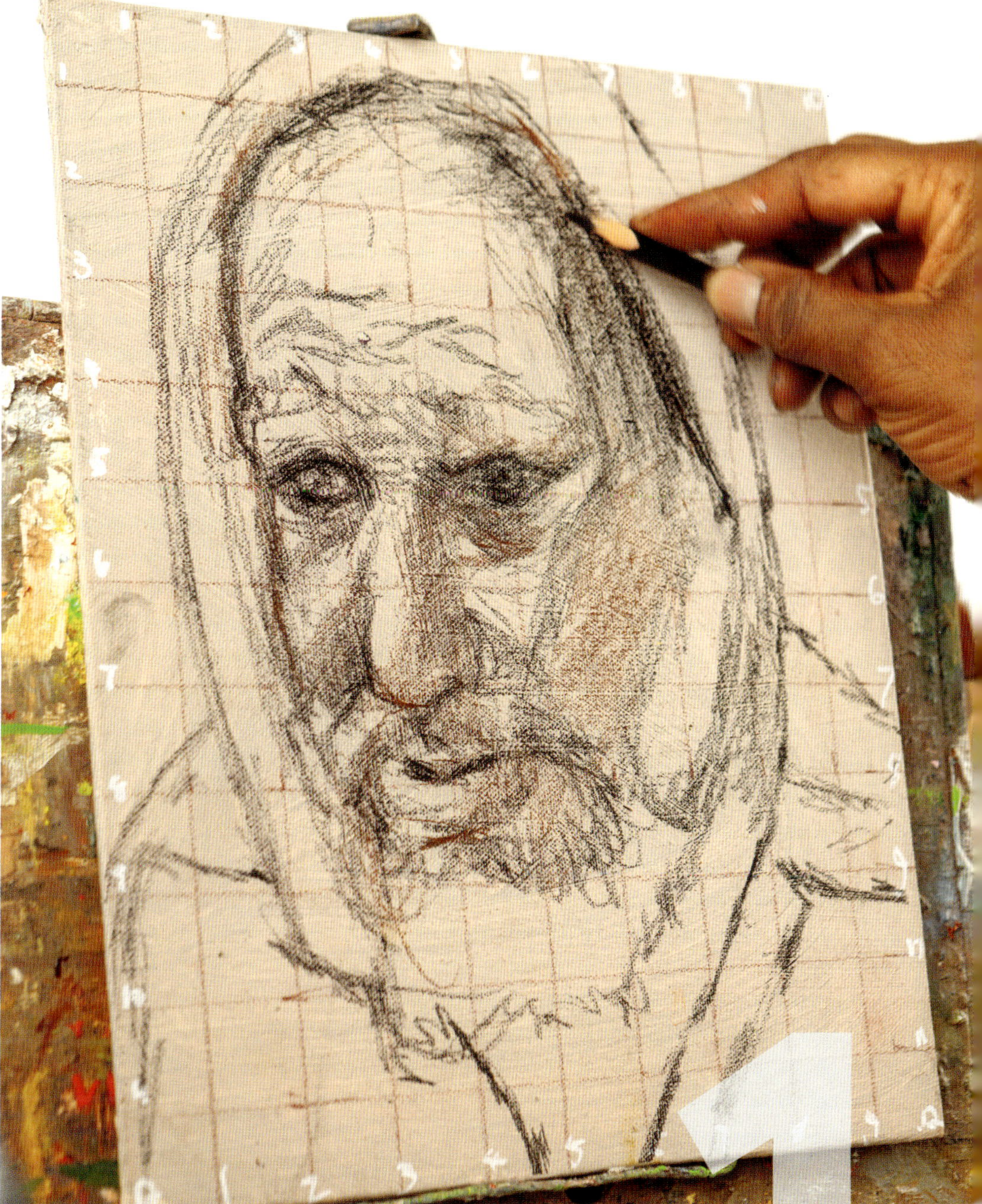

First sketch

Use the grid to help you get the sketch in place on your canvas board.
Use the black coloured pencil for the main outline and brown for the tone.

   The aim of this stage is to set your table – to get everything ready
for the luscious paint later on. A lot of the hard work comes in here, so
concentrate on building up the line and tone, and you'll make the later
stages of painting easier and more enjoyable.

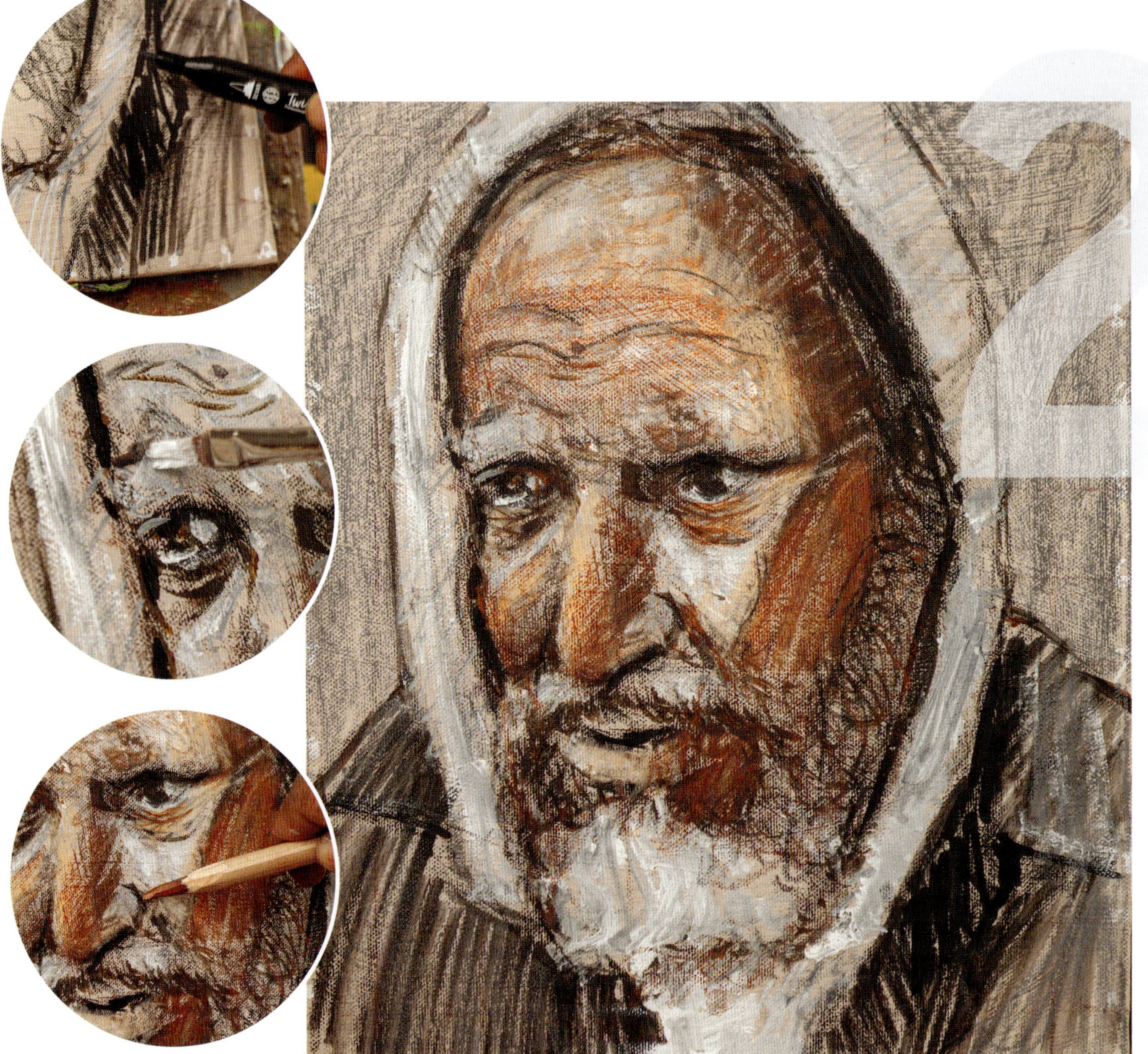

Sketching and tone

Before I begin to apply the paint, I start with layers of other media – burnt sienna and praline brush markers go in first to develop major landmarks in the face. These are not just the features; but the parts of the portrait that I want to emphasize. Here, the power of this figure is in his eyes; in the dense hair of his beard and the scooped-out shadow of his hood.

- With the midtones in place, I swap to Posca pens – white and almond – to add the lighter tints; then return to the brush markers (Winsor & Newton cinnamon and Decotime Twinmarkers: black 120; cool grey 5; cool grey 4) to further develop the marks.

- Use a small brush to add some punchy titanium white acrylic paint for the highlights to complete the tonal range.

When painting, I want to retain the details, so I go back and forth until I'm confident the tonal values are just right. I need the finished sketch to feel like a finished painting, but in a drawing. You'll notice that the grid is completely covered by this point.

Applying oils: darks

We'll build up from the deepest darks towards the midtones. The deepest areas are easy to see, so they're a great place to start – and we'll mostly be able to keep adding to one mix to gradually vary and lighten it, saving us from having to mix lots of different colours. I call this single varied mix my puddle.

- I never use one colour on its own. Even the deepest tones here are a mix of ivory black with a hint of cadmium red. I add a little Maroger to give it a slightly sculptural quality.

- Using a large and medium brush, I start to build up the deep darks with single strokes.

- Keep looking at the reference image and compare areas. Look for tone, but also hue. Add warming touches of yellow ochre and cadmium red to your puddle as you need to, and gradually build up the tones across the skin.

- For the clothing and hair, you may need some blue-tinged darks. The Zorn palette won't allow you to create genuine blues, but these areas can be painted by adding a hint of white to 'grey out' the colour.

- The goal at this stage is to find the darks and make them work. Tone is the most important thing. This is because I don't have enough colours to recreate things exactly. We can adjust the temperature: red or yellow to warm the mix; or black or white to cool it. However, tone is king.

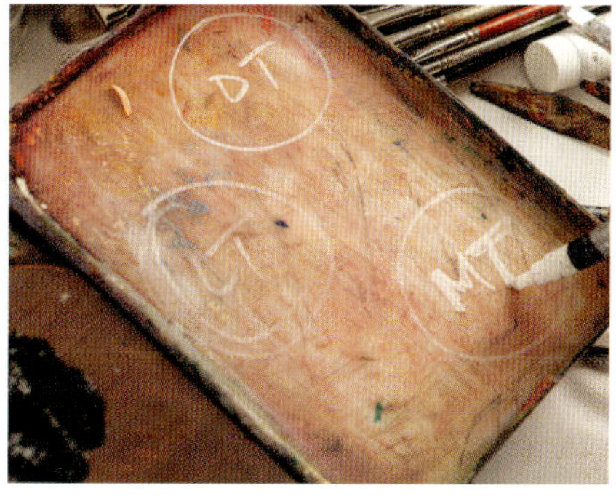

I draw small circles on my palette to help keep me organized: dark tones, light tones and midtones.

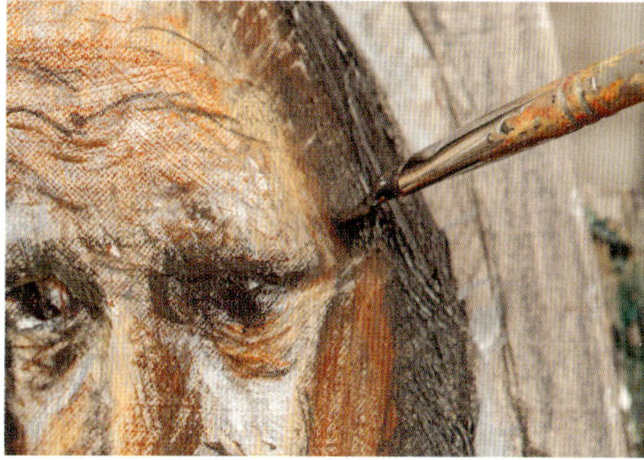

Don't mess about with it on the surface: pick up the paint, put it down, and pull the brush away with a bounce. This will ensure the painting has energy, freshness and vibrancy.

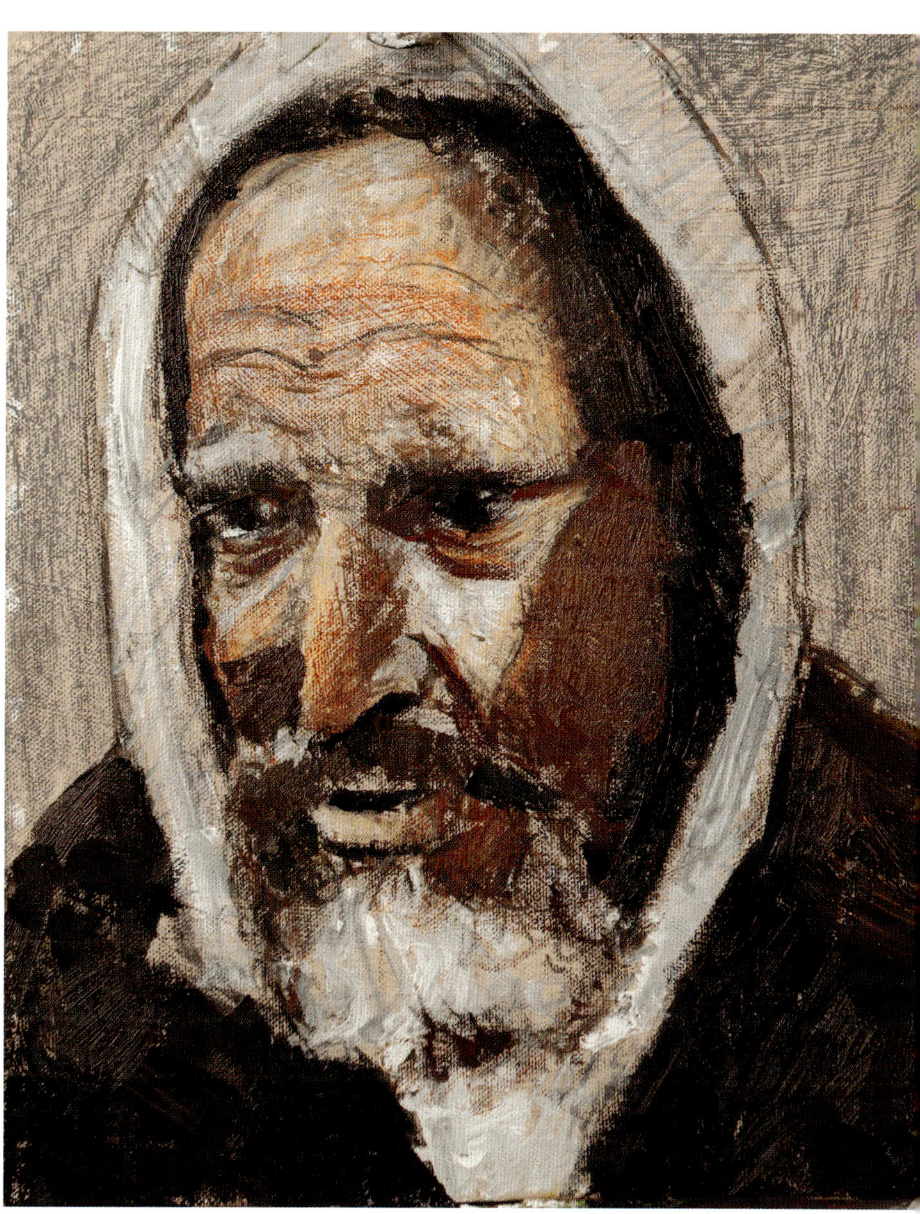

Midtones

Midtones are where the battle is won or lost. Here we'll work in three stages: start with the top third of his face, then the middle third, and then the bottom. There will be a temptation to go too light too soon: resist it. Handle your paint in a controlled way, and stick to the midtones.

- Create a puddle with yellow ochre as the base, then add cadmium red and Maroger to give you a base mix. To this, add a little of the dark mix from the previous stage. Apply this 'ashy' colour to the shaded area of his forehead using the size 8 and size 5 filberts, then begin to work outwards. Look carefully at the reference, and adapt the puddle, gradually adding touches of red or yellow to warm it, and small amounts of black or white to adjust the tone.

- If an area of skin 'shouts' too much and jumps out at you after you apply it, the tone is wrong. Gradually work into it with more of the correct hue.

- The hair of the eyebrows does not need a separate mix: just add more black and white to your base puddle to desaturate the colour and make it ashen.

- The subject's nose and cheeks are redder, with more blood. However, be careful not to go overboard with red when enriching your midtone puddle. You can warm it with a little cadmium red, but moderate it with yellow ochre, too, to prevent it looking too pink. Pay attention to the soft edges on the cheeks, and also bring in a little of the reflected light.

- At the bottom, the beard and moustache have almost greenish tinges, so bring in ivory black and yellow ochre to reflect this. Use the tip of the brush to get finer marks.

- With the face in place, paint the background. Make a new puddle for this from ivory black and titanium white. This neutral mix will ensure that it doesn't compete with the human tones of the skin. Add more white to the mix for the hoodie. Once the background and clothes are painted, go back and adjust to bring in some warmer hints with the addition of tiny touches of cadmium red or yellow ochre.

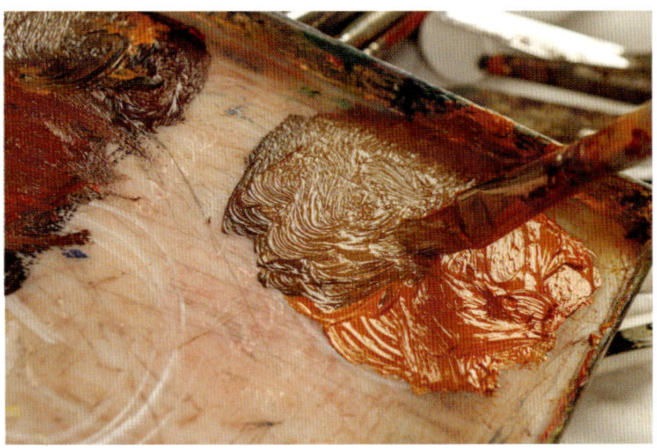

The old dark mix (visible at the top left) is being added to the new base mix. Note that some of the new base mix puddle is kept separate.

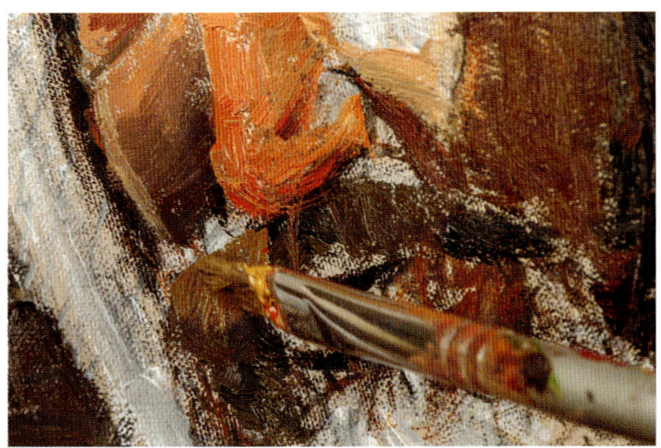

Apply the paint with light touches of the filbert – you want to apply the paint lightly on top, so if it touches dark-toned paint from earlier, you won't mix on the surface.

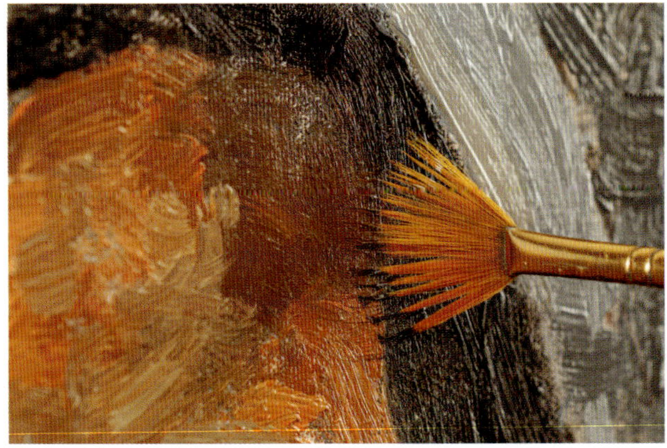

You can use the fan brush to soften some of the harder transitions, lightly drawing the brush from area to area to blend a little. Don't overdo this; you want to keep the textural quality where you can.

For the lips, continue to concentrate on tone. You do need a bit of red here, but it shouldn't shout. Use the tip of the size 5 filbert at various angles to apply the paint – this will help to keep the surface interesting.

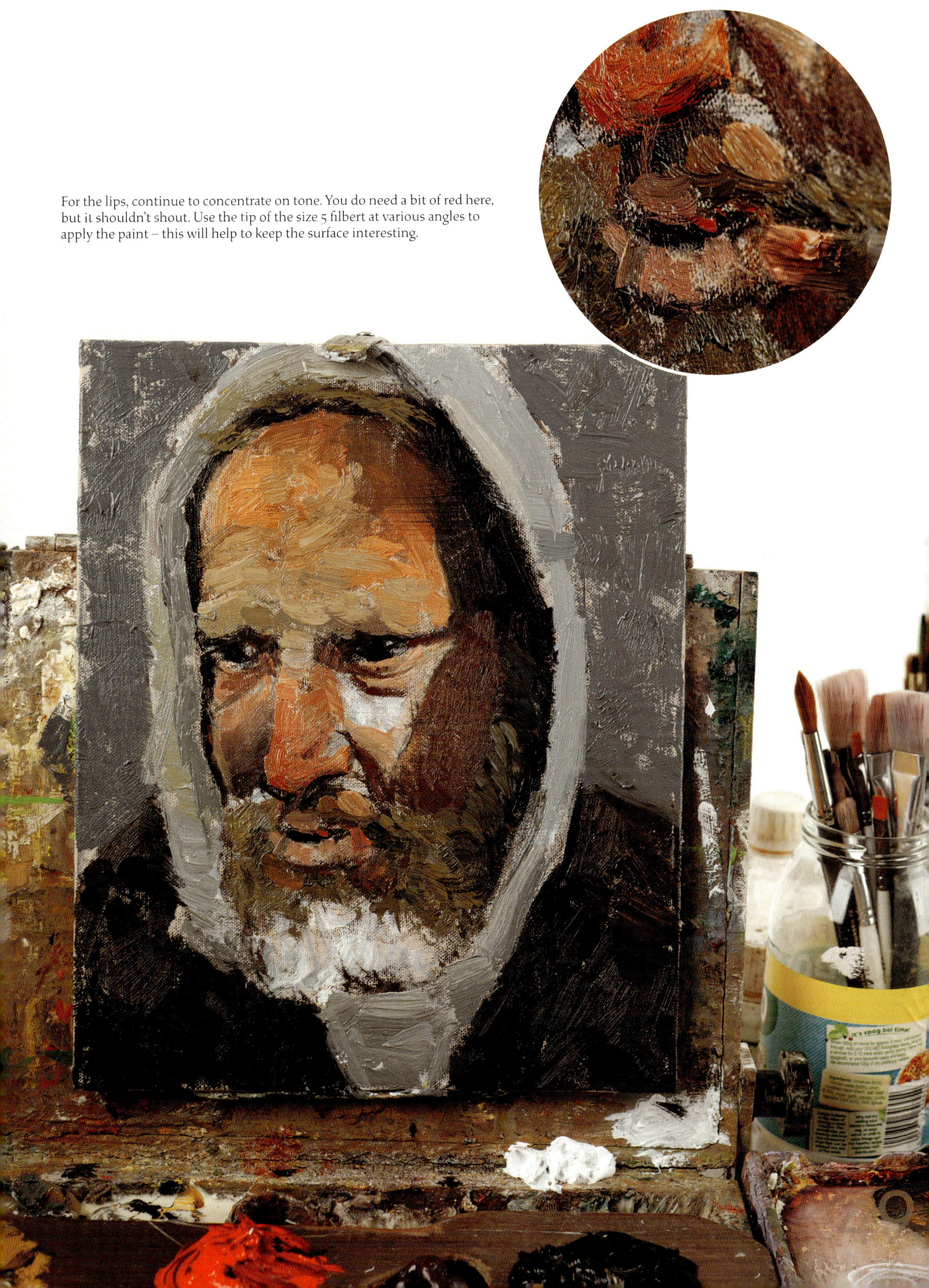

Lights

This is where the painting really starts to come alive. It's the stage I like best. I want a brush that can handle detail, so swap over to your two smaller brushes. I'm using a size 3 filbert and what was a size 6 round – but like the others, I've trimmed it down so the tip is more flexible (see page 13). This means that when it touches the canvas, this brush applies the paint but gives you control over where it goes.

- The paints used for the lights will be thicker – this helps the paint to stand out and catch the eye. Create a light puddle with titanium white with a little yellow ochre. I add a lot of Maroger here to ensure we can make punchy, sculptural marks. However, although the paint is thick, we want to ensure a human feel, so pay close attention to the soft edges and make sure your brushmarks aren't too hard and flat.

- Temperature is key here: ask yourself with every area, are you looking at a cool light or a warm light? On his brow, for example, we need a cool, ashy highlight, so add a hint of your neutral midtone puddle to ensure there's plenty of white and black in it. On his cheeks, however, there's warmth, so bring in cadmium red and yellow ochre. All the while, keep tone in the back of your mind – remember this is the highlighting stage, so things need to be light.

- For the beard, the highlights need to be sharp and thick. Add lots of Maroger and Liquin, plus plenty of titanium white to create a mix that is almost like a thick, rich and sumptuous dessert. Nothing needs to be perfect here, so enjoy the game of painting: touch your brushes on the surface to apply the paint.

- Use a small brush to touch in the paint in the eyes – we want to use these important areas to ensure the viewer understands the feelings and emotions of the man in the picture. The whites of the eye are never really white, so knock the tone back a little. Again, we don't have blue, so add ivory black to the mix for the man's blue irises.

- Switch to a size 2 brush for the final details, and use the mixes on your palette to refine and develop the painting until you are satisfied. Once you have restated the vital lights and darks, it's done. Don't be tempted to overwork the painting and spoil the immediacy and impact of your earlier stages. All the foundational work was done in the sketching stage; but we've developed it further, so don't break down your sculptural impression with too much fine detail.

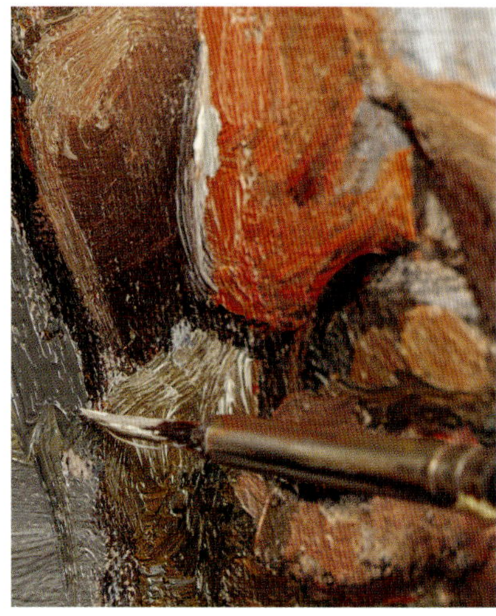

I love the cool light on his moustache, so I spend a lot of time here, drawing the brush carefully to work over it. The balance at this stage is ensuring a sculptural feel without rushing. Work carefully so that you don't overwork or obscure the marks you've made with new brushmarks, but ensure that you're accurately describing the individual you're painting.

A size 2 round is small enough to add in the very fine detail of the subject's eyes and the deep furrows in his brows. The sketcher in me loves to pick out these characterful details.

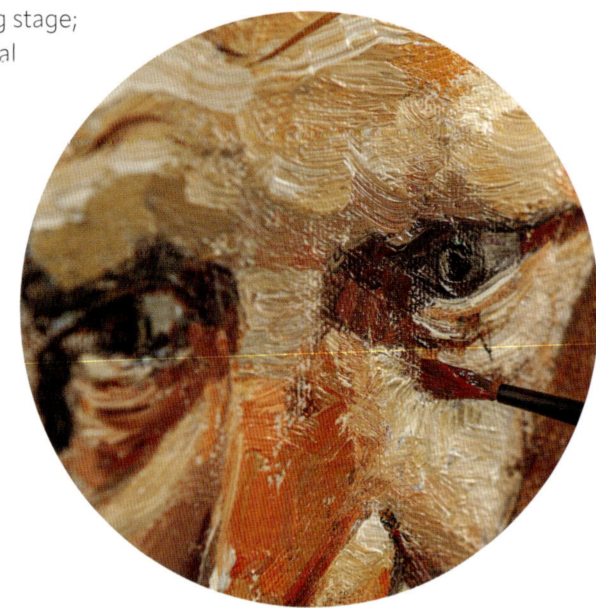

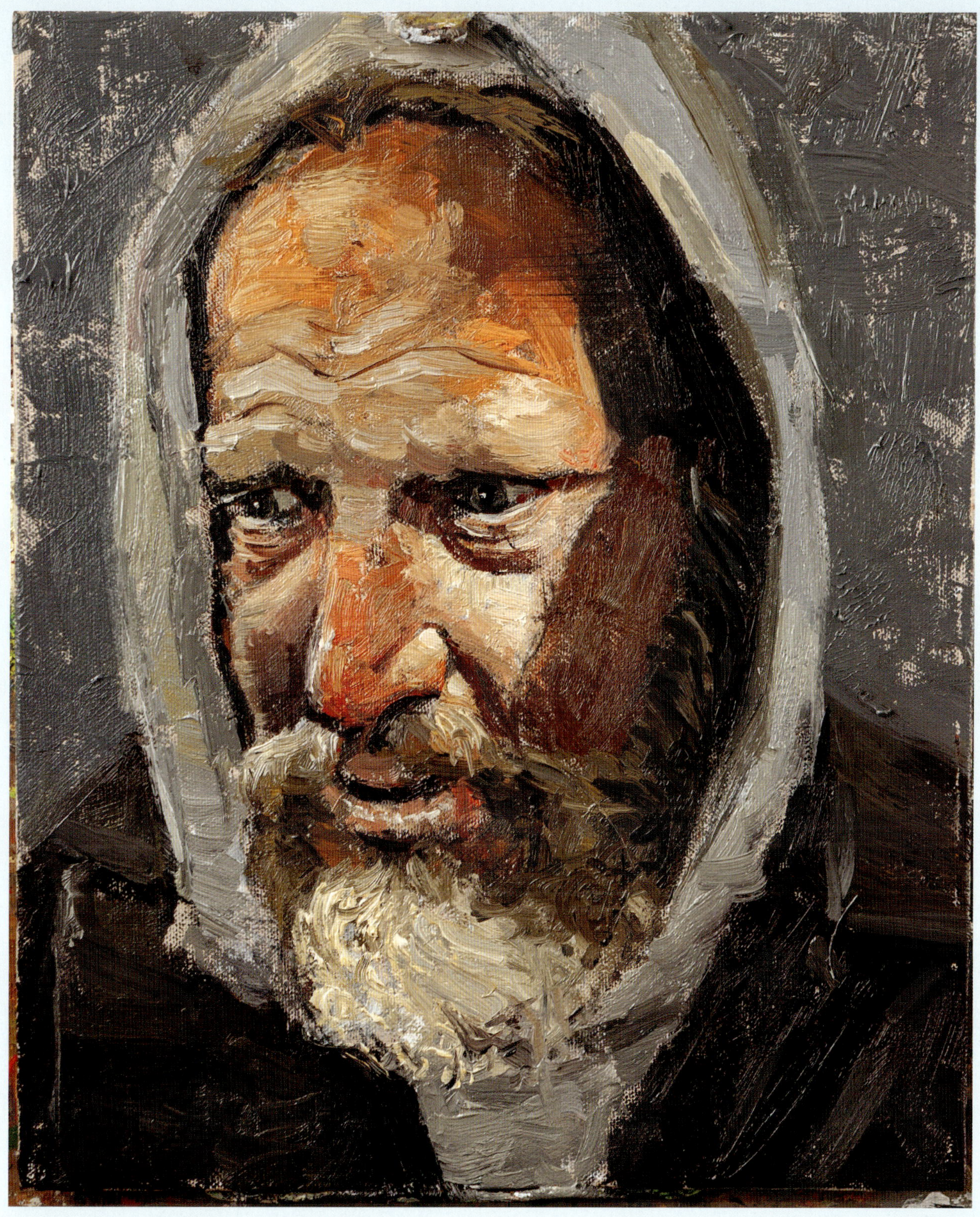

The finished painting

Commission work

When you paint for yourself, you can compose as you wish; but I wanted to include some examples of commission portraits, where the sitter had some input into the work. Their ideas and wishes can lead you to different, enjoyable challenges.

Painting *Chris Eubank*

I painted this portrait of champion boxer Chris Eubank from pictures, studies and sketches made when he visited my studio in Chelsea in 2016, as part of a series of paintings commissioned by *The One Show* (BBC One). The theme of the series was 'a brush with fame', and I got to interview, sketch and paint different celebrities and know a bit more about their journeys to stardom.

I used oils, because it was the only befitting medium for the size he recommended – I had been planning to do a smaller piece, but he simply insisted he 'doesn't do small', so I changed my plan and did this larger size.

For this traditional, formally posed piece, I used the inside-out technique (see page 29), working from his head outwards until the work was complete. Working in oils gave me the freedom to work wet in wet and not have to worry about the drying time – I had plenty of time to work one phase of the work into another.

Chris Eubank   100 × 100cm (39 × 39in)

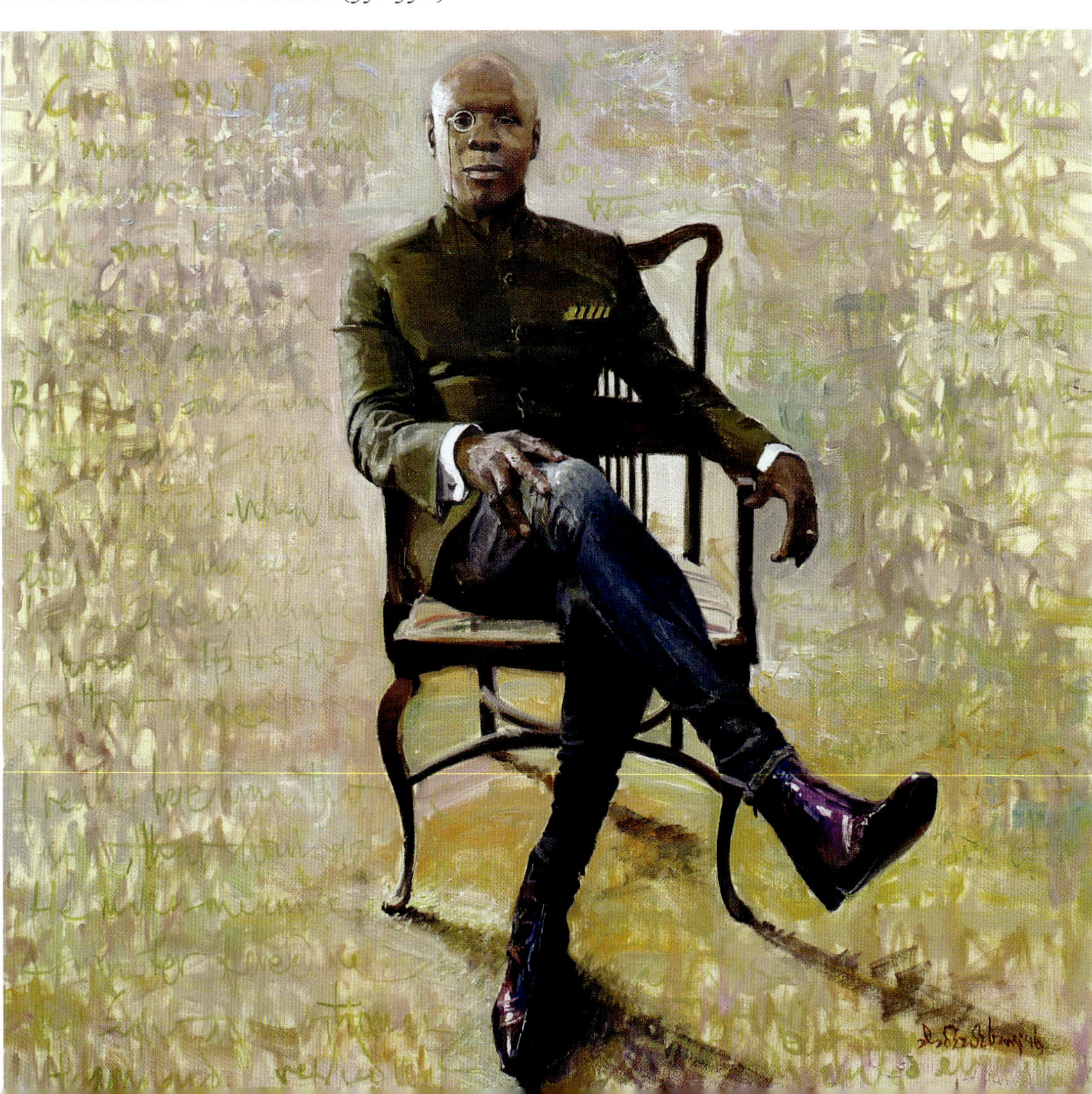

Painting *Professor Sir Ed Byrne*

This was a commission for the public collection of portraits at King's College London. Sir Ed Byrne was leaving and it is customary that the outgoing Principal gets their portrait painted by an artist. I was contacted by the College on the recommendation of Sir Ed's wife, Melissa Byrne.

I met Ed at his office at King's College and asked how he would love his portrait to be painted. I sketched him and took loads of pictures to formulate a few studies for him to choose from. After some discussion he mentioned that he wanted the College in the background. I then decided to make the College as a painting in the background while still maintaining his position indoors. He and the College were pleased with the idea – and the result.

I began with a very thorough gridded picture sketched onto the canvas as seen to the right, then worked with the inside-out technique to complete the painting.

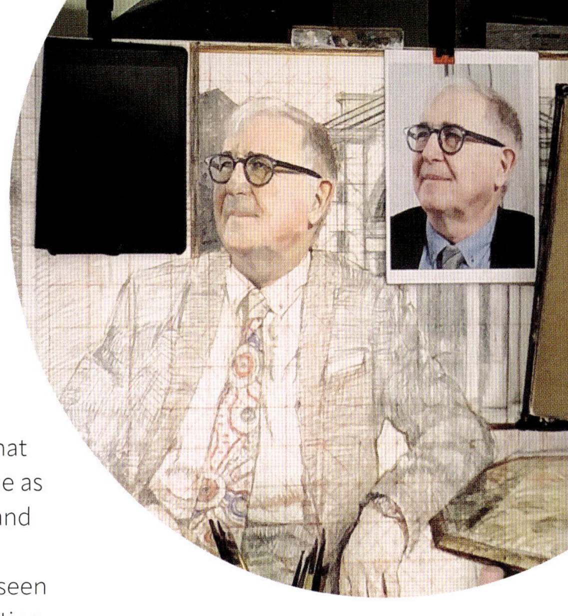

You can see in this work in progress picture how I keep my reference very close to the area that I am working on – in this case, the face.

Professor Sir Ed Byrne   101 × 76cm (40 × 30in)

Sir Ed Byrne was President and Principal of King's College London from 2014 to 2021.

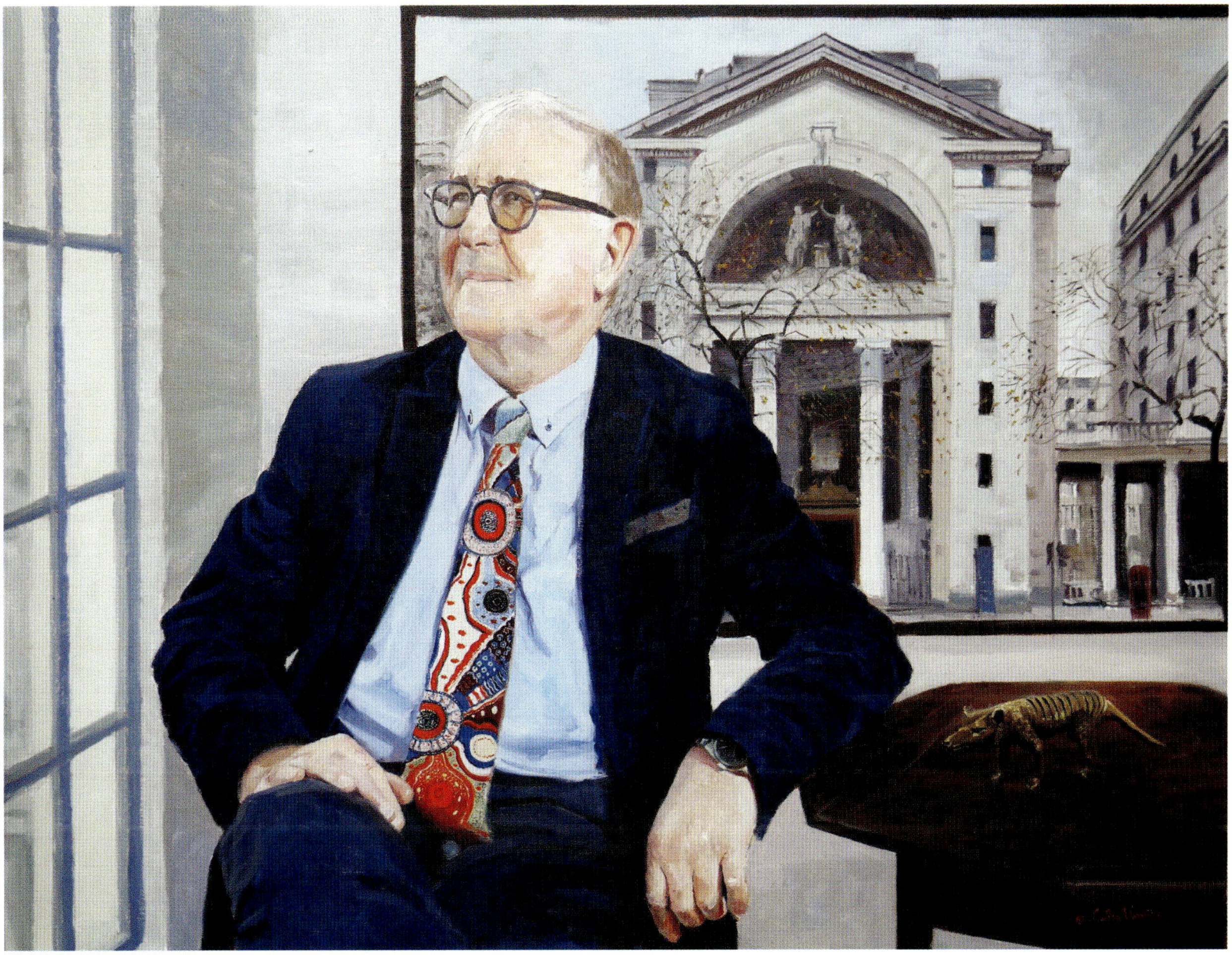

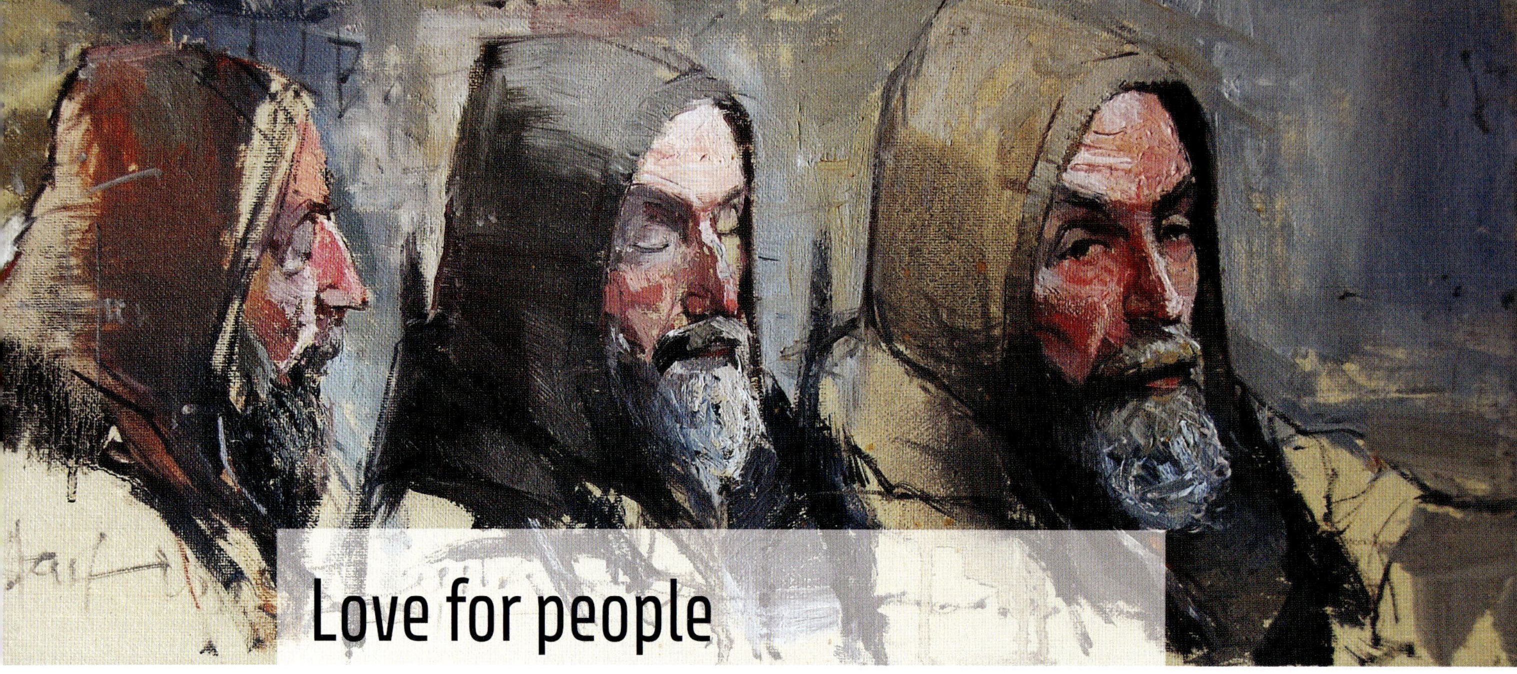

Love for people

I simply love the beauty, emotions, textures and movement of the people around me – it's these things that made me literally fall in love with painting people, whether up-close with a personal portrait, in the context of a broader scene, or as part of a massed crowd.

There's a subtly different appeal to painting people than places, where my interest is grabbed more by the mood, atmosphere, weather, historical importance and details of the architecture.

One aspect, however, links both – and is key, in fact, to whatever I'm painting – and that is the effects of light and shade.

Observation

Really looking at people is important if you want to paint – and fortunately, I love looking at people's faces. I can lose myself people-watching for hours, taking in the effect of light on faces, the mood, the beauty – whether in the innocence of a child's gaze or the weathered ruggedness of a homeless person's face. I'm simply a people person; and so I love sketching and painting portraits.

Don't be shy to ask if you can sketch someone. I have an outrageous habit of boldly asking people who I find fascinating or interesting to paint if they wouldn't mind being sketched, or if they wouldn't mind me taking a photograph so I can paint them back in my studio. Most people agree, some think I'm crazy, and sometimes I get an outright no! As with everything in life, you can only get what you put effort into getting.

Practice

Consistent sketching will come in handy for teaching you accuracy, and I regularly sketch people's faces on my journeys on public transport. This everyday exercise helps to build good hand–eye coordination, which is an important element in painting portraits from life.

I don't rely so much on my freehand sketching when painting portraits from photographs or a screen. Instead, I grid the reference picture so that nothing is left to my imagination or freedom: I must nail it when it comes to portraits, so I don't take chances. The lesson, whether working from life or from reference, is that accuracy in drawing is key.

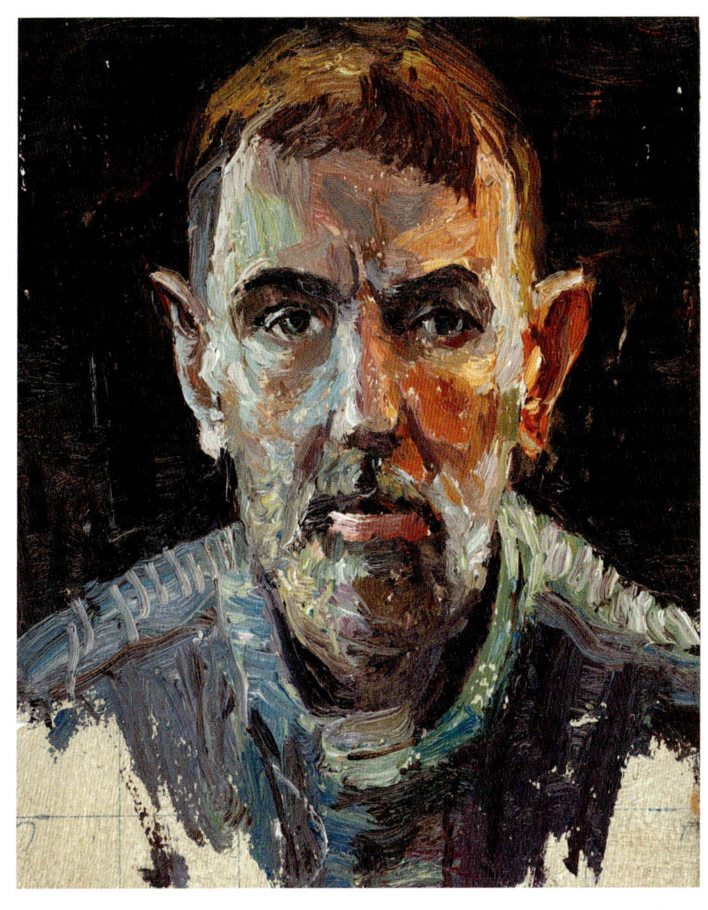
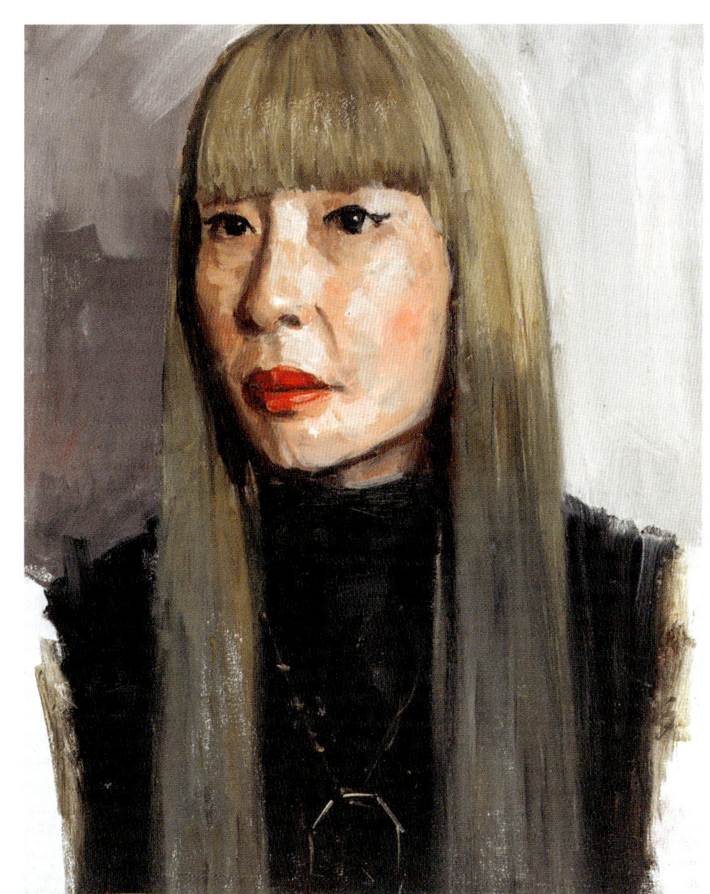
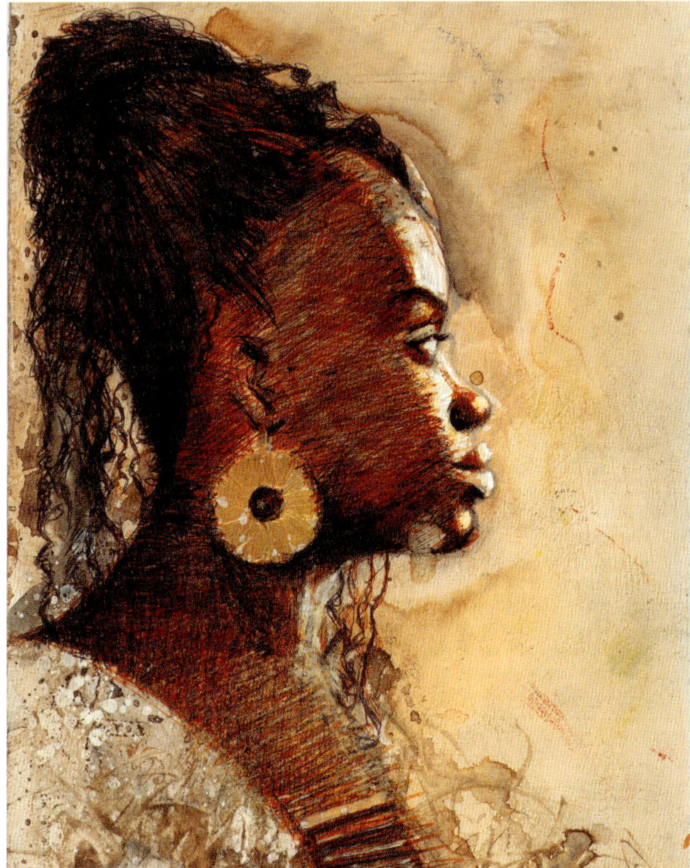
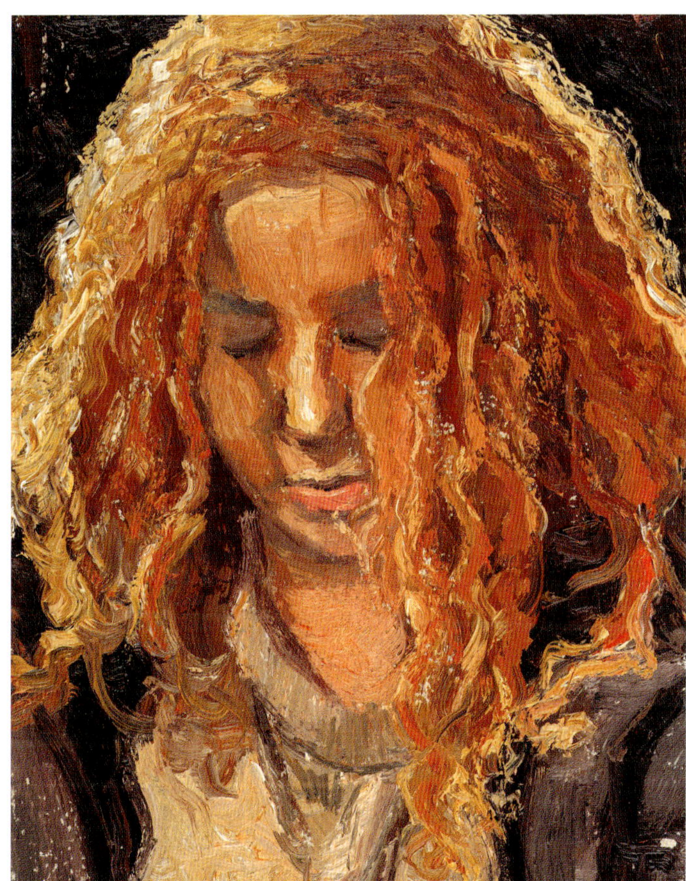

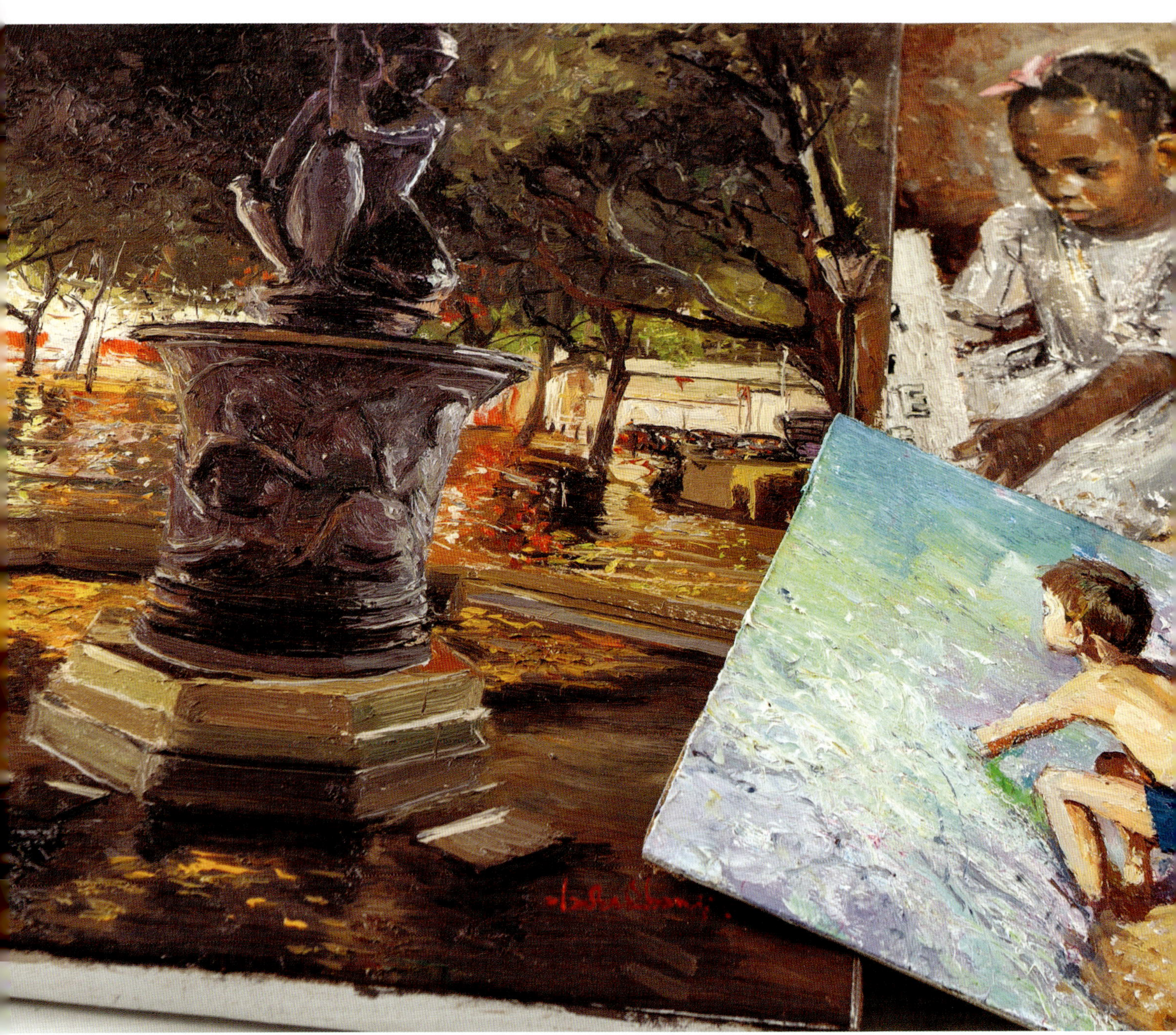

FIGURES

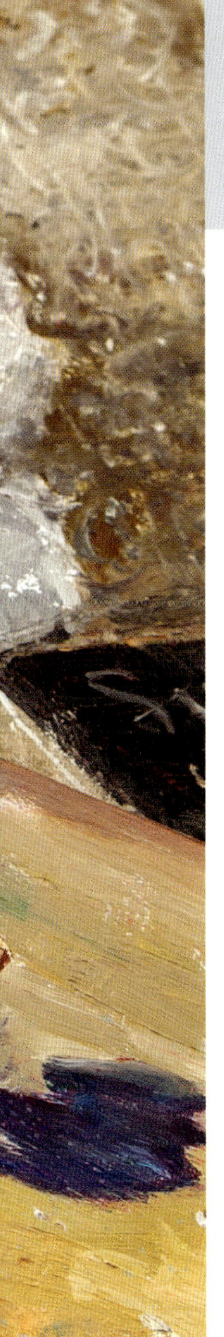

Whether indoors or outdoors you'll always see figures – perhaps people interacting or just someone taking a quiet walk. They could be a lone figure in a gallery, a child painting, a boxer, people playing snooker, a busker, a ballet dancer... the list goes on for everyday scenes that focus on figures interacting – whether with each other or their surroundings. Everywhere you go you will see potential material for paintings. This is precisely why I always keep my sketchbook and my phone camera with me – and why I am constantly recording scenes from my everyday life. Figures are the fuel that I use for artworks.

The key thing to note when painting full figures and groups of figures is the overall shape or shapes of the person or people you are painting. Unlike portraits, you never want to get bogged down with details. Instead, look for any connections and shapes in the scene that can make the depiction of your figures easier. Again, your sketching skills are vital. That is your ticket and password to producing convincing and accurate figurative work.

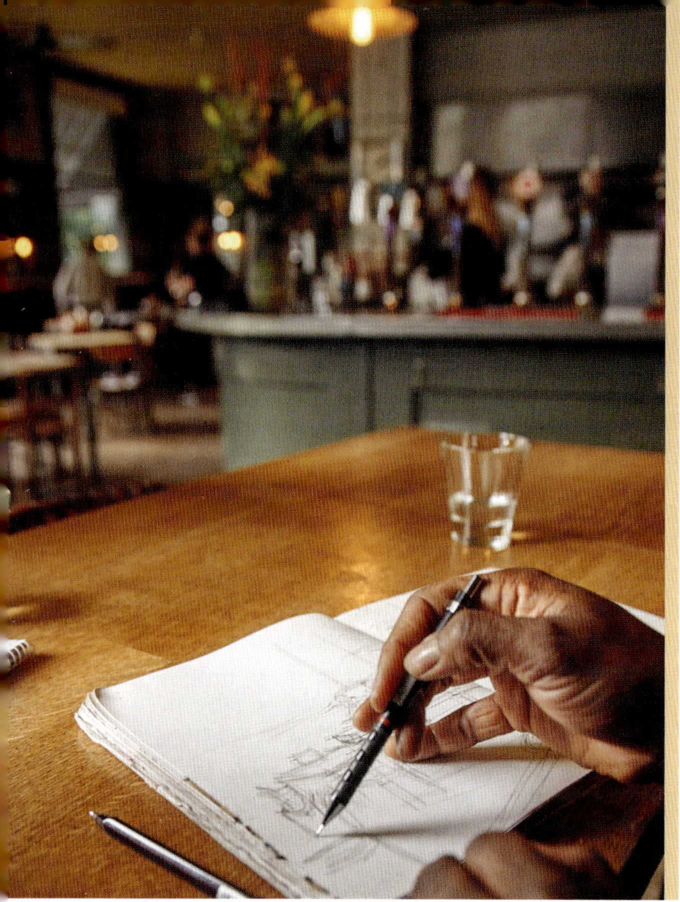

Interiors

When painting people in interior spaces, it's important to include some suggestions of the background as this will add interest and context to your painting and give a bit more of a story than a portrait would.

While the background should be included, it's important to strike a balance between framing and giving context to the figure, and distracting from the focus. In general, I suggest you aim simply to suggest enough of the surroundings to complement the figure: this will help to ensure the viewer's eye remains on the main figure (or figures) in the painting – as in the examples on these pages.

In *Creative Depression*, the complex background surrounds and seems to bear down on the focal figure, reinforcing the oppressive mood. In contrast, in *Mesmerized by Laura Knight*, the background is represented with very simple marks and little eye-catching contrast. The painting that the man is looking at forms an important part of the narrative – so it is this alone that is developed and refined as much as the figure. The rest of his surroundings are left very simple.

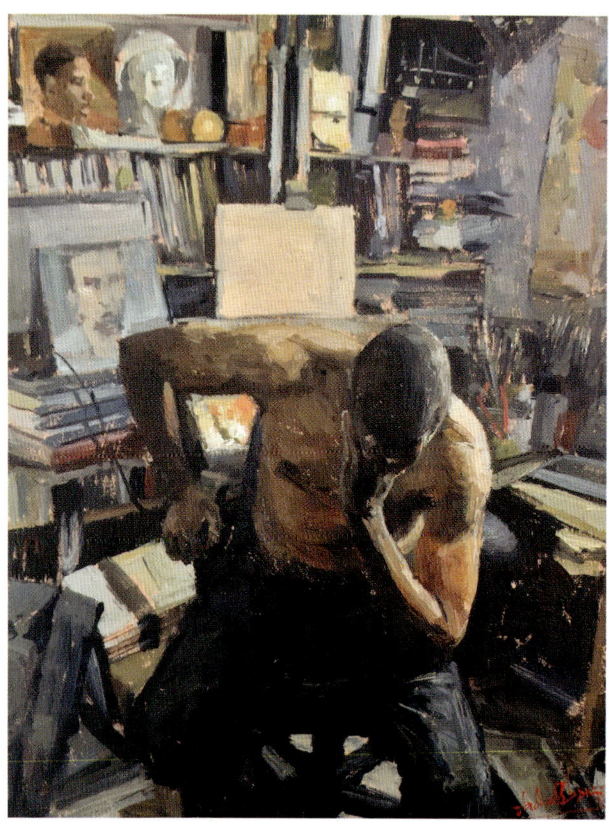

Creative Depression   35 × 45cm (14 × 18in)

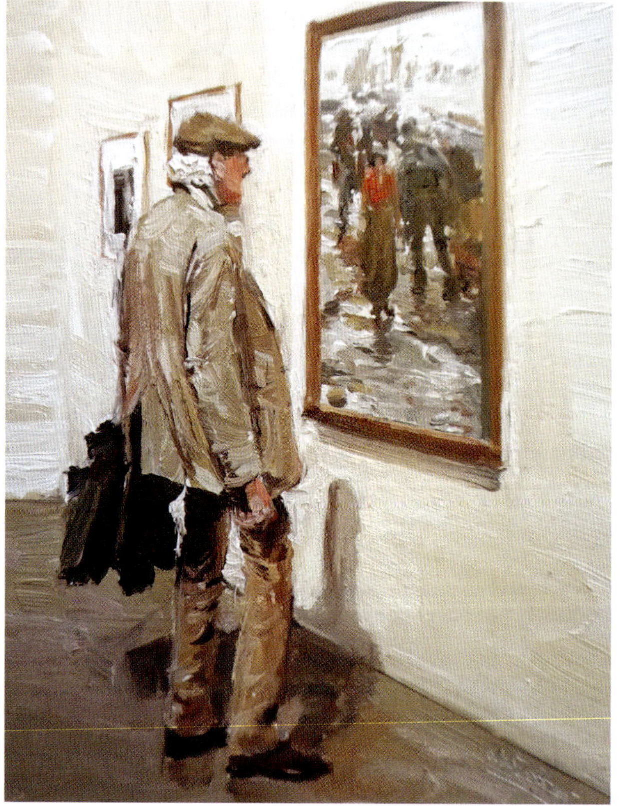

Mesmerized by Laura Knight   25 × 30cm (10 × 12in)

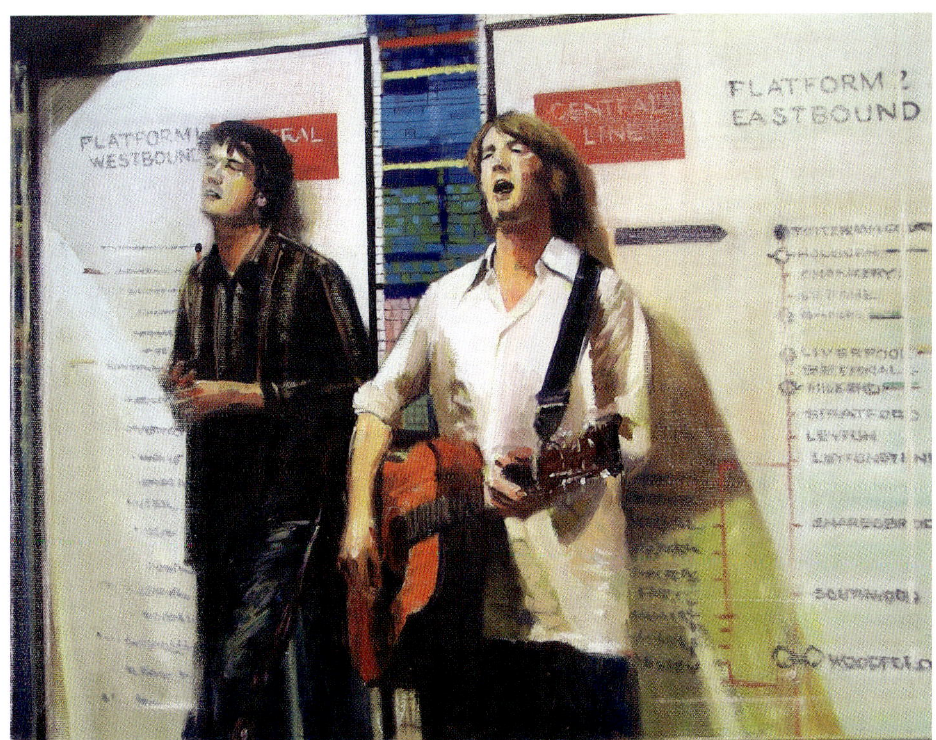

Buskers   67 × 60cm (26¼ × 24in)

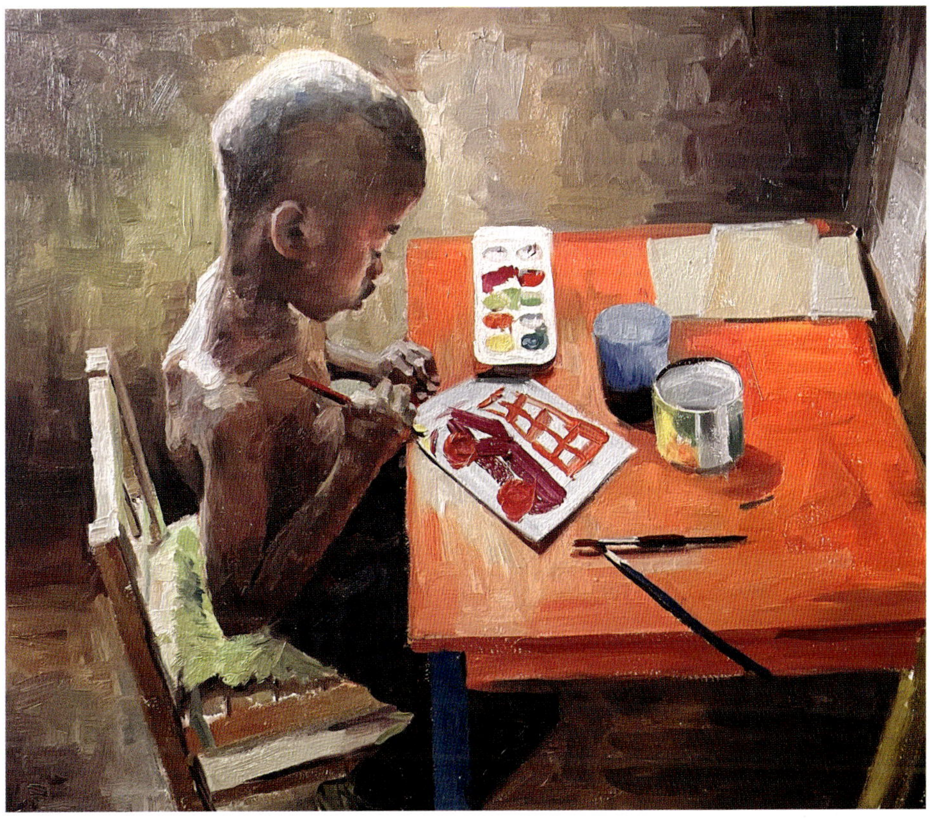

The Little Artist II   60 × 50cm (24 × 20in)

Paint: The Little Artist

Successful *alla prima* figurative work needs to strike a balance between being lively and drawing the subject well enough to be recognizable. The key area needs to be refined enough to draw the eye, but not so tight that it becomes overworked. If you treat every area like a detailed portrait, you'll end up with a dead, tight result.

Here I'm using an inside-out approach (see page 29), tackling each part in turn, shape by shape by shape – the hat, the easel and so forth. Each part is resolved in turn, rather than gradually developing the whole painting at the same time. Inside-out is a slower process, but it's so rewarding as it builds up. It's a good way to tackle paintings of people where you're not that fond of the background. The clutter becomes abstract shapes or is left out entirely, so that the focus stays on the subject.

I think all of us need to get back to the child in us. We were born to be creators! Too often we overthink our painting, and that leads to procrastination or fears that we won't be good enough. Have a child's ease with paint: forget about what people are going to think about your art, and just do it. That's the way of the artist. Not all passion needs to be loose and dangerous – the grid will help you get the best of both your childlike enthusiasm and adult control and skill.

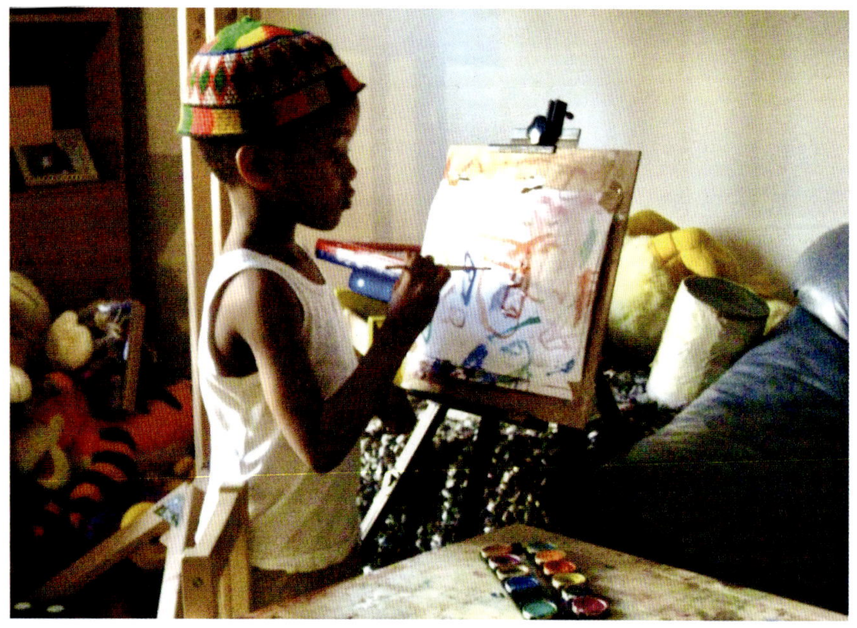

The original photograph is in 4:3 proportion – common to most smartphones – which makes converting it to a 16 × 12 grid easy.

As we're working on a light-coloured base, I've used black Posca pen. Note that I've also numbered the grid across the centre. This is useful when working with a bigger grid, and helps you to find the centre quickly.

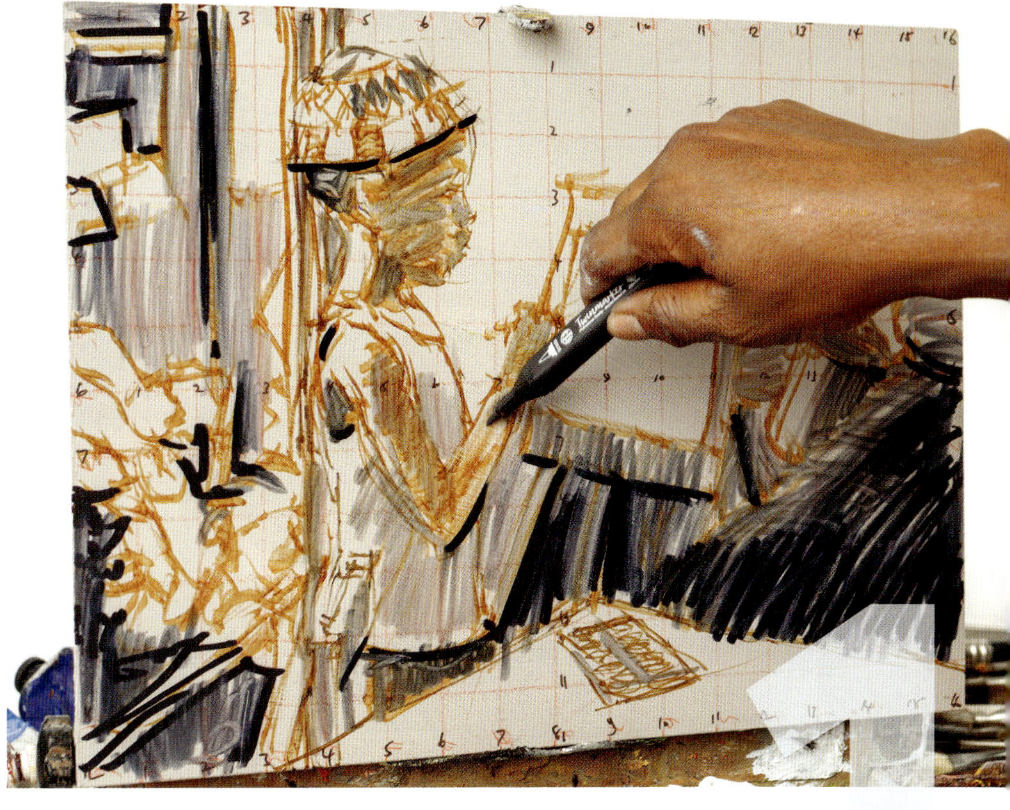

Sketching

Confidence comes from practice, so I encourage you to sketch, sketch, sketch before you even think about painting. The creativity will come through in your painting, later – but for the sketch you need to be a good follower, just copying with as much detail as possible. Close your right-brain creativity for the moment and copy what's in front of you.

You can start from coloured pencils if you prefer, but here, I'm confident that I can lay down all I need with brush markers; partly because I'm planning to simplify the background, and partly because the grid makes things easier. With the grid in place, there's no need to second-guess things: all the information is there. Be faithful to the grid so you don't lose your way to the destination.

- Use burnt sienna for the major lines, making sure the child at work is clear; then bring in darks with the black Twinmarker, and midtones with cool grey 5.

- Think in painting terms; block in the large dark areas loosely, freely and quickly. Don't get bogged down: enjoy your sketching.

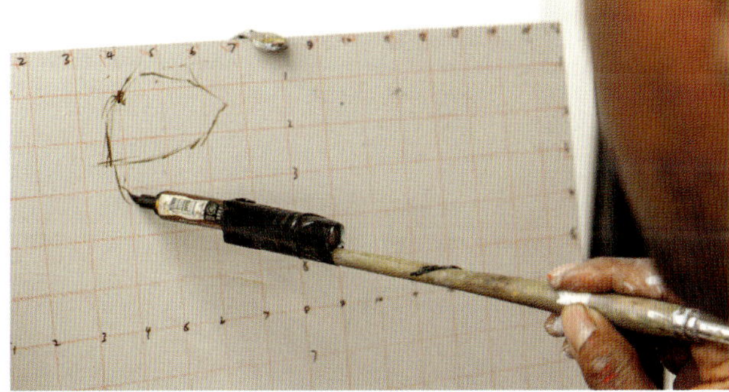

To get more of a brush-like feel, and create some distance between you and the surface, tape your brush markers to paintbrush handles.

GETTING SET UP

Paints

Titanium white
Yellow ochre
Cadmium red
Ivory black

Mediums

Liquin Impasto
Maroger
Alkyd
Bob Ross Odourless Thinner

Brushes

Sizes 8 and 2 filbert
25mm (1in) flat
Size 2 round
Trimmed fan brush (see page 66)

Surface

40 × 30cm (16 × 12in)
  canvas board, prepared
  with a 16 × 12 grid

Other materials

Smartphone, tablet or gridded
  reference photograph
Posca pens, 0.9mm: black, white
Brush markers: Winsor & Newton
  burnt sienna
Decotime Twinmarkers:
  black 120; cool grey 5
Coloured pencils: Faber-Castell
  Polychromos black
Liquitex Heavy Body Acrylic:
  titanium white
Small palette knives

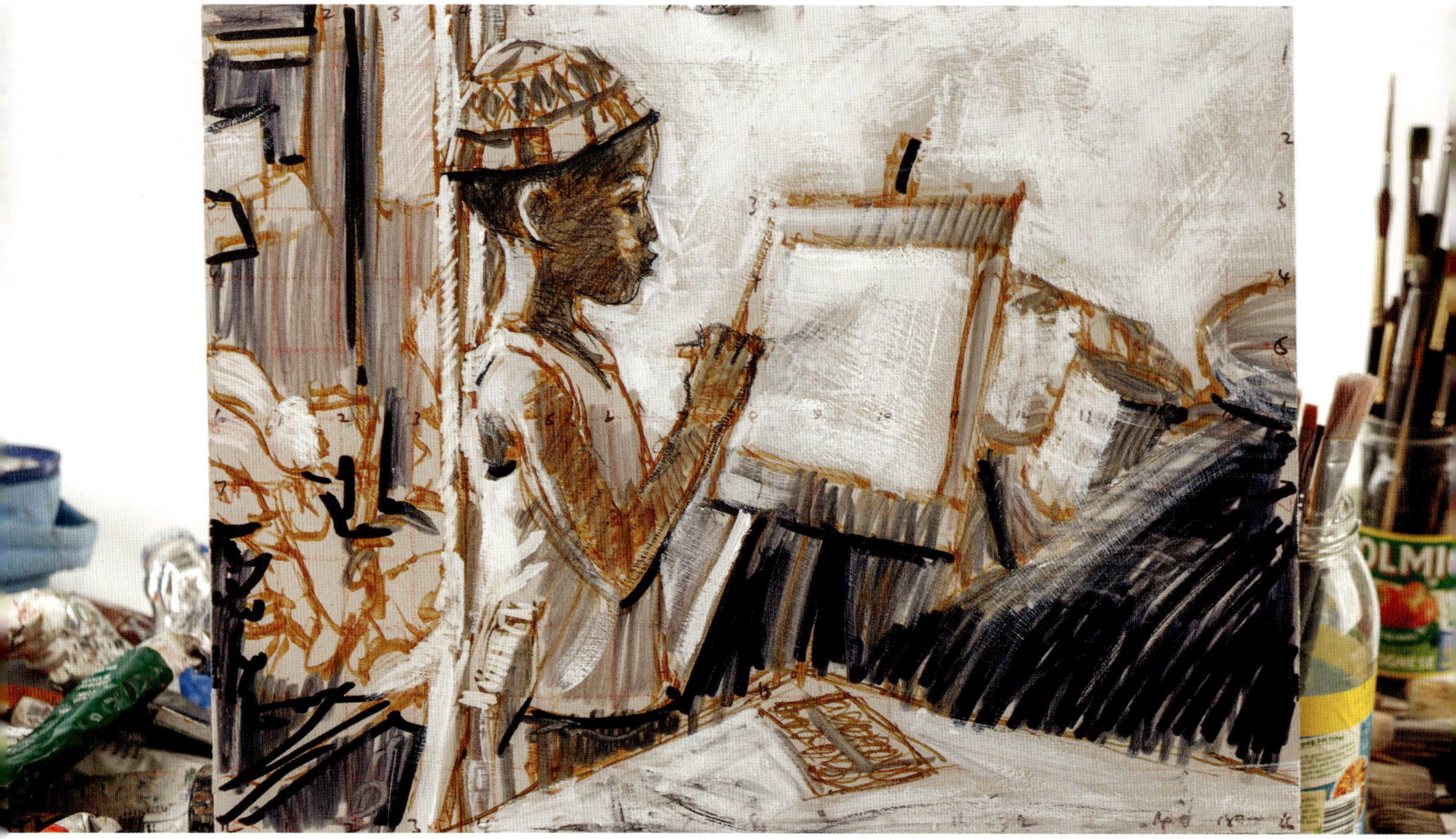

This is my equivalent to a traditional underpainting – I love sketching so much that I want to bring the visceral feel of it into my oils; and I've found using a mix of media the best way to get a good drawing on the surface.

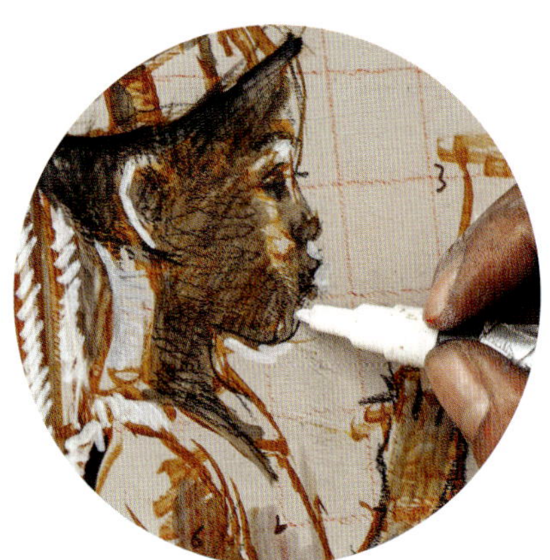

The white Posca pen lets you cut back in over dark tones to refine shapes.

Refining the sketch

The finished sketch should be a 'false painting': everything in place, the tones and shapes accurate and ready to make your painting easy and enjoyable. Avoid areas that you don't like – I've ignored the clutter visible between the boy and the easel.

- Bring in some black coloured pencil and white Posca pen to add some impact in the tones and vary the textures.

- Use titanium white acrylic paint to build up the large light areas and fill in the background. Now that the lines and shapes are in place, the grid is no longer necessary, so you can paint right over it.

- Use choppy, loose marks even at this stage – it's how we'll handle the oils later on, so let's start as we mean to go on. This establishes the texture to give us something to work on.

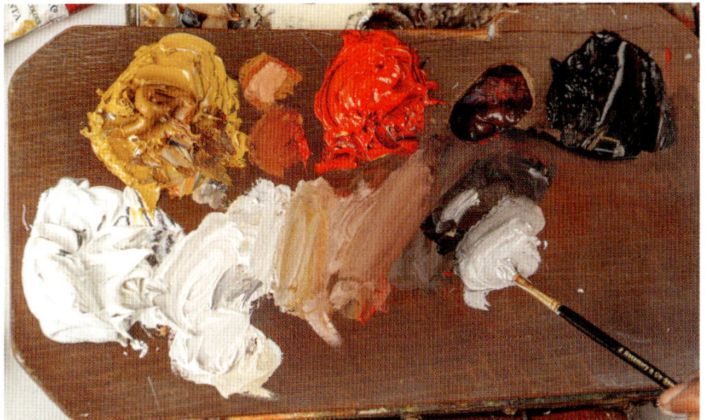

The Zorn palette makes colour mixing easier as you need only consider four options: black to deepen the tone, white to tint it and red or ochre to warm it and get the hue right. Add both black and white to desaturate the area.

Starting the painting

With the inside-out approach, colour and tone need to be considered equally. It's a lot to bear in mind, but you only need to work shape-by-shape. Work slowly and steadily and build up brushstroke by brushstroke, working outwards. If you can, zoom in on the area of your source image that you're focusing on.

First, I concentrate on the face and the hand. These are the key areas that add intimacy to the painting, so they're particularly important. The brushstrokes here will be more controlled than elsewhere, and in the finished painting, this extra detail will draw the viewer's eye.

- Pick a particular area of your source image to focus upon. Mixing the colours as you go along, and using a size 2 filbert for detail and control, break down the shape into small areas. Squint to help better see the major shifts in tone and edge. Anything that disappears when you squint is irrelevant.

- Pick an area – I started with the forehead – and mix a colour that matches. Here that was ivory black with yellow ochre and some cadmium red to warm it a little. Place the colour with a single brushstroke, then work outwards. Pay attention to the exact tone and hue of the mix and adjust as you need to.

- While painting, try to put ideas like 'face' or 'easel' out of your head. Just look for shapes and edges. When you place the next brushstroke, does it need to be lighter or darker, warmer or cooler, richer or more neutral than the brushstroke next to it?

From known to unknown. If you can't decide what colour an area is, compare it with nearby colours. The red on the hat obviously needs lots of cadmium red, and so you know the nearby green needs none of that – just a combination of the other three.

Painting the background

Now I've got the important focal area complete, it's time to paint the rest. While I still need to pay attention to shapes, tone and temperature and the other 'bedrock' parts of painting, I don't want the background to compete with the intimate heart of the picture. Bigger, freer marks are the key here, along with particular attention to the nature of the edges.

The hard work you put into the sketch earlier will pay off now, and make the painting easier.

- Use a large, squarish brush, like a 25mm (1in) flat so that you are unable to overstate areas. It'll force you to work with larger, more open brushstrokes.

- The base mix is titanium white, ivory black and yellow ochre, with plenty of Liquin and Maroger. As before, each area is built up brushstroke by brushstroke, and the particular tone and hue considered with each stroke. The brushwork is vital. I don't want any of the brushwork to be boring, so I use a variety of angles and pressures to vary the marks.

- The room is full of clutter, but using a big brush forces us to work out how to represent it with big marks – and that means losing details. That's a good thing: the more mysterious these items are, the more they will intrigue the viewer.

- There's no right way to work. I started from the top centre and worked almost clockwise round. When I reached the edge of the table, I jumped over to paint the bottom of the figure. This was to ensure that I could get a good clean line on the foreground table. The left-hand side of the painting has some more cadmium red in the mixes: the right-hand side of the background has almost none at all. Pay attention to your reference image to ensure you're matching the colours.

- The right-hand side is considerably more complex and complicated than the left. Switch to a size 8 filbert to give you more freedom for variety of marks as you build up the shapes.

- Try to strike a balance between accurately representing what's in front of you and keeping things free, open and abstract. All of the shapes are interlocked. Nothing stands out as individual. I'm giving nothing away, but instead inviting you to look closer and create your own details from the hints I've suggested.

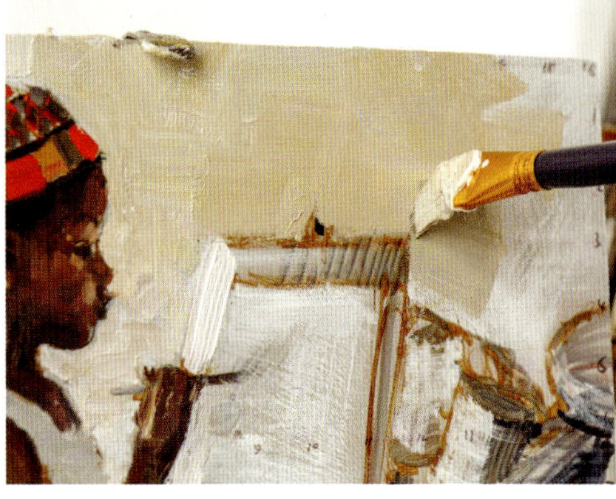

You can see here how the larger brushmarks are put in at a variety of angles for texture and interest.

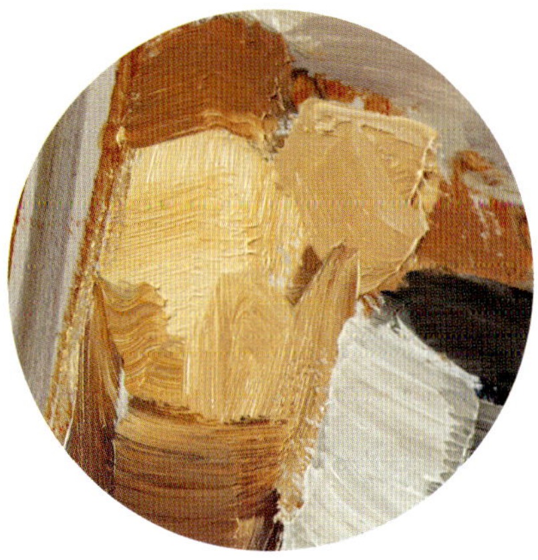

The background shapes are almost abstract. There's enough there for the viewer to read into, but not so much that it distracts from the figure.

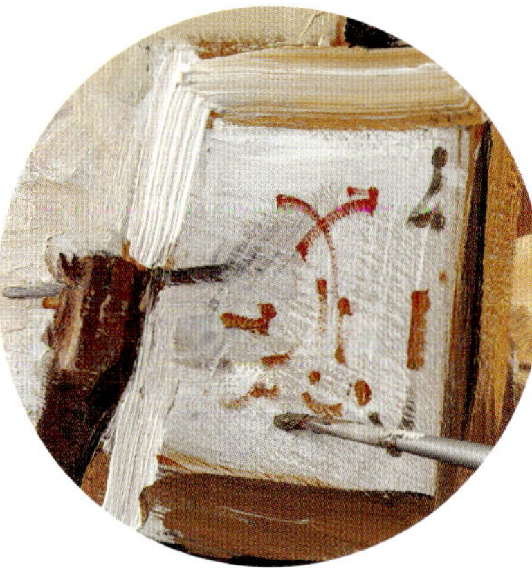

I left the canvas here as the colour of the primer, and used the size 2 brush to add a few scribbly marks before filling in a few of the blank areas with touches of a pale mix like the background.

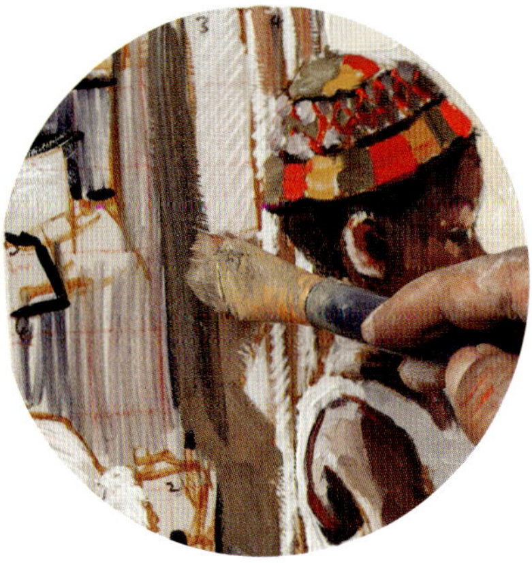

Hard edges, even relatively small ones, like on the easel or shelf, can be tackled with the edge of the 25mm (1in) flat brush used like a blade.

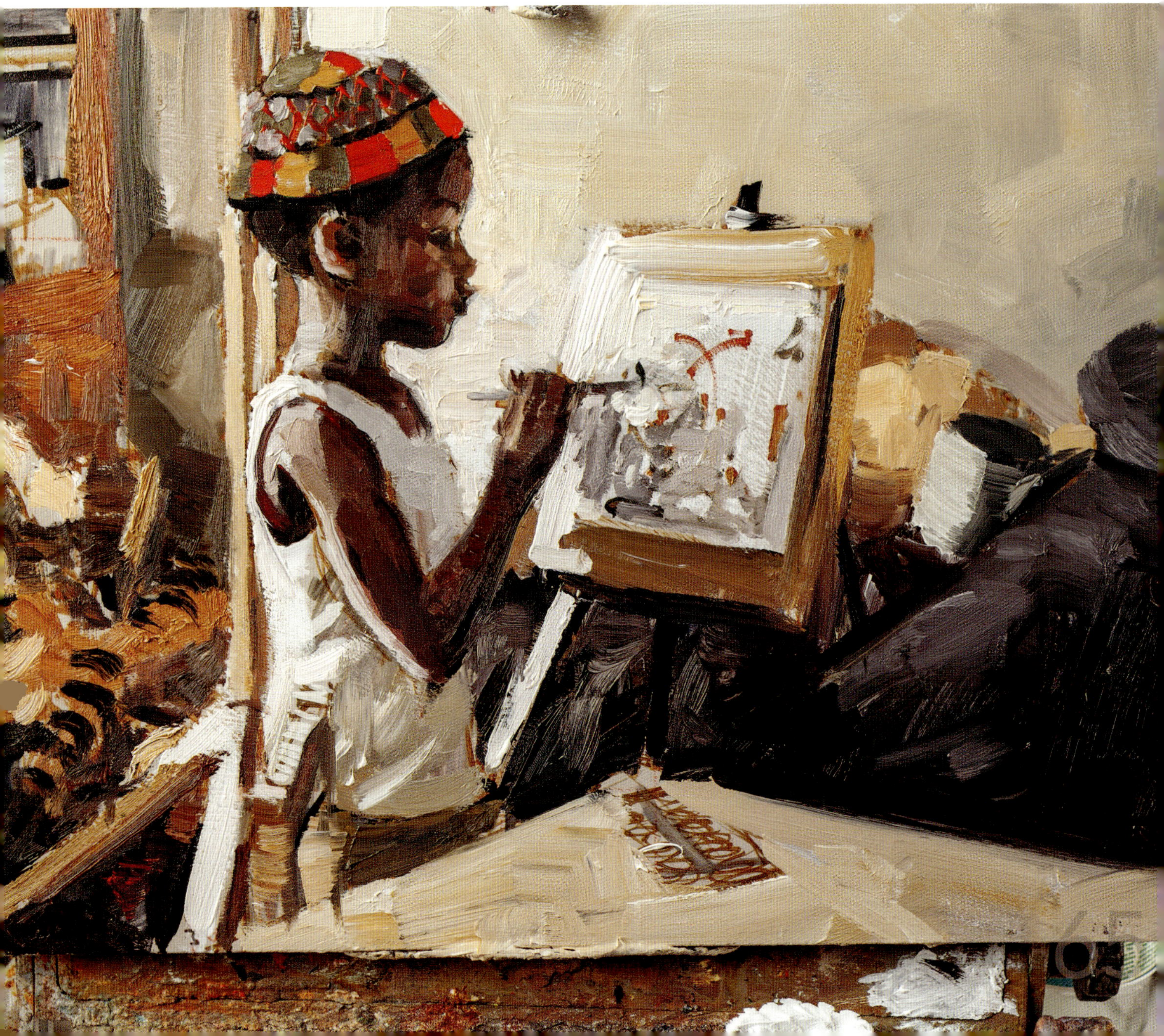

Refining and finishing

Once you've got the background in place, step back and consider. Use the mixes on your palette to revise, refine and fill in any missing areas in your mosaic of shapes. Having just three colours and white in your palette means every part of the painting will include some of the same colours, which in turn means a harmonious result will naturally happen. You won't miss the vivid greens and blues when the overall painting hangs together so beautifully!

• Be careful not to overwork the background. Keep your marks clean, clear and large so that the more controlled, finer marks of the figure remain the focus. The key thing is to keep the background light and loose so that the figure sings out.

• Swap to a size 2 round brush for the final details. Again, use the same mixes on your palette, or dip into the pure paints on your palette for the colours in the child's palette. You won't be able to recreate some of the hues on the palette in the painting, so concentrate on getting the tone right.

• Where to stop adding detail will come from experience. It's largely intuitive, but stopping every so often, stepping back and asking yourself 'what did I want to say with this painting?' will make sure you keep the overall finish in mind. If you think you've said what you want to say, then stop.

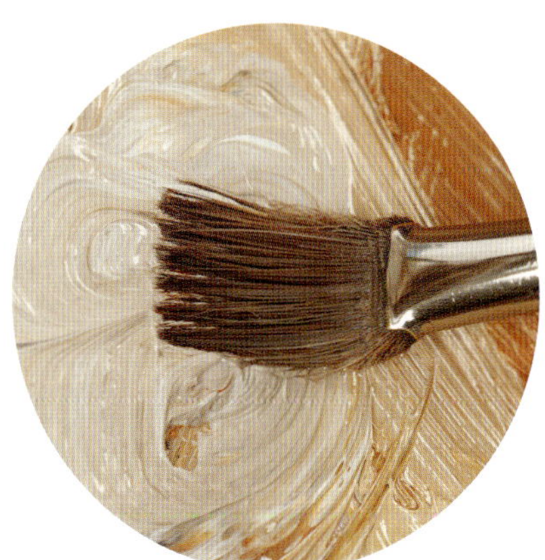

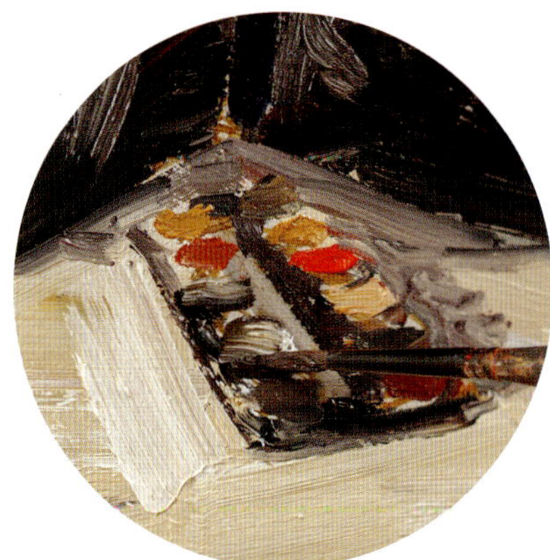

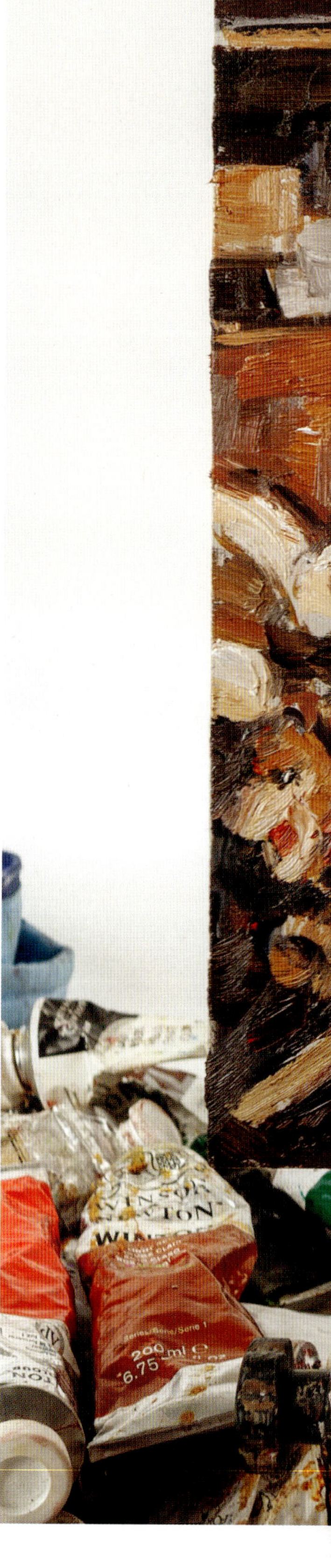

I use a customized brush for this stage. It was a fan brush, but I trimmed off the sides so that the paint goes just where I want it. You could use a size 6 flat, the size 8 filbert or something similar, but the advantage of a trimmed fan brush is that they don't have much hair, so you get a naturally light touch.

The lack of hues might seem a drawback for details like the child's paintbox, but this painting shows the strengths of the Zorn palette in giving a harmonious result – and that you don't need to represent everything exactly as it appears. It'll help you to make those artistic choices that can be paralyzing.

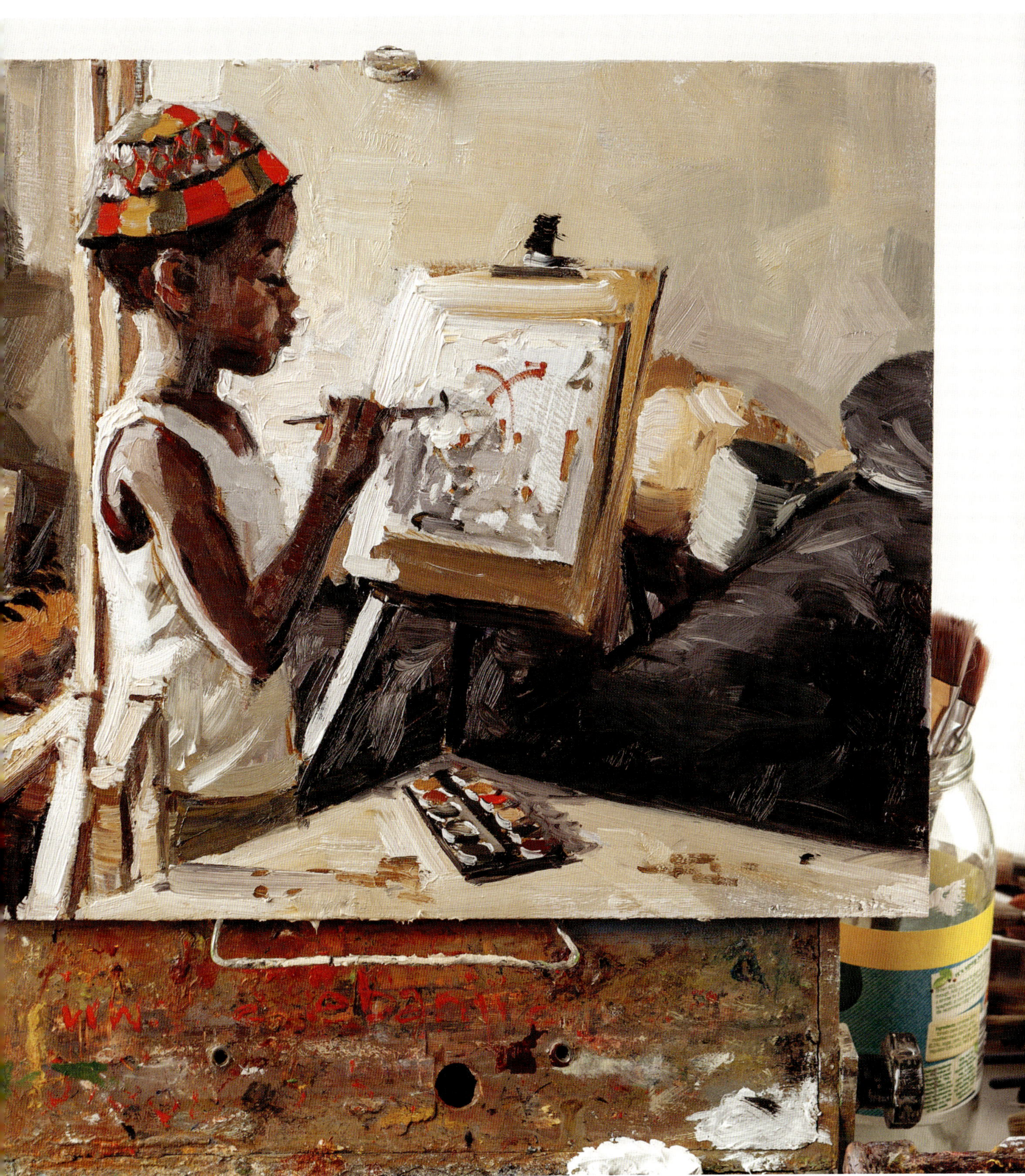

The finished painting

Figures outdoors

There is an abundance of material and references for painting figures outdoors. The simplest advice I can give is if you are interested in people, go to where people are – parks, cafés, train stations, airports, bus stops – and sketch them from life. That's the way to get the first-hand information about figures.

Look for body postures, gesture, movement and the negative spaces in between figures. All this comes down to having a flair and passion for people in places. Don't be intimidated by anatomy and other details.

When adding midground or distant figures to a landscape or urban landscape, my advice is to keep the heads small and try to minimize the feet – especially if they are moving figures.

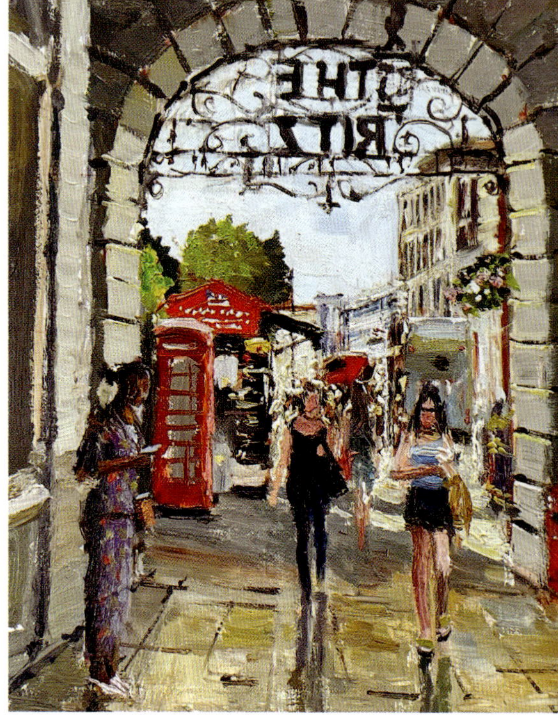

The Ritz, Backlit Summer Light I
20 × 25cm (8 × 10in)

Painting the Ritz

London is such an important part of my body of work, and these paintings, of the Ritz Hotel from Green Park, add to my repertoire of iconic London scenes.

The picture was first conceived as a *plein air* piece: I wanted to capture a sense of the flow of figures emerging from outside the archway to inside and the effect of the backlighting. But when I did the *plein air* piece (see above), I wasn't able to capture the backlighting effect as the light changed ever so quickly.

I returned the following day and took a picture of the scene when it showed the flow of figures and the strong shadows and backlighting. The new painting, made in the studio, was easier to control as I was not under any pressure and the lighting was right. The key thing I noted was not to make the shadows too dark: photographs often exaggerate the tone in shadows – hence the importance of informing your work indoors with lessons from painting outdoors (see page 30).

These pieces are the start of a future series of paintings of the Ritz archway – I also want to capture it when it's wet and grey, and also at night when the artificial tungsten lights add interest to the dark alleyway.

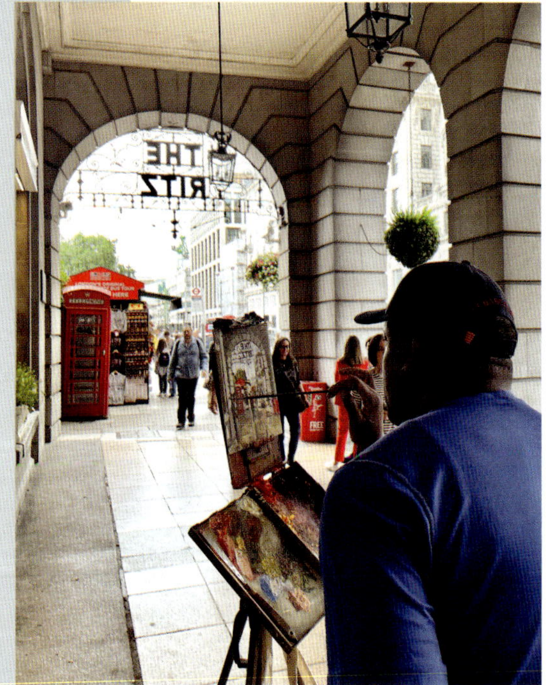

Painting *en plein air* the people walking through the arch at the Ritz from Green Park, London.

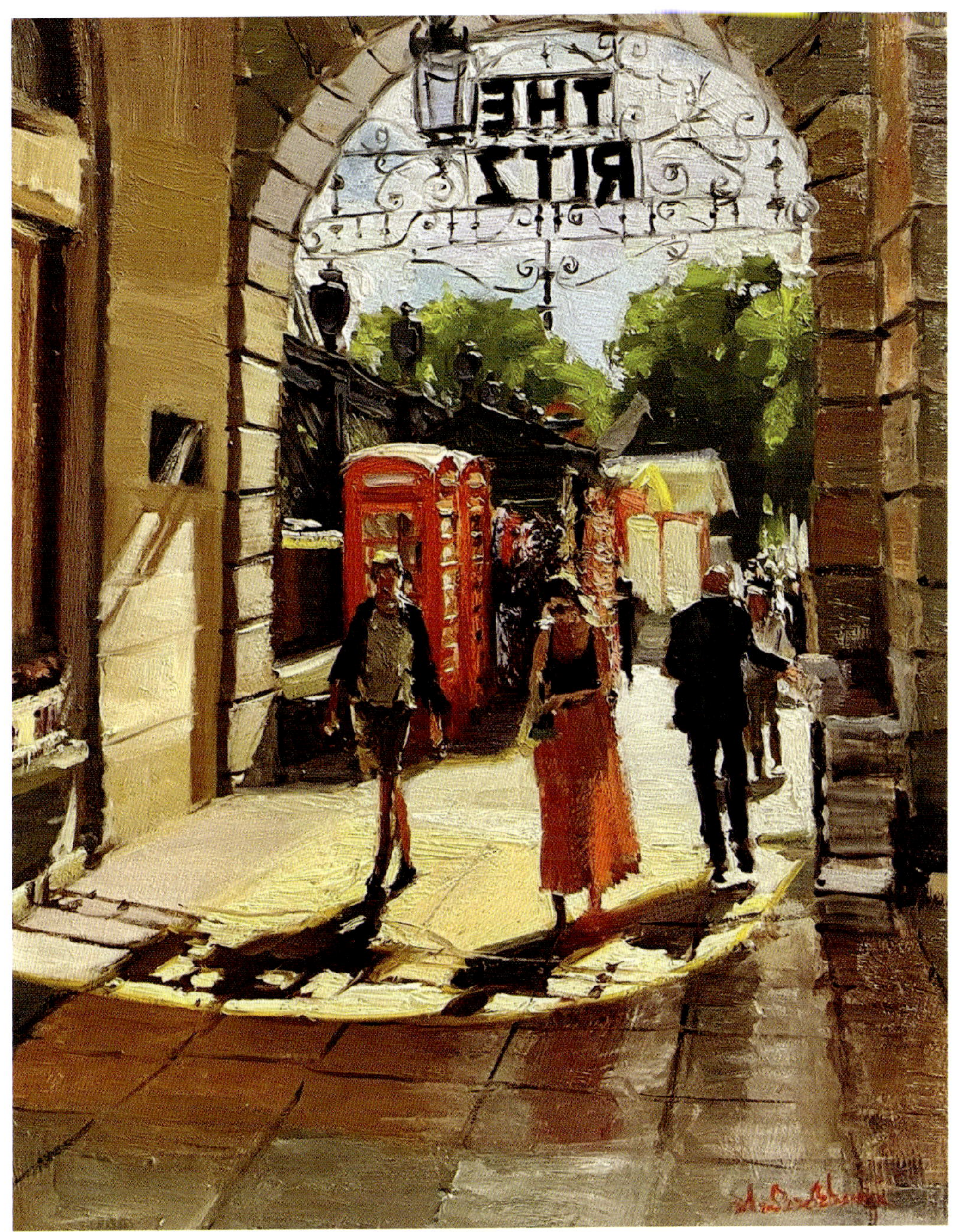

The Ritz, Backlit Summer Light II   30 × 40cm (12 × 16in)

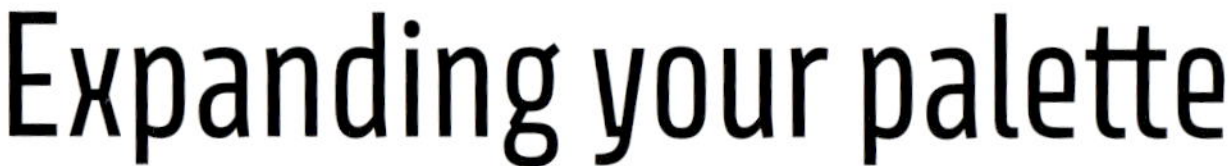

Expanding your palette

Versatile as the Zorn palette is, you'll likely want to explore colours beyond it, particularly for subjects like figures, where a broader palette can help capture specific colours.

   The colours of my full or extended palette, shown here, cover the entire colour wheel. I always lay the paints out in the same way – doing so helps you to become familiar enough that you barely need to look at your palette while painting, helping to avoid breaking your concentration. With the palette shown I can mix any colour I see by using two or three of these in varying proportions.

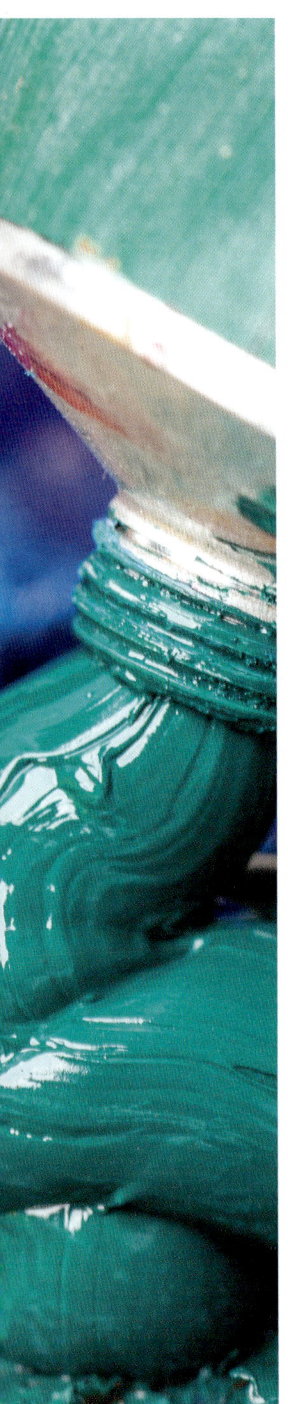

Titanium white (a) Opaque and with great covering power, I only use this white. There are varieties of this colour in the Michael Harding range: I use both their standard and fast-drying titanium whites, as explained on page 42.

Winsor lemon (b) This is a cool yellow for light and cool passages. Cadmium lemon is a good alternative.

Cadmium yellow medium (c) My standard yellow for all mixtures, this is my 'go-to' warm yellow.

Cadmium-free yellow deep (d) Sometimes substituted with cadmium orange, this colour is here mainly for convenience. I use this to avoid muddying my yellows and reds when mixing oranges.

Yellow ochre (e) A familiar face from the Zorn palette, I couldn't paint skin and trees without this – a precious colour!

Light red (f) A lovely reddish brown great for a variety of mixtures, especially greys when mixed with greens and blues. Terra rosa is an alternative to this useful paint.

Transparent red oxide (g) A lovely colour that is used for all my brown mixtures. I prefer transparent red oxide to burnt sienna because it doesn't dry so fast, but burnt sienna is otherwise very similar.

Cadmium red (h) The purest warmest red on my palette. I usually use the version made without heavy metals, simply called 'cadmium-free red'.

Permanent alizarin crimson (i) The coolest red available, this is great for darks too.

Magenta (Winsor & Newton) (j) This paint has a reddish nature, useful for all my red-tinged purple family mixtures.

Ultramarine blue (k) Called French ultramarine in some paint ranges, this is the truest blue in my palette. I use it mainly for warm blues, and it's invaluable for darks, too.

Cobalt blue (l) The best cool blue ever, this is quite expensive but worth every penny.

Viridian green (m) Neither too bright nor too dark, this is a versatile part of my full palette.

Ivory black (n) I inherited this black from the Zorn palette, and it is simply brilliant.

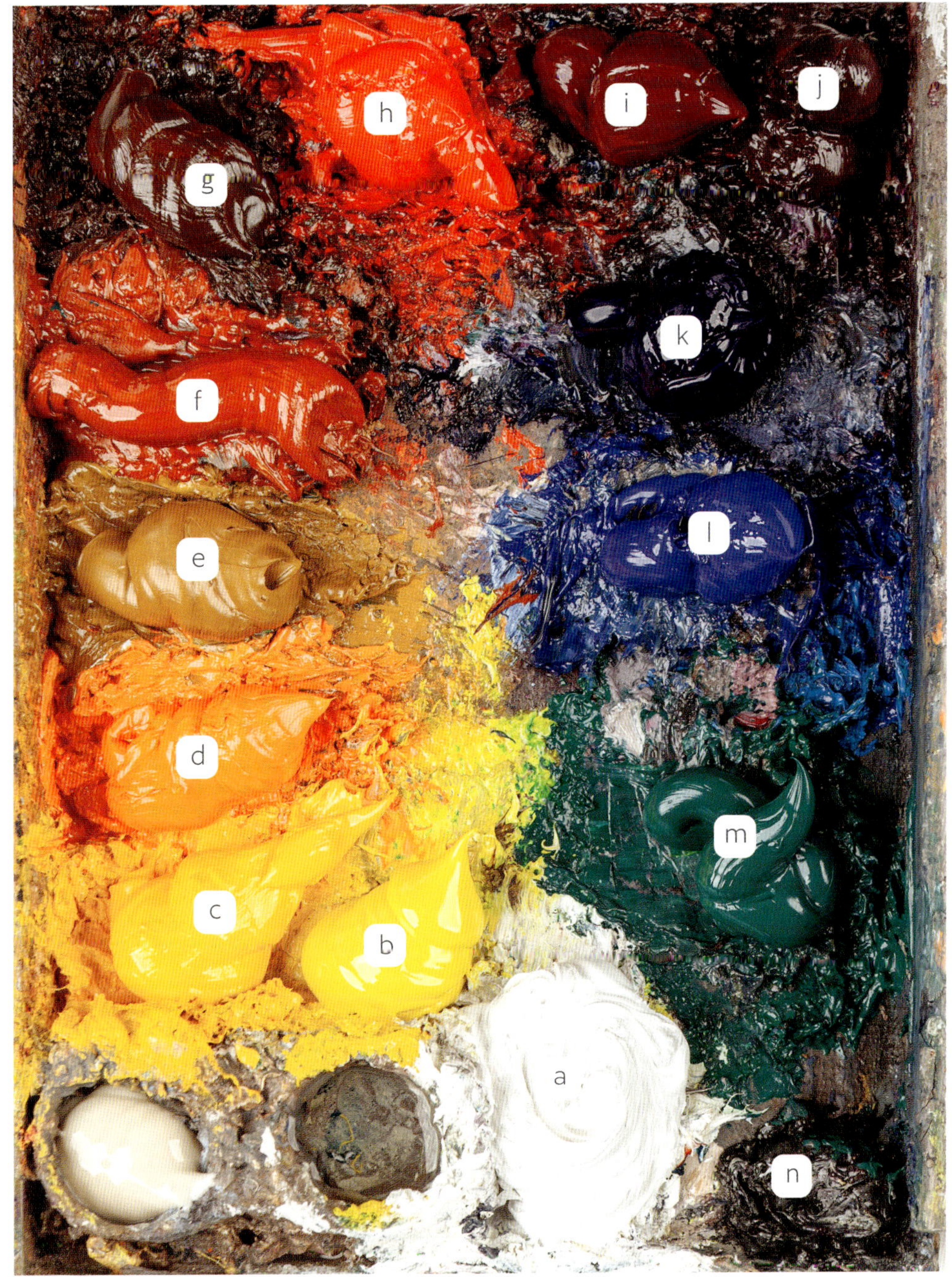

Supplementary colours

Colour is very subjective and the comments on my palette are based purely on my experience of using these paints. I encourage you to experiment and find your own favourites – here are two that I use on occasion:

Cobalt violet (Old Holland) This is a violet with a bit of blue in nature, quite expensive too, but worth it for the magic it brings.

Magenta (Old Holland) Quite different from the Winsor & Newton magenta, this has a more pinkish tinge.

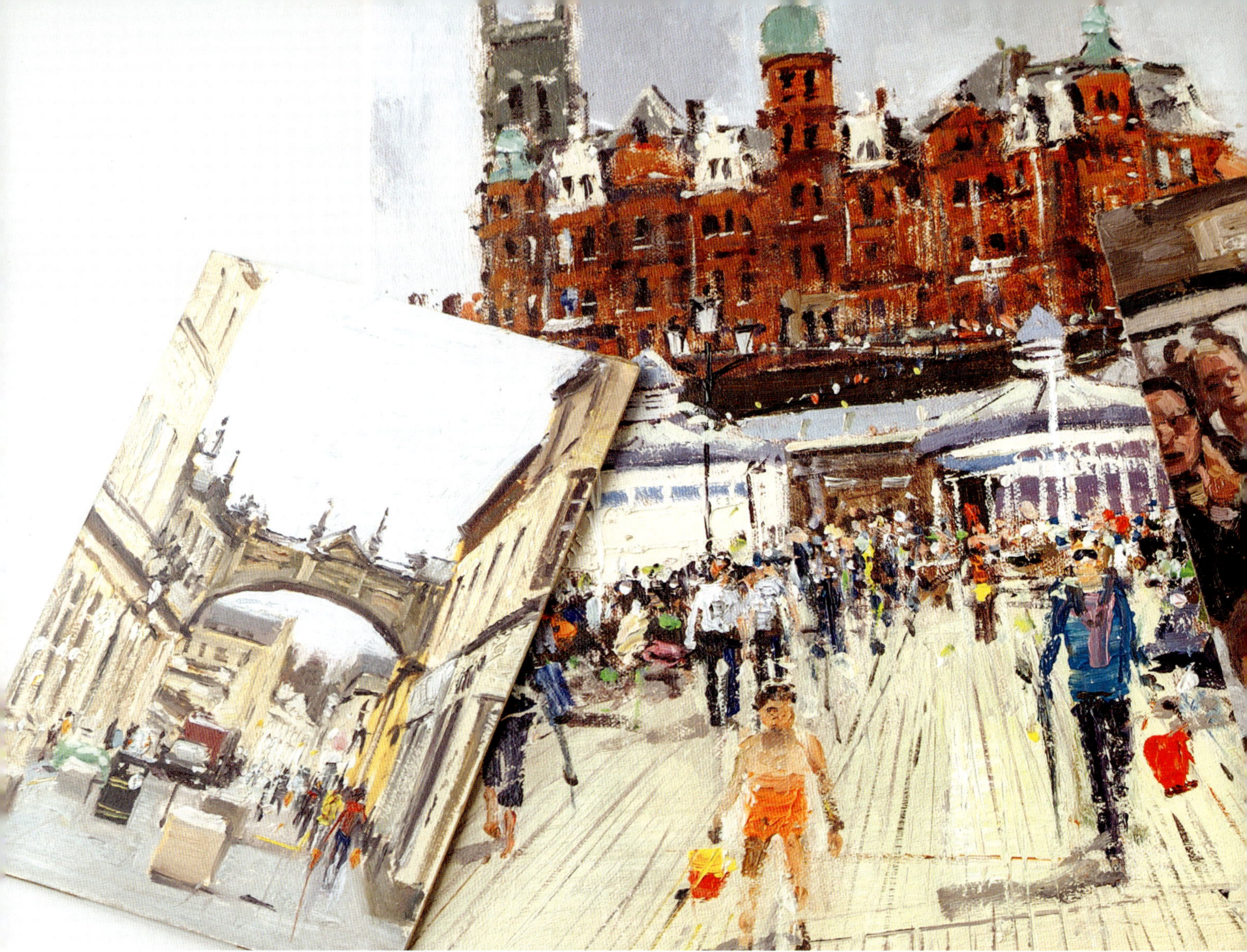

CROWDS

I got hooked on painting crowds after seeing John Singer Sargent's (1856–1925) brilliant painting entitled *Gassed*: it is literally my favourite painting ever. I love it not because of its theme – it has a very melancholy war narrative – but because of the way he handled the individual figures, capturing them as parts of a greater crowd while simultaneously investing each with an individual touch. I want every crowd scene that I paint to have both energy and a sense of harmony, so that the overall piece looks like it has been woven from the same thread.

Another artist that inspired my love for crowd scenes is the great Australian painter, Sir Ivor Hele (1912–1993). I was completely mesmerized by his painting *Australian Troops Disembarking at Alexandria after the Evacuation of Greece,* as it is a perfect example of how crowds can almost take on an abstract quality yet remain representational in every way.

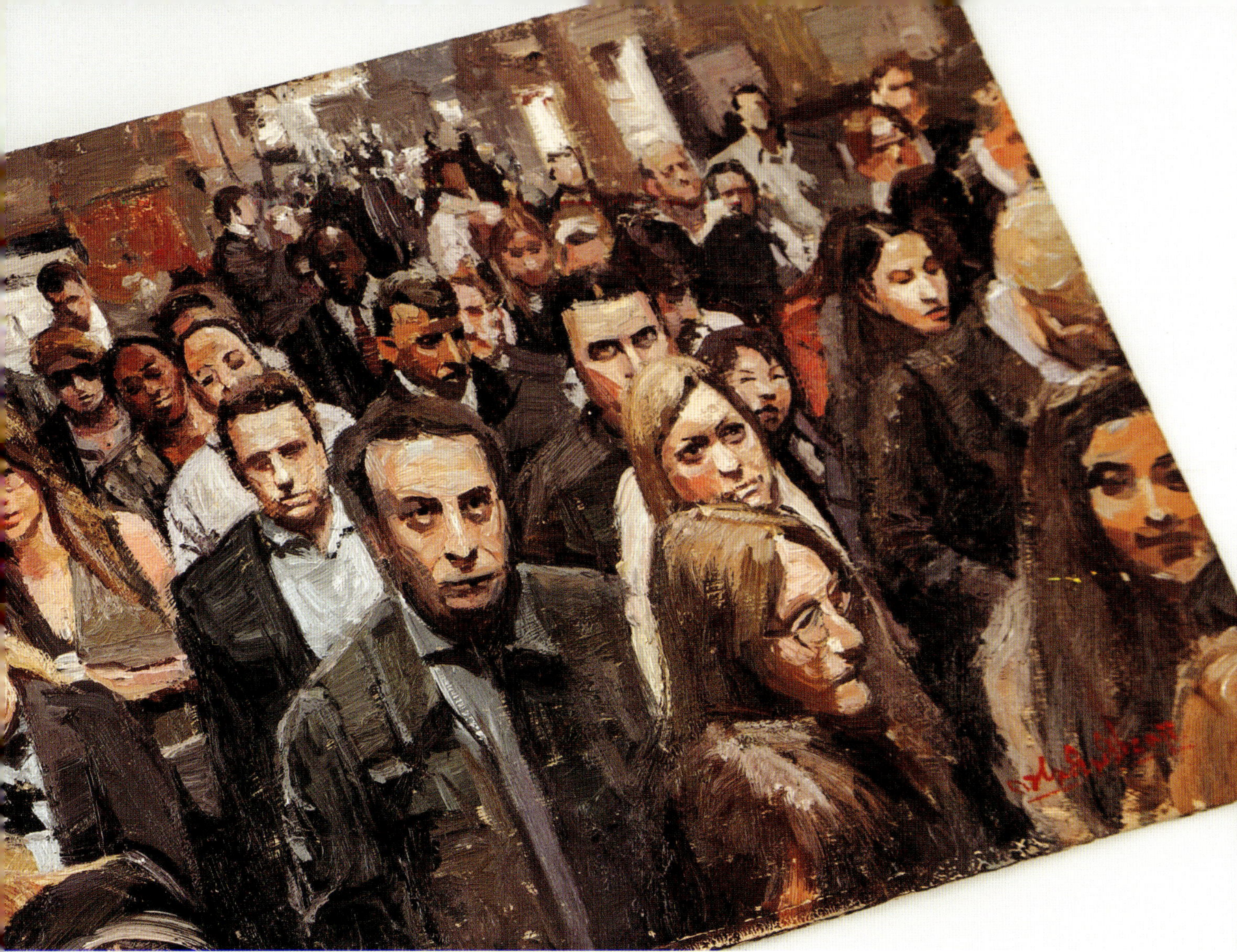

When you paint crowds outside, it's key to make sure you look at the overall shape and feel of the crowd, rather than seeing the individuals. It's the only possible way to capture the impression in time.

If you are planning to paint crowd scenes in the studio, this is less important. I still suggest you think that way when planning the scene, but because of the added luxury of time available in the studio, you have a lot more freedom to give each individual some attention – I call it some personal love and care.

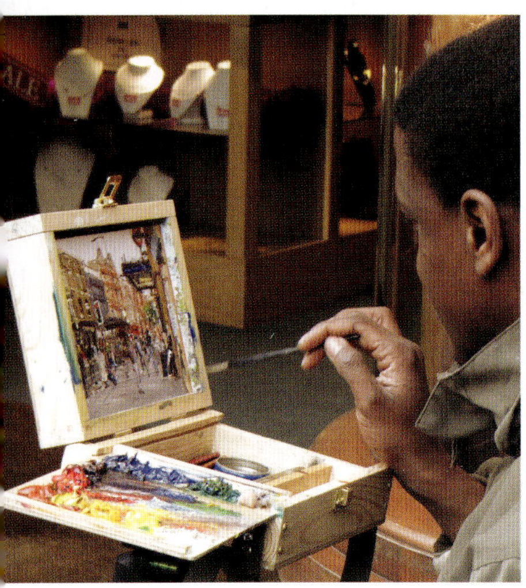

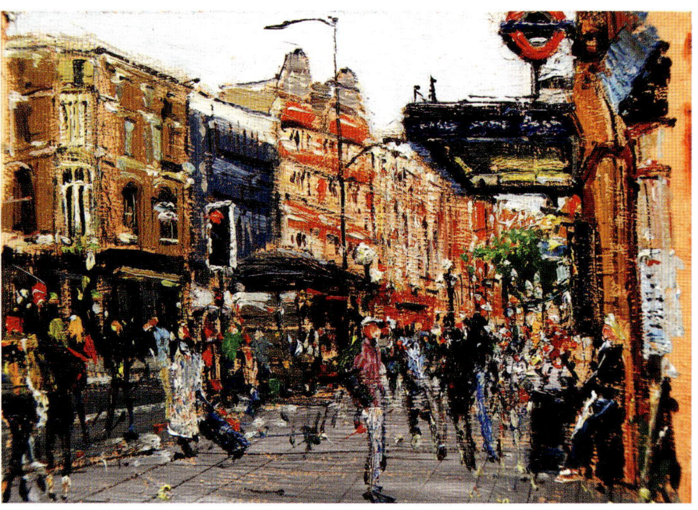

Simplifying

When you are painting outdoors with little time available, and want to capture a crowd, the best way is to look for the the overall shape of the mass of people then add dots to represent the heads of individuals. From here, vary the negative shapes in between the figures to pick them out. This will give a convincing impression of the crowd over time, rather than a snapshot of a particular moment.

Working under time pressure means that you'll have to sacrifice the urge for a perfect snapshot – unless you have enough experience to allow you to work effectively from memory, which also helps.

London Rush Hour   100 × 50cm (39½ × 19¾in)

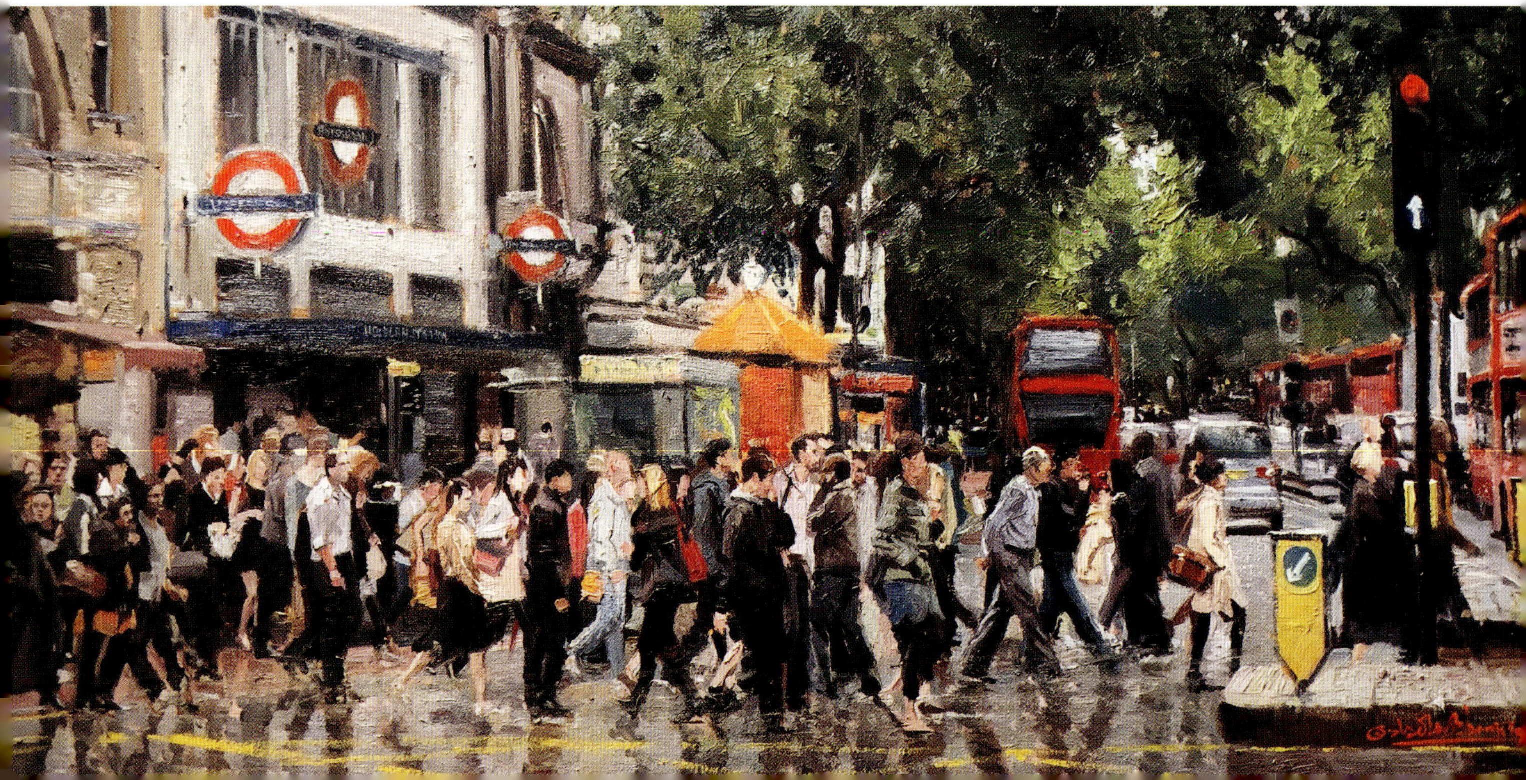

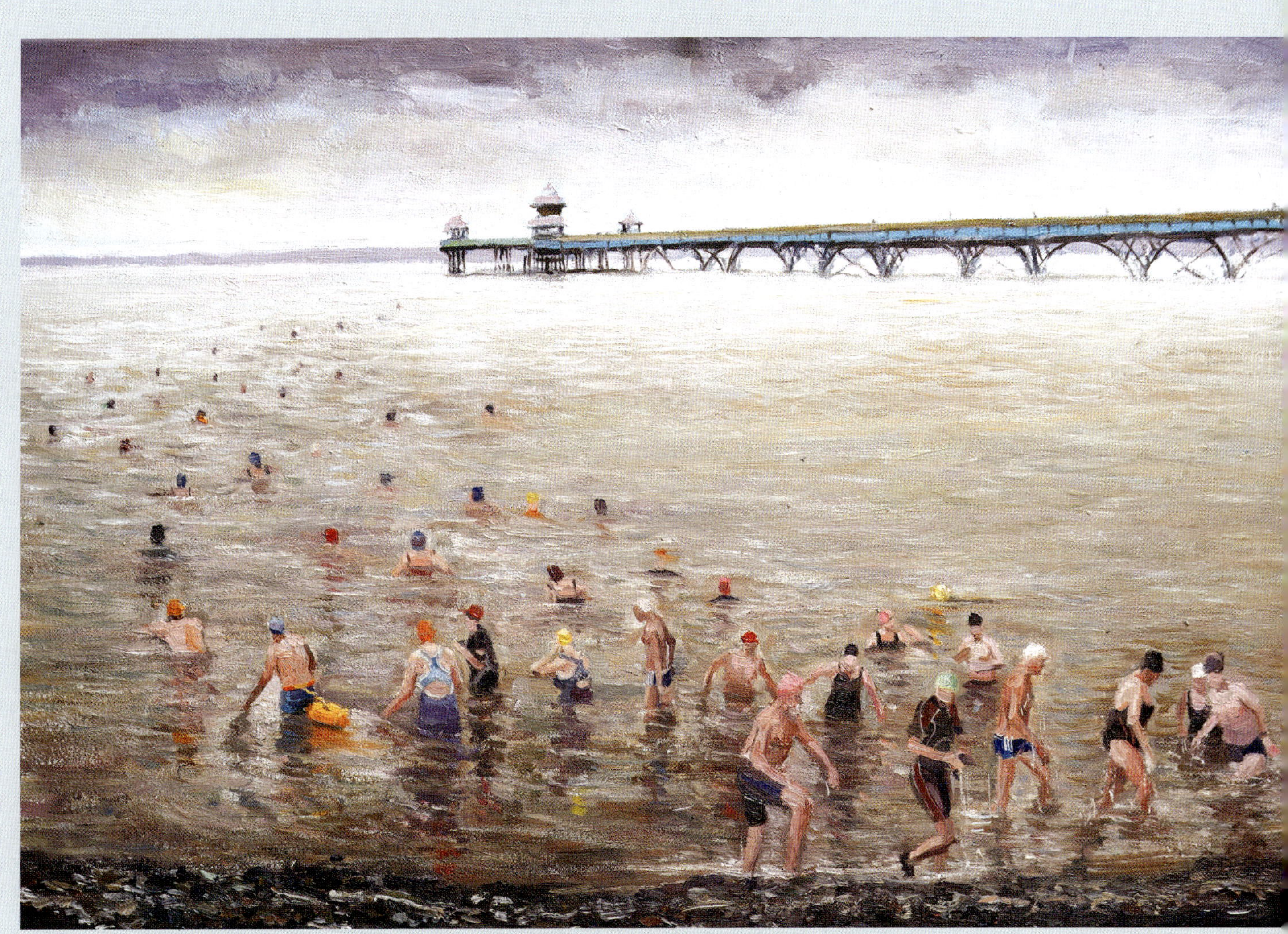

High Tide Swimmers, Clevedon   76 × 50cm (30 × 19¾in)

Paint: Rush Hour

This is a complicated scene with lots of figures, and the first thing we need to work out is how to tackle it. The answer is to simplify. Because the figures are moving, you don't need to get the details exactly right for it to look right. Edit out the unnecessary and focus on the important. Tonal values, lights and darks are all important, but the individual figures need only be part of the crowd. Don't be intimidated by the people: to an artist, a crowd is just a mass of shapes.

As you might expect, we'll use an inside-out approach (see page 29) for the painting: working shape by shape and gradually growing the painting, rather than trying to tackle it all in one go.

This project teaches the lesson 'every journey starts with a single step'. Even a complex crowd like this can be broken down, and down, and down, until you're just putting two or three strokes into a small box. You then move on to paint the next box, and the next, and the next. Before you know it, you'll have a finished crowd scene.

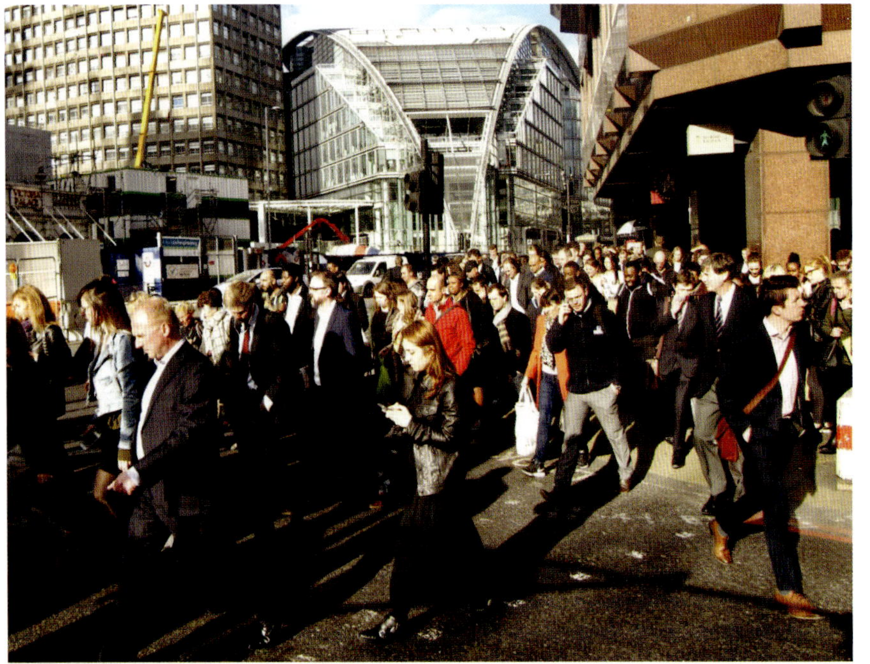

I snapped about forty shots for this photograph, and what I was looking for was an interesting distribution of light and shade. Here there's a mass of dark, with light breaking in and passing through. The crowd of figures makes an interesting shape – and that makes for a good composition.

The original scene is very busy, so a grid helps us to break things down and make it less intimidating.

We're using a 16 × 12 grid here, converted from a 4:3 ratio.

GETTING SET UP

Paints

Extended palette (see page 70)

Mediums

Liquin Impasto
Maroger
Alkyd
Bob Ross Odourless Thinner

Brushes

Sizes 8 and 2 filbert
25mm (1in) flat
Size 4 rigger

Surface

40 × 30cm (16 × 12in)
canvas board, prepared
with a 16 × 12 grid

Other materials

Smartphone, tablet or gridded
reference photograph
Posca pen, 0.9mm: white
Brush markers: Winsor & Newton
burnt sienna, cinnamon
Decotime Twinmarkers: dark
wood 119
Coloured pencils: Faber-Castell
Polychromos red
Liquitex Heavy Body Acrylic:
titanium white
Ruler
Duct tape
Masking tape
Craft knife

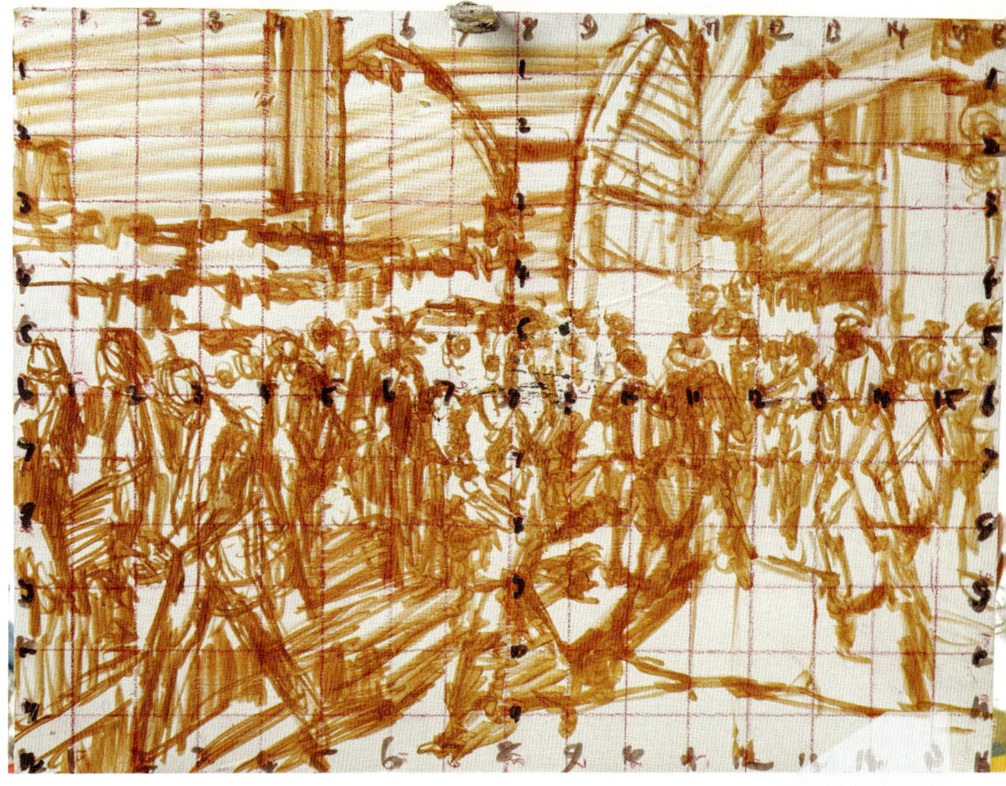

Midtone sketch

Getting the numbers laid out on the grid immediately makes the photograph less overwhelming. To make it more approachable still, zoom in on just one half. Let's start on the left, using a burnt sienna brush marker.

- The focus is on the crowd, so start with the people and block in the darks as you work from left to right. The grid shows you that almost all of the heads are within a horizontal strip just above the centre line – the eyeline. Once you spot that, it's already less daunting.

- The individuals should be sketched in their simplest form. Look to capture their gestural shapes and a sense of movement, rather than anything about them as people.

- Once you've filled in the crowd in the lower half, sketch in the buildings above them. Each square in this compositional grid contains a simple abstract shape. Look closely, and you'll see there are just a few shapes or lines there – easy! Sketch the shapes in and then move onto the next square. It's all you need to do.

- Once you've finished one half, move on to the right-hand side. You'll be finished before you know it.

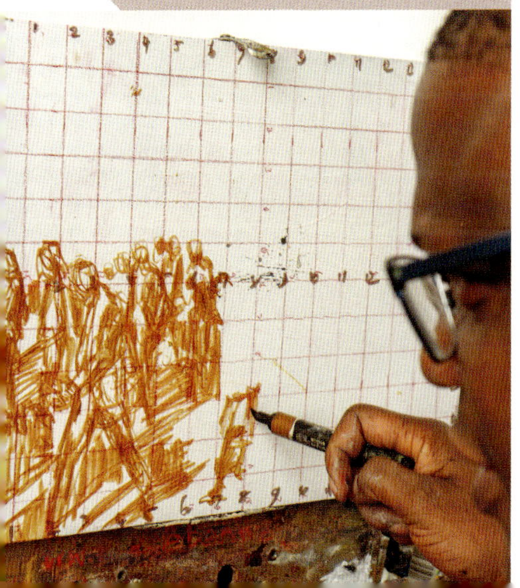

One step at a time, one shape at a time, you'll tackle this.

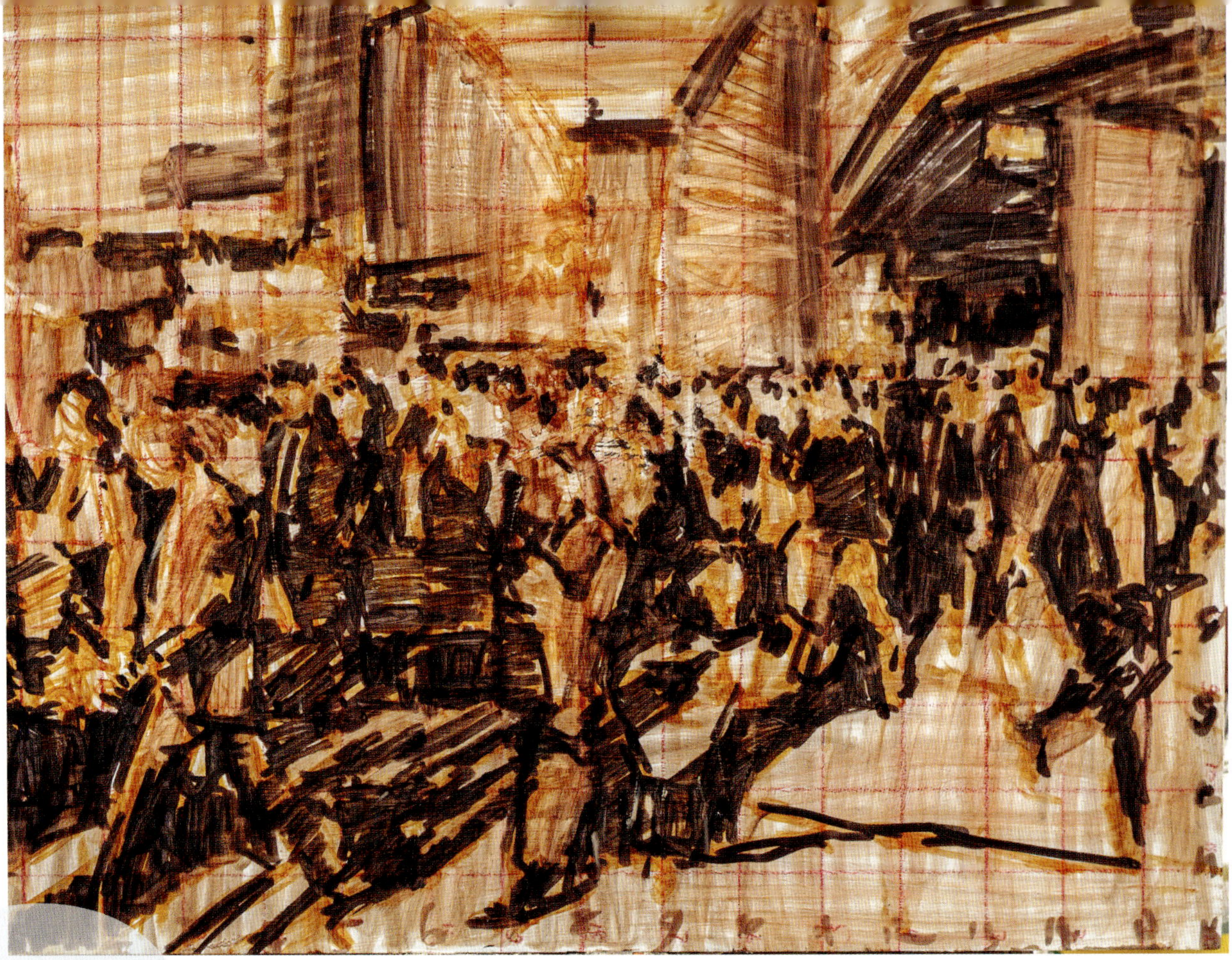

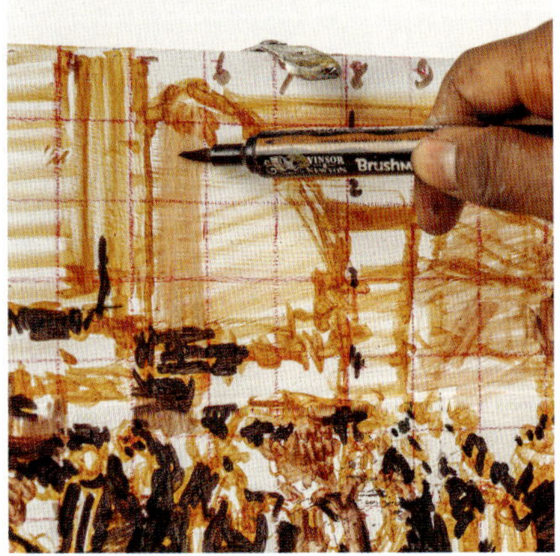

Adding tone

We've got the structure and the feel of a crowd, but now we need to add some depth and tone to make a bit more sense of things. I've extended a dark wood Twinmarker by taping it to a paintbrush handle for this. As before, work one half, then the other.

- Think just in terms of filling in shapes. Pick a shape in each square, fill it in, move on to the next shape then, when the square is finished, move on to the next square. Think in abstract terms of shapes and tones, and it will make the confusing scene less complex.

- The lower half, with the crowd, has many more dark tones than the background buildings in the top half – these are just a symphony of midtones. If you can't decide whether a shape is dark, but it's definitely there, then it's probably a midtone. Use a cinnamon brush marker to fill in the shape.

- I do use the sketch that's already in place to guide my placement, but mainly refer to the photograph. If I've made any small errors, identifying the darks will help to bring this out – and I can then correct as I go, simply by putting the darks in the right place.

- At the end of this stage, I work over the whole surface with the midtone marker, leaving me with a picture of midtones and darks.

I don't want to get to the next stage and think 'this looks hard to paint'. Building good foundations here will make the painting stages enjoyable.

Midtones over the whole surface. Note that the cinnamon marker used for this doesn't mix with the dark markers, so the areas remain clean and clear.

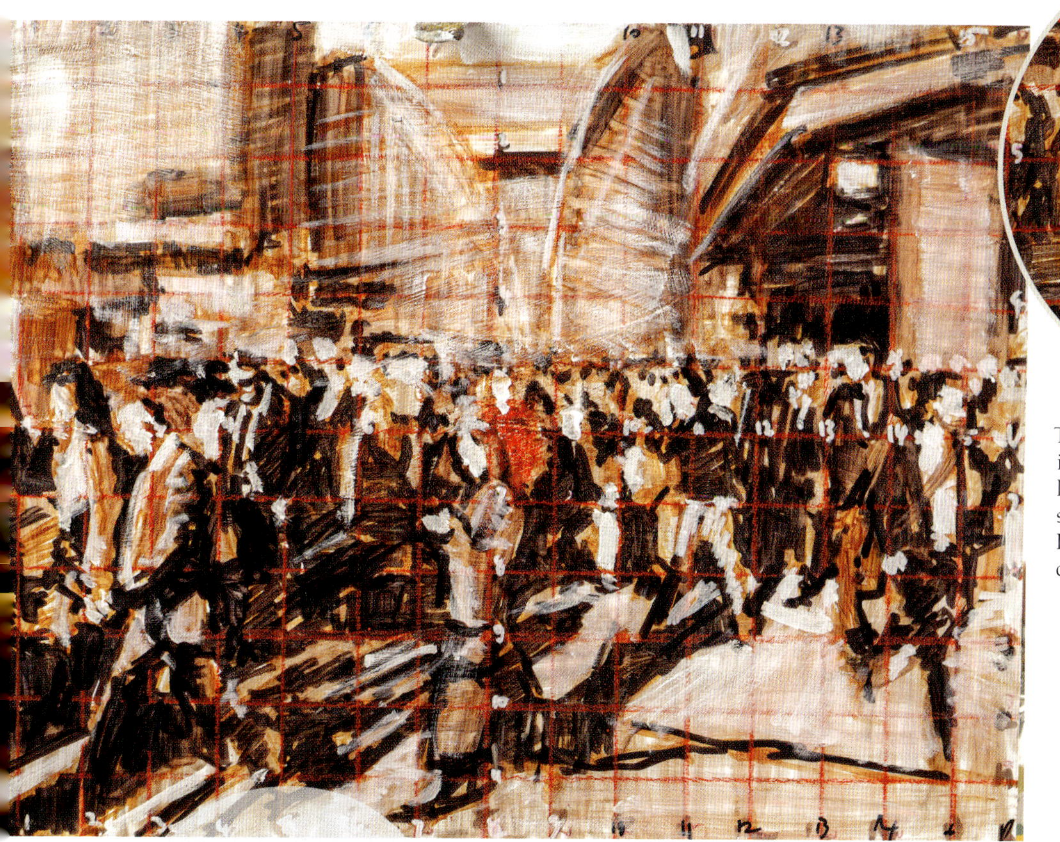

The figure in the dead centre is a key element – he's the largest red area in the painting, so I want him to stand out. I colour in his coat with red coloured pencil.

Bringing in the light

Once the darks and midtones are in place, it can still be complicated. To make sense of this chaos, I reinstate the grid with a ruler and red coloured pencil (make sure it's not water-soluble) before moving on. This will stand out, even against the whites we're about to add. This'll give me a little safety net.

- Over the grid, I start to add the light areas using a white Posca pen taped to a brush handle (this ensures I don't get too fiddly), or titanium white acrylic and a size 2 filbert brush. There aren't too many highlight areas, so you can either work outwards from the first you find, or just fill them in as they strike you.

- You can vary the tone of the white depending on how much paint you apply. By using thick white acrylic, you'll create a bold white; by using less paint and a drybrush technique (barely any paint on the brush), you'll get a more subtle highlight.

- Sometimes I might go back and touch in a dark or midtone – either because I've missed them earlier, or because a particular detail, like a tie on a white shirt, or the shadow under a figure's jaw, only becomes available to draw once the lights are in place. It's a process of small refinement that distills the picture into simpler terms. At the end, you'll have a 'false underpainting', made with pen and acrylic rather than oils.

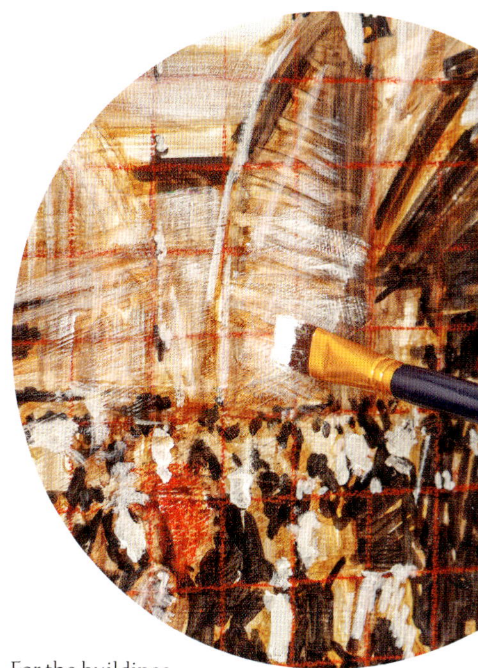

For the buildings, use a larger brush (like this size 8 filbert) with barely any paint on it. This'll help you block them in quickly and prevent you being too fussy and contrived.

Foreground – piece by piece, bit by bit

Pick a brush that's large enough to stop you being fiddly. For these 2.5cm (1in) squares, I'm using a thinned-down (see page 13) size 8 filbert, which is big enough to fill a square in about three brushstrokes, but will still allow for finer detail if necessary.

- Stick to the script. Use your sketch to help you, and forget about what the scene is. Try to treat it as an abstract; or think of the brushstrokes you're making as tiles of colour.

- The crowd is made up with cool shadows, because the morning light is warm. This means you need to use greens, purples and blues. Start by making a mix of ultramarine blue with cobalt violet and the two magentas, with plenty of Maroger. Use this to begin filling in the shadows. Don't think about what the thing is: just follow your sketch and reference image. Trust them. They'll help you because if the tone of your paint is wrong, it'll jump right out at you.

- Nothing should be predictable. Vary the direction of your brushstrokes to create a textural, calligraphic feel to the painting. After every three marks, vary the mixture by touching in some more or less of the different colours, or introducing touches of alizarin crimson (a cool blue-tinged red), viridian, yellow ochre, titanium white or other cooling colours from your palette. As long as the mixtures are cool, the colour is secondary to the tone.

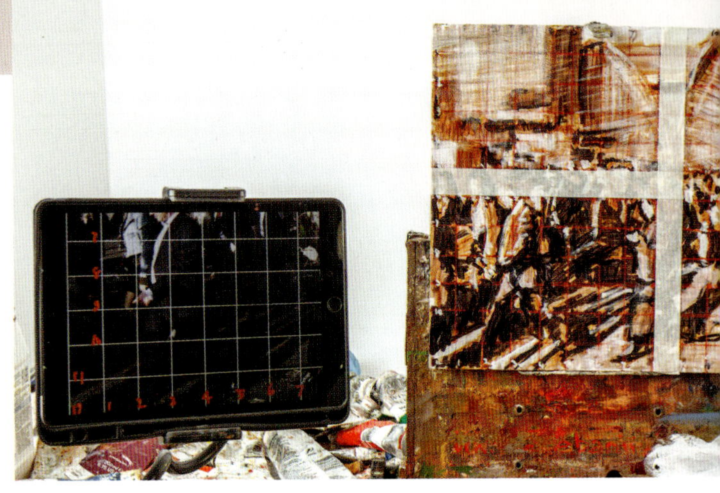

Having your reference picture at the same size as your painting makes things easier. If you can zoom into a section on a tablet, that's great. Use masking tape to frame a part of the painting to make quick reference easier.

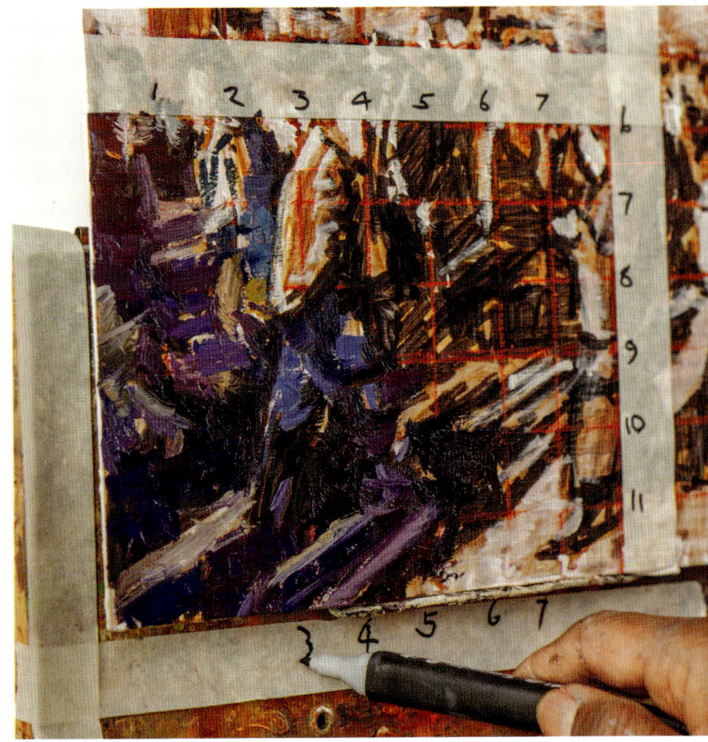

As you paint, you'll gradually cover the grid and the numbers on the surface – don't worry: you can add the numbers on the masking tape framing the area.

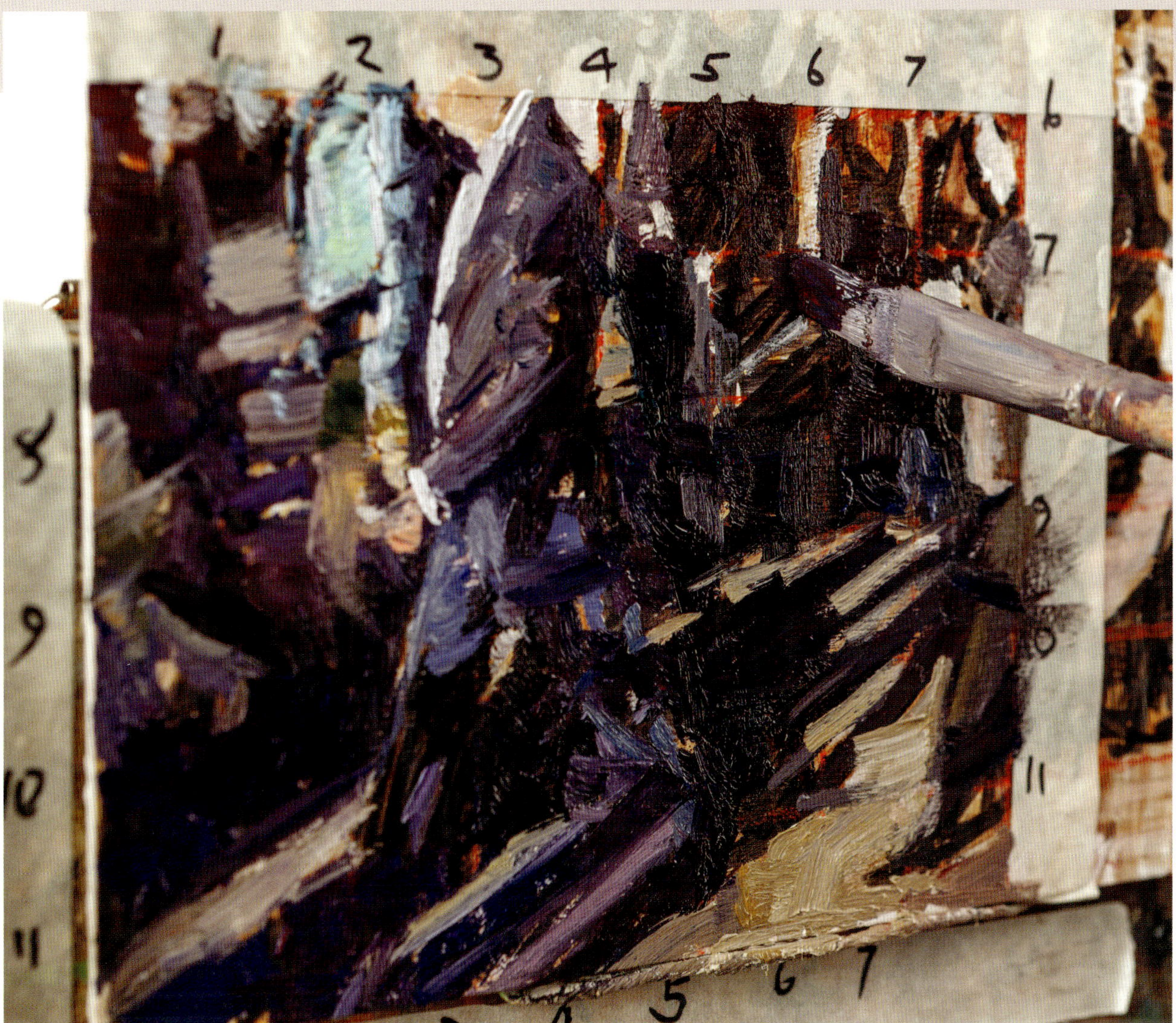

- Painting from the inside-out means tackling the area all in one go, so where you need to introduce 'tiles of colour' that are warm, start small new mixes and introduce warming colours like lemon yellow. These will come in particularly where the morning light strikes the figures.

- Go slow. Don't rush. Navigate through the painting slowly and carefully, following exactly what you see, shape-by-shape. Step by step, we'll conquer this mountain.

Don't make judgements on what's important. Just paint what's there. If you decide 'I can skip that bit', it'll show in the bigger picture.

Everything matters. Whether it's someone's face or a patch of pavement, treat it in the same way. Look for the tone, look for the colour, make the mix, and apply it in interesting ways.

- Work right to the edge of the area you've masked out. Don't worry about getting paint on the masking tape; we'll remove it once the area is complete.

- Combinations of yellow ochre, lemon yellow, cadmium red and titanium white can be used for the majority of the skintones in this photograph.

- Once you've filled the area, remove the masking tape and frame the next area. Clean down your palette and start again from scratch. Treat this new area as the only thing that matters; like it's the whole painting. It'll simplify things, help you focus, and make it feel like painting a series of small, simple paintings rather than one big intimidating one.

- Don't worry if you've cut through a figure at the border: if anything, it's good that you have, as it'll help you think in abstract terms. Remember that it's all just shapes; tiles of colour. It's fun, so don't burden yourself with thinking what that shape represents.

You don't want to put masking tape over the wet oil paint, so for the lower left area, put a strip across the top as shown. I've also made a little L-shaped piece of foamboard, attached to the back of the painting for the right-hand side and bottom.

A filbert is perfect for crowd scenes. It gives you lots of options for interesting marks, can put a lot or a little paint down at once, and lacks the hard corners of a flat brush that might tempt you to get lost in the detail.

Combine cadmium red and cadmium yellow deep for a punchy eye-catching 'bang' of colour on the focal hot spot.

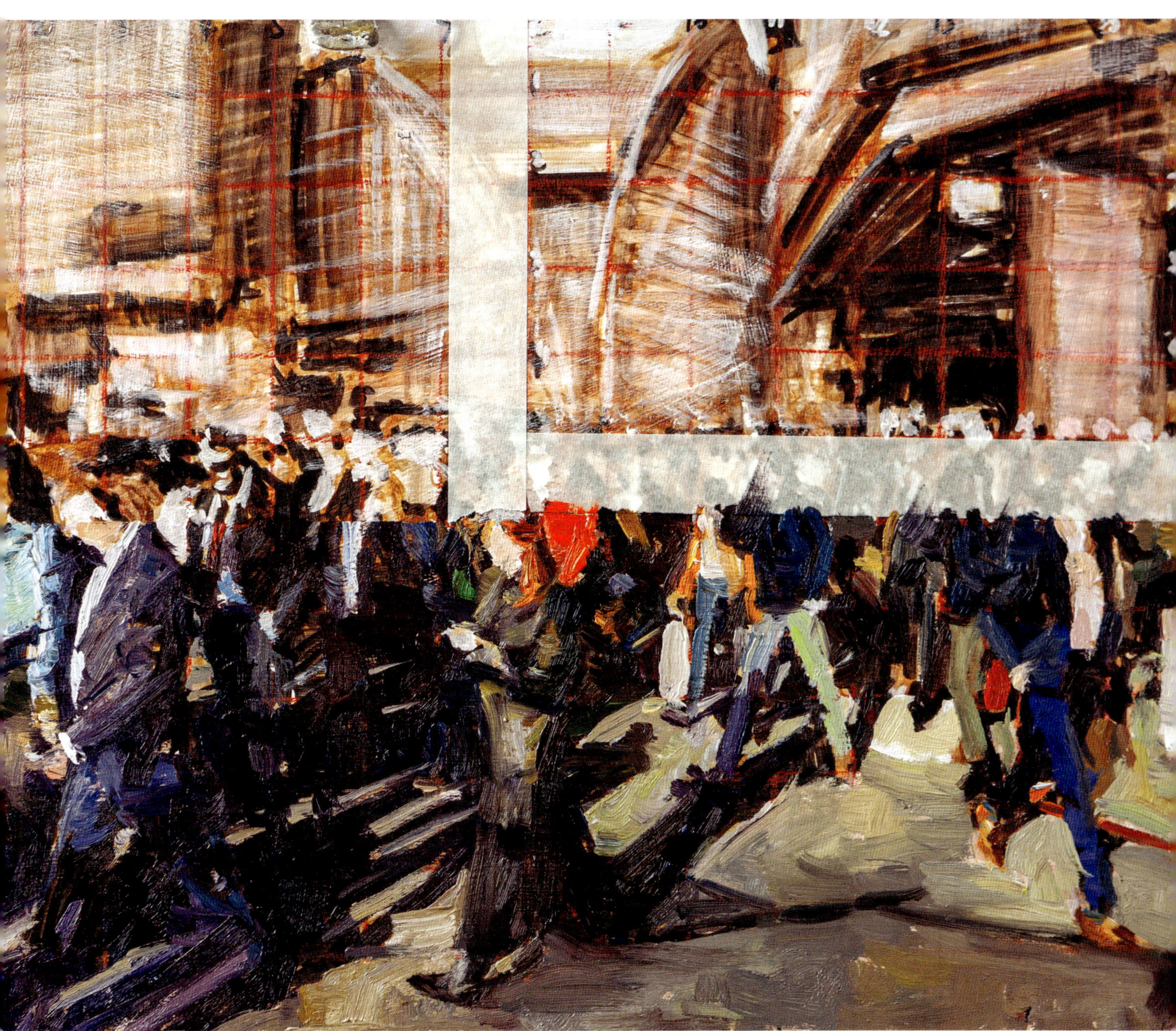

Building the background

Phew! The painting stage is effortless. You can play with it, enjoy it – and all because you put the time in earlier. You would have to think more deeply without the strong foundations. With a strong underpainting in place, you don't have to check the tones; you know them already. Painting gets easier as you move on and the anticipation builds to see the finished painting. Let's move on to the next area: the top right. Set up your masking tape references as before, and clean down your palette.

Because this area has a lot of heads and I want it to feel a bit more 'human', I'm going to swap down to a size 2 filbert or size 4 rigger for the faces. Aside from this, the same lessons as earlier apply. Look at a square, identify the tones, mix the colour, and paint the surface with interesting, varied marks.

- Switching to the smaller brush for the strip of faces on the eyeline will naturally make the strip more complex, interesting and eye-catching: perfect for drawing the viewer's eye. I want to give a little bit more interest and detail to this focal area, but balance this against making it too detailed.

- As soon as you've finished the heads, switch back to the size 8 filbert for the buildings. Broadly speaking, the buildings are much lighter in tone than the foreground area, so reflect that in the mixes you use. Other than keeping that in mind, you should tackle them in the same way as the foreground; looking closely for the right colour and tone, and varying the way you apply the paint. Again, leave the building detail to the architects – just capture the broader shapes and curves.

- Once you've completed the top right area, remove the masking tape and move on to the top left. Paint the faces using the size 2 filbert or size 4 rigger, then change to the size 8 filbert for the larger buildings, and work down from the top, square by square. The last thing we want in this area is for it to appear busy. Clean, controlled brushstrokes here provide calming contrast with the hectic foreground and provide somewhere for the viewer's eyes to rest.

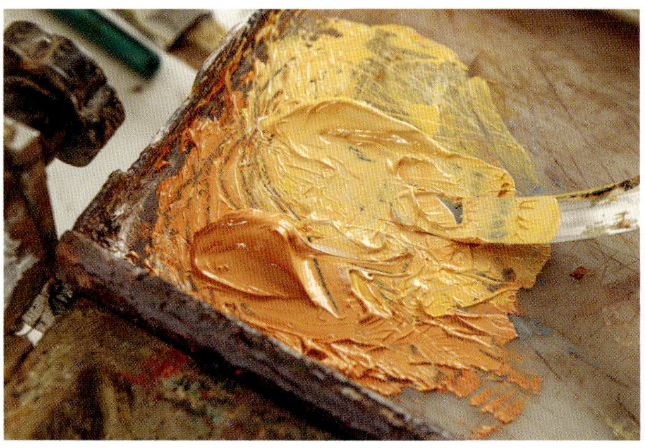

Preparing a puddle of cadmium red or bright red, yellow ochre and lemon yellow will give you a good start for all of the flesh tones. Make a bleached-out version to one side by adding a lot of cadmium yellow medium and titanium white.

Cadmium red, alizarin crimson and ultramarine blue make a good dark mix from which, with a bit of variety, you can paint the majority of the shadows and hair.

For black skin, combine the two mixes above. Try varying the proportions of each mix for different tones.

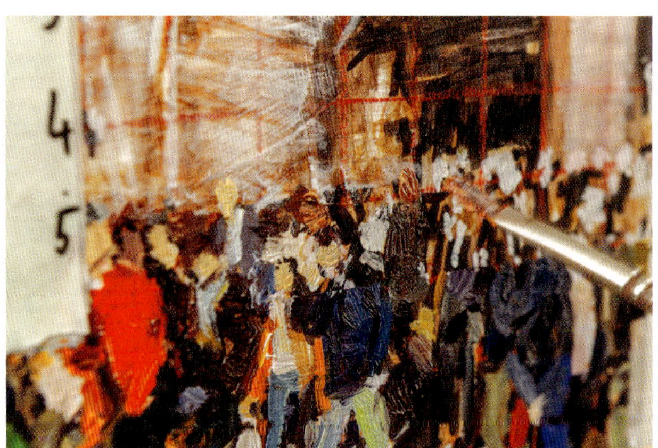

The danger is getting too attached to the idea of faces, rather than abstract shapes. Don't over-labour things: keep a fresh, light feel. Keep moving!

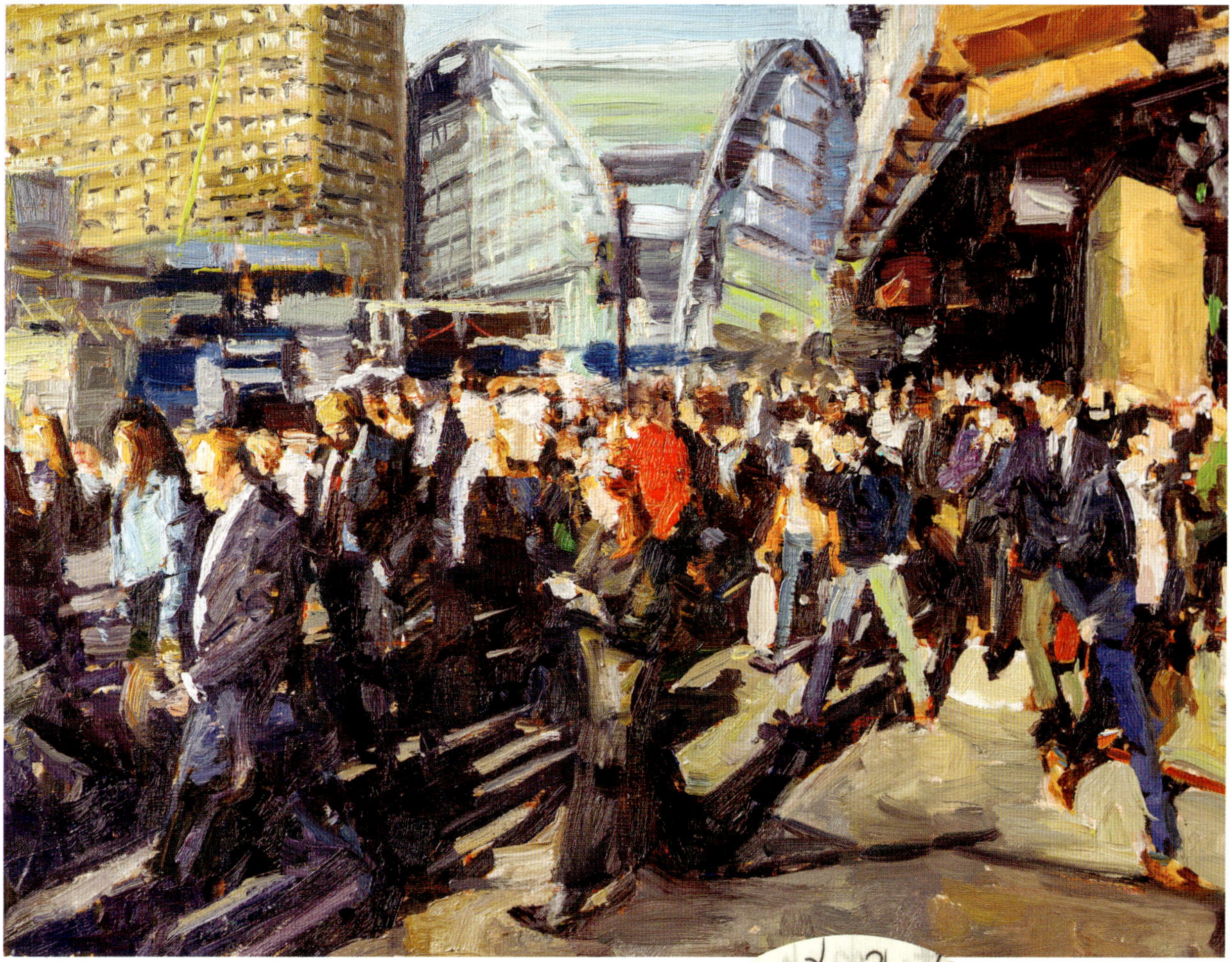

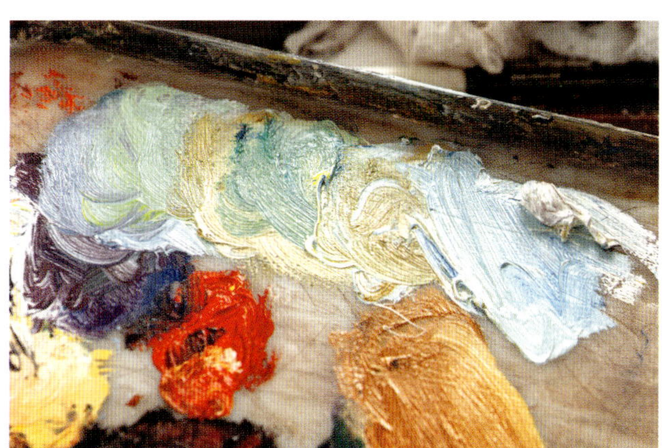

Mixes for the buildings are much lighter in tone, particularly the glass ones. There's at least a little titanium white in all of these mixes, which otherwise primarily involve ultramarine blue and lemon yellow.

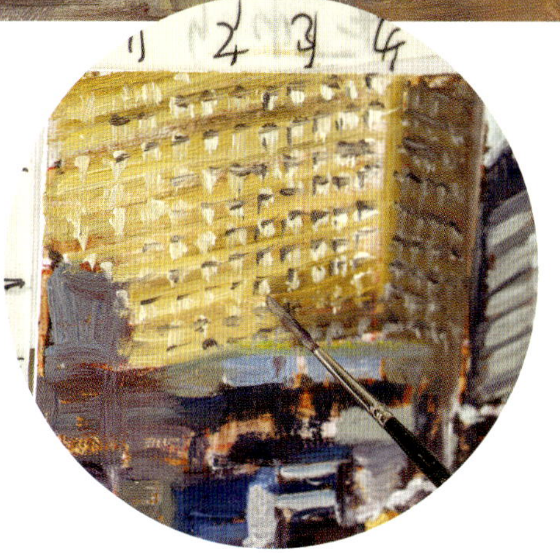

For the windows, just hint at them; using the tip of a size 4 rigger to give a suggestion of orderly rows of windows. The important thing is that they're proportional to the building.

Accents

Getting involved with the details earlier on in the painting is a bad idea – it'll distract you from the overall scene and the crowd. For that, we needed to be in abstract mode; looking just for shapes, colours and tones. Now that the surface is covered, however, it's time to add some tiny details.

Switch down to a size 4 rigger and zoom right in to your reference to bring a few important areas to life. A little bit of attention to the closest figures will help them to stand out and give some humanity to the overall crowd. In other words, we're turning up the resolution of some areas in the painting, because we want the viewer to be able to relate to them.

- Change your brain from abstract mode to detail mode. Forget the overall painting and focus on individuals. It's tricky to know who to resolve and who to leave looser. I say look at the first three rows of people, and add detail to these only, with less detail as they recede. Beyond that, let the abstract shapes stand. With the front figures further developed, use the rigger to just touch in blobs for faces further back.

- In the shadows, where everything is dark, add some 'motion strokes'. These are brushstrokes that are analogous with the background colours, but suggest direction and movement. You want to subtly give a sense of motion so that the dark areas don't look dead. This applies to the colour, too; develop the foreground shadows with ultramarine blue and magenta mixes, cooled with titanium white. These need to be cool to contrast with the warm light areas.

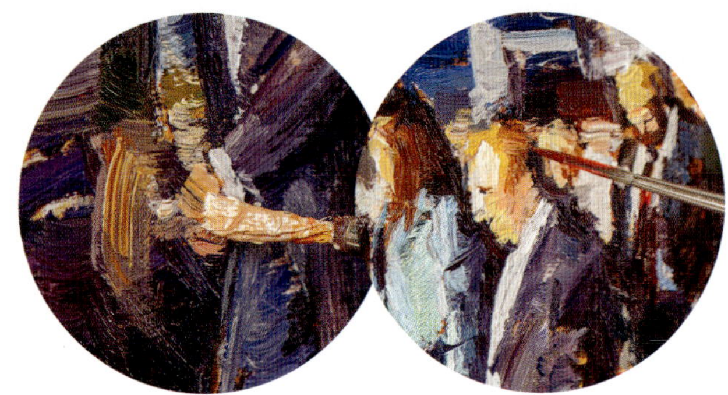

Motion strokes are almost flicked on, with quick directional strokes. They should be subtle.

You don't want anything around human figures to look cold; a little red added to the dark surrounding his face suggests a little heat and life.

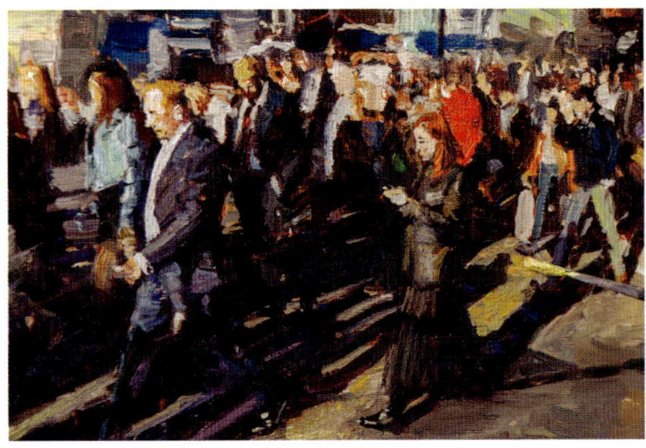

This is a warm morning, the sun is out, and the crowd is going to earn their day's wage. Bring a sense of light and optimism and energy to all the light areas in the foreground – even the road's surface – with mixes that incorporate warm touches.

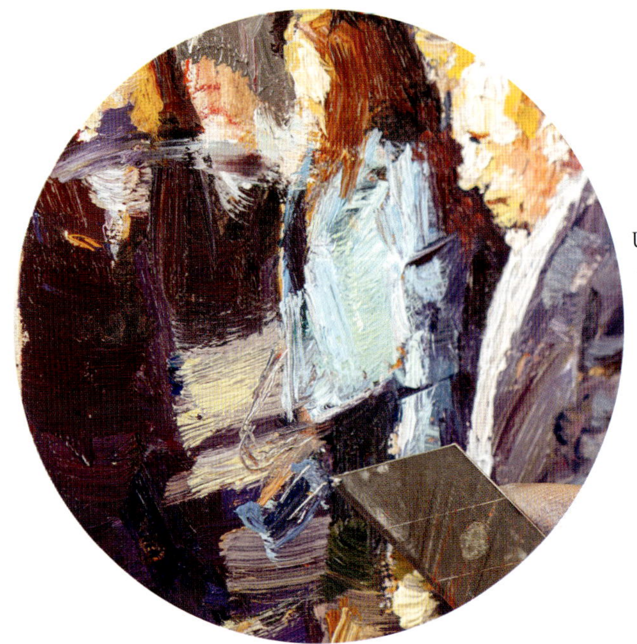

Use a craft knife to gently scratch away the surface for very fine details, like the wire from the headphones to the phone.

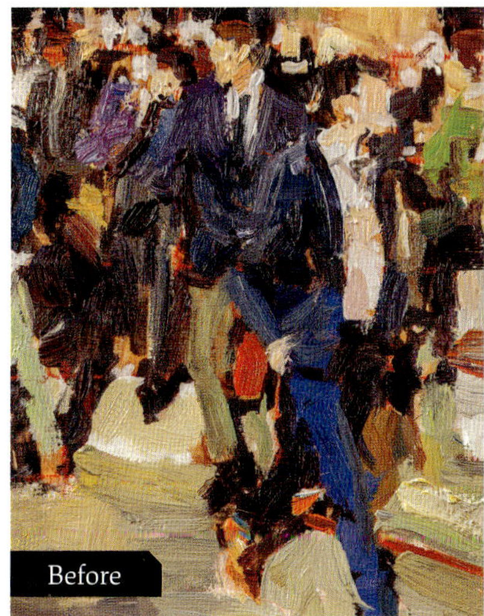 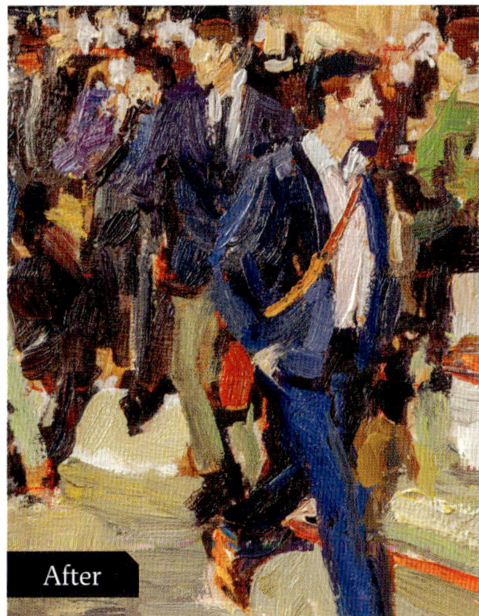

Resolving the foreground figures puts the people into the place. It humanizes the crowd and reminds the viewer that everyone here is an individual, with their own thoughts and hopes.

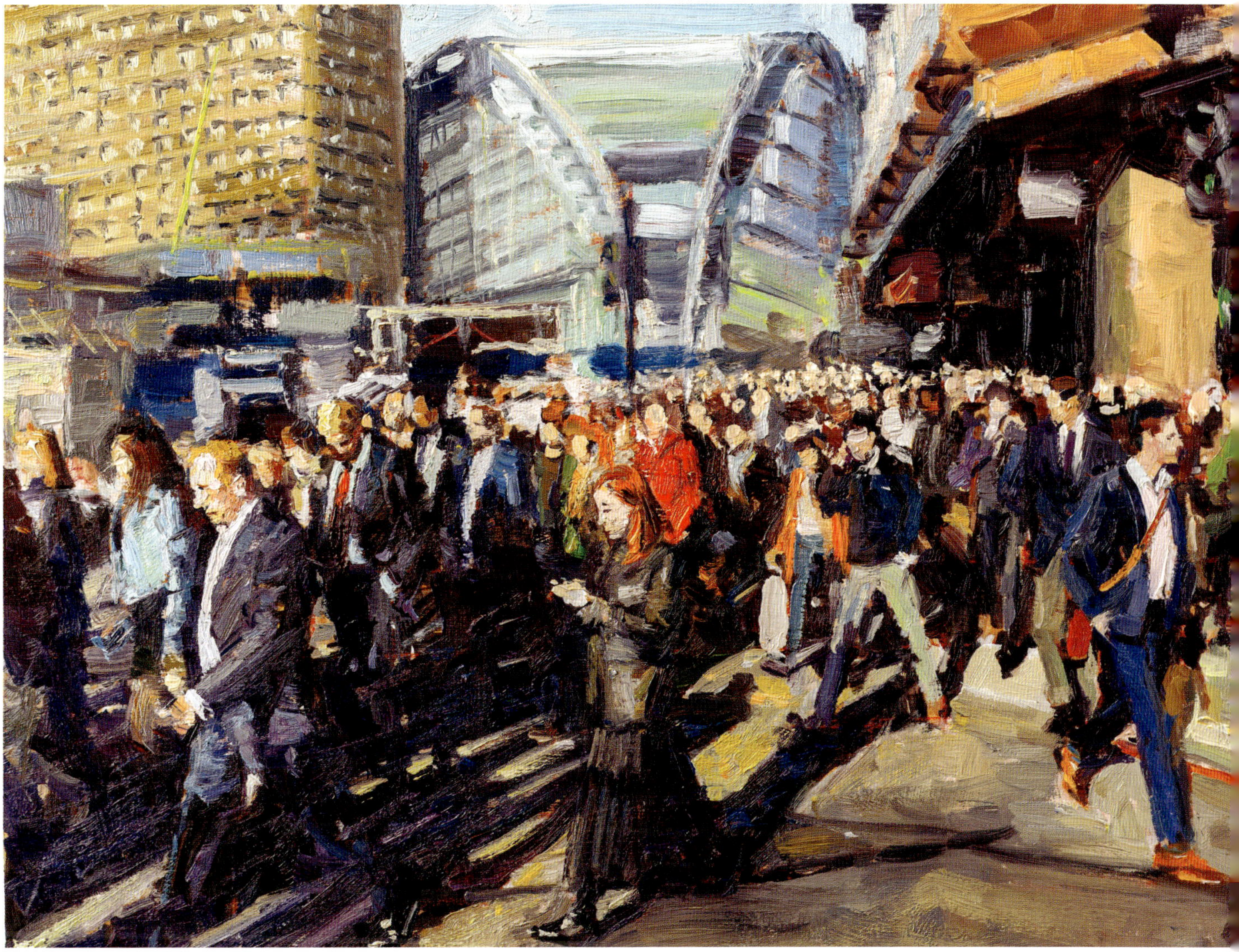

The finished painting

Different viewpoints

Try altering your own viewpoint. This can create interesting variations to crowd scenes, as shown in these examples, one from slightly above head height, and the other looking down from an escalator.

Both of these were composed from lots and lots of pictures I took while at London Bridge Underground station. I always visualize what I might be able to get from a particular crowded area from different viewpoints; and what might make my next crowd painting. I'm always walking with a painting idea in the corner of my eye – there's no dull moment, it's exciting!

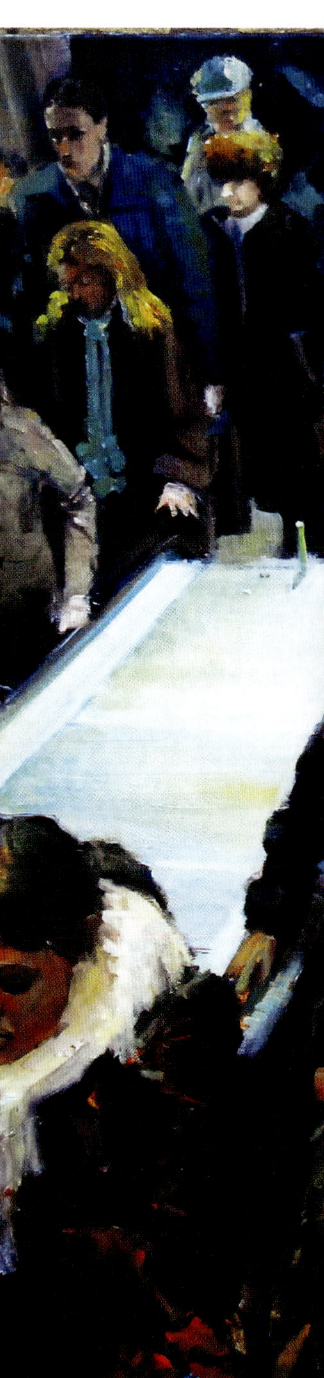

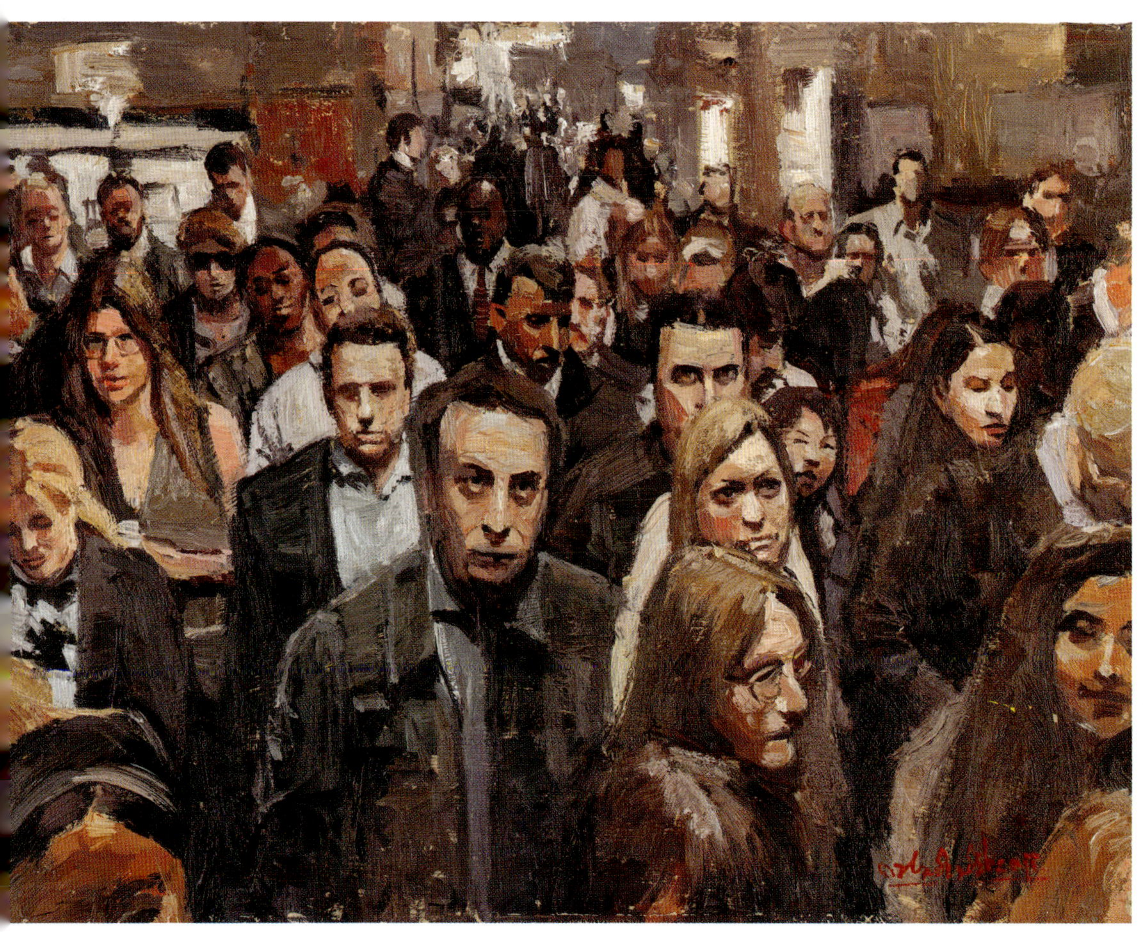

Londoners, Rush Hour   40 × 30cm (16 × 12in)

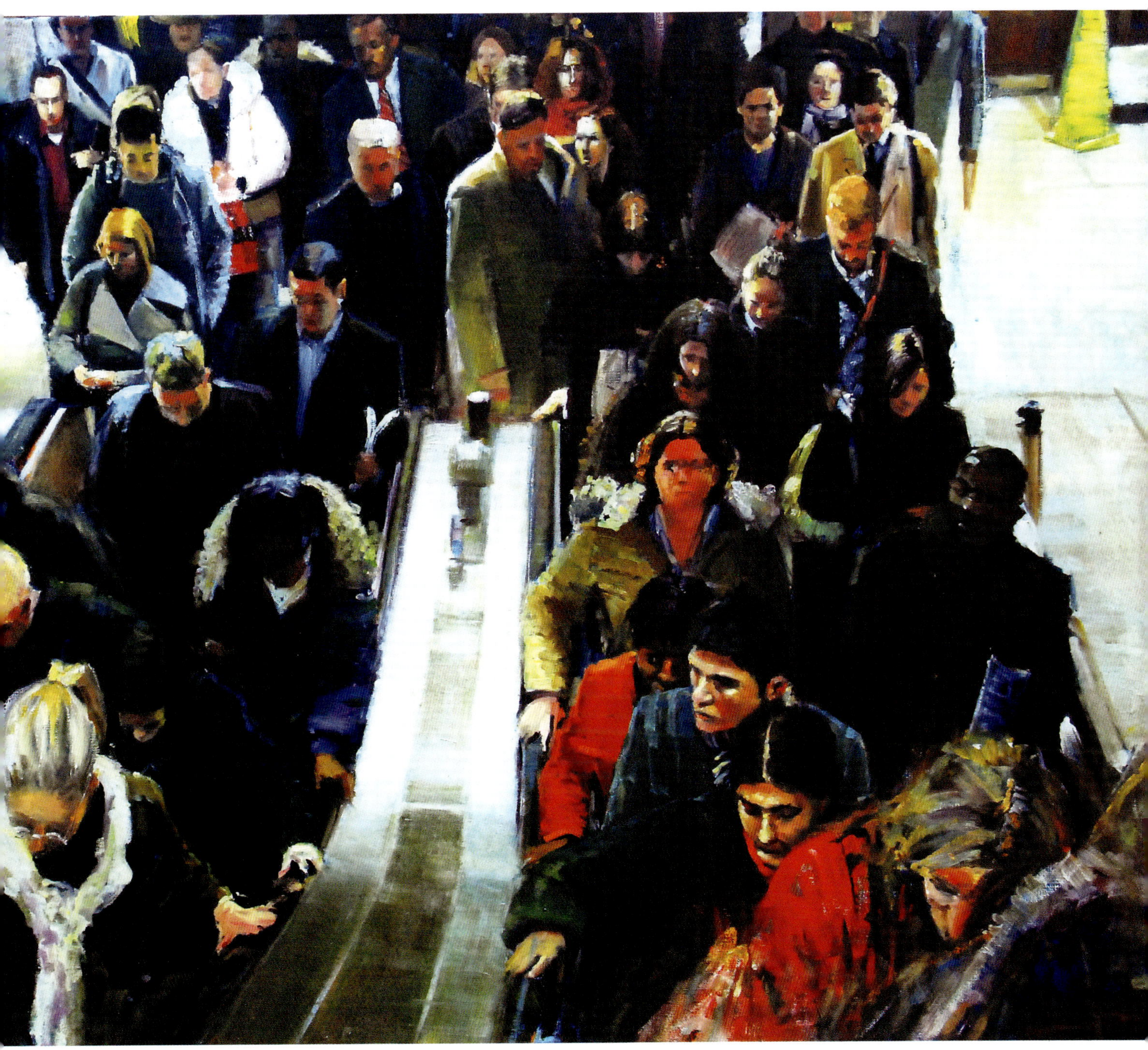

Rush Hour IV   100 × 80cm (39½ × 31½in)

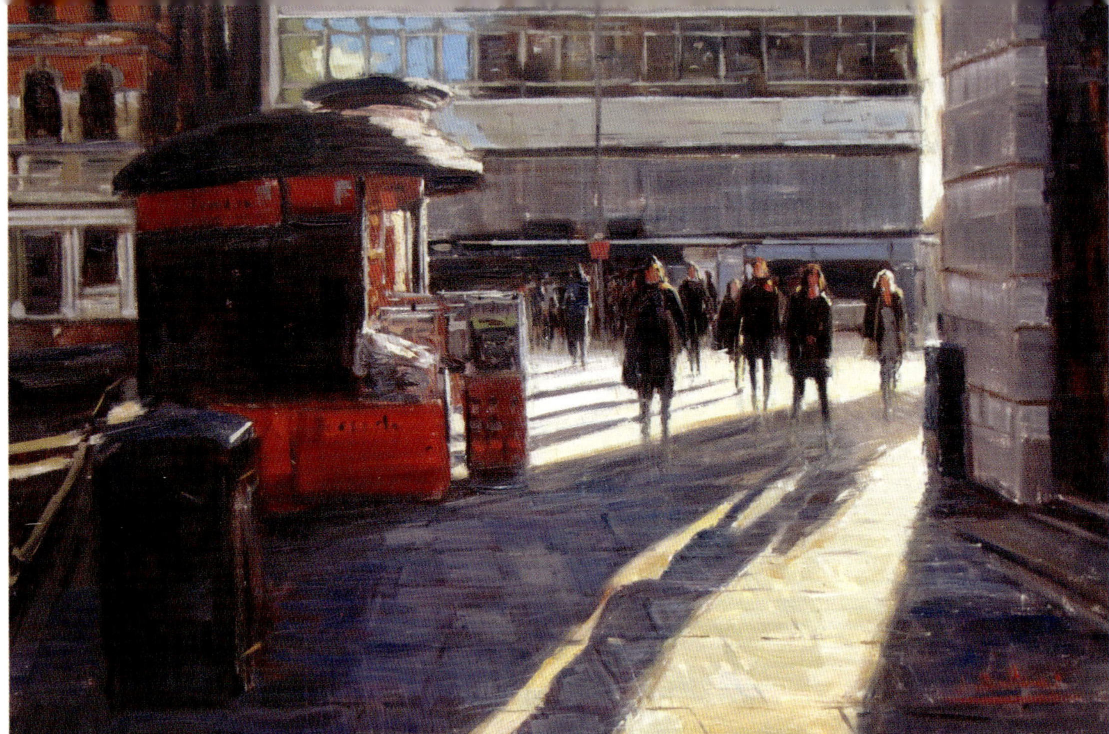

Light

Light makes a massive difference in my work. In fact, it's often what the light is doing in a particular scene that attracts me to paint it.

Light changes everything about a composition, and the more dramatic, the better. Dramatic light creates interesting shadows which help the composition to have variation in values and in design. When I see a crowd of people interspaced with the right light and shadows, I can almost smell blood – for me, that's a painting on the horizon!

As you can see from the paintings here, the right lighting enhances the scene, making it easier to bunch up crowds into congested shapes while enhancing the shadows and the light that comes in between.

If painting a crowded scene, make sure you record the most interesting light before it changes. Even a quick snap on your smartphone will come in handy towards the end, or if you finish it up in the studio.

Always paint the colour of your shadows. They are seldom dead darks: look intently, look carefully, and you'll see they always have colour in them. Your ability to paint coloured shadows can transform your paintings drastically. Likewise, in painting the light, check out its colour. The more variety you can put in your lights, the more believable your work will be.

Have the curiosity of a scientist when dealing with light: see what it does, right from the source to piercing through the figures.

Top
Morning Light, Sloane Square Station   76 × 50cm (30 × 20in)

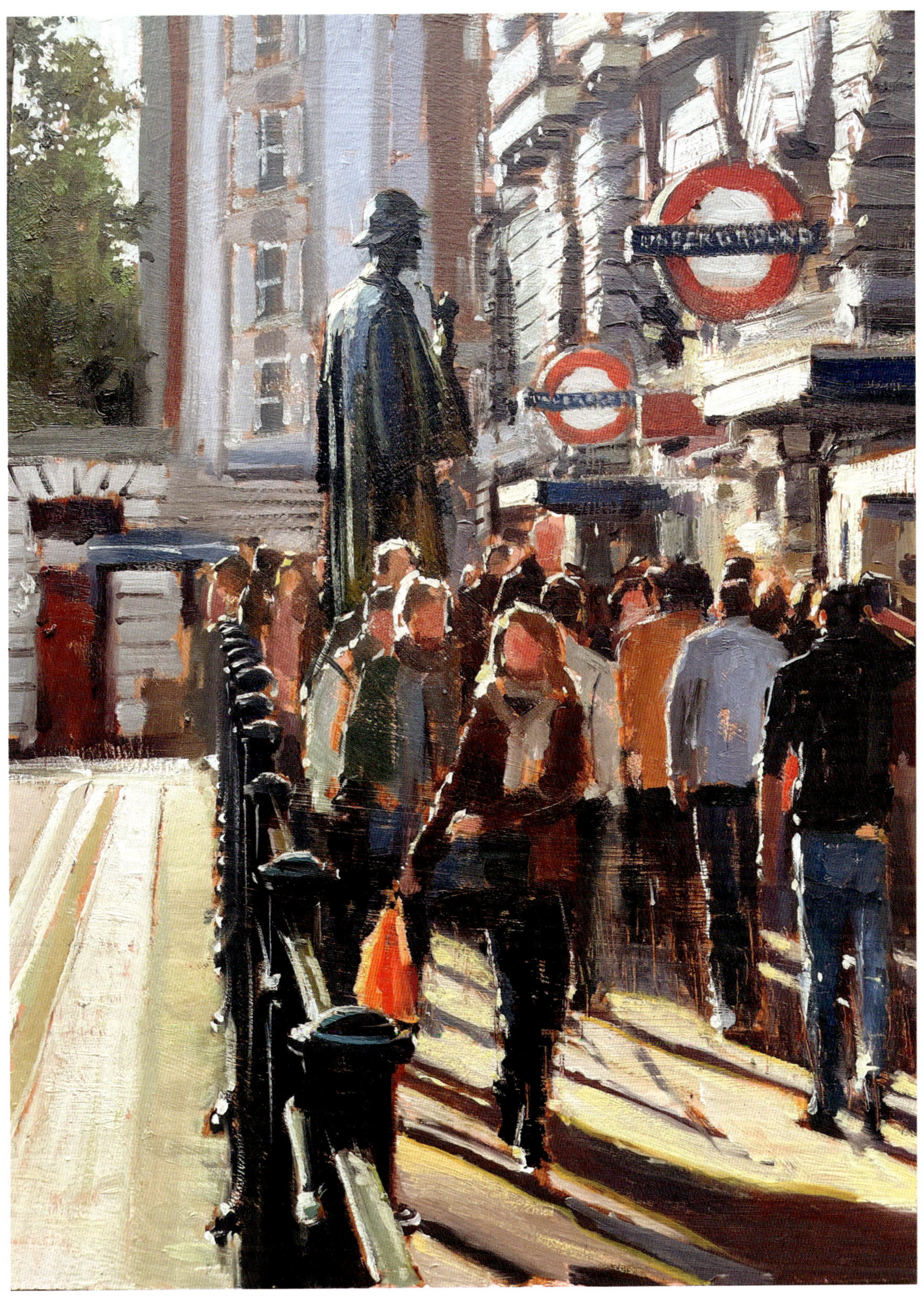

Morning Light, Baker Street Station   12 × 16cm (30 × 40in)

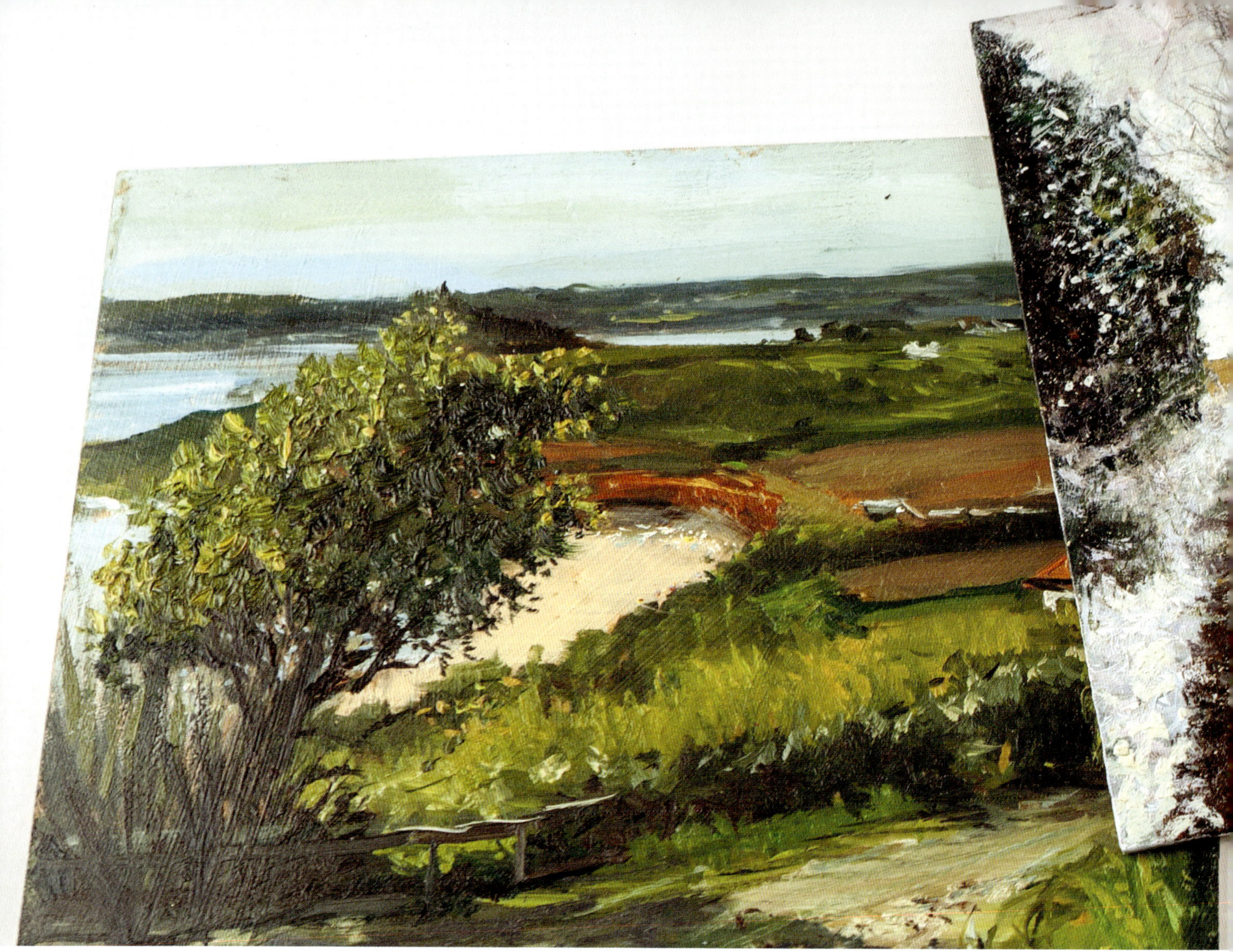

LANDSCAPES

Oh for the glory of landscapes! This is the sort of subject matter that brings out the child in me. I say this because most of the elements are purely organic: trees, rivers, hills and mountains all have a sense of flow about them, with few hard lines and sharp angles. Being purely organic makes landscapes simultaneously one of the easiest and most challenging themes to paint.

I get into my core element while painting landscapes and the process becomes pure fun. I would encourage any artist who loves nature to venture into the wide and wild unknowns with your kit and just have fun. You'll never regret it.

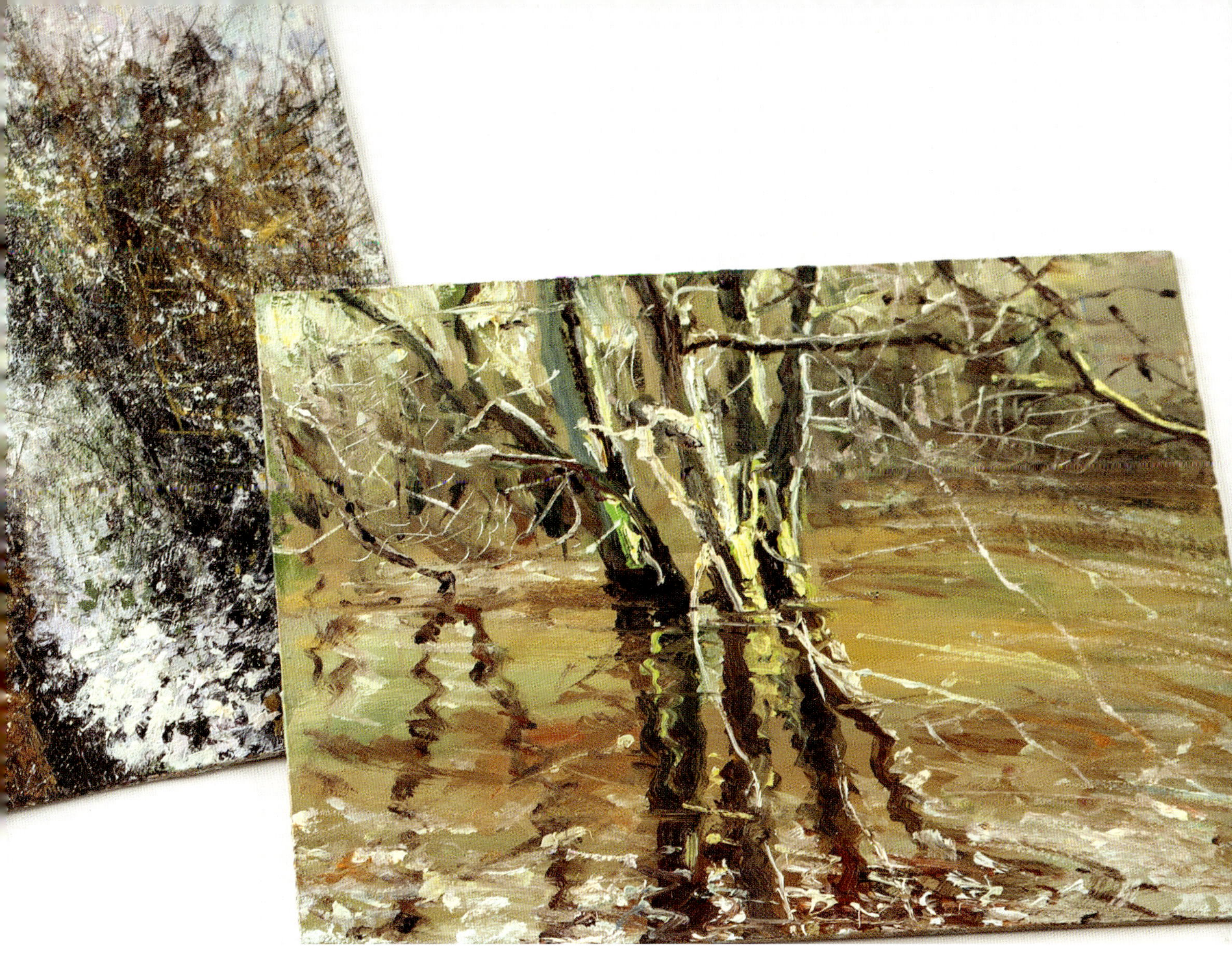

Greens are ever-present in the natural landscape, and they are also delicate. How to handle mixing and using greens with oil paints is one of the major challenges in painting landscapes for the amateur or beginner artist. I have a way of adding yellow ochre to all my greens even before I lighten or darken them so that they are not raw or acidic. Just a little bit of warmth can alter any landscape from looking dead to becoming a well-accomplished piece.

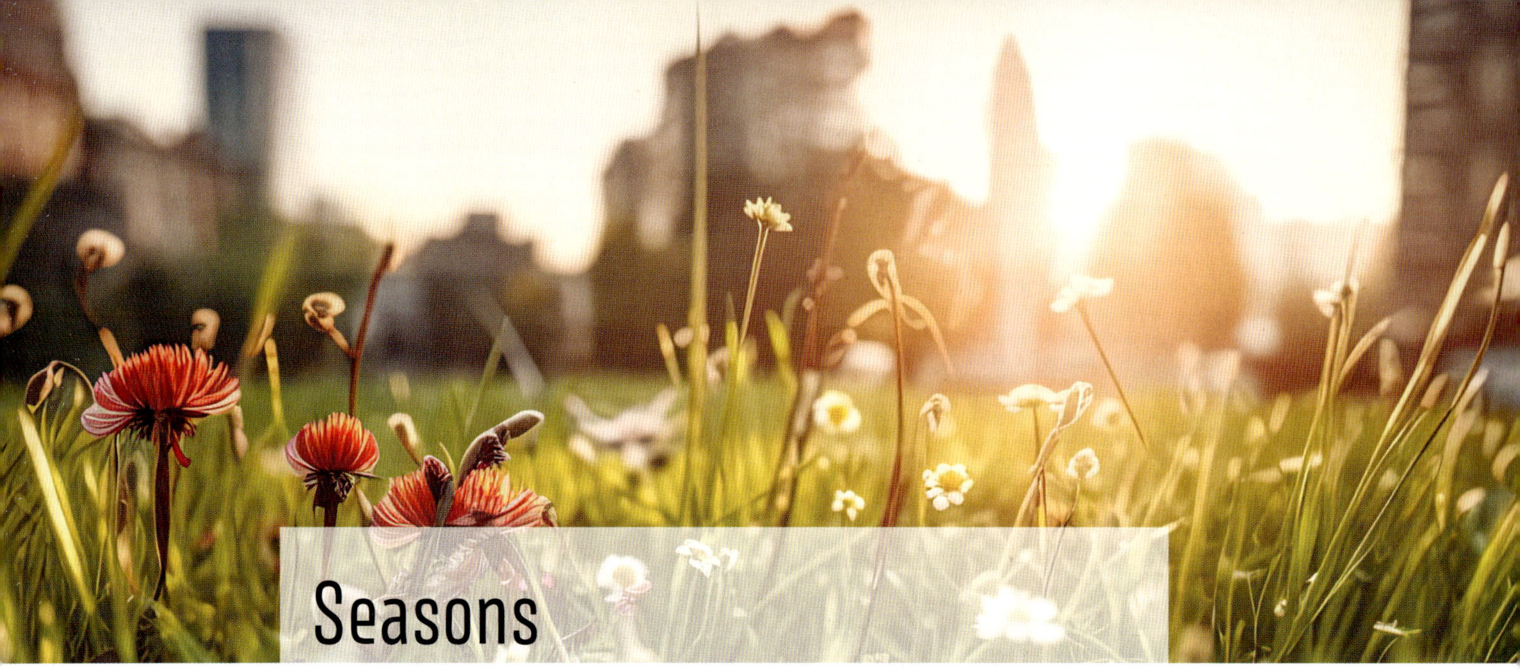

Seasons

Different seasons affect the landscape, making it interesting to paint all year round. I love the fact that there is something unique about each season. Spring has brightness as the flowers bud and shoot up. Summer is gloriously green and lush; while in autumn you see the beauty of browns and oranges. Winter brings out the skeletal beauty of the death of it all.

Whichever season you find fascinating will depend on your own tastes, but don't miss the opportunity to paint outdoors when the weather is warm. It's harder to paint outdoors in the cold months, but entirely possible if you gear up to keep warm. I normally wear lots of layers – so many layers! – during the winter months. To cover my hands, I put a sock over my fingers and poke a hole in it so my brush can stick out. Whatever you do, just don't forget to have fun.

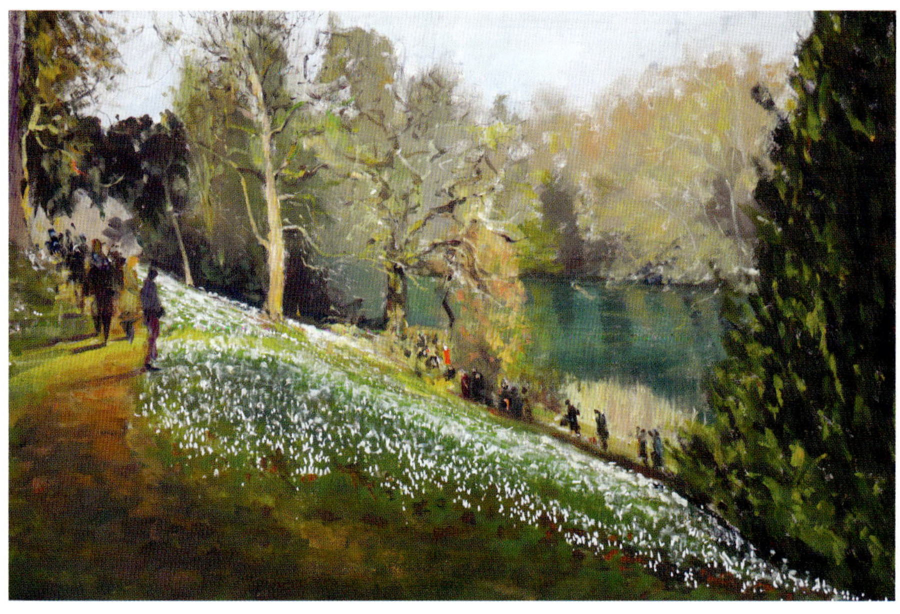

Snowdrops, Colesbourne Gardens   91 × 60cm (36 × 24in)

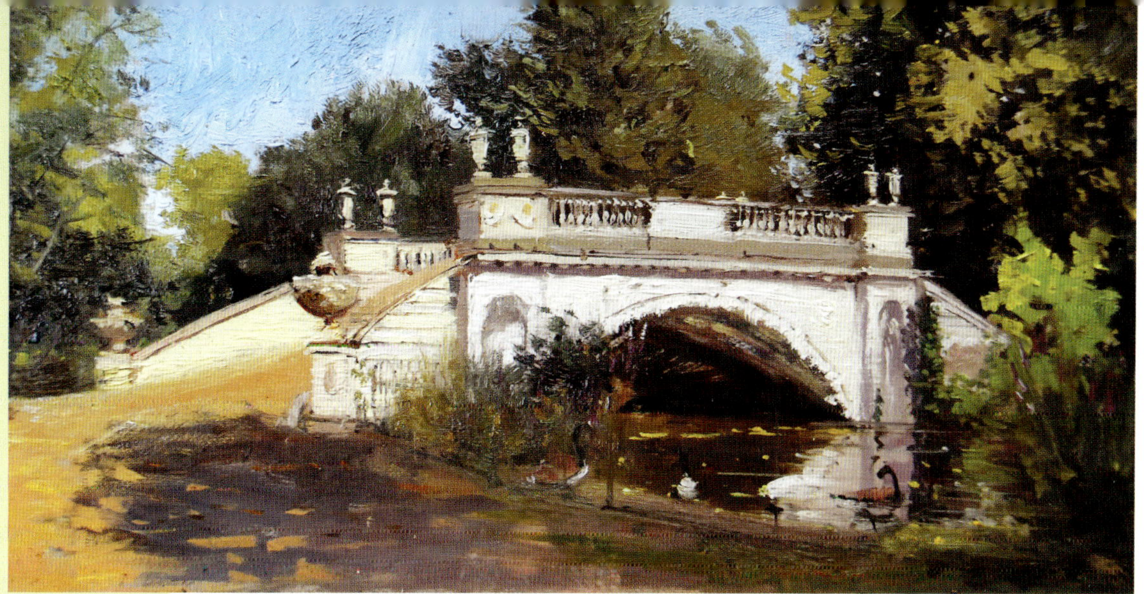

The Classic Bridge, Chiswick   40 × 20cm (16 × 8in)

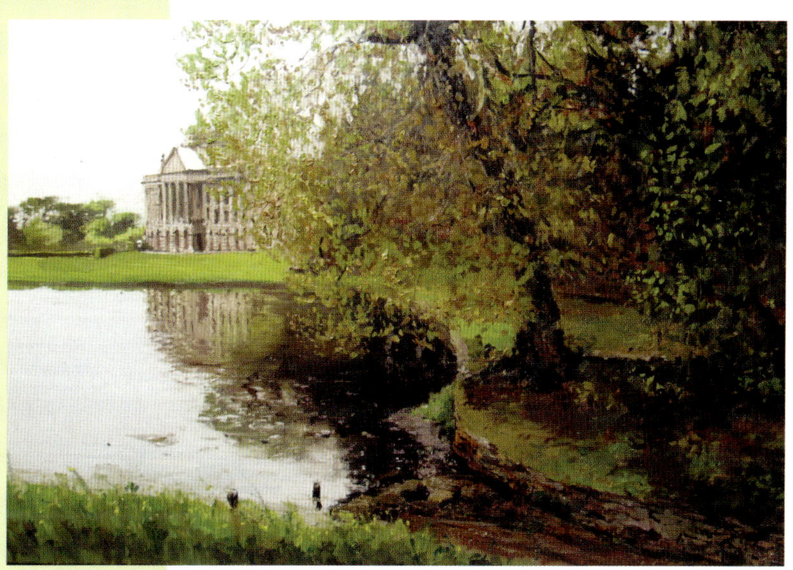

Autumn, Lyme Park   91 × 60cm (36 × 24in)

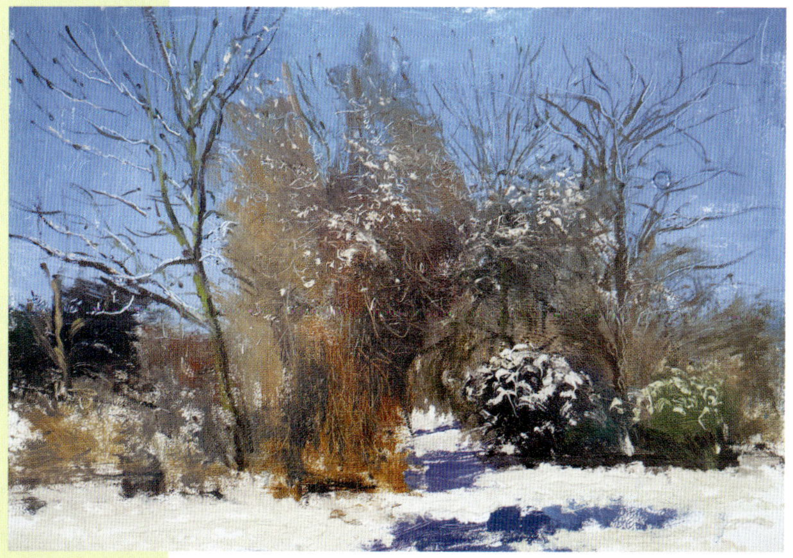

Snow, Sunshine & Shadows   40 × 30cm (16 × 12in)

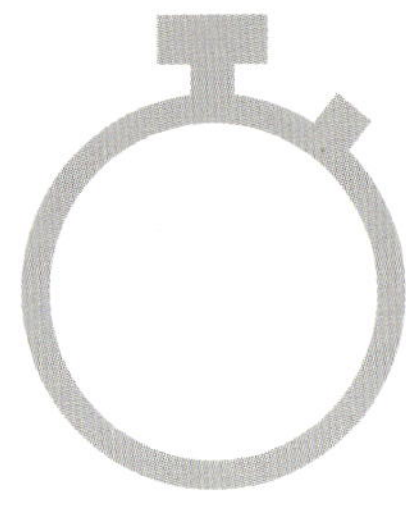

Paint: **Summer Light in the Evening**

This project will let you explore the fun of working quickly. We're going to break it into 15-minute stages.

   This composition is of a lovely park near my old studio, and it's just tree, land and sky. There's nothing scary here. It's a small, simple painting that you can really enjoy exploring. I hope that it gives you more confidence – so whether you go straight outdoors to play, or have a go inside first, it's all good.

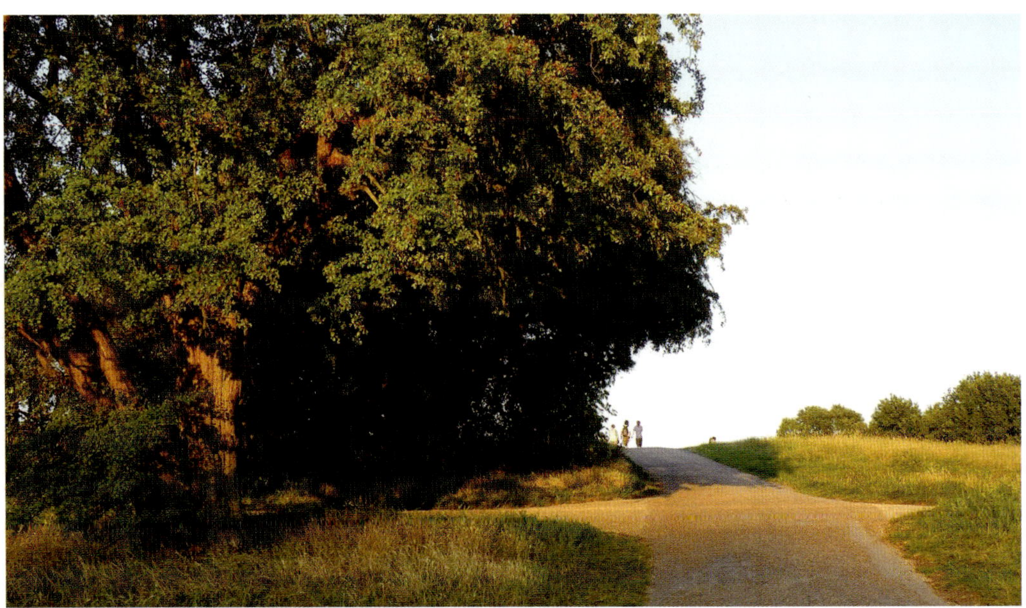

There's no grid necessary here, mostly because it's a small surface, and secondly because it's a natural subject: no-one's going to notice that something's slightly out of position in the same way as, say, a city street not being straight. This frees us up and means we can get straight into sketching.

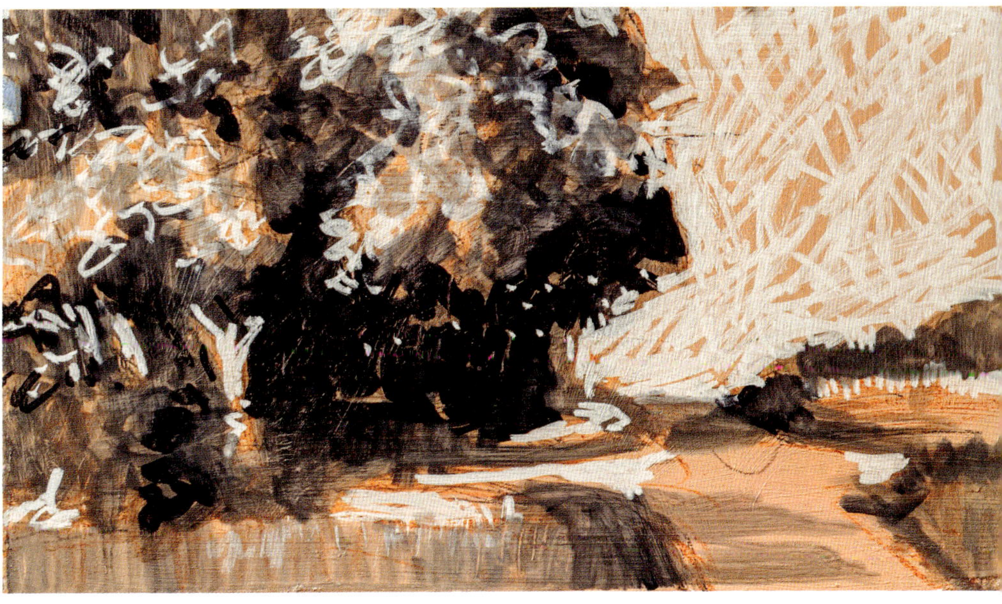

First 15 minutes: sketch

Start by placing the horizon. We want unequal land and sky – we either
have more sky or more land. Here, the horizon goes in a third of the way
up from the bottom.

- Rough in the bulk shapes with the brown coloured pencil, working very
  loosely. Don't worry about accuracy as you would with a portrait. The
  tree's not going to be angry with us if we get a branch in the wrong place.
  Swap to a black coloured pencil to develop the tone. The goal is a tonal,
  monochromatic 'false underpainting'.

- Swap to the brush markers and use them to develop the tone. Start with
  a blue-grey for the midtones then add in the punchy darks with a black
  brush marker. What I'm following here are the shapes of the foliage in
  the tree. Look for shapes – again, squinting is going to help you. Trees
  always look busy, but all you need to do is squint and look for those three
  tones: darks, lights and midtones.

- Use the white Posca pen to add the sky in. The sky is bare, but we want
  the surface to look interesting. Haphazard strokes will give you a sense of
  movement and energy.

- Touch in the other light areas and highlights with scribbly organic marks.

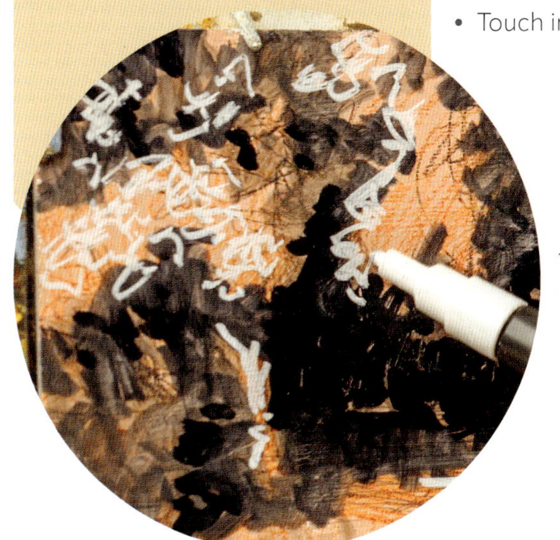

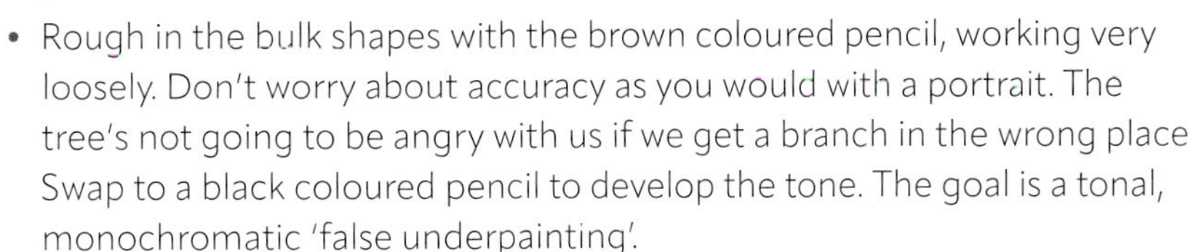

Treat the strokes you make with the pen as a
rehearsal for what you'll later do with paint.

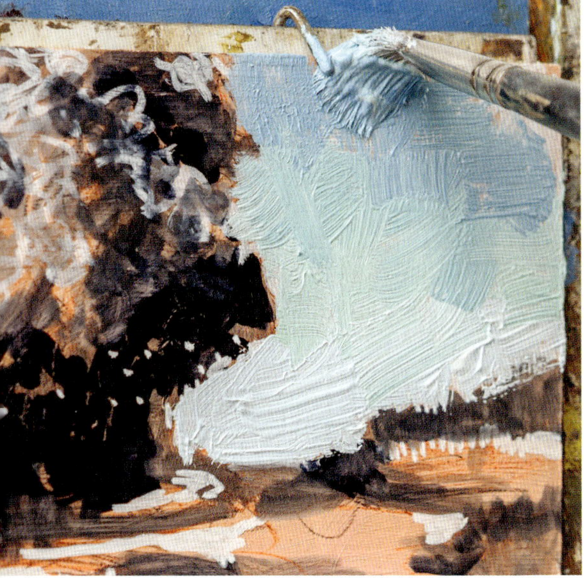

Second 15 minutes: sky and land

It's a small landscape, so let's go thick and luscious with our paints. Create a paste of Maroger and Liquin on your mixing surface, then begin adding your colour mixes. I'm considering aerial perspective, and we'll work from the horizon up.

- Paint the sky with a mix of titanium white and hints of cobalt blue and cerulean blue. As you work upwards from the horizon, add increasing amounts of cerulean blue, cobalt blue, and also a hint of lemon yellow. At the very top, add a little ultramarine blue.

- With the sky finished, swap to a size 6 round brush, which is small enough to give you some control. Add a little Old Holland magenta and alizarin crimson into the sky mix to create a cool shadow mix. Use this to paint the shadow on the distant path.

- Use viridian and yellow ochre to make a green mix. Add a little of all three yellows (lemon yellow, cadmium yellow and cadmium yellow deep) and a hint of the sky mix to paint the distant trees. Vary the amount of cadmium yellow deep and yellow ochre to vary the hue. Cut into the treeline with the sky mix to suggest gaps in the trees.

    - Paint the grasses on the right-hand side with variations on the green mix. Use more yellow ochre for the areas where the grasses look baked and dry, and some of the sky mix and lemon yellow for the area in shadow.

    - Mix alizarin crimson and viridian for the shaded area of the main tree's foliage. You don't want your greens to look acidic, so some yellow ochre will warm them and make them look more natural. I call this 'ochreizing' my greens.

- Look at your reference to see how the greens relate to one another. Adjust them as necessary using the colours above – where there are some dried-out looking grasses introduce light red.

- Throughout, always ensure that you apply the paint with interesting brushstrokes. It's a simple scene and a small canvas, so we want to pack it full of interest and movement and texture.

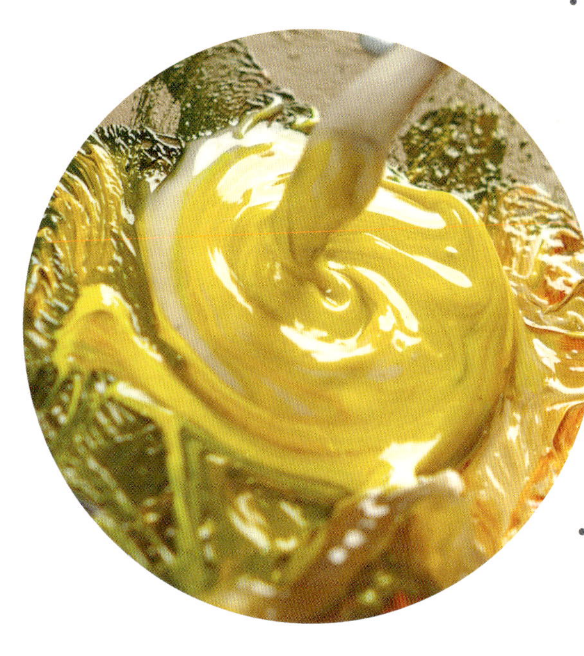

Adding plenty of Maroger gives you great impasto textures. Don't be shy of surface texture. It's going to turn this little canvas into a heavyweight with lots of interest.

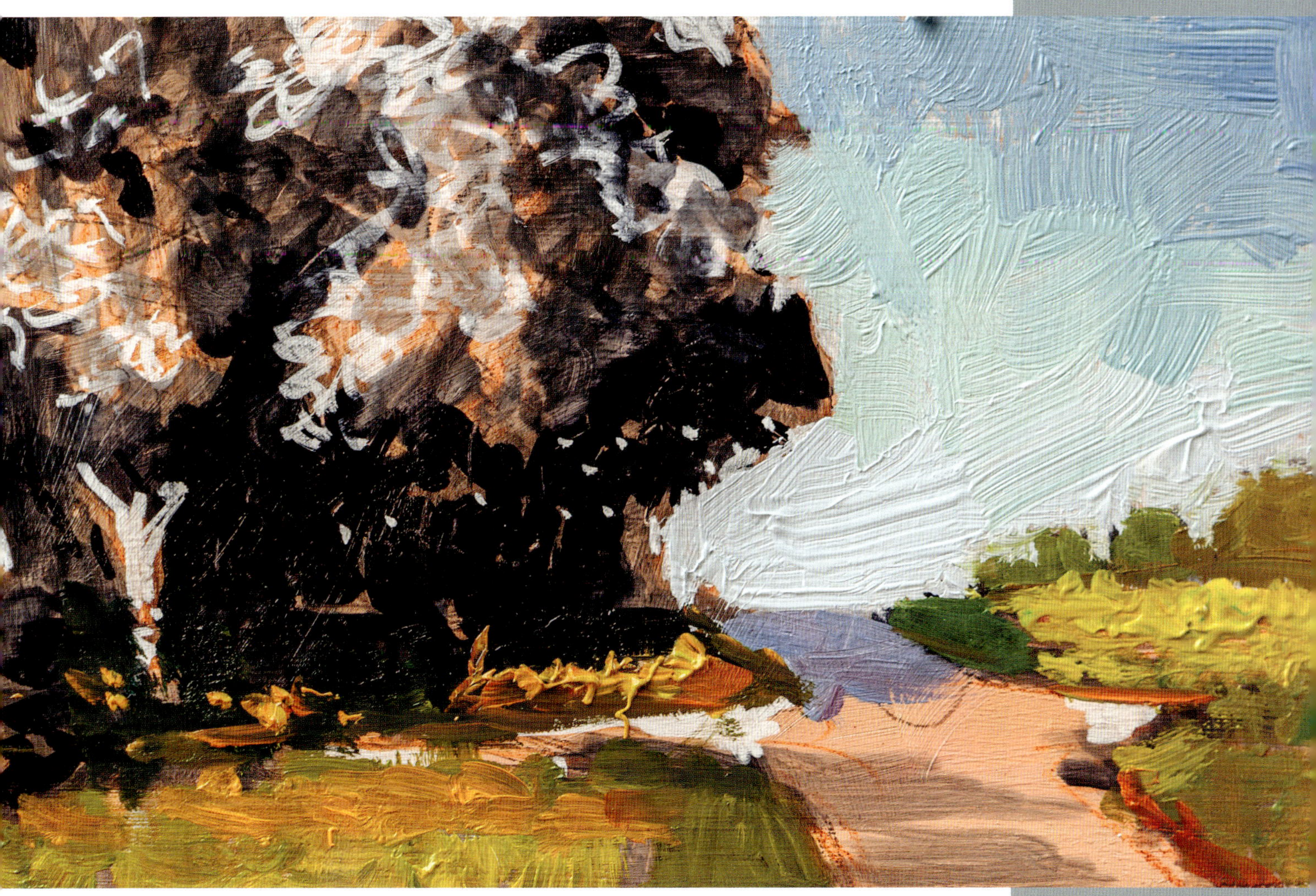

This shift in colour and tone emphasizes the distance and size. The brushstrokes should be vigorous and interesting. You're not plastering a wall. Get some movement and texture in.

Third 15 minutes: road and tree

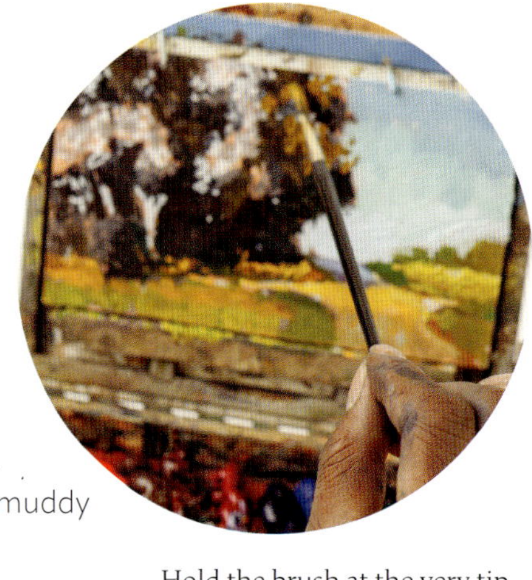

Hold the brush at the very tip to ensure a very light touch.

The tree is the pinnacle of the scene, and we don't want any distractions. Painting it is where the painting will be won or lost. Clean your palette to ensure you don't accidentally get murky, muddy mixes. You need a fresh start.

- Swap to the size 2 rigger for the path. Even the road has a yellow tinge, so we can use the dry grass colour on your palette to quickly block it in with vigorous brushmarks. We want it to have interest and variety, so look at your reference. The path becomes shaded and grey, so add some cerulean blue to the path mix.

- Mix ultramarine blue and Old Holland magenta and add a touch of this deeper colour to the shadow on the path where it meets the bolder middle-ground path.

- We'll be moving from dark to light, and adding in pockets of sky. I want a brush that can give a very light touch, so I'm using a size 2 egbert.

- Prepare your mixes. For the darks of the tree, combine alizarin crimson, viridian and a bit of cobalt blue and yellow ochre. In the deepest shadows, you'll barely notice these marks, because they're sitting on top of black pen. Towards the edges add more ochre to ochreize the colour and bring in some more warmth.

- For the brighter greens, play around with viridian, yellow ochre and a little cadmium yellow deep.

- For the midtones, alter the proportions and use a mix of viridian and cadmium yellow deep with just a little yellow ochre.

- Use the underpainting to guide your placement. Have fun using varied dabbing motions to place interesting marks and shapes.

- Like the foliage, the bark is worked from dark to light. Start by adding alizarin crimson to the dark foliage mix on the palette and paint the darker areas. Next, make a mix of yellow ochre with cadmium yellow with plenty of Maroger. At no time of the day except the evening, and no time of the year but summer, will you get these golden tones on bark. Use these for the midtones. Vary the colour a little with tiny hints of cadmium red or titanium white.

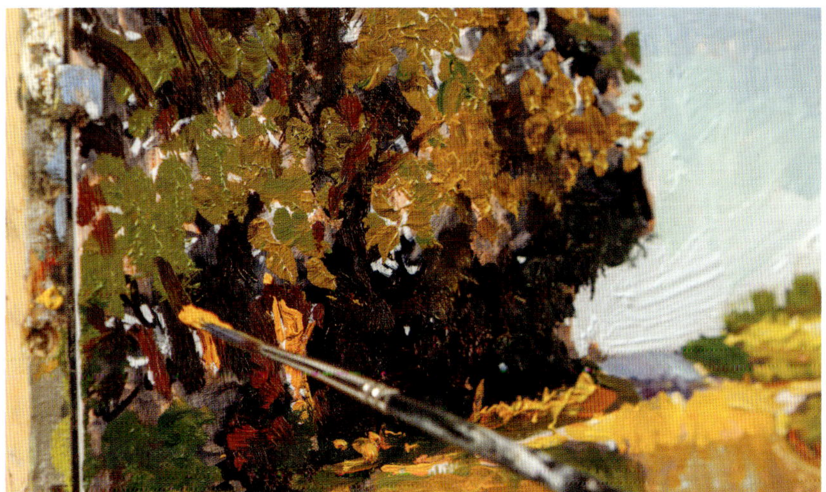

It doesn't matter what size the canvas is. If you adjust the brush to match, you'll get a painting that does it all. Get the colours right and the brushstrokes right, and it'll do the work of a huge painting – but you'll have it done in a short time. Great when you're chasing the light.

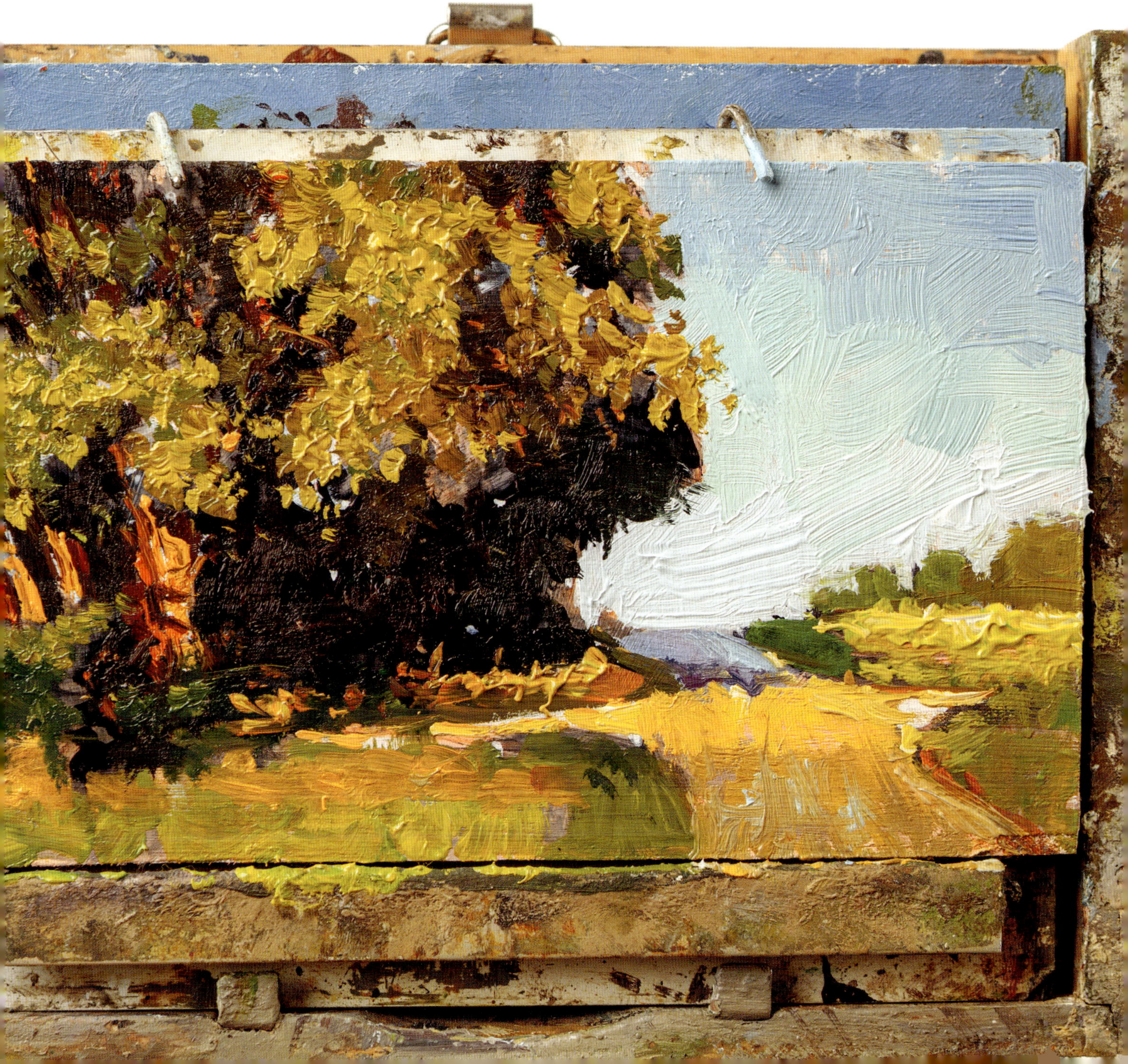

Last 15 minutes: finishing touches

For the highlights on the foliage, create a mix of viridian with yellow ochre (to stop it being too acid) with lots of titanium white to lighten it, and a little cadmium yellow and lemon yellow to prevent it being too chalky. Combine this distinctive mix with the midtone mix and begin building up the lighter passages, and gradually 'sneak up' to using the bright highlight mix on its own.

Next, reinstate a few darks – use the mix on your palette, and add some mystery with a little cadmium red and/or ultramarine blue to create new varieties – then add in some sky windows with a very bright mix of cerulean blue and white. Just touch these on with the tip of the rigger.

Whatever you do, don't overwork it at all. Keep it short and sweet.

The final marks are on the horizon. Add a fine, very bright line of titanium white mixed with a tiny hint of alizarin crimson to make a very, very pale pink. Finally, add two distant figures on the path with the tip of the rigger and the dark mix on your palette.

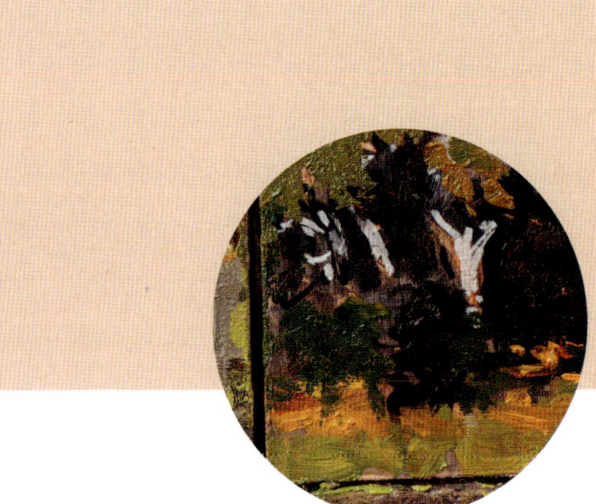

The foreground bushes are a more vibrant green than the tree. Add a little cerulean blue, cobalt blue and viridian to the midtone to enliven the colour.

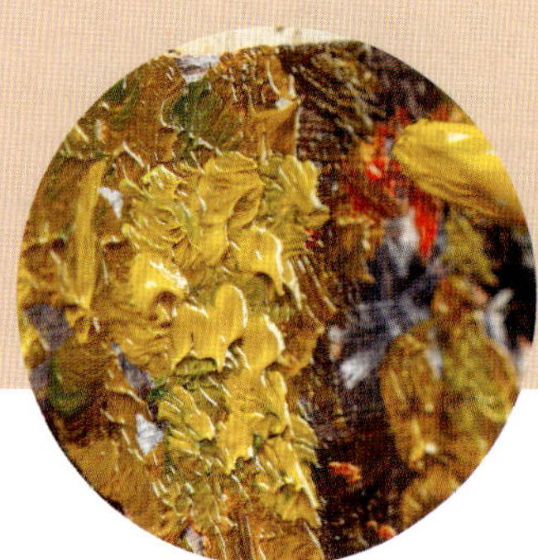

For these final touches, add plenty of Maroger to give the paint body.

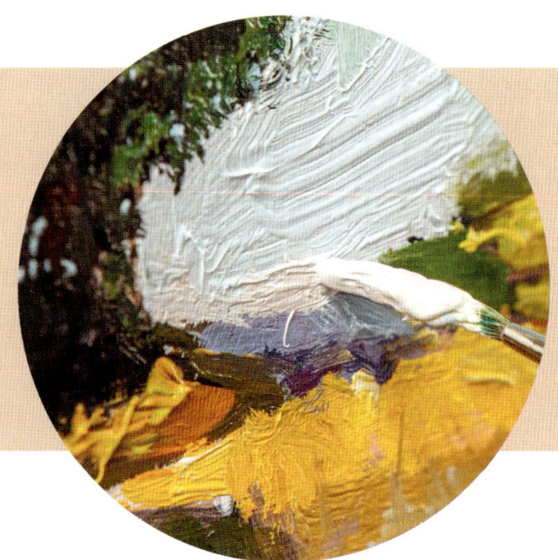

Compare the cool pink used on the horizon with the warm oranges of the foreground tree trunks.

The use of blue-tinged pink on the horizon has the effect of making that particular area more distant, as it obeys the laws of atmospheric perspective, which say colours get cooler and lighter as they recede.

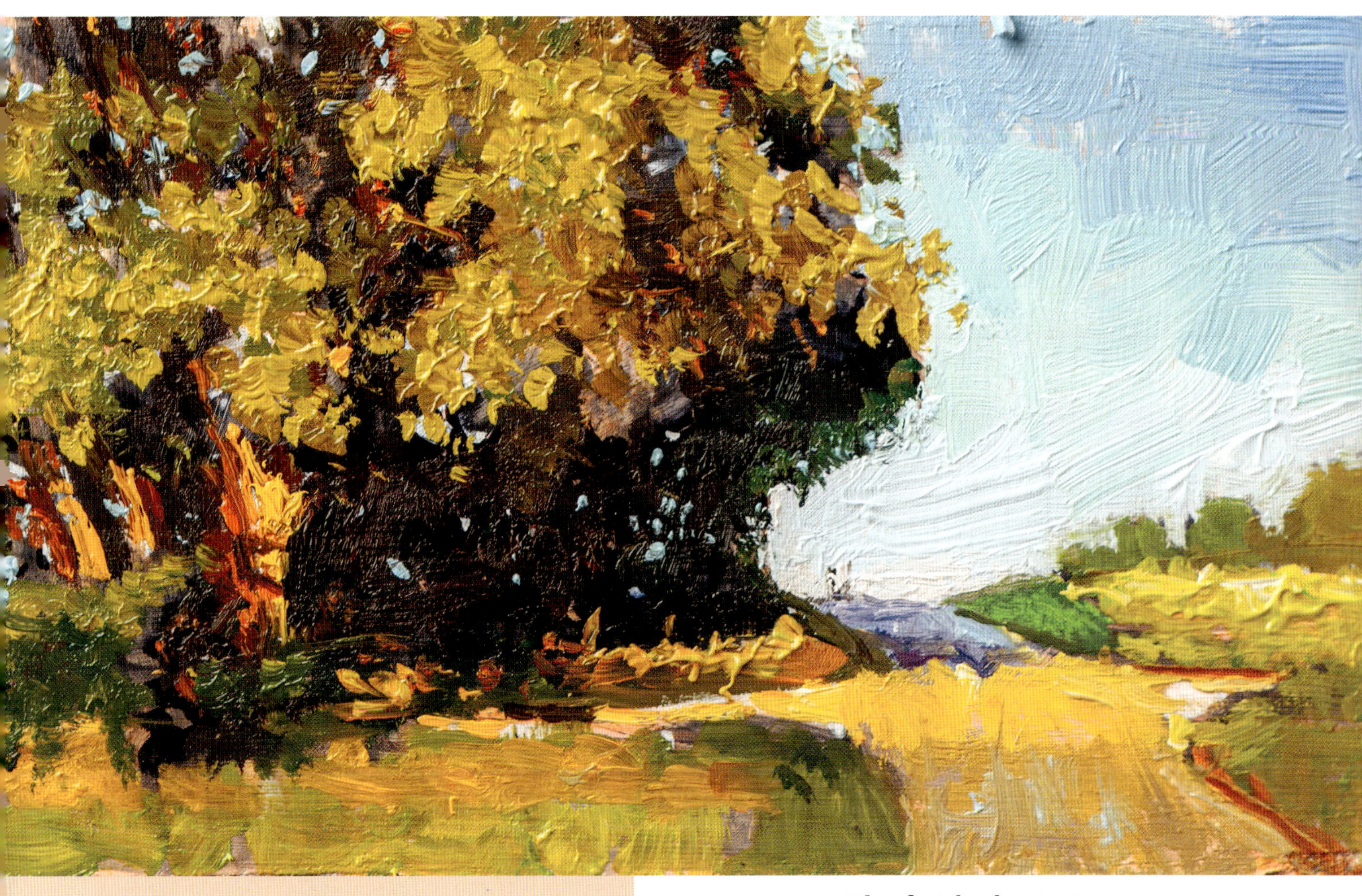

The finished painting

Mood and atmosphere

There is nothing that excites me more than encountering a scene with a clearly identifiable mood. Whether the scene is notably bright, grey, dull, wet, hazy, foggy or blazing with contrasting light and long shadows, if the simple twists and turns in the atmosphere have made for a naturally striking scene, you need do nothing more than record it. Capturing the specific combination of effects that was before you is what will allow the viewers to understand the mood and atmosphere that you experienced.

The sometimes sudden changes caused by light are what makes painting landscapes interesting. Subtle changes matter more than you might think, and this is what you need to look out for when you encounter a scene. If you want to capture atmosphere, you need to really be looking closely, and recording faithfully what you see.

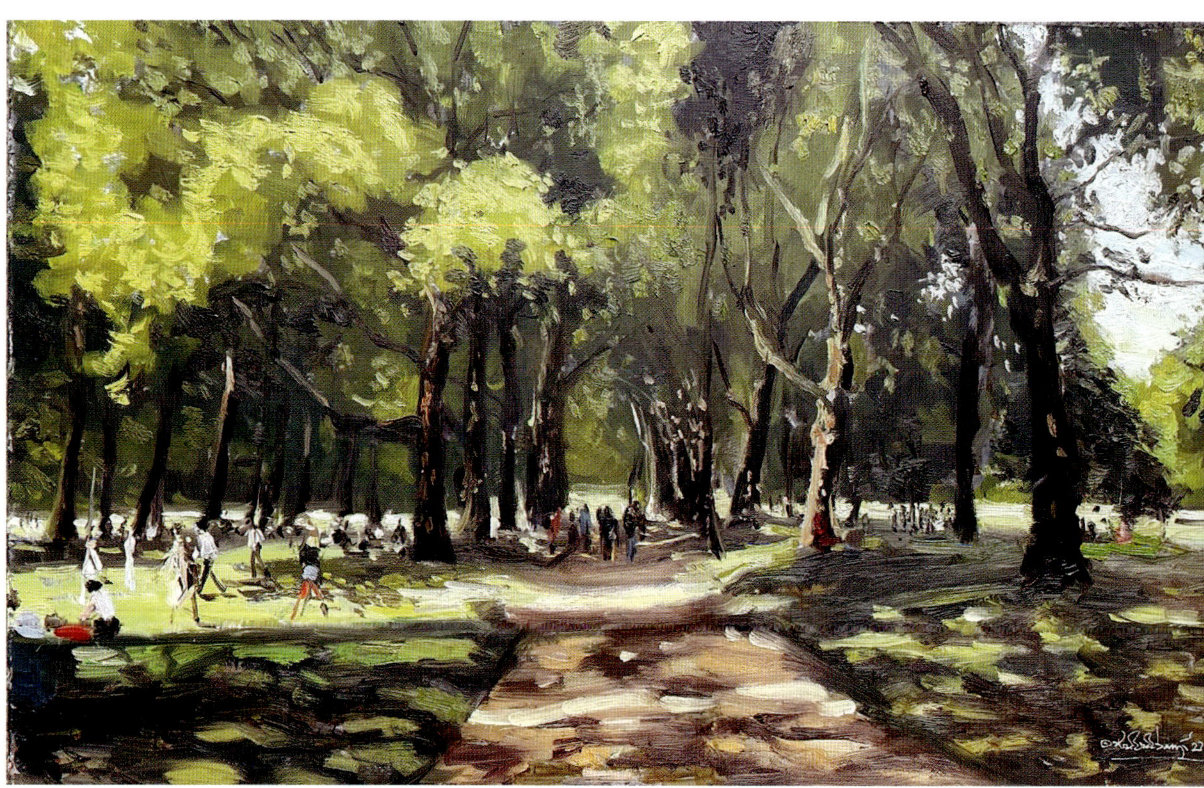

Summerlight Shadows, Green Park   50 × 30cm (19½ × 12in)

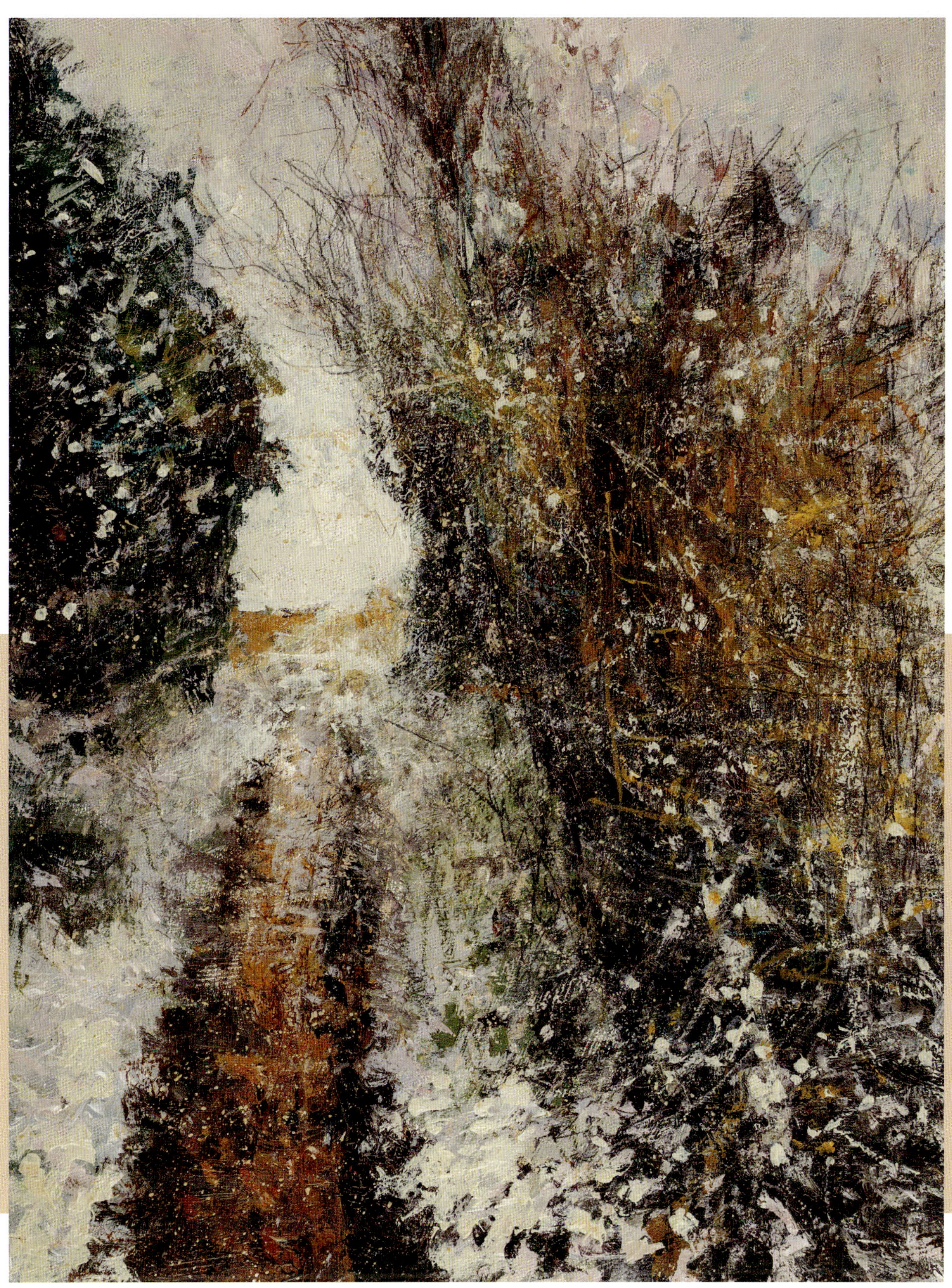

Snow Inspiration I   15 × 20cm (6 × 8in)

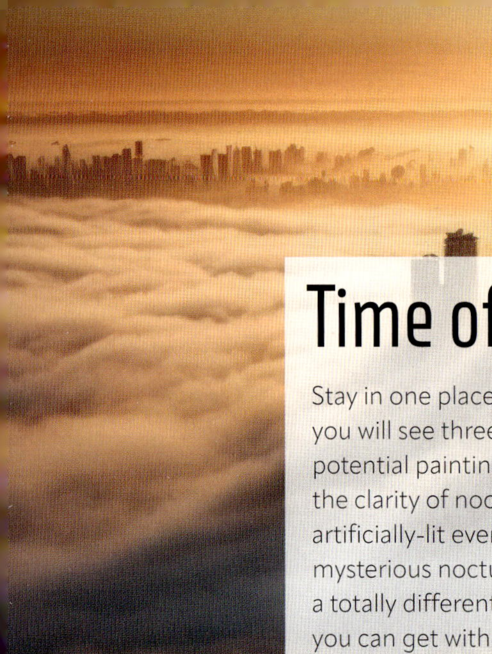

Time of day

Stay in one place for a whole day and most likely you will see three or four completely different potential paintings. Fresh morning sunrise, the clarity of noontime light, hazy afternoons, artificially-lit evening scenes or perhaps a mysterious nocturne, every time of day will bring a totally different feel to an area, and thus to what you can get with your painting.

The key thing to note is the sky. The sky is the first place that gives away the mood; both through its colour and tone.

The other thing to note about capturing the mood of a particular time of day is to vary the contrasts between the tones used. Well-lit times near the middle of the day give high contrasts, while tones are more closely knit around early morning and late evening – though note that this also depends on the weather, so trust your eye.

The final thing to be aware of is that if you are faithful enough to paint in the right tone and in the right temperature, very naturally your painting will always have the mood and atmosphere you are trying to convey.

Mornings and evenings These are the best times for dramatic results. I love these for their injection of contrasting lights and long shadows, which make creating interesting compositions easier.

Noon Pieces made in the middle of the day are likely to be more vibrant, with shorter shadows that can really highlight very interesting contrasts in light and shade.

Sunset Blazing sunsets can be really enchanting – but very quick. Photographs don't do sunsets justice as the camera never picks up the right tones and colour temperature, so it's important to either take colour notes or paint rapidly. The best way to go about capturing a sunset is to make fleeting studies on site, then elaborate on them in the studio.

Nocturnes Night scenes are the best! The light doesn't change, and as long as you accompany your easels with an external light attached, you can get the best pieces done at your own pace. You can work from pictures, but again, it's best to take colour notes from life.

Colour temperature only comes into play where strongly warm- or cold-tinted artificial light affects the surroundings, so it's more important to focus on tone than temperature.

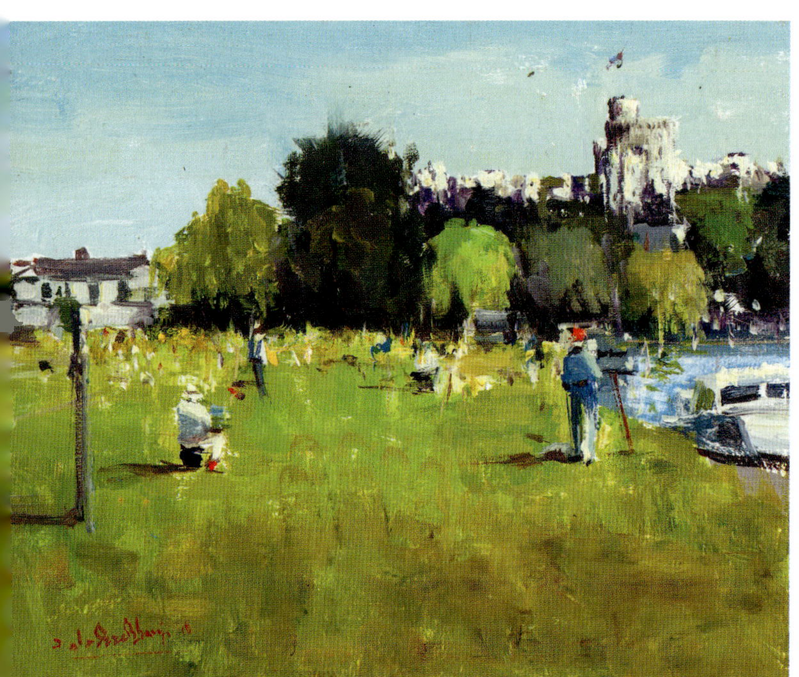

Summerlight, The Brocas, Windsor
25 × 20cm (10 × 8in)

Evening Light, Cornish Farmyard   25 × 20cm (10 × 8in)

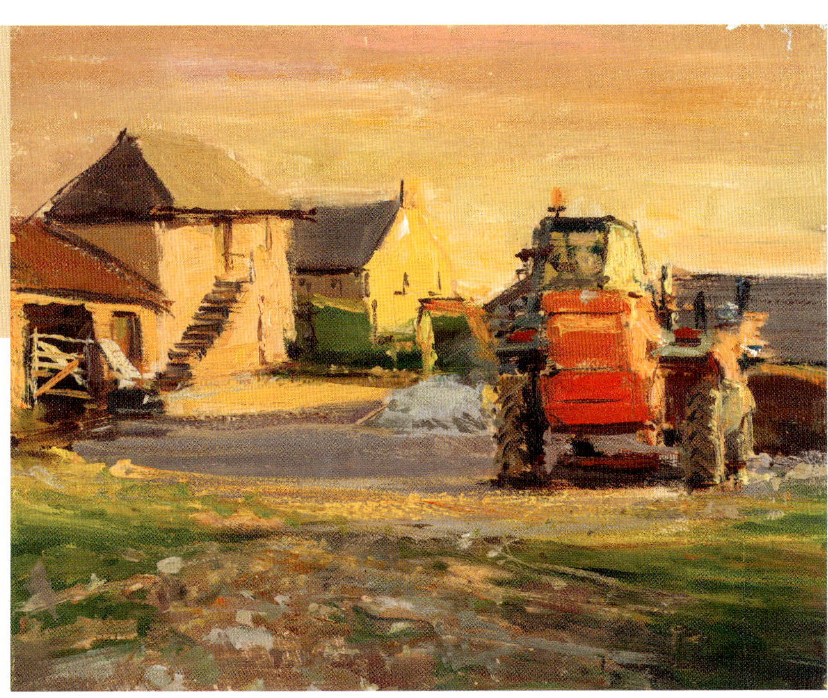

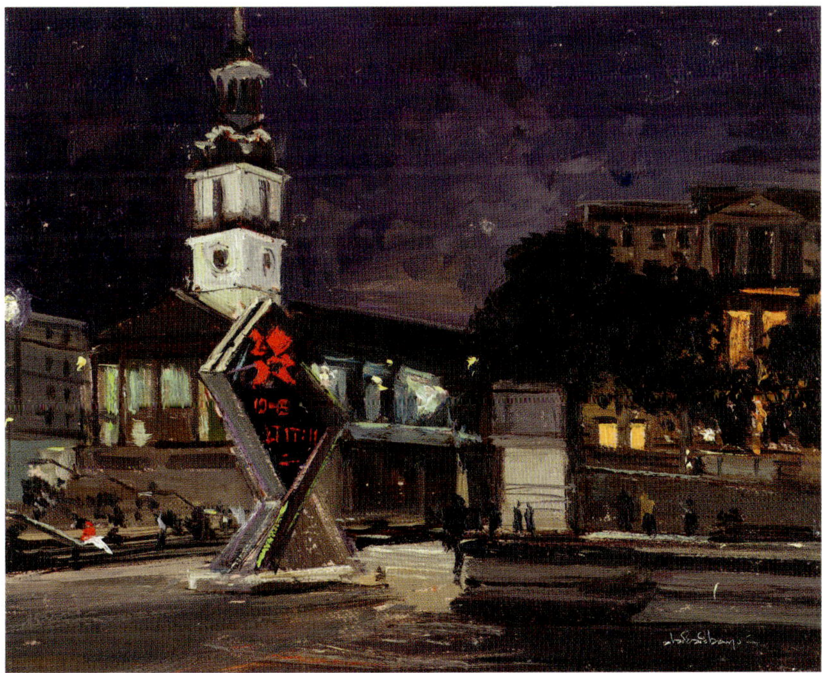

London Nocturne I   25 × 20cm (10 × 8in)

URBAN LANDSCAPES

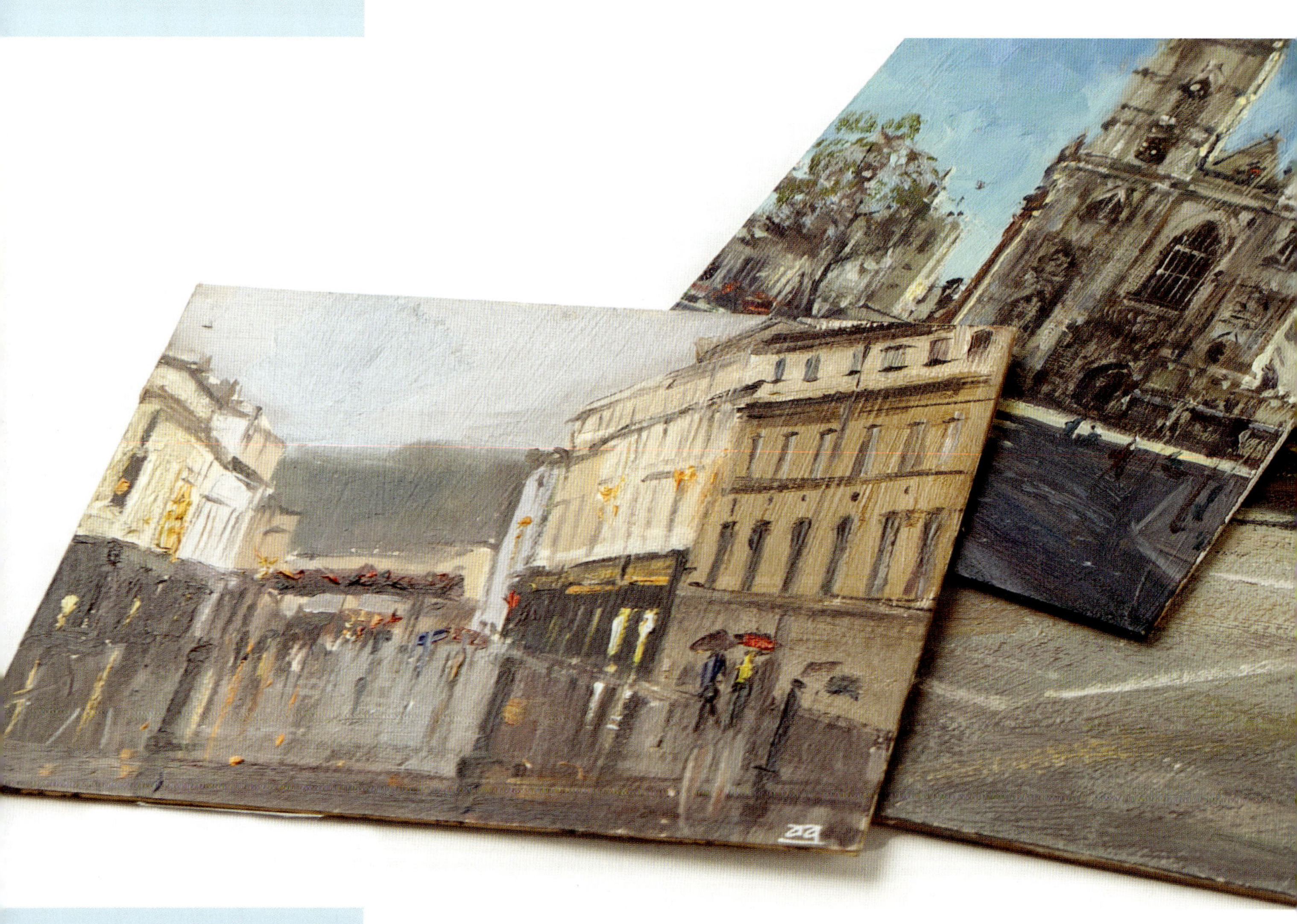

The urban landscape offers the oil artist some of the most fascinating and interesting subject matter. It gives you the opportunity to explore so many elements in one picture – you can include architecture, vehicles, people, trees or street lamps all in one picture – and have space for the traditional landscape sky.

Whether you call this sort of work urban landscape, cityscape or townscape, the name is quite irrelevant: the main draw is the opportunity to capture all the parts that make up a typical contemporary, modern part of our living on this planet!

Most of all, I love cities for their buzz and excitement, and I must say, most of my work focuses on this subject matter.

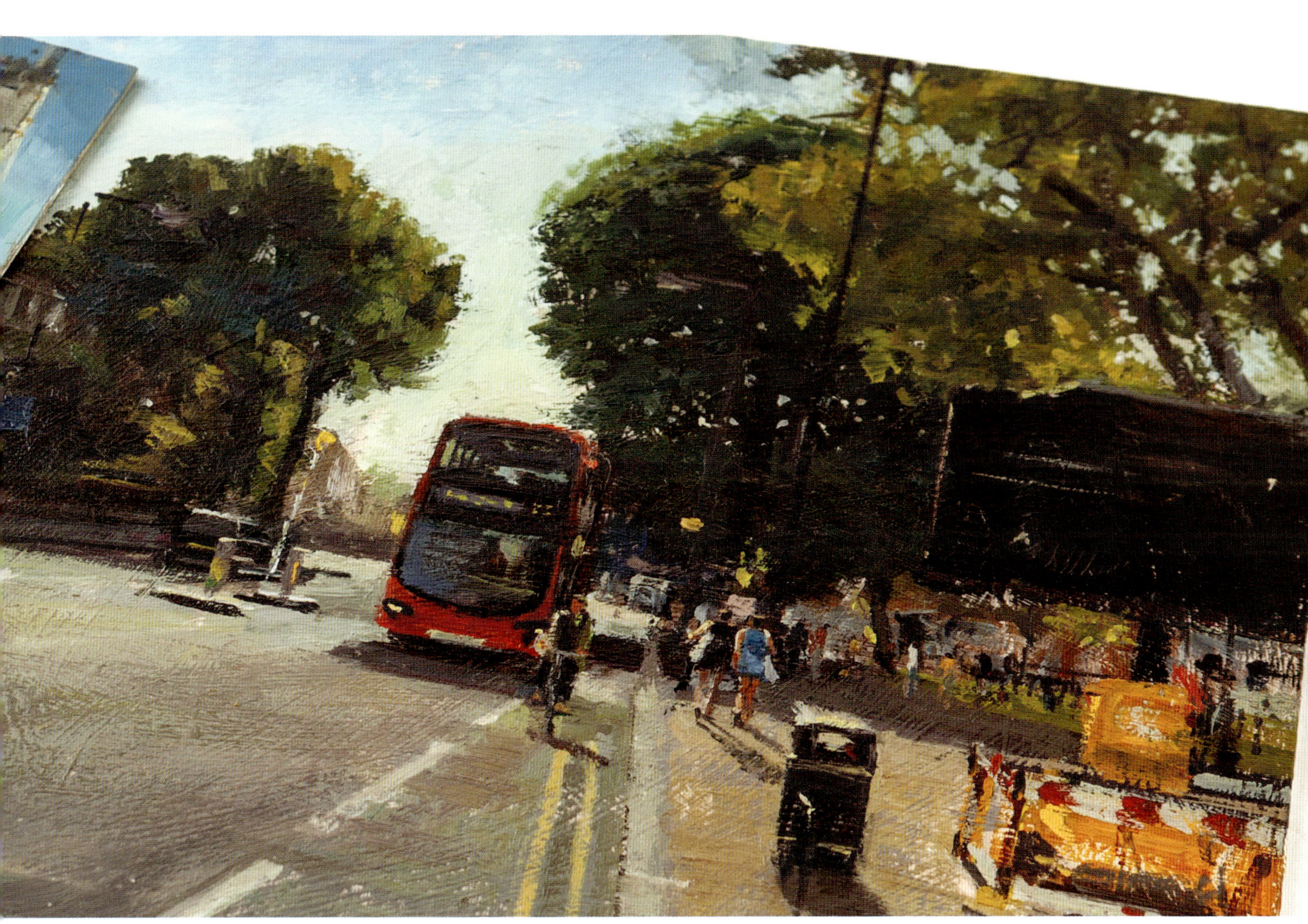

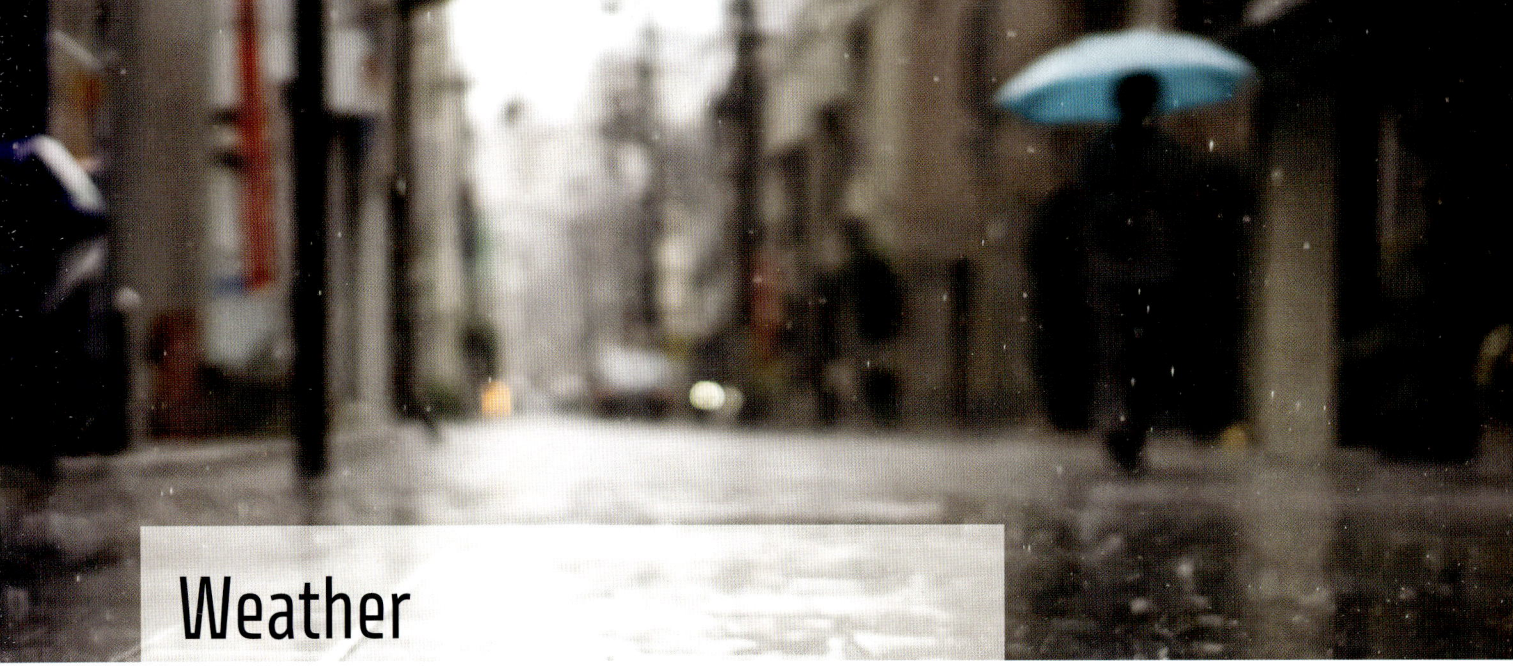

Weather

The weather makes a big difference to how the urban landscape appears; and therefore how you paint it. My general advice for making the best for each weather situation is to make sure you are fully prepared, have the right gear on for colder days, and lighter gear with a sun hat for warmer days. The right protection from the elements means there is less to worry about, so you can just concentrate on painting.

Cold and grey Everything will be clear with a lot of detail available, but the light will be flat: it will have few, if any, interesting contrasts, colour or shadows and you'll have to work around that. The advantage of this sort of weather is that you can work for longer periods outdoors without worrying about the light changing – great, particularly when you are just starting out with *en plein air* work.

Hot and sunny You'll be blessed with some of the best moments in an urban landscape with this weather. Bright sunlight throws lively shadows, which makes finding an interesting composition eaiser. There is a slight reduction in the details you'll see, since there will be larger dark shapes and values against smaller shapes and values or vice versa.

Rainy days Of all the weather situations possible in an urban landscape I love rainy days the most. It's a real challenge to paint outside on wet days, and usually I prefer to take great pictures and paint in my studio. This is due to an experience I had while painting *en plein air* in the city of Bath, UK: the weather had been great, when all of a sudden it started raining so heavily that half of my painting was washed off the surface! I hadn't positioned my umbrella properly and ended up forced to repaint that half. Ever since that day I haven't tried venturing out on a rainy day.

Weather and people

Just as with their surroundings, weather will affect how you see people. When the day is grey and dull you will see their forms more clearly, while when the sun is out you will get stronger shadows and silhouettes, which can help to add interest and drama to your painting.

It's perhaps less immediately obvious, but bear in mind that the weather will also affect the people – they'll move more quickly and be more hunched-over in cold, wet weather; and stand more upright in fine weather. Pay attention to accurately recording their shapes, even if you're only getting glimpses.

Clothing tends to be brighter on sunny days, too – though as you can see opposite, umbrellas can offer a focal flash of brightness on even the gloomiest day.

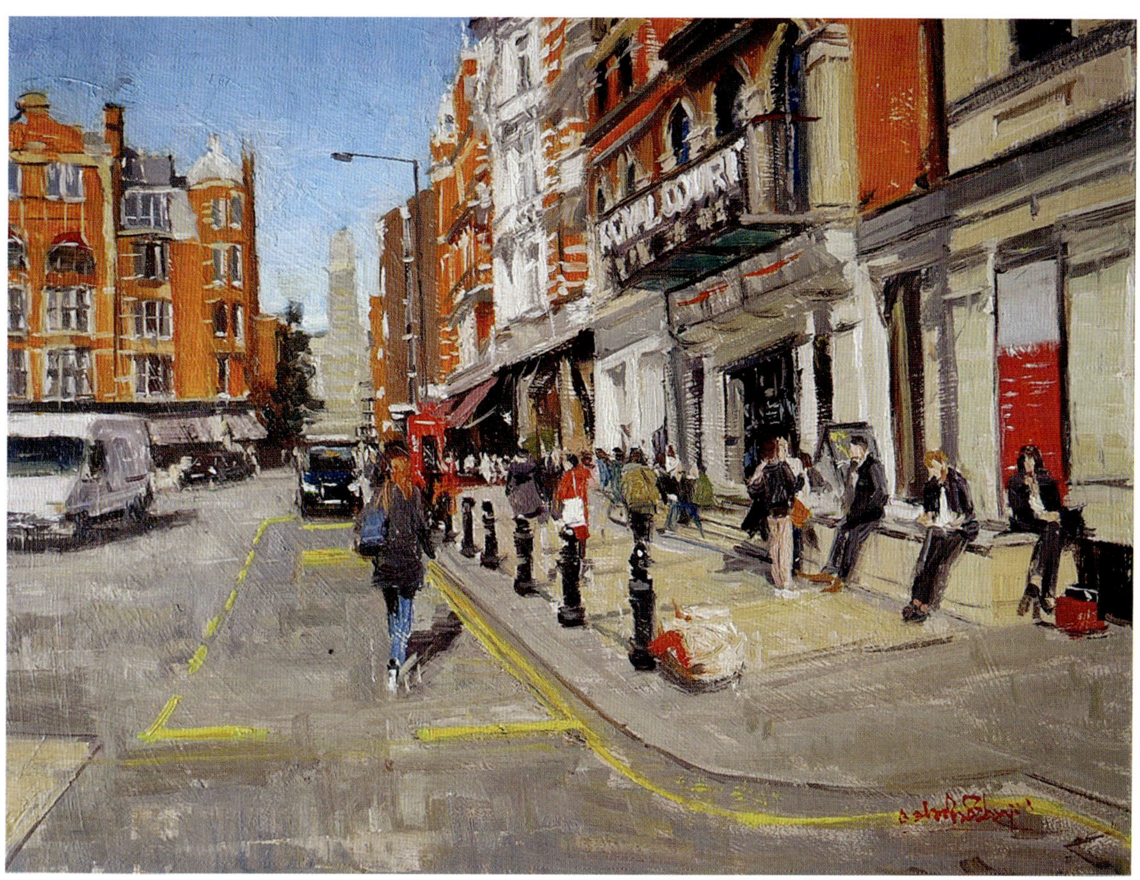

Sparkling Spring Light, Sloane Square 40 × 30cm (16 × 12in)

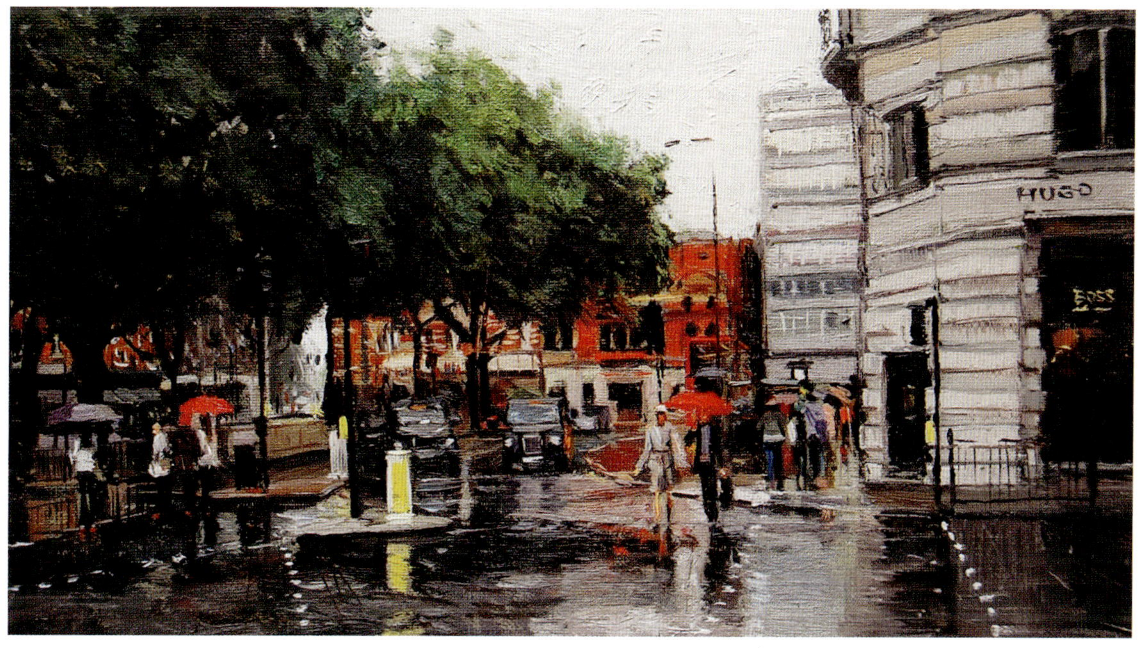

Wet & Rainy Day, Sloane Square 30 × 18cm (12 × 7in)

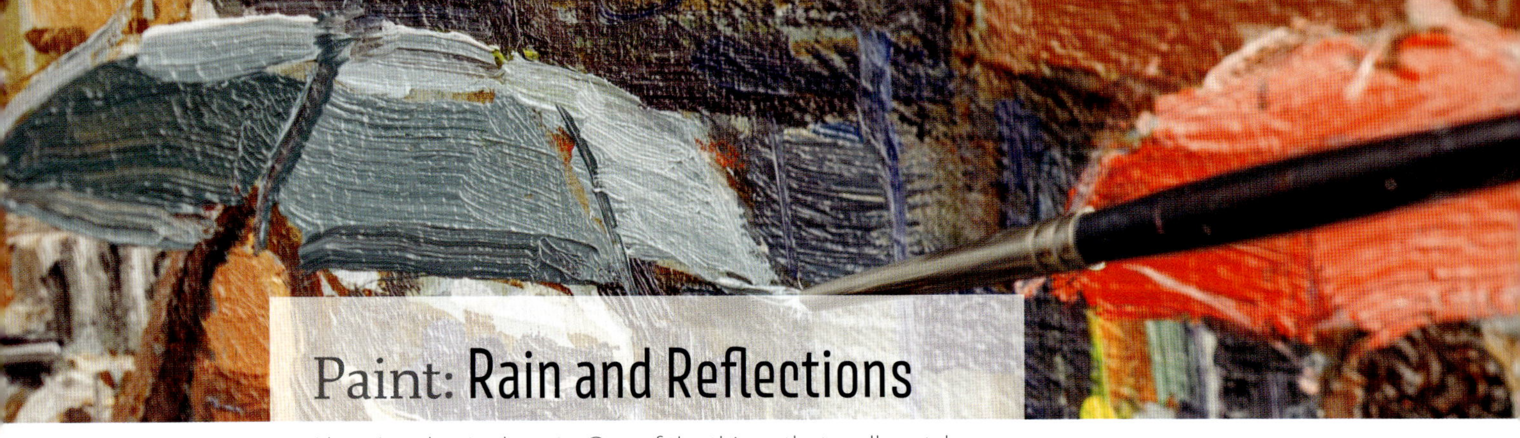

Paint: Rain and Reflections

I love London in the rain. One of the things that really catches my eye is the variety of tones that you get on the pavement during and after heavy rain. This painting is an experiment in making the pavement as interesting as possible. I'm no huge fan of a wet, rainy day in and of itself, but it does offer a brilliant opportunity to explore the greys and muted coppery tones that appear on the surface.

Success will come down to passion. To paint this kind of scene successfully, you need to have a buzz or interest in the region you're depicting.

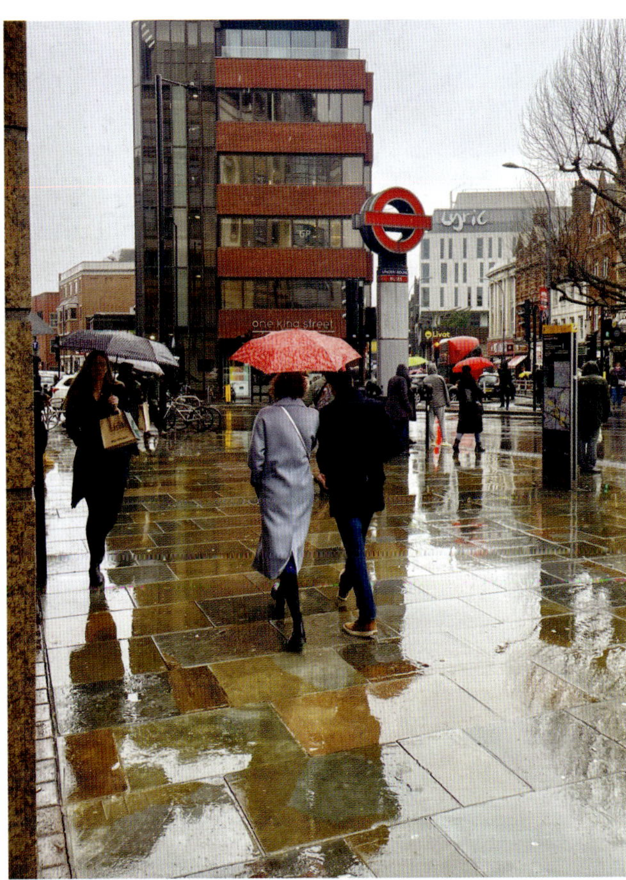

The portrait format of this picture is largely because I was working from a smartphone – the upright extended portrait format is one that increasingly influences us as artists; and will be familiar to lots of us, so I thought it'd be a good choice here.

Of course, since we're interested in the figures and reflections – effectively doubling the height of the people – a portrait format is a good choice that makes the most of the subject.

Because of the format, we'll use a 12 × 16 grid for this project, converted from a 3:4 ratio.

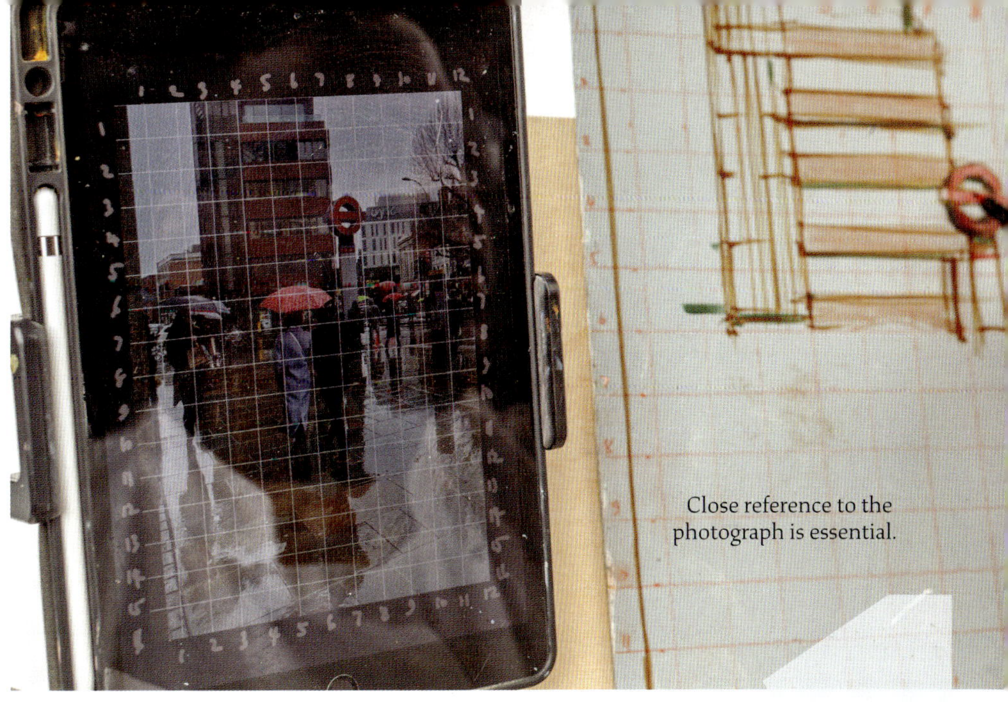

Close reference to the
photograph is essential.

Starting the sketch

Because I'm working indoors, I have the luxury of time, so I'm going to take off my oil painter hat and be an illustrator for a while. There are a lot of details in this photograph, and I want to have precision in this underlying stage. The paint can be loose, but the sketch must be tight.

- Work on a table or on a desk easel at an angle to give you more control.

- Use the brush markers to build up the sketch, with close reference to the photograph. You'll note how the straight lines of the buildings can be a useful addition to the grid lines for placing other objects.

- Use the burnt sienna marker for most of the lines and tone, bringing in colours as and when you need them.

- Work section by section, and take your time. You'll cover all this with oils, so it's important that each part makes sense to you in isolation.

- Work the background and righthand side first.

White Posca pen is added to give a rough sense of the sky.

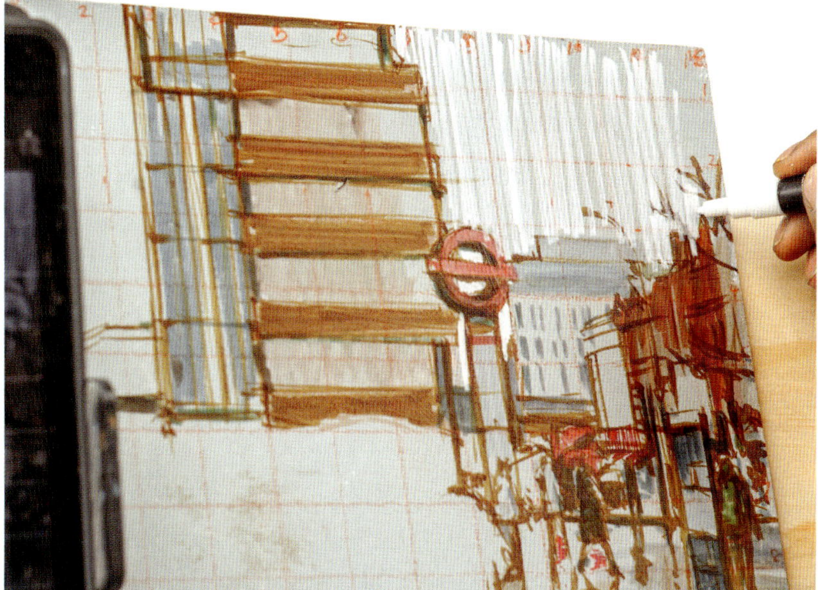

113

Refining the sketch

By the end of this stage, you should be familiar with the painting, and have everything in place to make your painting enjoyable. Don't rush the sketch; it's your chance to get to know what everything is – even the complex areas, or those far from the centre.

- After the right-hand side is completed to your satisfaction, work on the left-hand side before building up the paving.

- The pavement area in particular is critical to the painting, so I need to see the reference lines. Use the grid to line up the angles, and try to make the lines in one swift stroke. This will help to keep the paving clean.

- This will leave just the central area to work on – and this should be easier now that you've built up useful reference points around the sketch.

- If the markers build up and cover the grid, stop and re-establish your grid lines using a coloured pencil and the ruler before continuing.

- Tape your white Posca pen to a brush handle to pick out reflections and highlights. It'll give you a more painterly feel as you prepare to move over to oils.

- It's critical to get the tone right. The advantage of brush pens is that you can layer and glaze, working them over each other.

- As you build up tone, use the movement of the pens to reflect the area: make horizontal marks back and forth for the paving, for example, but vertical marks in the sky and on the tall buildings.

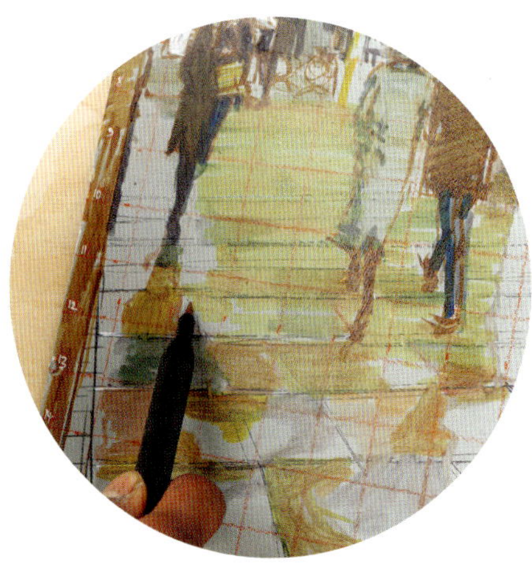

Pay attention to the colours of the paving slabs; and note how they're much more obvious in the reflections of the figures.

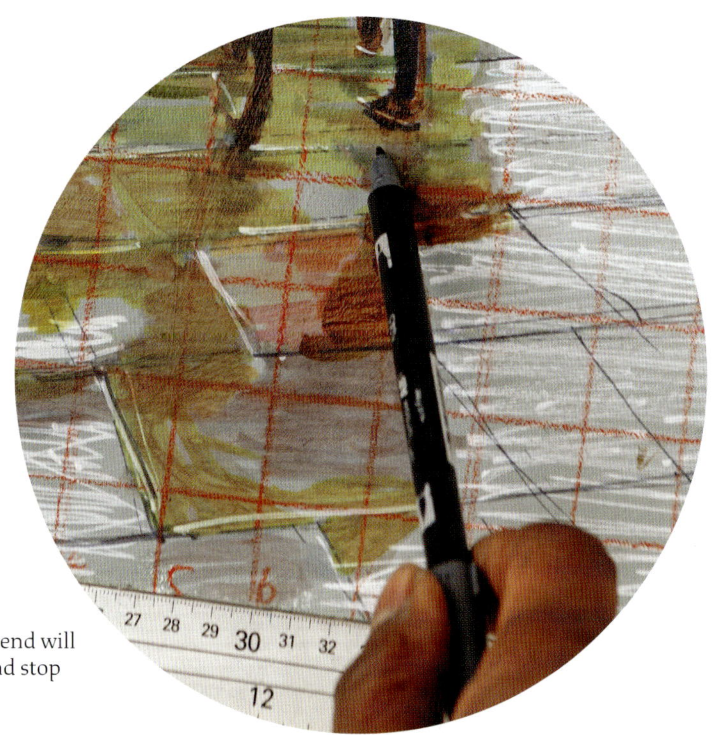

Holding the pens near the end will help to give a looser feel and stop things getting cramped.

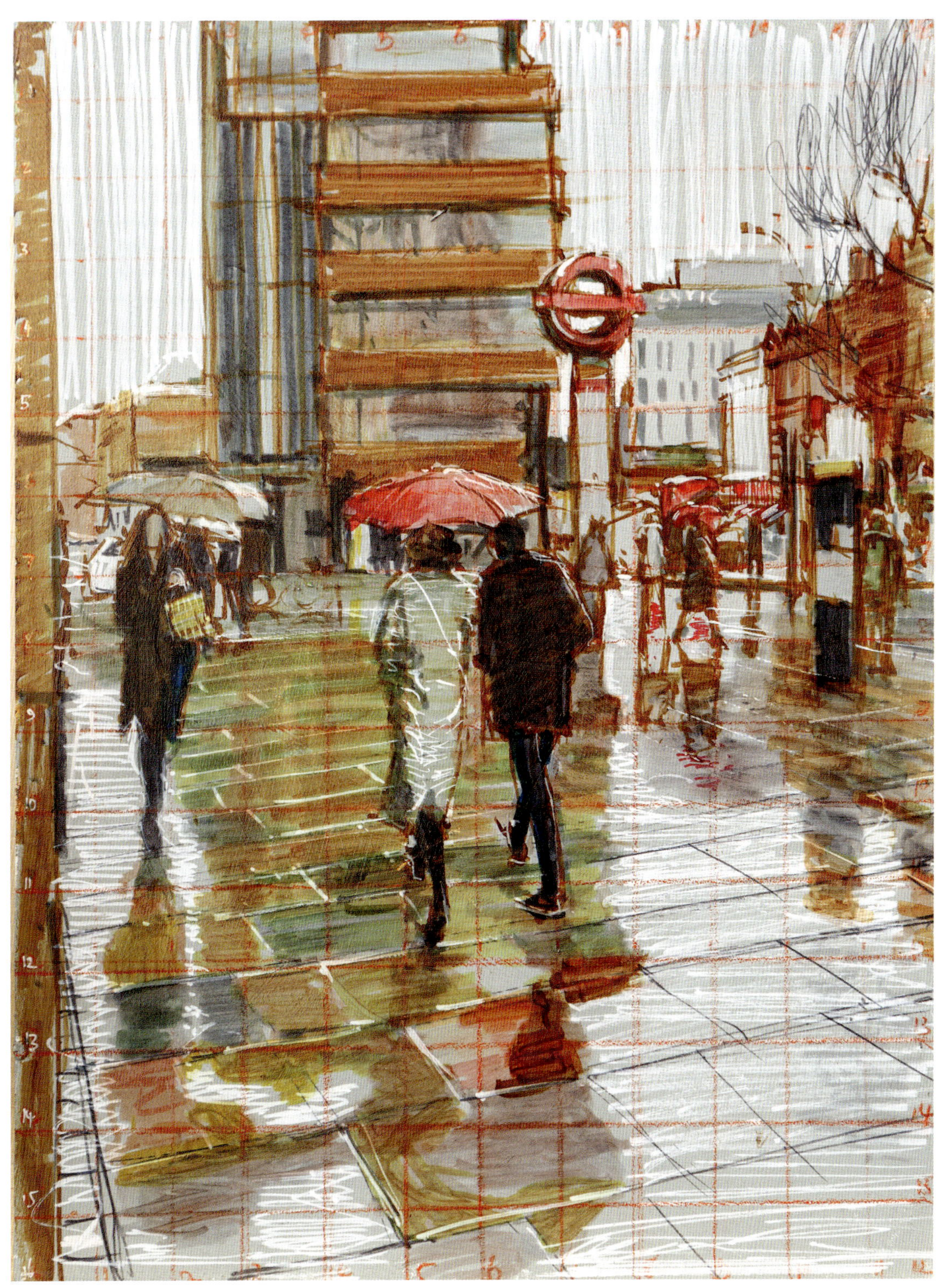

Sky and buildings

I have a formula for breaking down a painting like this: I start with the sky, then move onto the architecture, then the wet pavement, and only then move on to develop the figures.

  The type of brushes you use for this painting is important. It's a complex scene, but we want it to be easy on the eye. For this reason, it's going to be impressionistic – deliberately simple. This means the brushes need to be able to depict each section of the painting in as few strokes as possible.

- For the sky, we're going to make long, vertical flat marks. Pick a brush that's got a decent width – I'm using a thinned-down size 6 filbert. Use a mix of titanium white with a little cobalt blue and a touch of magenta to grey down this dead, muted mix. Vary the proportions slightly to give some interest, but keep this subtle.

- How you place a brush in a particular area will help to convey the mood. For the pavement, vary the horizontal brushmarks with vertical ones to give a sense of movement, and stop it feeling flat.

Make sure you've got plenty of mixing space – there are a lot of colours needed here.

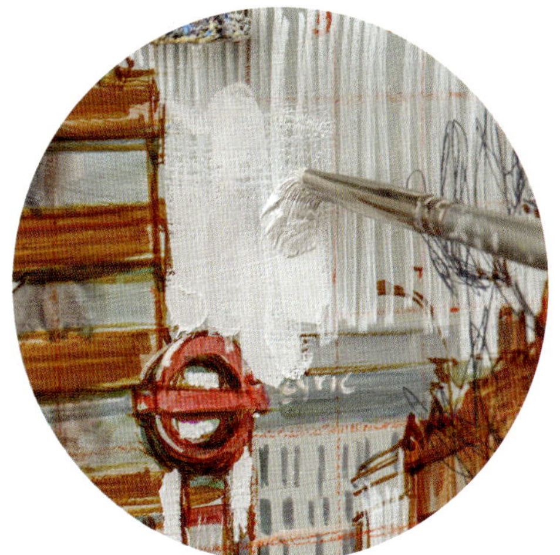

I want to give the feeling of a wet, pouring day: the vertical marks of this dead, unattractive mix, give a convincingly gloomy day.

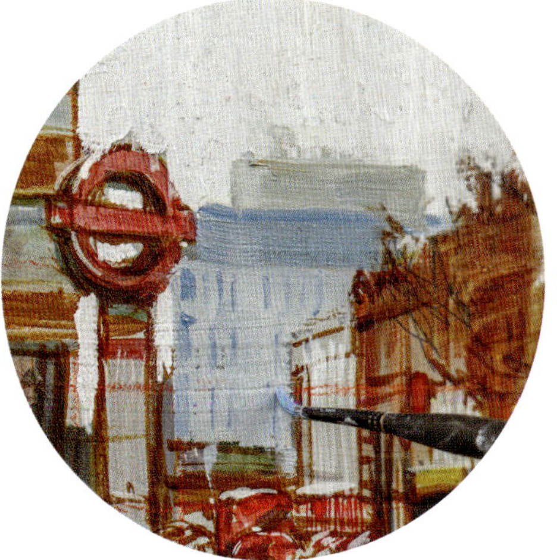

You can use the sky mixes as the basis for the distant buildings, adding just a hint of yellow ochre. Most colours for the background are cool in temperature.

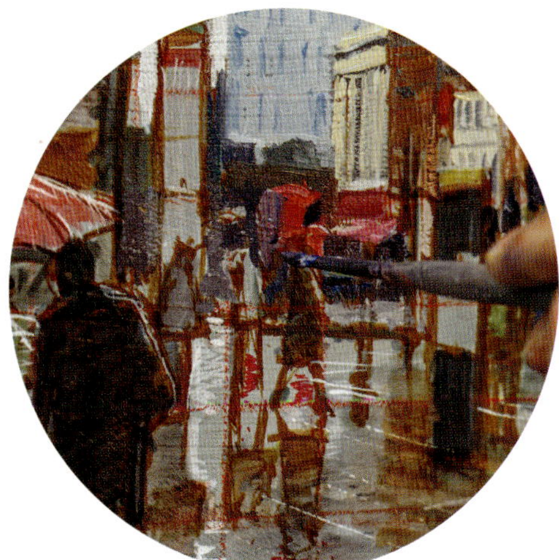

Consider the placement of each mark carefully, but don't be too precise when actually making the brushstroke. This will ensure the distant areas look loose and fresh; you can make more important areas sharper so they stand out.

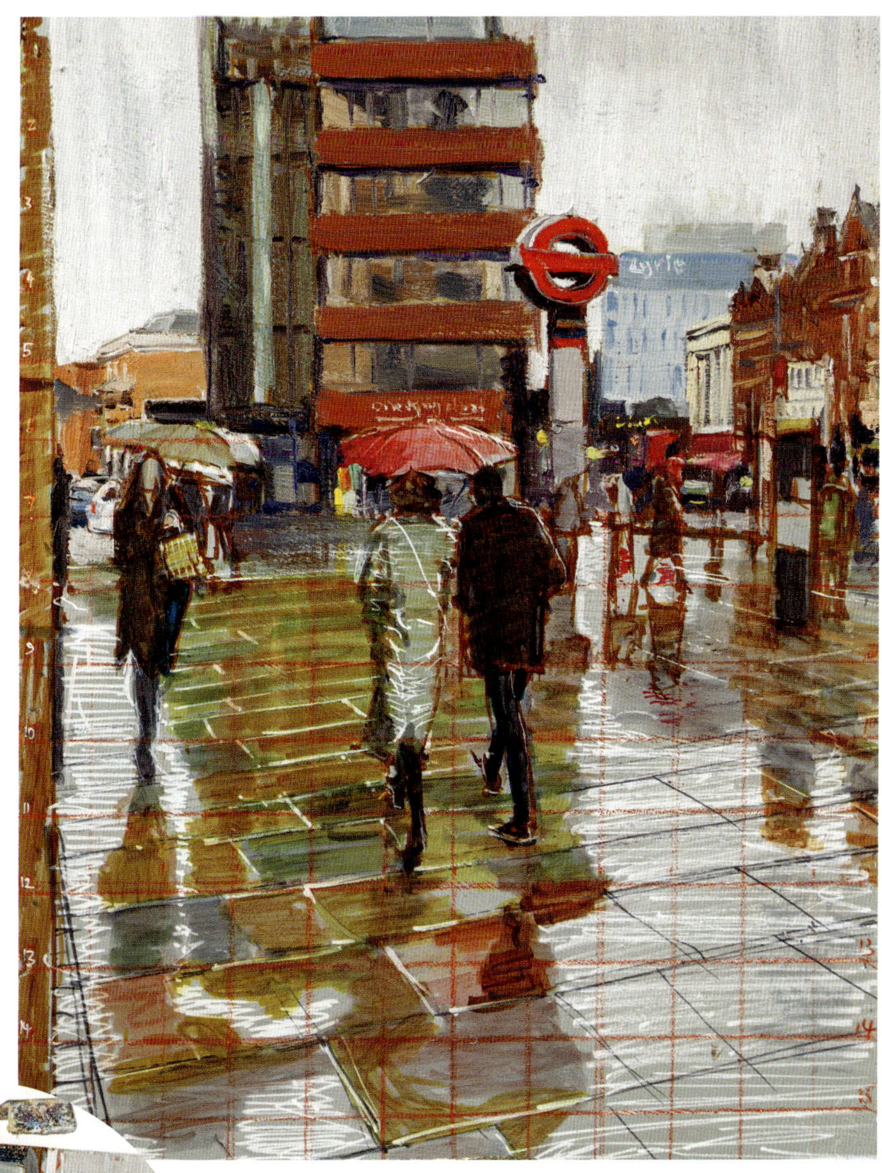

Use the colours of the underlying sketch as a prompt to help you mix the right hue.

- Work each area up to completion as you come to it. It's a good way to ensure you can keep the detail in mind as you paint over it – just swap to a size 2 round brush and get the area finished before moving on.

- Match the colour temperatures as closely as possible. When looking at a particular area, try to work out which two colours on your palette will bring out the closest result to the hue. If it's cool, for example, use a combination of a cool blue and a cool brown.

- The main building is made up of lots of muted browns. Yellow ochre, viridian green, burnt sienna, terra rosa and similar hues are useful for the mixes here. Don't over-detail this building. Summarize and combine detail to simplify, and keep the contrast between tones low.

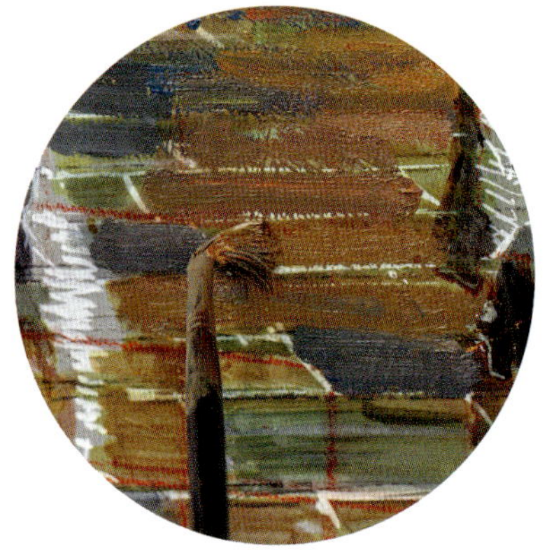

Most of the brushstrokes in the paving will be broadly horizontal, but vary things to ensure interest.

4

Pavement

The pavement is the key to the whole painting, bringing everything else together. It's a perfect opportunity to explore colour mixing.

This painting is approached in an inside-out way (see page 29), so it's been gradually built up by working smaller areas to completion before moving on. Treat the pavement in the same way. Don't rush, pay particular attention to the tones and colours, and build up the flagstones gradually.

- Swap to a square-ended size 2 flat synthetic brush for the bulk of the paving. This is ideal for the hard edges of the flagstones, as you can use the edge, flat or corners of the brush depending on the mark you need.

  - Work from the horizon line downwards, and try to use slight variations of your mixes for each brushstroke. This will ensure that everything works harmoniously, and that there's enough complexity and interest to make a feature of the paving.

    - Treat the highlighted and shadowy areas just the same: paint them as you come to them, rather than treating them as distinct areas.

    - For the strong highlighted reflections of the sky, add Maroger and plenty of titanium white to your mixes. This gives heavily textural results that add interest to the area.

- The wall on the left of the picture helps to frame the image and give it a sense of intimacy. Use a ruler to help keep the line clean, but vary the stroke to suggest brickwork and texture.

- Once the paving area is complete, make very, very light, flickering up-and-down strokes with the size 2 rigger. These will pick up the textural surface and just add a sense of scattered highlights, movement and rainfall without looking static or contrived.

  - The key to successful reflections is that lighter objects appear darker in reflection, while dark objects appear lighter. Bear this in mind when painting figures and their reflections – you can often slightly adjust the original mixes to get the right colour.

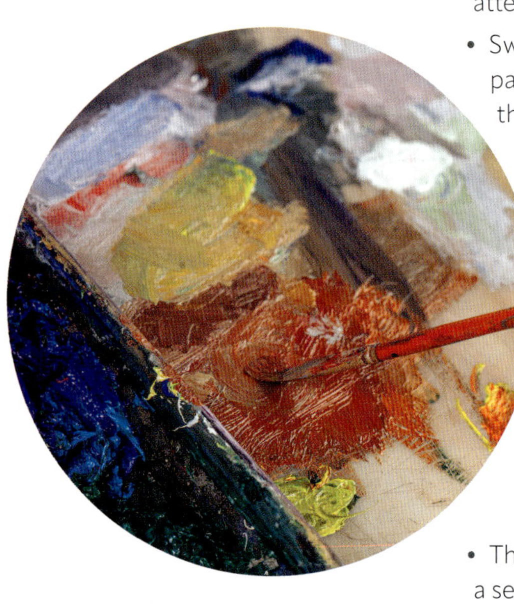

Light objects reflect dark; dark objects reflect light. Get the tone right and don't overwork the reflections: keep a loose feel.

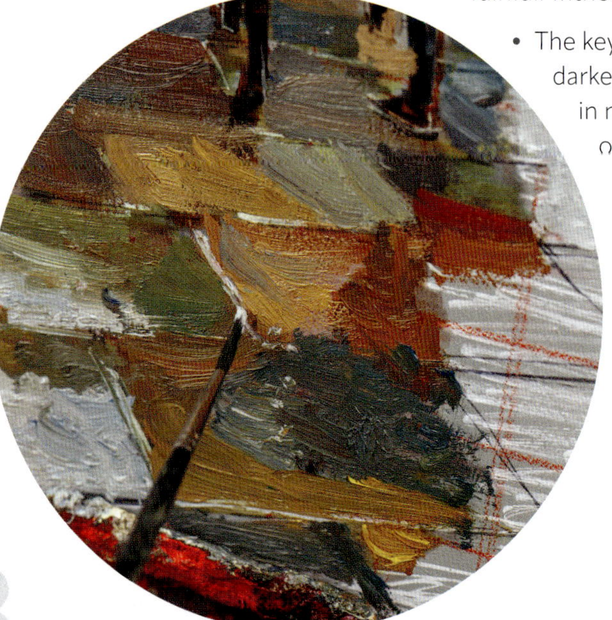

Use the size 2 round brush to draw in very faint lines to give shape to the paving. Use near-white in darker areas, and a very dark mix in the bright areas.

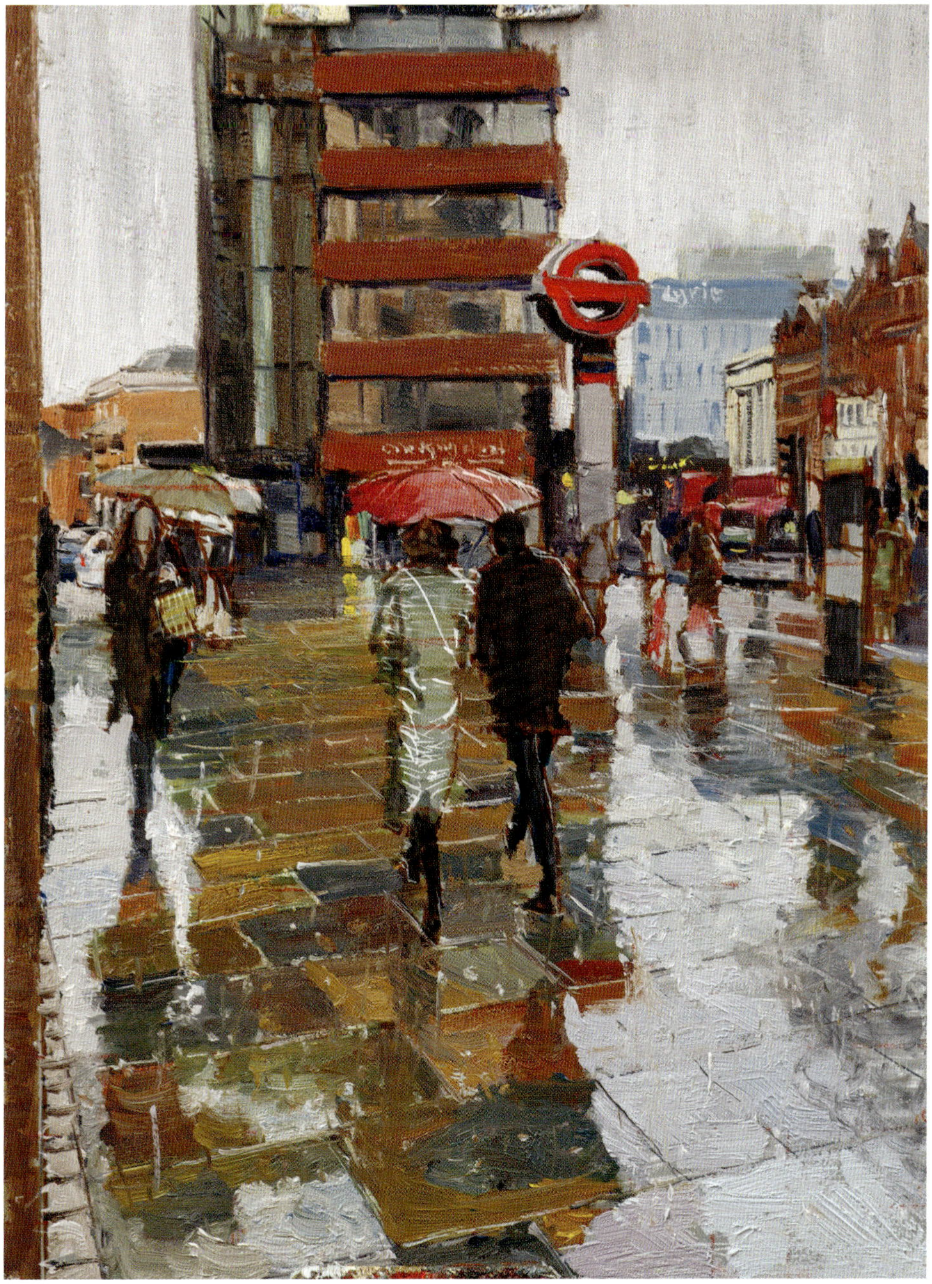

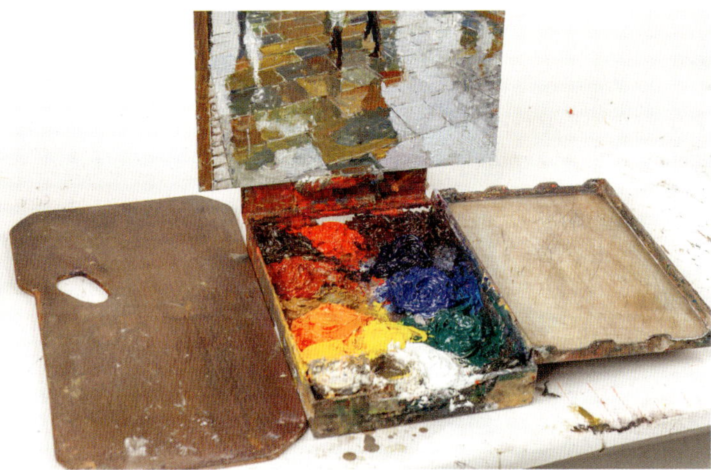

Before moving on from the paving, spend some time cleaning up your work area and your palette so you can approach painting the figures and other final elements with the right mindset.

Having a fresh, clean workspace (and a few minutes of mindless cleaning) will give you a break from the intense concentration you've been working up while painting the paving.

Figures and finishing

The figures are the icing on the cake.

- Use a dark mix of viridian green, yellow ochre and a little cobalt blue to paint in the trees on the upper right-hand side. Paint in the main branches with the size 2 round brush, but swap to a trimmed fan brush (see page 66) to add the suggestion of the finer branches – one or two quick, light, upward strokes should do.

- If you spot any gaps, fill them in at this stage.

- Start with the small, distant figures on the right-hand side, working carefully and slowly as you refine the shapes established earlier.

- Before you start on the central figures, spend some time looking at the negative space surrounding them, and develop or refine any details such as lights, signage and so forth. The better developed these areas, the clearer the shapes of the figures will be.

- Use a size 2 filbert for the central figures. Identify the major tones in the figures, and work up from darks to lights, painting each tone in turn.

- When working on the final figures, work from the back to the front. This gives a more natural result.

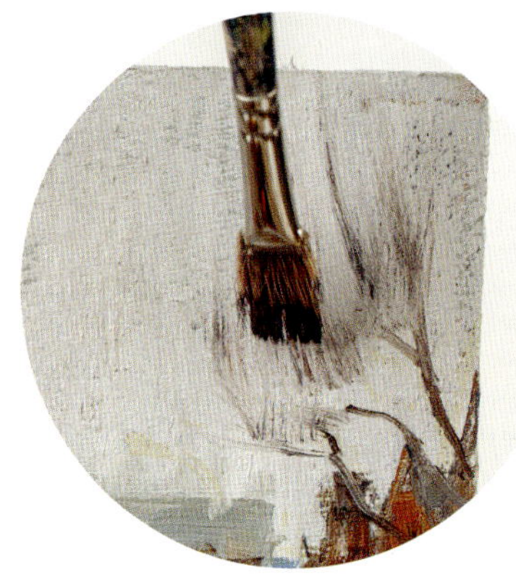

The trimmed fan brush is great for broken marks like this – and much better for an impressionistic finish.

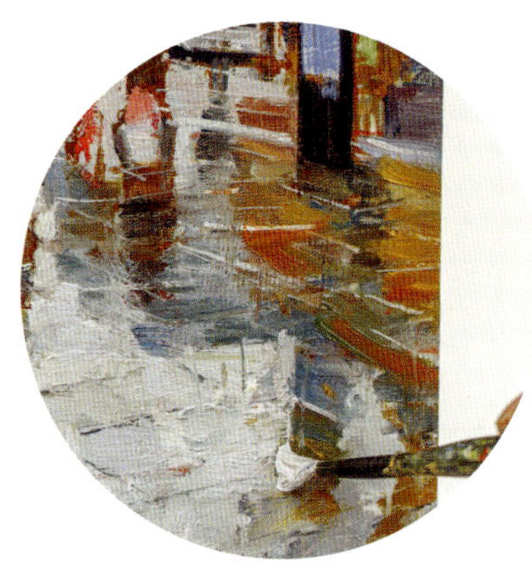

Here I'm straightening a little reflection of the street furniture – reflections should always be directly below the object.

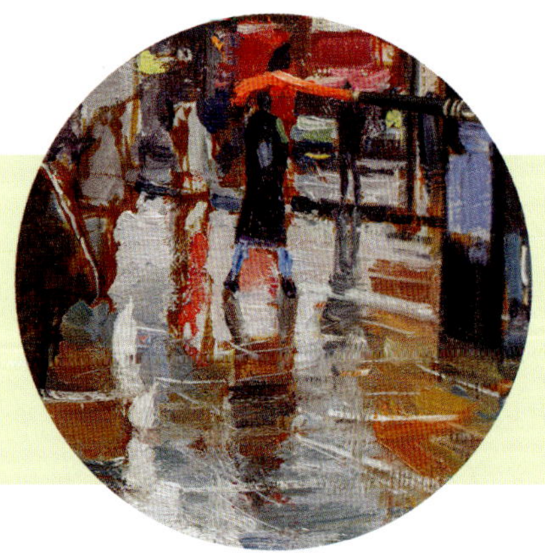

Refer to the source photograph closely for the colours, and remember that reflections of dark objects should be slightly lighter in tone; and reflections of light objects should be slightly darker.

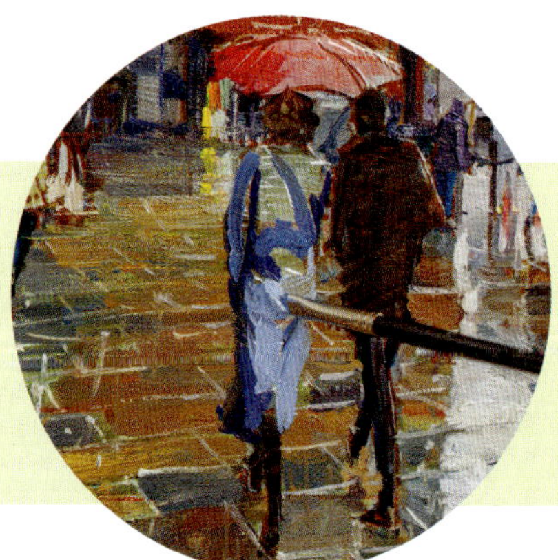

I used a combination of cobalt blue, viridian green and a little alizarin crimson, thickened with Maroger, for the darks on the left-hand main figure. Look for simple shapes within the coat, and work up through the major tones.

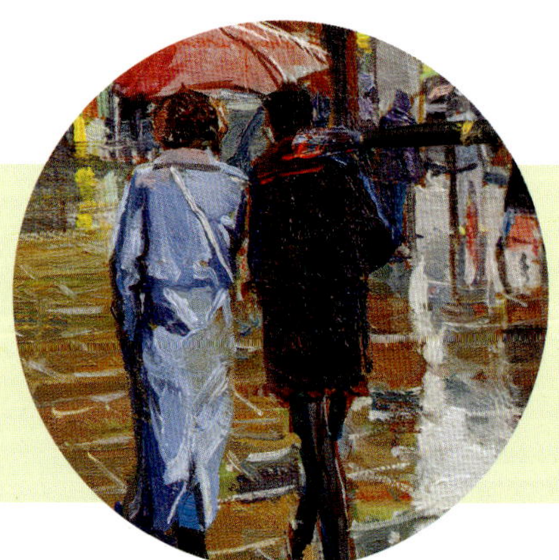

Although the man's coat is dark, be careful not to make it one tone. Add subtle variations of colour, and vary your brushstrokes.

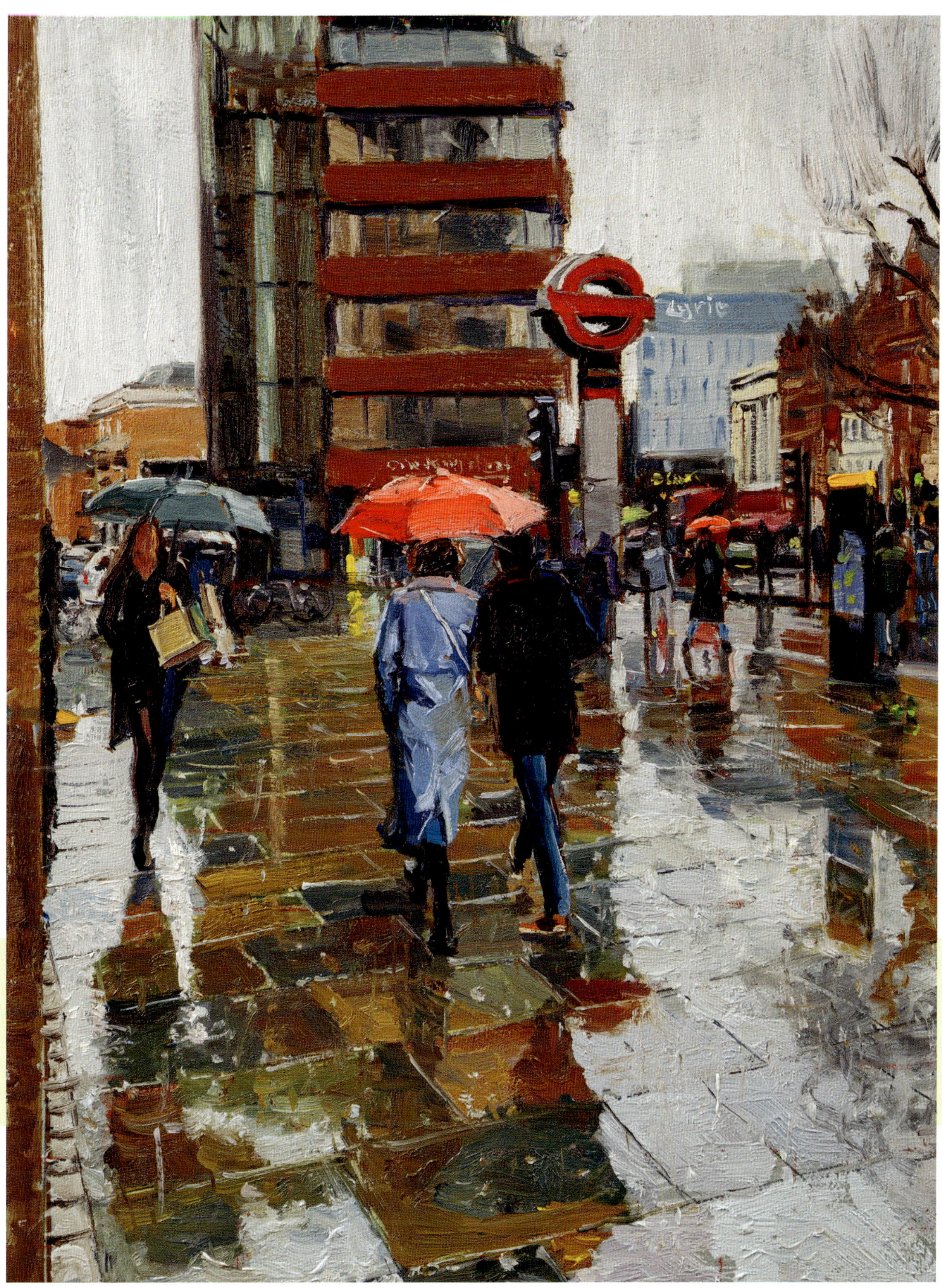

The finished painting

When to stop

You can brush a painting to death, so you must know when to stop. This is a big problem with amateur painters. There's a tendency to want to make sure everything is 'tidy', with every stroke perfect and every passage refined – but this misses the beauty of direct painting: the spontaneity that it brings, the variety of the brushstrokes, the freshness of the colours and the immediacy of the paint application.

After watching me demonstrate, students often ask me how I know when to just lay a stroke and leave it there – that is, how I resist going back to refine it. The answer is simple. I take the time to really observe what I'm seeing, analyse it and only then respond with the fewest and simplest possible strokes to depict it. Rather than taking ten strokes to paint something, I reduce it to five. Vibrant brushstrokes are how you give life to a painting, but if you continue to work into strokes and constantly refine them, they – and the painting – will become flat and dull.

Success will come from understanding that in direct painting, less is more. This method of painting aims at a feeling or impression: totally different from indirect painting, where layers of glazes are constantly refined to bring out depth and detail.

The point to stop is as soon as possible after you have laid in all the big shapes, and put in the major details. If you find yourself starting to circle around and fidgeting without knowing where to lay the next stroke, it's time to stop. When you've said all you need to say about a particular scene, you don't need to say any more.

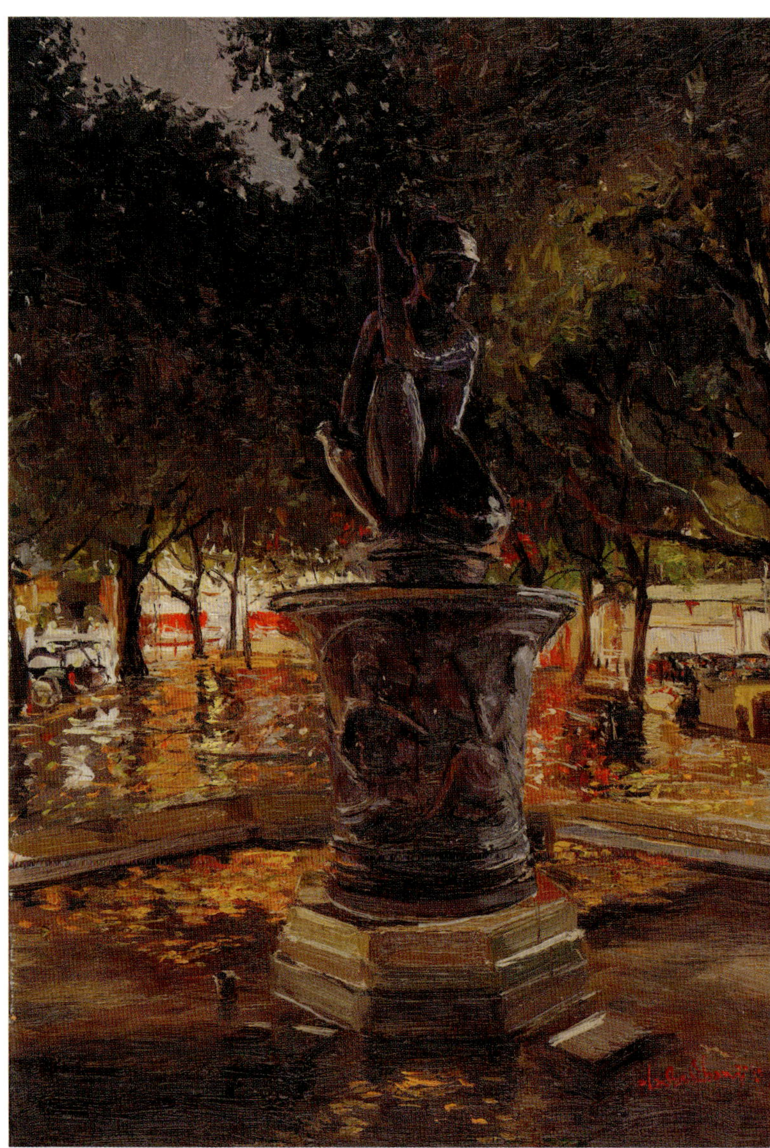

The Nocturne, Sloane Square
30 × 40cm (12 × 16in)

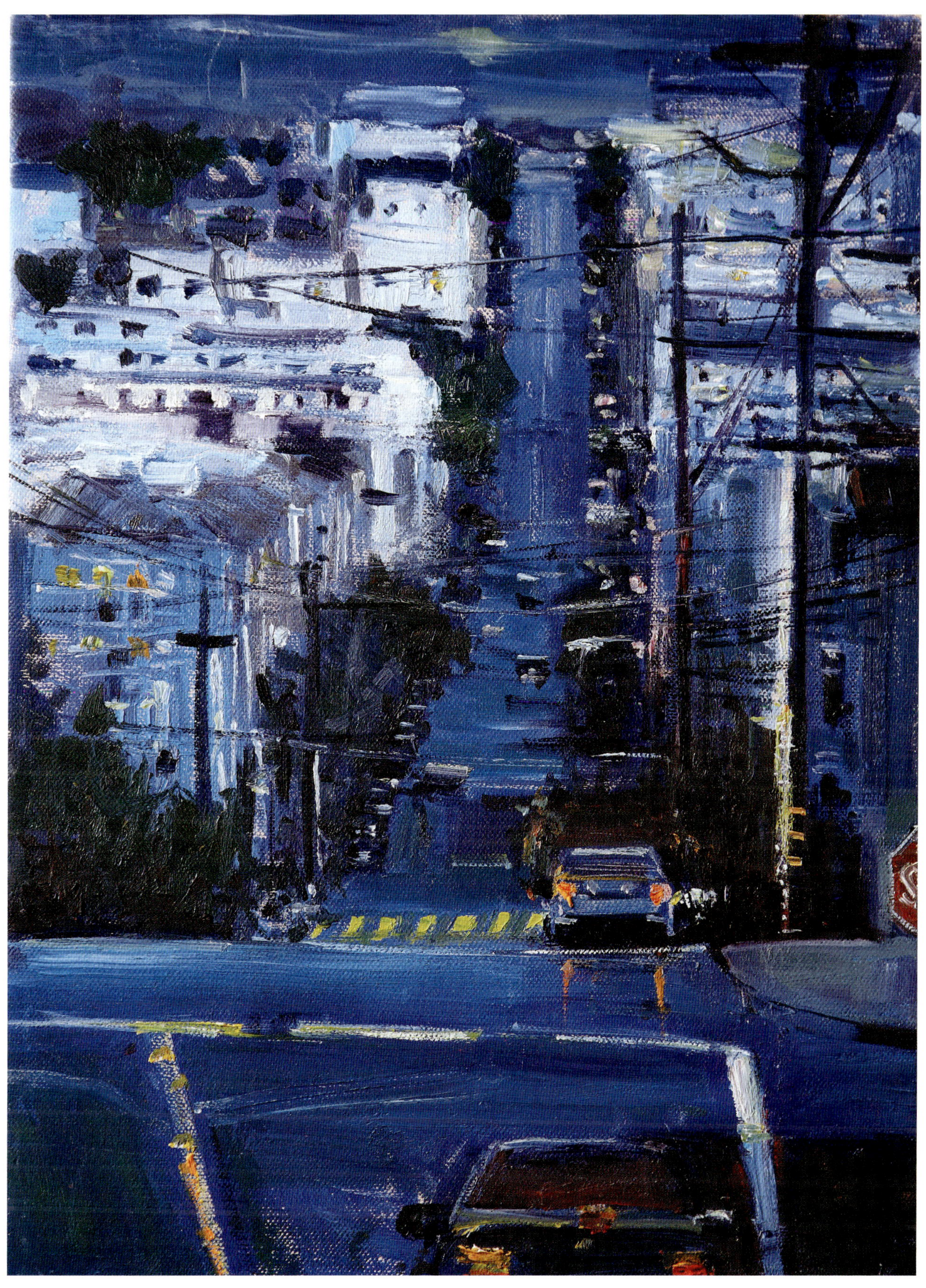

San Francisco Blues   30 × 40cm (12 × 16in)

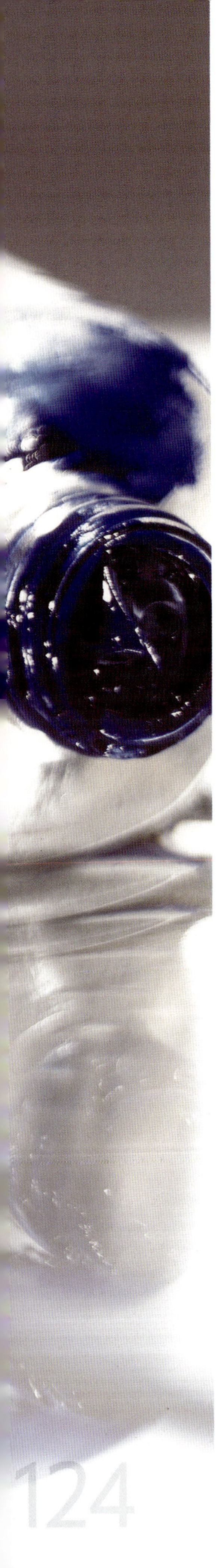

Introducing other media

I have always been a fan of working in other media besides oil.
More specifically, I love mixed media pieces which combine watercolour,
gouache and coloured pencils, as in the example below. I think it's the
sketcher in me that makes me want to work in media where I can get an
immediate effect without having to worry about the drying time. These
different media can be handy, especially for work on the go.

Watercolour

I never use watercolour all on its own, but
there's no better medium than watercolour
for allowing the underlying sketch to show
through – a particular favourite effect
of mine.

The is normally done as for oils, usually
in coloured pencil alone. I then lay
watercolour over the top to add colour.

Towards the end when I have almost
finished, I like to add accents here and
there using more coloured pencil and
perhaps a touch of gouache for any
opaque areas that need strong light.

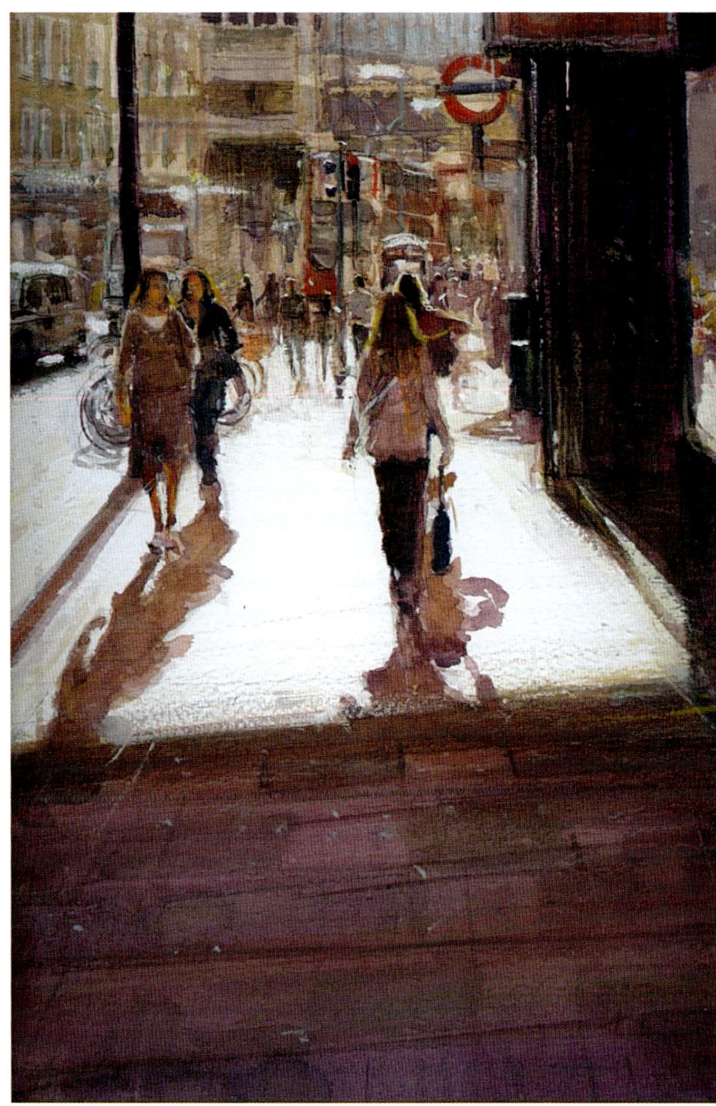

Summerlight, London Bridge
20 × 28cm (8 × 11in)

Acrylics

I think working with a different medium helps to develop the ability to understand how to tackle subject matter from that particular medium's point of view.

Acrylics are naturally faster drying than oils, but they offer perhaps the easiest jump in terms of technique. Watercolours and pastels are very different disciplines, but you can easily apply all the lessons of oils to acrylics. The main differences between acrylics and oils is that oils give a richer finish, and acrylics have a shorter working time.

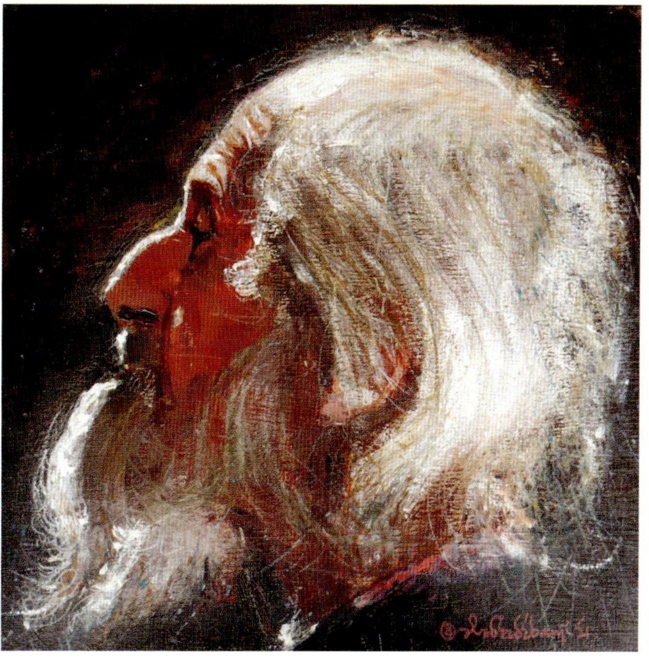

After The Storm VIII
20 × 20cm (8 × 8in)

Mixed media

In the painting below, I started off with a sketch in coloured pencil, built up layers with very opaque gouache and finally gave it some punch with coloured pencils and ink. As long as I can get the effect I'm looking for, it doesn't matter to me what medium I work it into the picture.

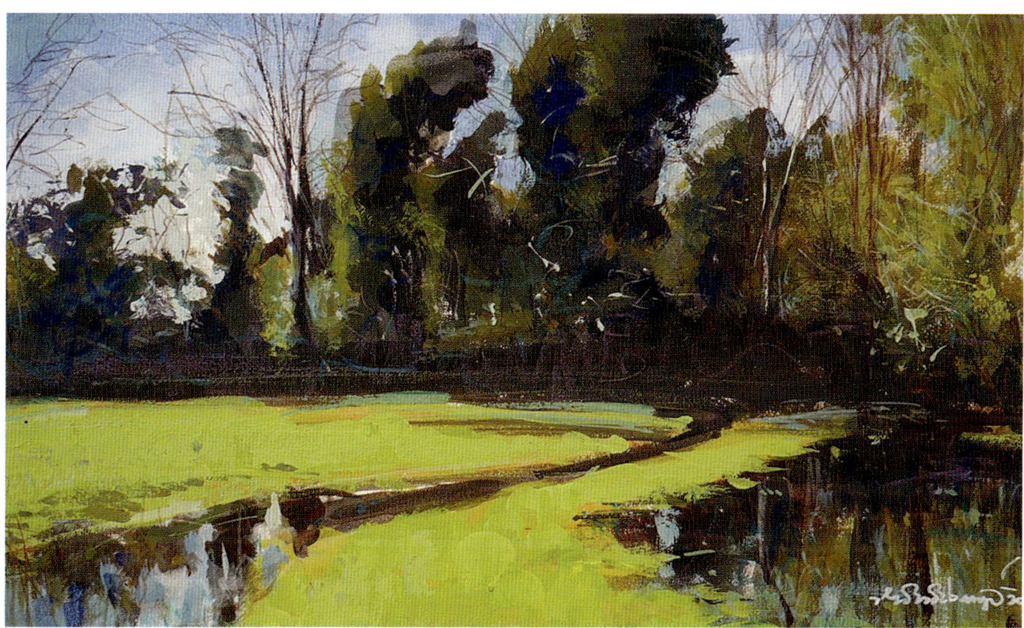

Black & Green Landscape I   23 × 14cm (9 × 5½in)

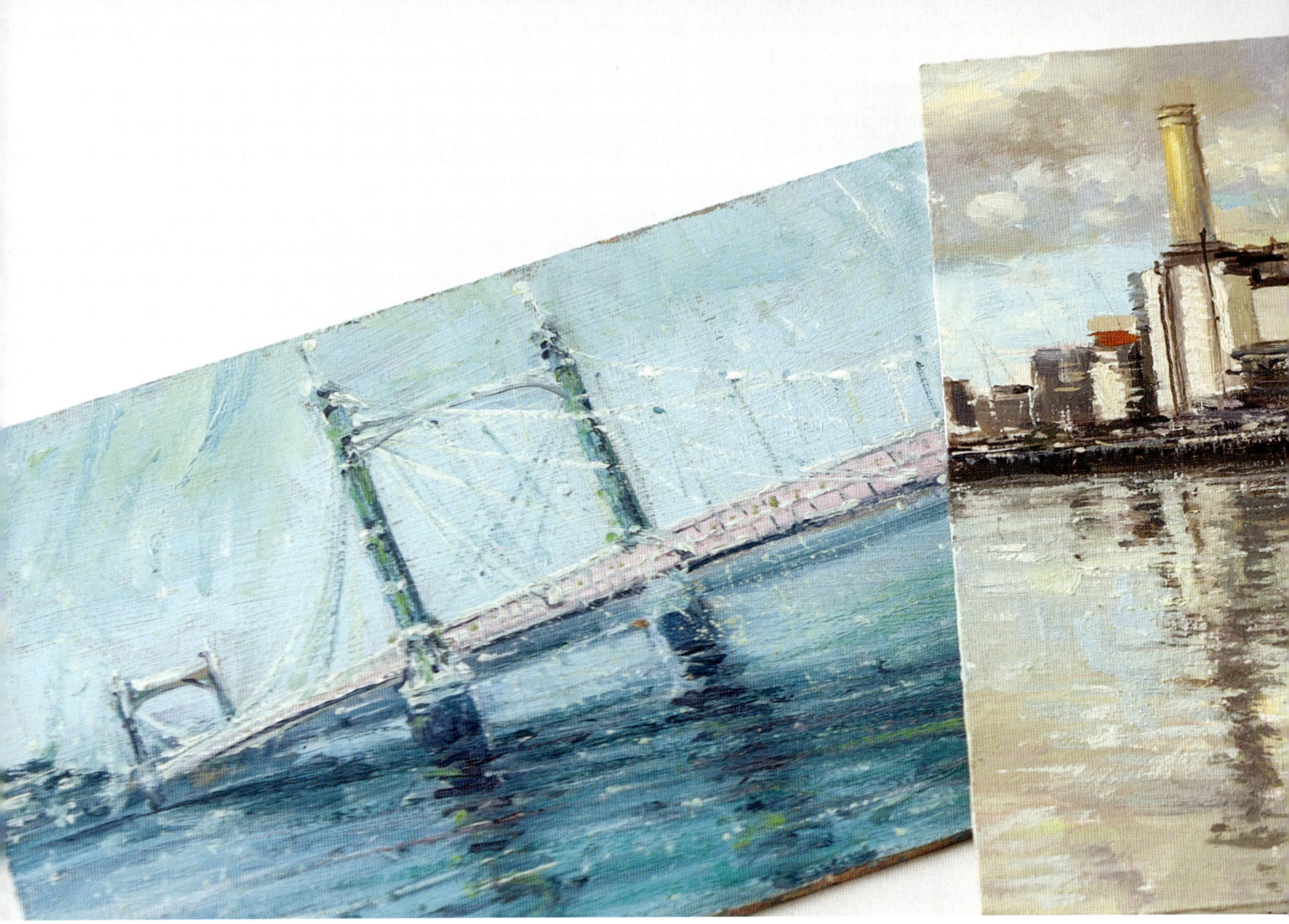

SEASCAPES

I simply love seascapes, mainly because of the freedom that painting water gives me. When taking it on, you can attack the canvas or board with sweeping strokes which can be very organic in nature. The key factor that really helps me to enjoy them – and which is really important to success – is the ability to mix colours. This is because the tones are so closely knit when it comes to painting moving water. Seascapes demand really keen observation in capturing the colours as closely as possible.

Reflections on and around the sea also help to bring the reflected building or boat to life. Here, it always helps to remember that dark objects appear lighter and lighter objects darker when reflected.

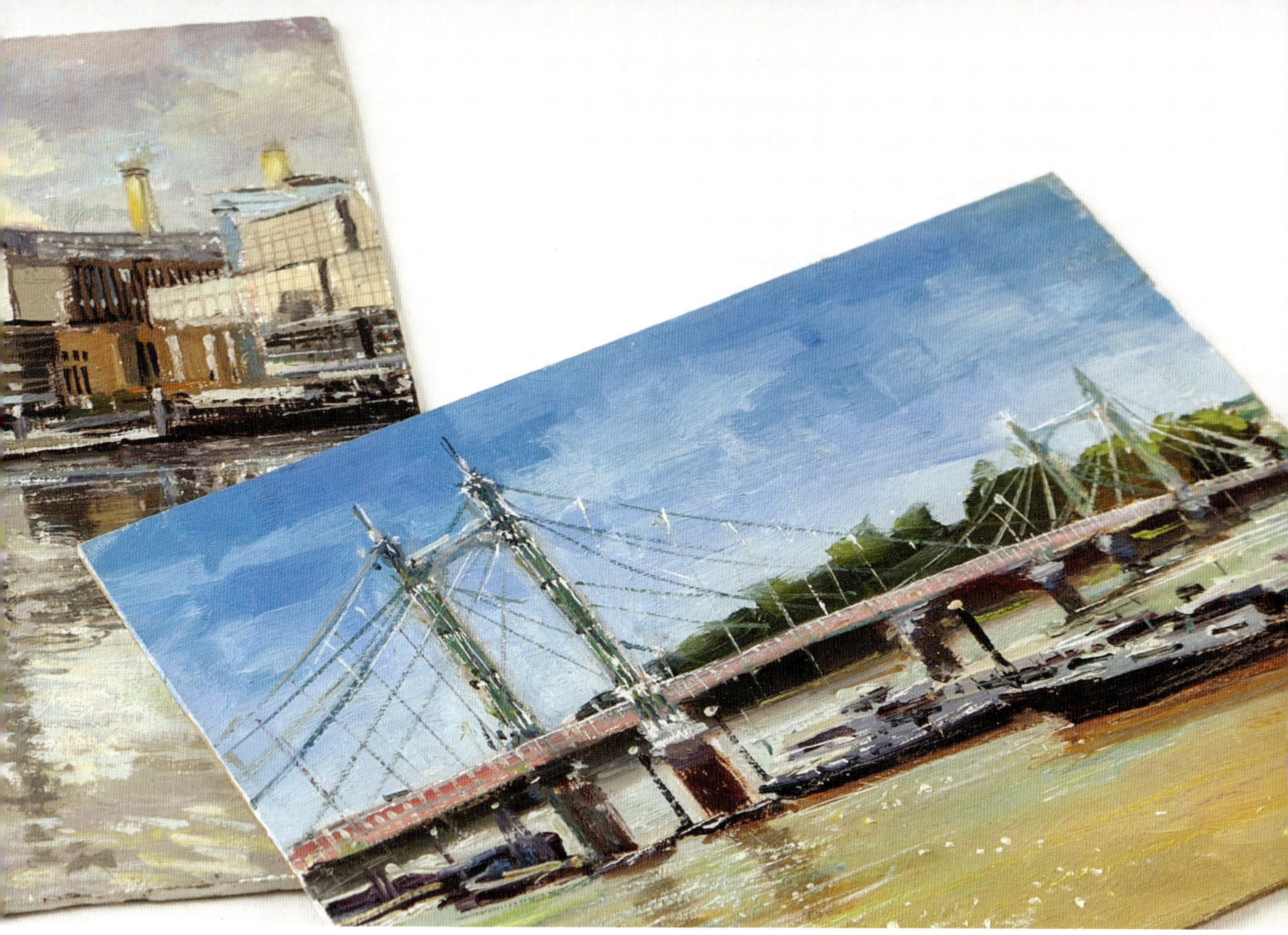

Bridges on rivers are a particular favourite of mine because they give me the opportunity to add reflections in the water. Well observed and well painted reflections add power and punch to the painting and make the viewer believe what they are seeing. The accuracy with which you paint the reflections in a seascape can be the reason why the painting is effective or not.

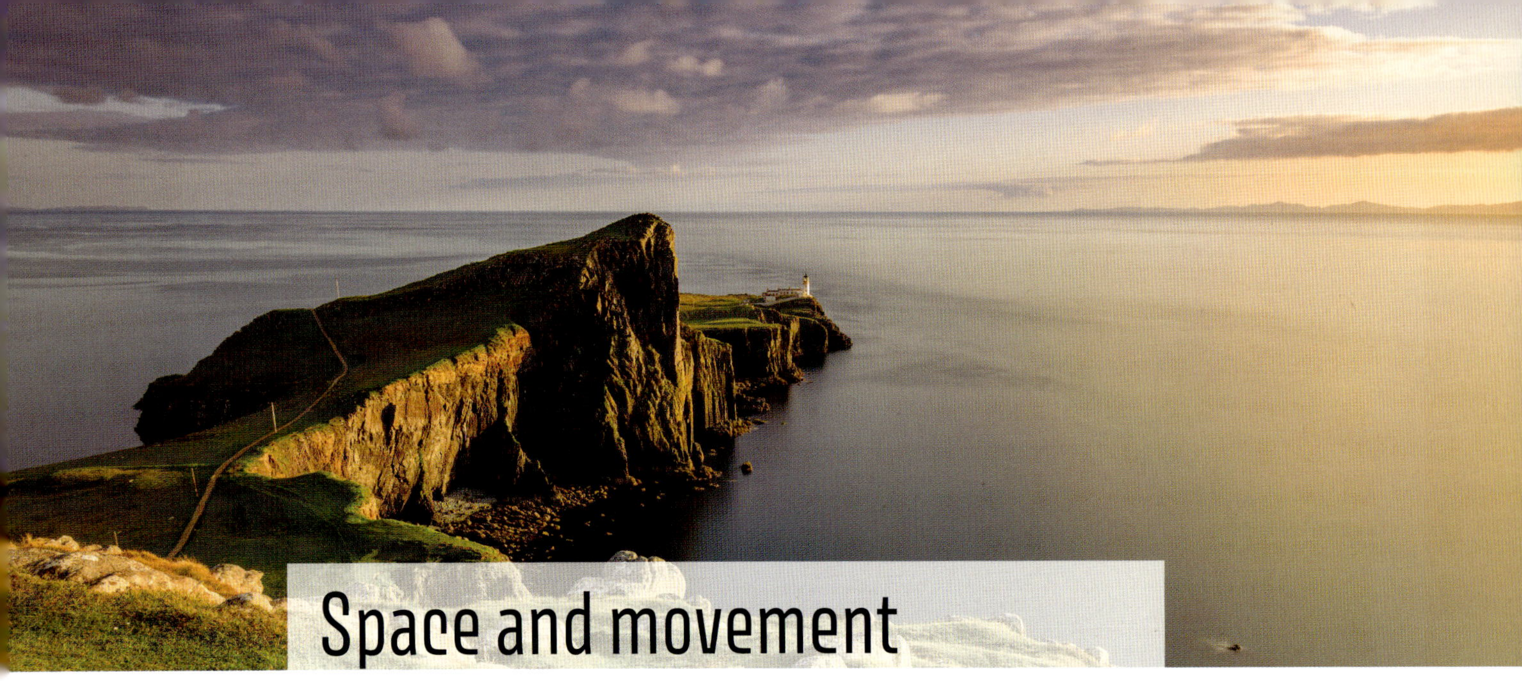

Space and movement

You can create action, restful moments, splashes or calm moods just by the way you apply the paint to the canvas. All the effects in my paintings that give them dynamism and movement are created through the ebb and flow in pace and pressure at which I make the brush hit the surface.

Active effects are achieved with faster, more staccato brush applications while restful, calm effects are achieved with slower, smoother passages where the brushstrokes just glide along the surface.

I am constantly reacting to what I see and the way I see it. Besides getting the colours right, the way in which you paint will convey what you are trying to paint. This applies to all art styles – it's why abstract painting can still show feelings of certain kinds, without a concrete object in sight – and all subjects. It's particularly clear in seascapes, as we'll see in this chapter.

Take a look at the paintings opposite, and see what impression each one evokes. The water and sky in *Low Tide, Summerlight, Clevedon* are complex and draw you in – there's a sense of freshness and movement, which is enhanced by the briskly walking figures. In contrast, for *St Nicholas Chapel, Ilfracombe*, I used simpler, slower application in the water and sky to give a sense of space, stillness and serenity.

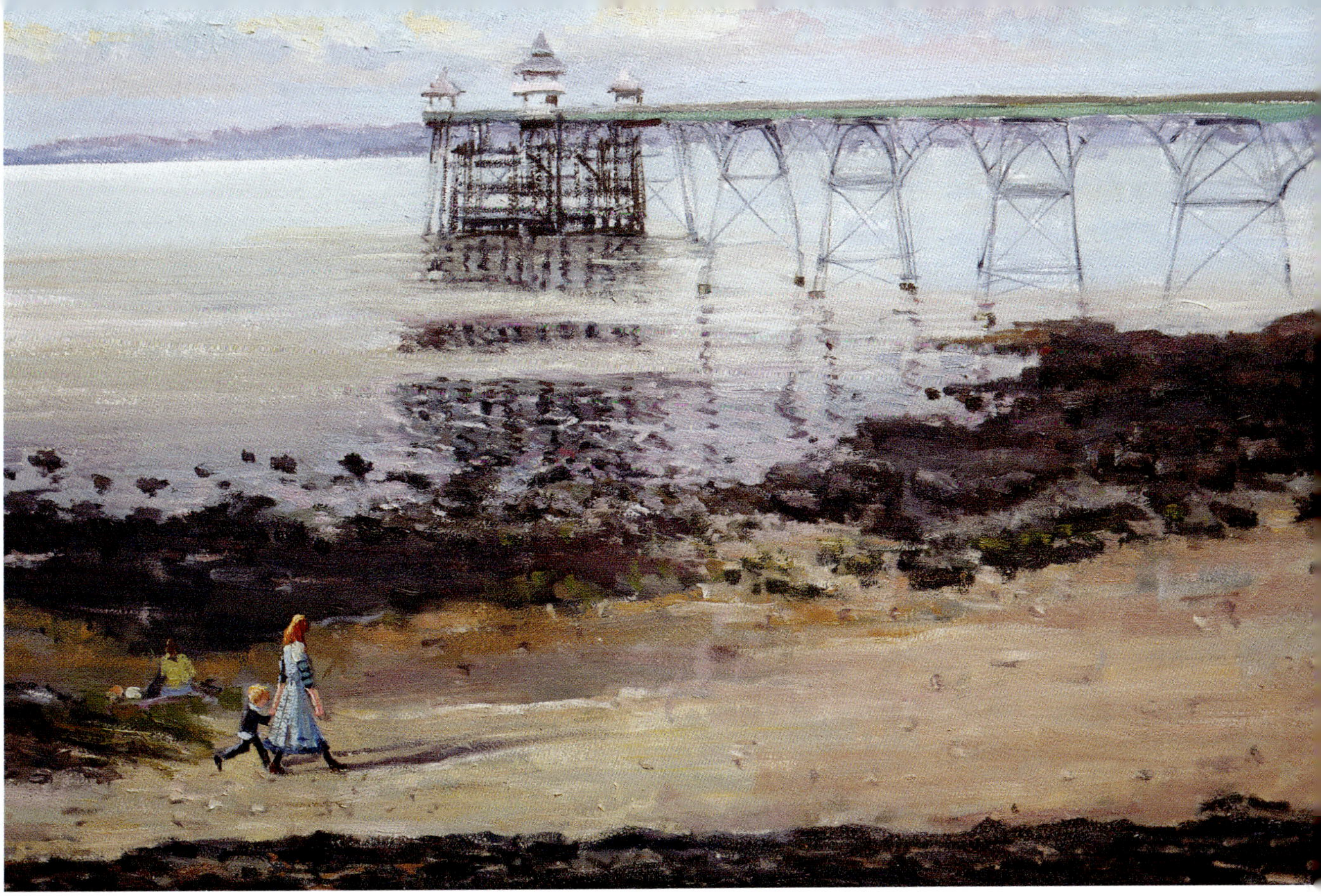

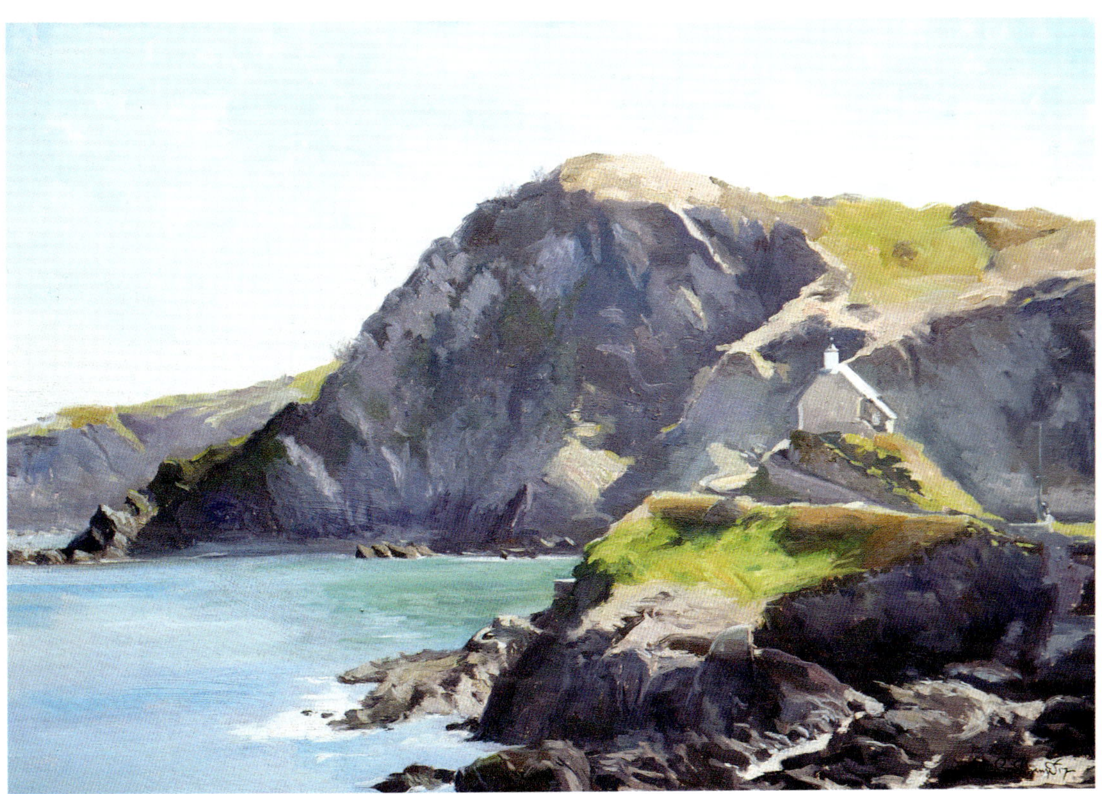

Low Tide, Summerlight, Clevedon   76 × 50cm (30 × 20in)

St Nicholas Chapel, Ilfracombe   100 × 70cm (39½ × 27½in)

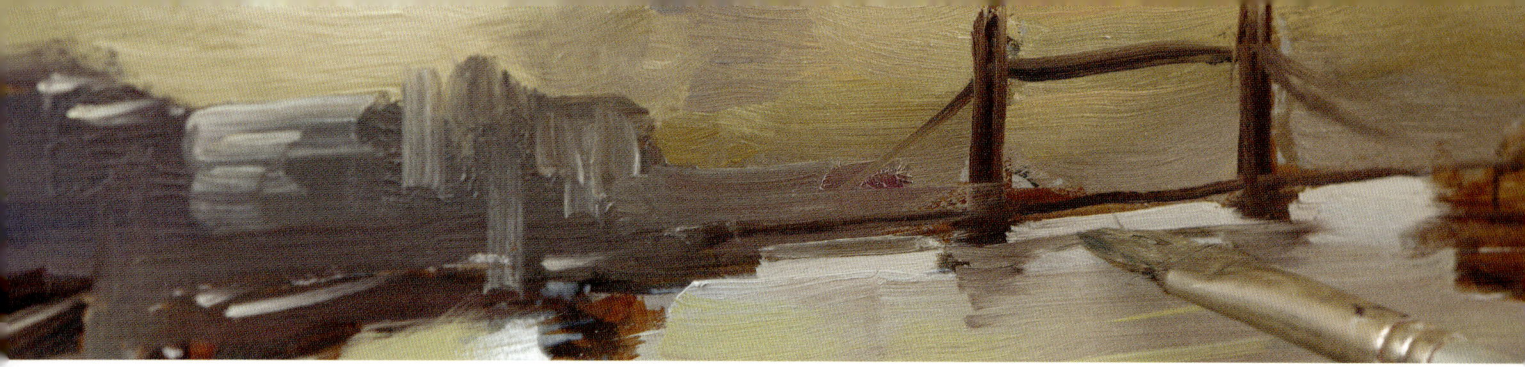

Paint: River Harbour

Unlike most of the other projects in this book, I'm not going to use a grid for this painting. This is because seascapes lend themselves to a looser feel, and doubly so with this morning scene, where the early summer light is throwing almost everything into silhouette.

Mood and the effect of light are the keys to this painting. I don't want any bright light shining through, so I've prepared the board with a cool underpainting made from a mix of burnt sienna, ultramarine blue and titanium white, with a spot of ochre.

Because there's not much detail, it's less important to create a grid. It's a very tonal picture that divides the painting into the right type of shapes, which enables me to organize things easily. For the purposes of the sketch, we'll just flow in an organic way – the impression of a morning river is far more important than exacting accuracy.

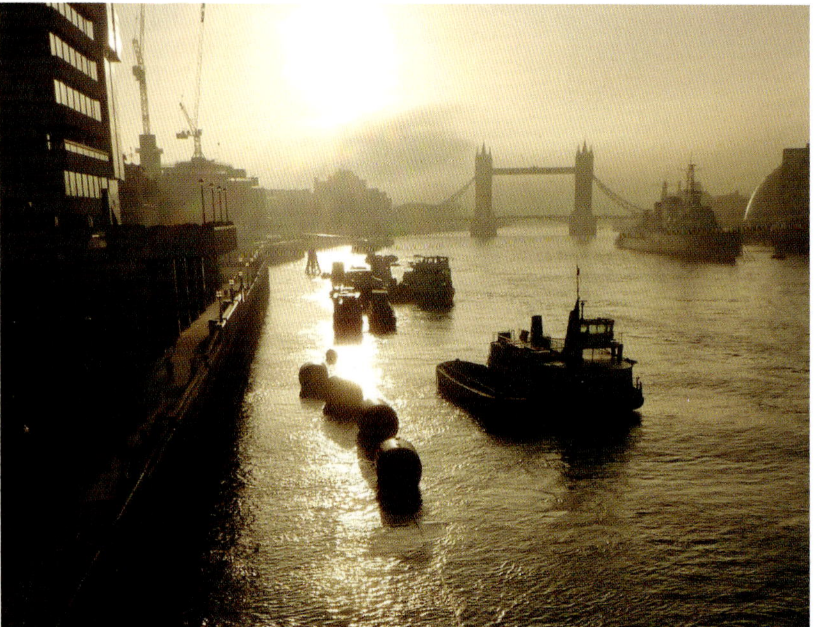

Although I'm not using a grid, note that the board is already in the same proportion (4:3) to the source photograph.

The horizon is off centre; with more river shown. Compositions with an even split of sea and sky look too balanced and are rarely successful

On the river's surface, it's easy to get lost without a grid or reference. Use the shapes you have established to help you – but equally, if a boat is slightly out of position, it won't be something to worry about.

Tonal sketch

Sketch in a loose, organic way to build up the forms and shapes. Work from left to right and background to foreground, blocking in the rough shapes. The source photograph will give you the basics, but there's no replacement for your own memory and experience of the light. Rely on your intuition to invest the sketch with your intepretation and enjoy it.

- Use the burnt sienna brush marker, taped to a brush handle for this midtone sketch, and darken the tonal values using the Zig pen.

- Make sure that you're as accurate as possible in representing the tones and shapes. These are the fundamental elements of the painting. Get these right, and you'll have the liberty and ease to add the paint at the later stages.

- You don't need to know what things are – just draw what you see in the simplest terms.

- Very little detail is needed to make the sketch work well. You don't want to overwork it, so a few horizontal lines on the river's surface will do.

- Add the highlights last, using the white Posca pen. Start with the sun, then see how it transforms the scene and makes it feel like it's a complete painting.

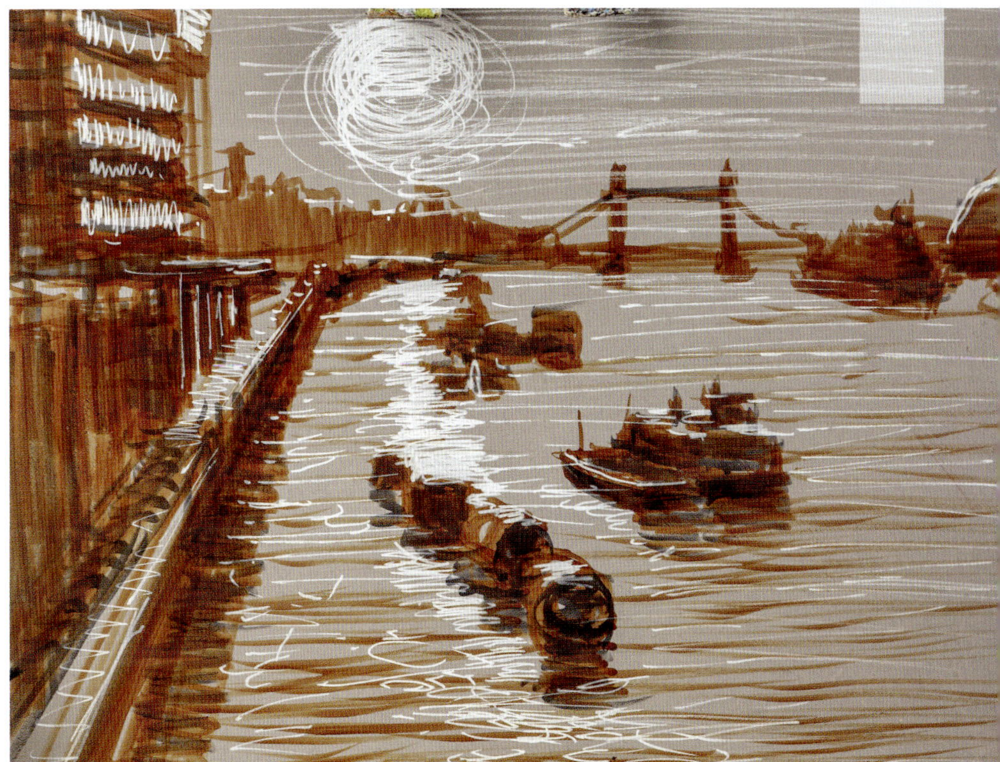

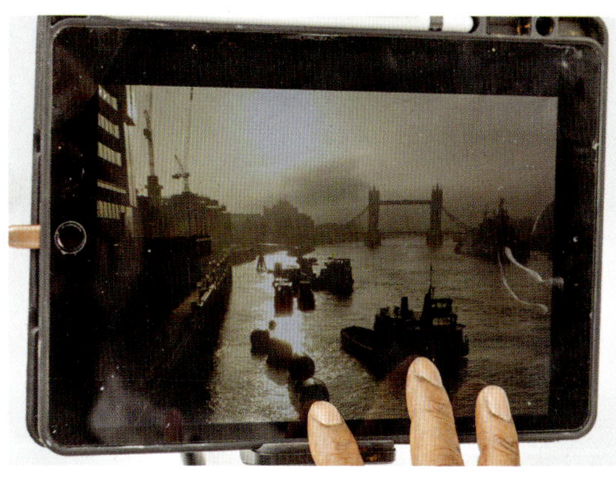

Sky and skyline

Even though this is a near-monochrome image, we're still going to use the full palette of colour. This is because it'll lend the tones a real richness, and improve upon the starkness of the source photograph. You want a symphony of greys.

- Start with a mix of lemon yellow and plenty of titanium white for the sun, using lots of Maroger. Apply the paint with the size 6 long filbert. Add a little more yellow for marks away from each other. Once the sun is established, leave it alone – work the sky around it.

- Create a misty grey using a combination of ochre and a little magenta and cobalt blue. Use the size 6 long filbert to build upwards from the horizon with soft overlapping strokes. There's no blending on the surface – that's important, or you'll lose the vibrancy of the colour. Closer to the sun, add a litle cadmium orange and the yellow and white sun mix from earlier.

- As you work upwards, add hints of magenta, viridian and ochre to the grey mix, as well as varying the proportions of the white and yellow. All of these colours help to add interest and develop the overall sombre feel.

Don't be shy in using technology – a great advantage of the tablet is that you can zoom in on a particular area.

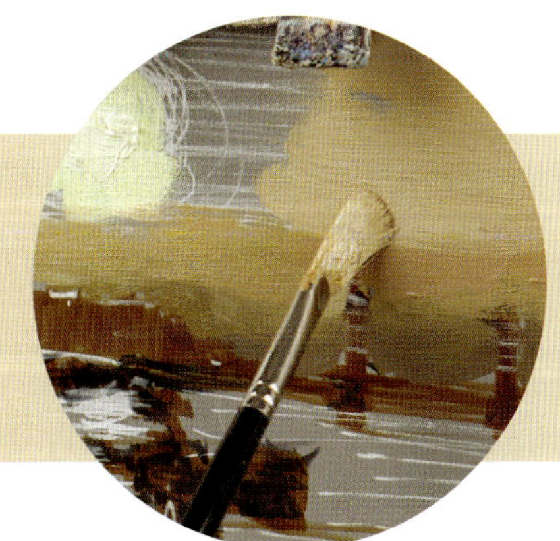

As you can see, the additions of other colours are all subtle. You want the sky to feel cohesive and unbroken. Connect each stroke to others, to avoid a hard feel.

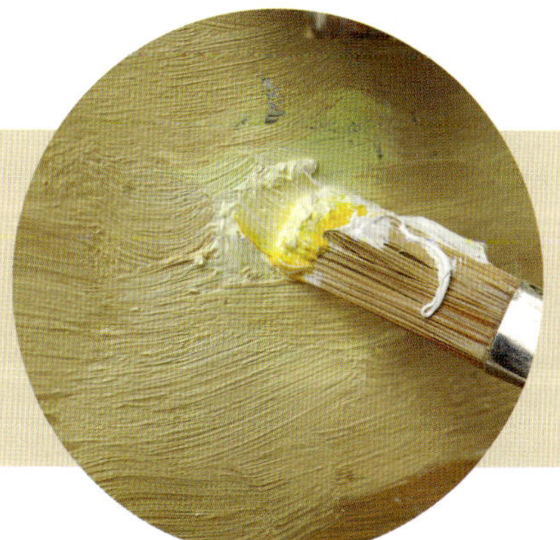

Increase the intensity of the tone nearer to the sun by adding more titanium white – and work into it, rather than out from it: this ensures the sun itself stays clean, but is soft.

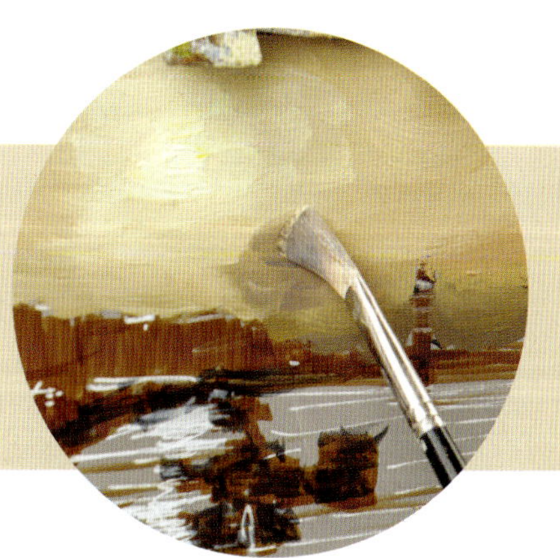

The cloud is treated as part of the sky, using slightly darker tones of the same mix.

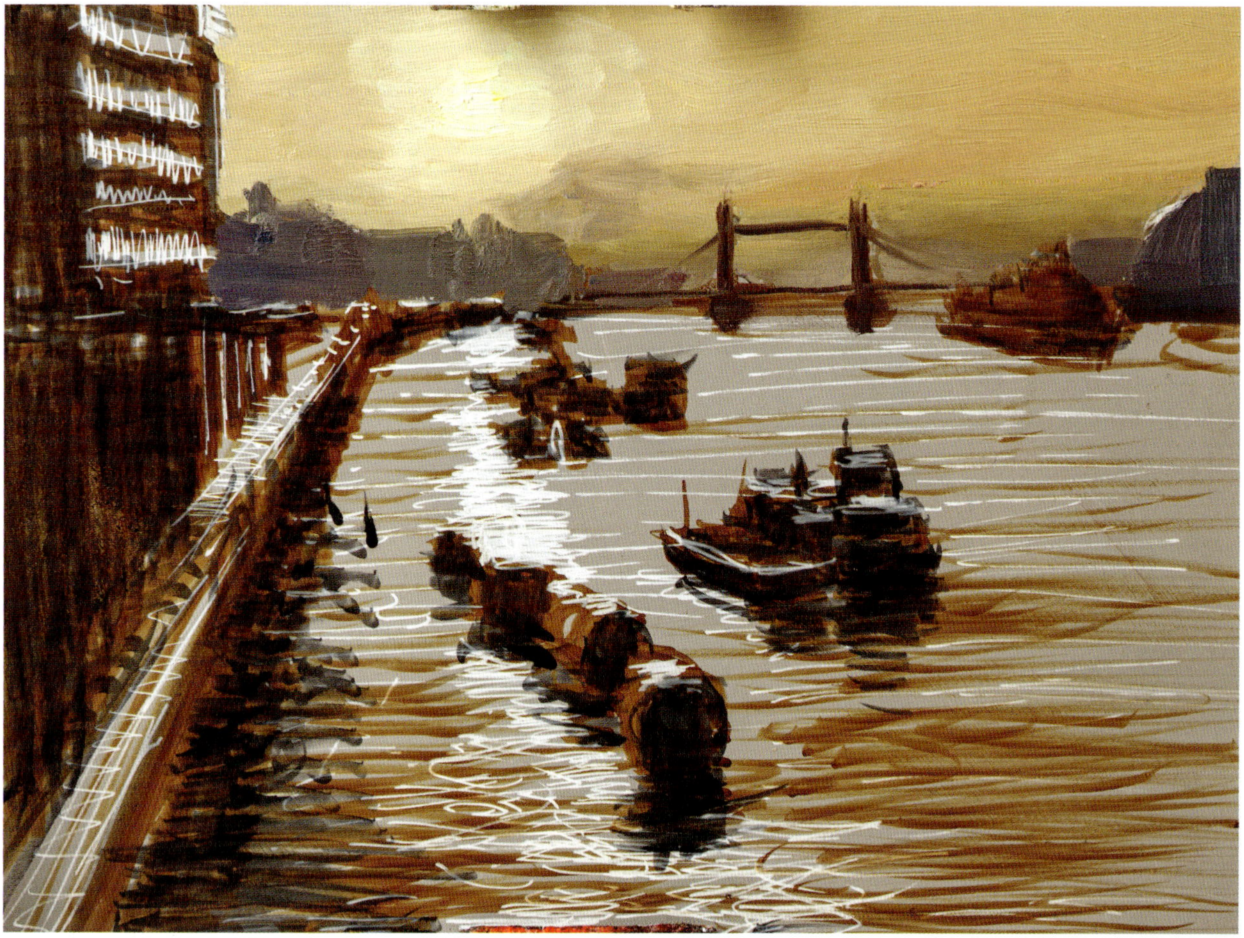

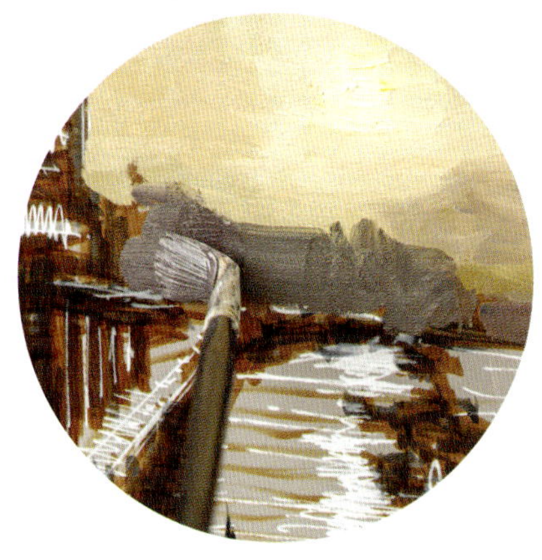

For the skyline grey mixes, swap between cobalt blue and ultramarine, both for variety and to alter the tone subtly.

- Mix cobalt blue or ultramarine blue with transparent red oxide and a little yellow ochre for the background buildings. Use the same brush and aim to create harder-edged marks. Mix your colours for the buildings on the palette alongside the sky mixes – this will also help to ensure overall harmony.

- As you advance, add transparent red oxide for the buildings. It's important not to go too dark in tone too soon.

- Swap to a cut-down size 6 long filbert (see page 13) and use single strokes wherever possible. This is to help ensure that your marks are clean, clear and unmuddied. The marks shouldn't look stark, because the tones you're using are still only subtly different from the sky.

Foreground

Now it's time to add some contrast in the foreground. I want the finished painting to give the impression that it's been done swiftly – perhaps on site – but that doesn't mean we should rush.

- Swap back to the untrimmed size 6 filbert, and mix a near-black dark from ultramarine blue, alizarin crimson and viridian green and transparent red oxide. Go straight in with knife-edged strokes to block in the darkest darks. Take your time with these angular strokes, applying them lightly.

- Add more viridian, alizarin crimson and yellow ochre to the mixes to create midtones. I call these 'sneaky greys' because they don't make much of an obvious impression – in contrast to the more obvious strong tones, they're sometimes hard to see, but important.

- For the windows catching the light, use a combination of the mixes on your palette, and block in each entire row with a single stroke.

- Show the pathway of light running down the street with a series of overlapping long strokes away from the light source (the sun). Gradually introduce darker and darker tones until the light peters out entirely.

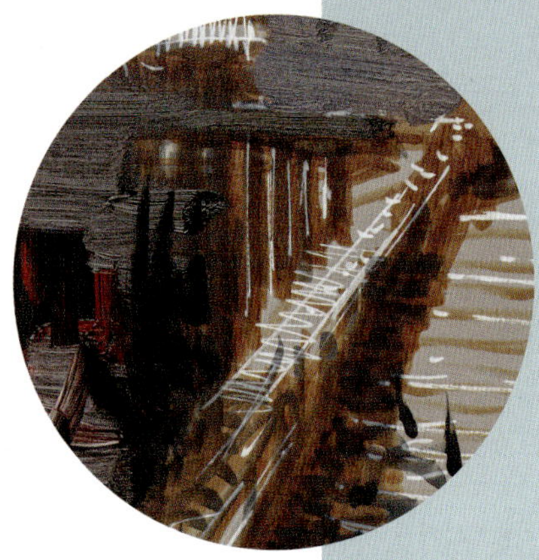

Avoid the darks becoming dead: vary the proportions of the colours in the mix and apply the paint with short, blocky marks made in different directions.

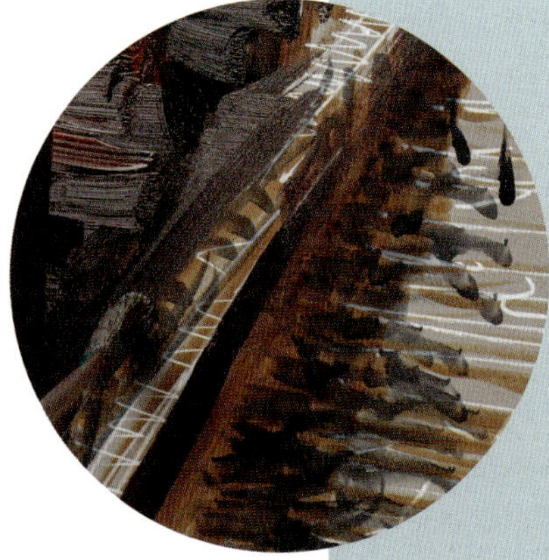

Use the direction of your brushstrokes to help the viewer make sense of the objects. In the architecture, follow the shapes of the structure: clean diagonals, horizontals and verticals.

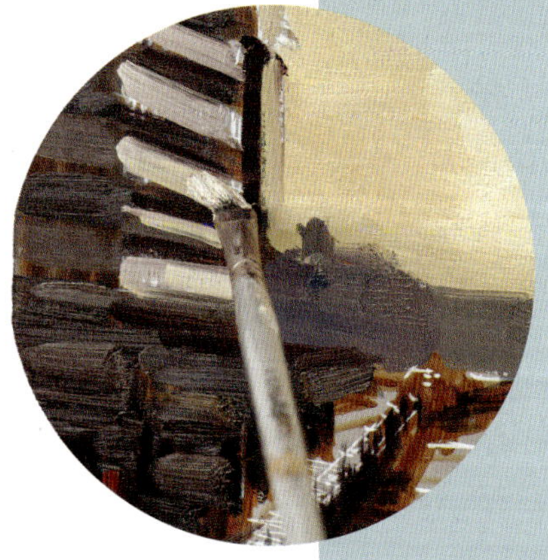

Add some details to the window blocks with tiny little vertical touches. Give the viewer enough to understand – but don't over-explain or you'll make the area too eye-catching and fixed.

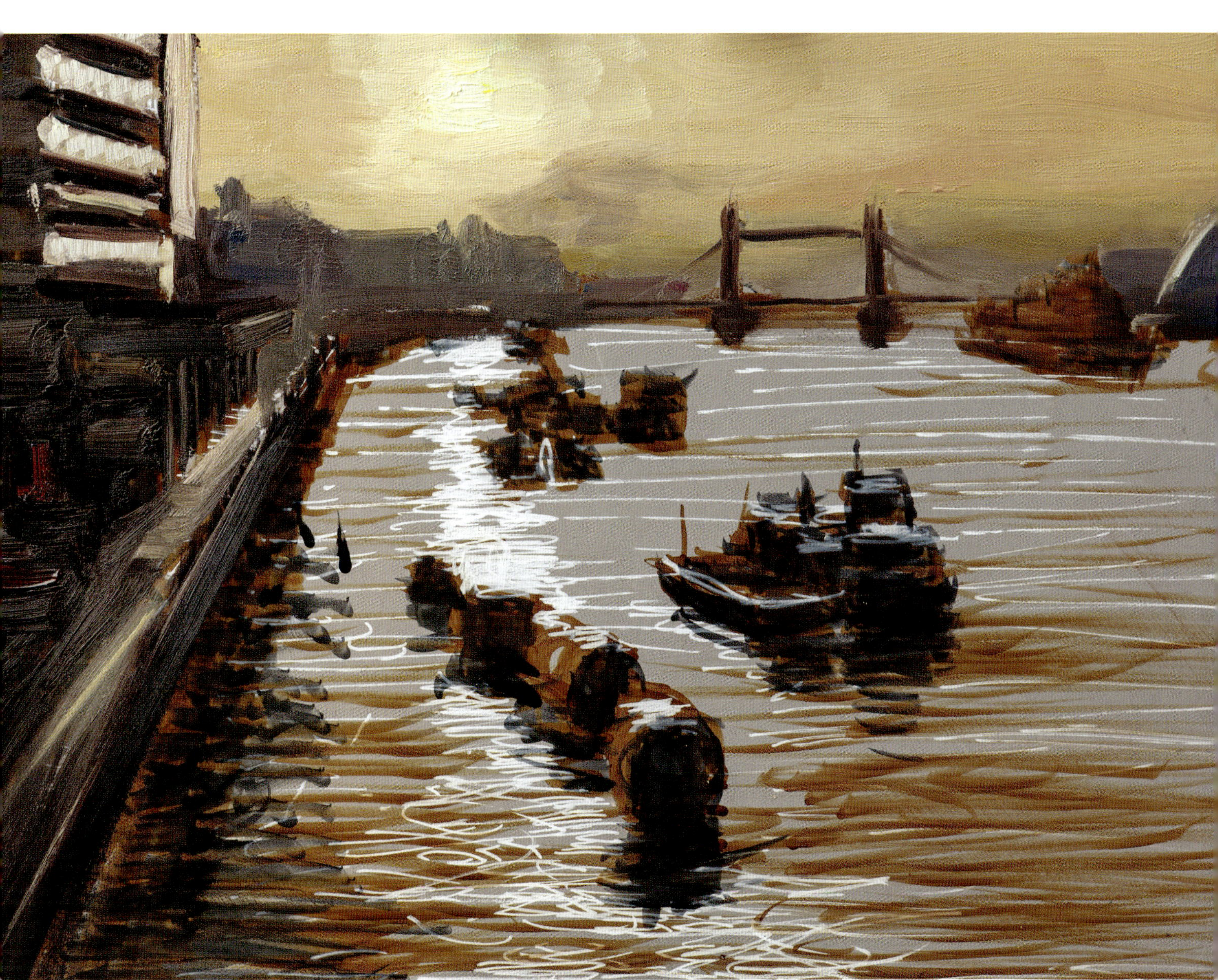

River and foreground

This stage is about creating visual flow between the background and foreground, so you want to create a continuous gradient from light to dark both into the distance and across the width of the river. The marks you make will create the right thoughtful mood, so consider them carefully. The colour of the river on the horizon is relatively light, and will get darker and a darker in tone as it advances. Everything is harmonious, everything is relatively close in tone.

- Create some light tones using titanium white, viridian green, transparent red oxide and cobalt blue. This will be used as the first rays of light on the river's surface. Apply the paint where the river and sky meet.

- Working with slow, broad, horizontal brushstrokes, begin to advance down the painting. Work down the right-hand side of the painting (further from the light) first.

- On the left-hand side of the painting, the buildings cast the river into deep shadow, so use ultramarine blue, viridian green and alizarin crimson for the mixes.

- Add yellow ochre and lemon yellow for the bright reflections in the distance, and cadmium yellow deep for the warmth in the middle distance.

- At the bottom of the picture, add more viridian green and cobalt blue to create heavy, murkier marks.

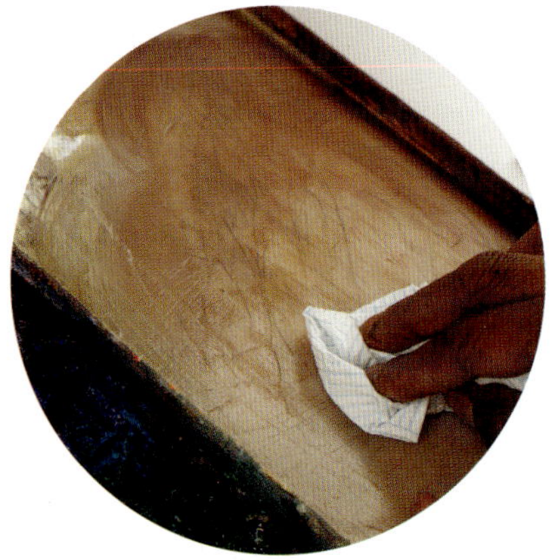

Clean down your palette before starting this stage to ensure clean highlights.

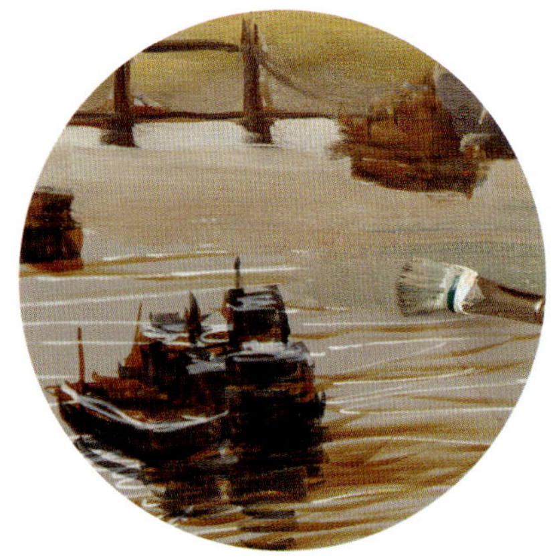

As you advance, introduce more cobalt blue and viridian – and some warming raw sienna – to avoid the river's surface becoming gloomy or dull.

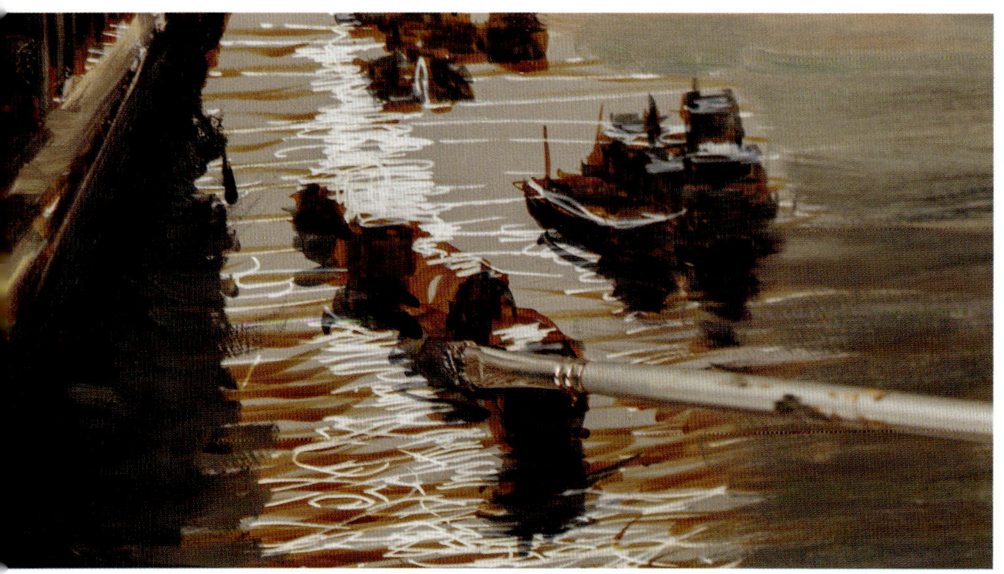

The dark reflections of the boats and river furniture can be painted in with the same darks as on the left-hand side of the river.

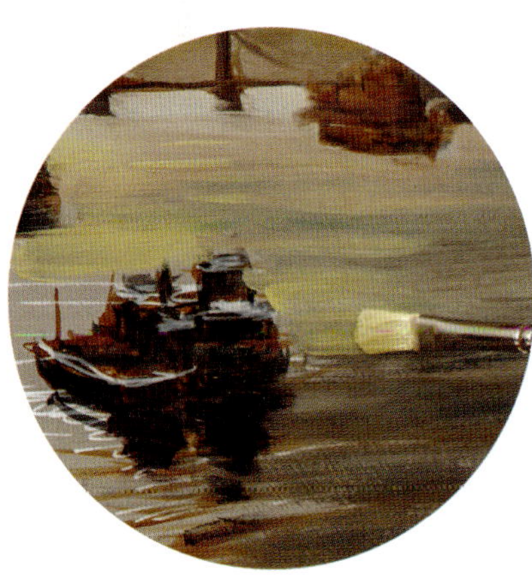

Overlap and use long, light brushstrokes as you advance so that every mark blurs into the next. You don't want to add marks that grab the eye.

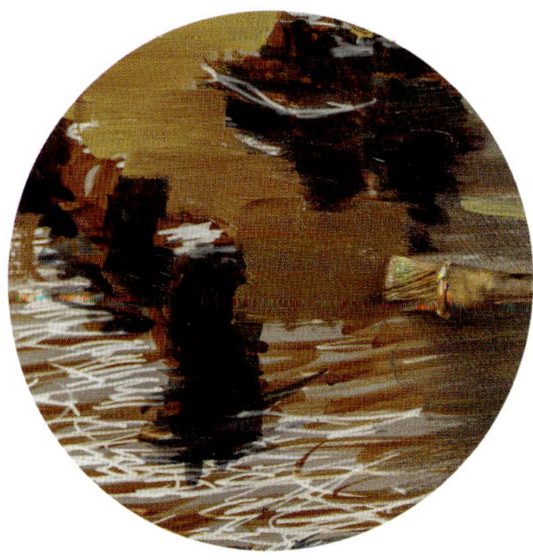

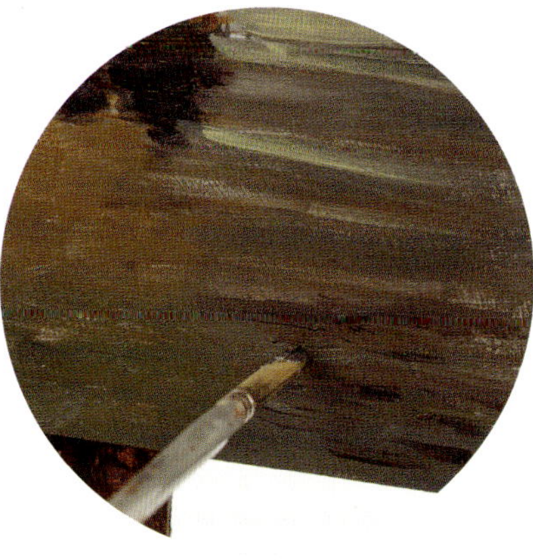

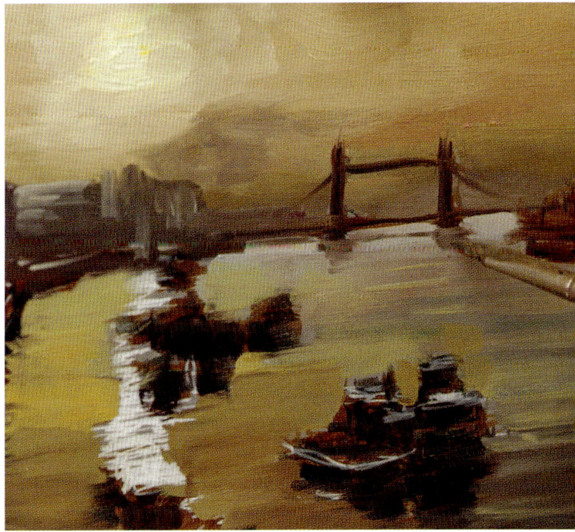

In the foreground, the introduction of cadmium yellow deep gives a warmth and orange tinge to the water. The colour is not in the photograph, but helps to replicate the colours in the sky for overall harmony.

Short, stabbing strokes made with the tip of the brush help to add a little detail and realism to the otherwise very impressionistic river, and make the painting more convincing.

With the river blocked in, you can return to add a few highlights to the buildings on the horizon, and reflections of Tower Bridge on the surface of the river.

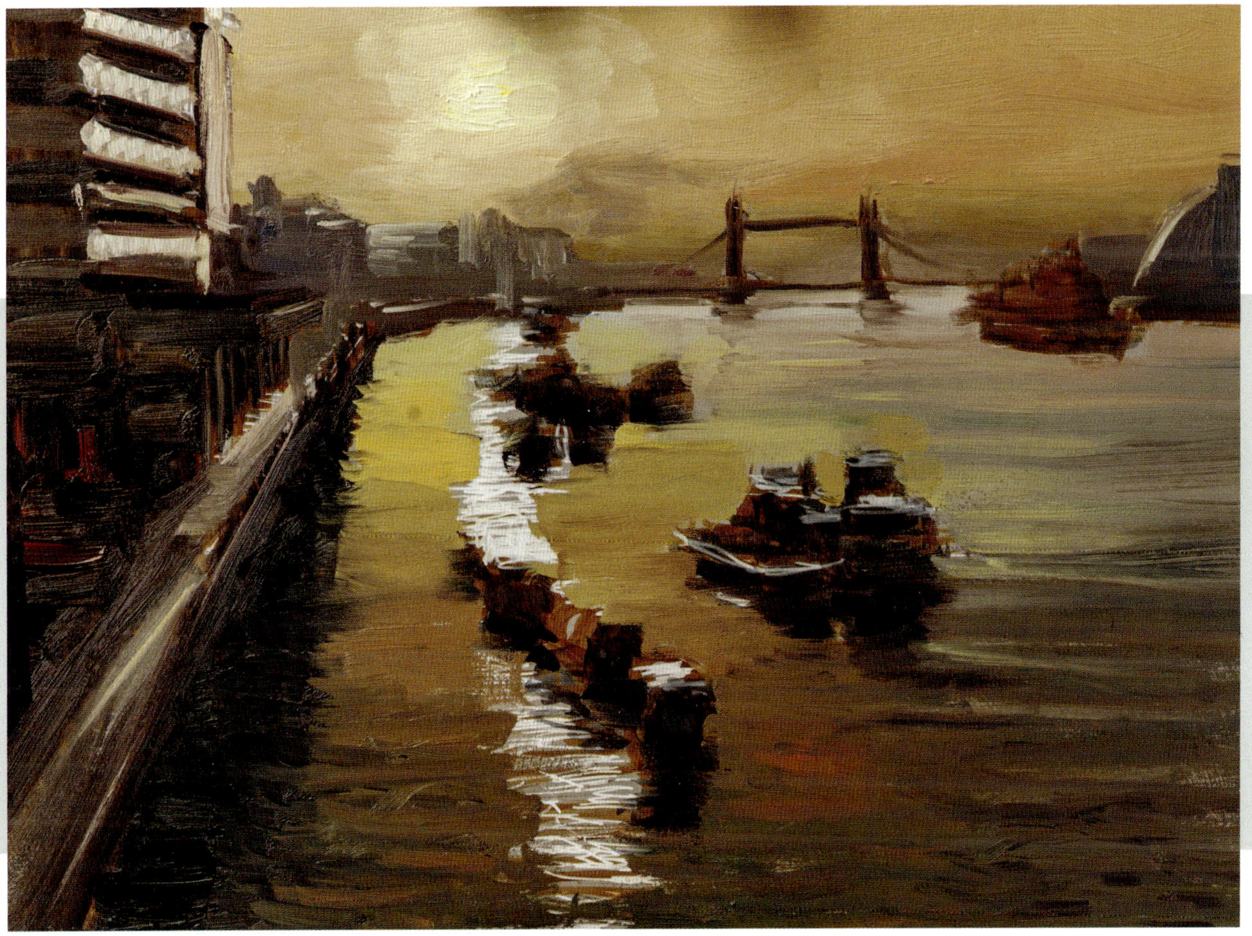

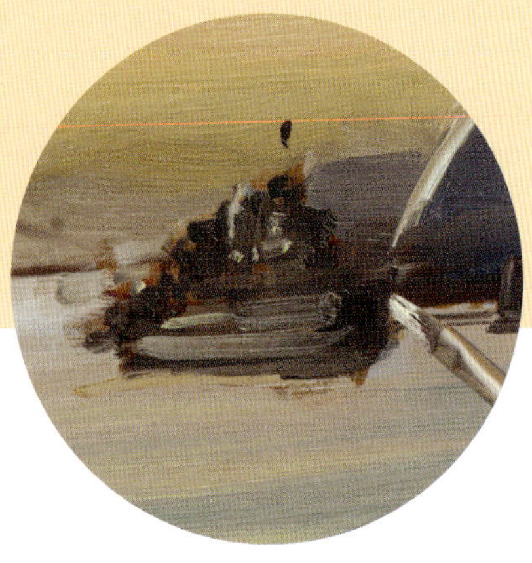

Don't neglect the water when developing the boats: use the same colours to add some marks on the river that settle them into place.

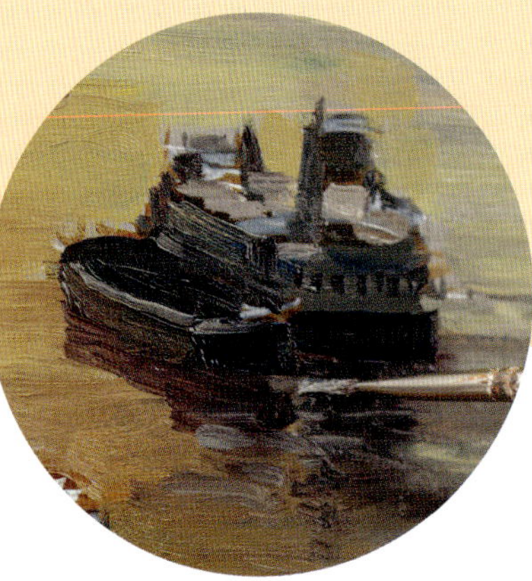

Feel free to swap down to a smaller brush early when adding fine detail. Here I'm using a size 2 round.

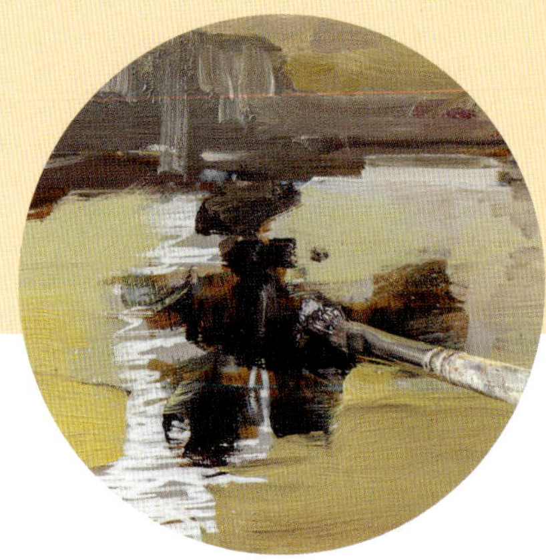

This central midground area is complex – even confusing – so just take it slowly and look carefully.

Boats and sunlight

There are two broad parts to this stage: painting everything on the surface of the river, and adding the striking highlights on the river. This is a stage of refining and developing, so don't worry if the sketch marks don't make sense immediately. The complex objects will take care of themselves if you look closely and build them up from simple shapes.

We're largely using the mixes on our palette at this stage, so there's no need to worry about mixing new colours. Concentrate on tone, mood and brushmarks.

- Swap down to a size 2 filbert for the distant boat. Nothing should stand out here: you want to create an overall impression of the boat using the mixes on your palette.

- Treat the shapes on the river as just that: shapes. Don't try to work out what they are; just look for tones and shapes and put the right tone in the right place and they'll gradually resolve themselves.

- The larger boat in the foreground will need a little more detail than the more distant ones, but you're still primarily aiming for an impression.

- For the very thick highlights on the water, swap to a size 2 filbert that's been cut down. Add a lot of Maroger to titanium white and lemon yellow. Working from the horizon downwards, begin to apply the paint to the rippled reflection of the sunlight.

- Blend in the heavy-bodied white reflections by combining the light mix with the colours on your palette, then swap to the rigger for the tiny details.

- From here, it's simply a case of refining until you are happy. Be careful not to overwork the painting. Just use the colours on your palette to add a few final details.

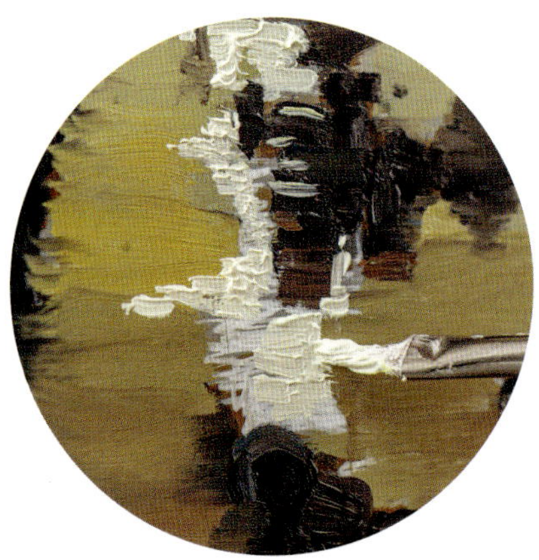

The sunlight adds life to the painting, so take your time and enjoy the process of applying heavy-bodied paint. The brush itself barely touches the surface; allow the paint to cling on where it touches.

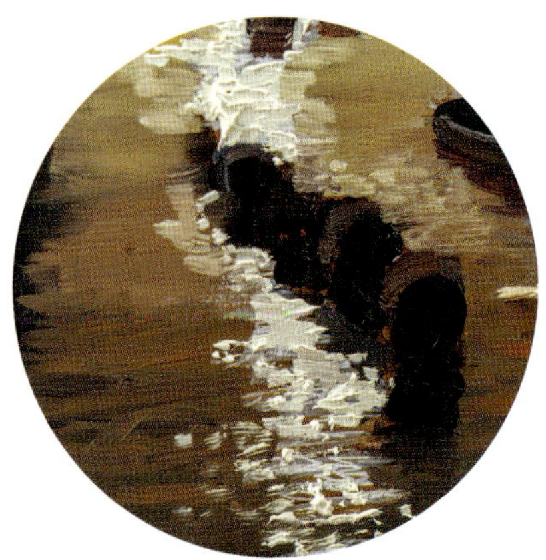

Take your time with the highlights and ripples to ensure a convincing complexity to the water's surface.

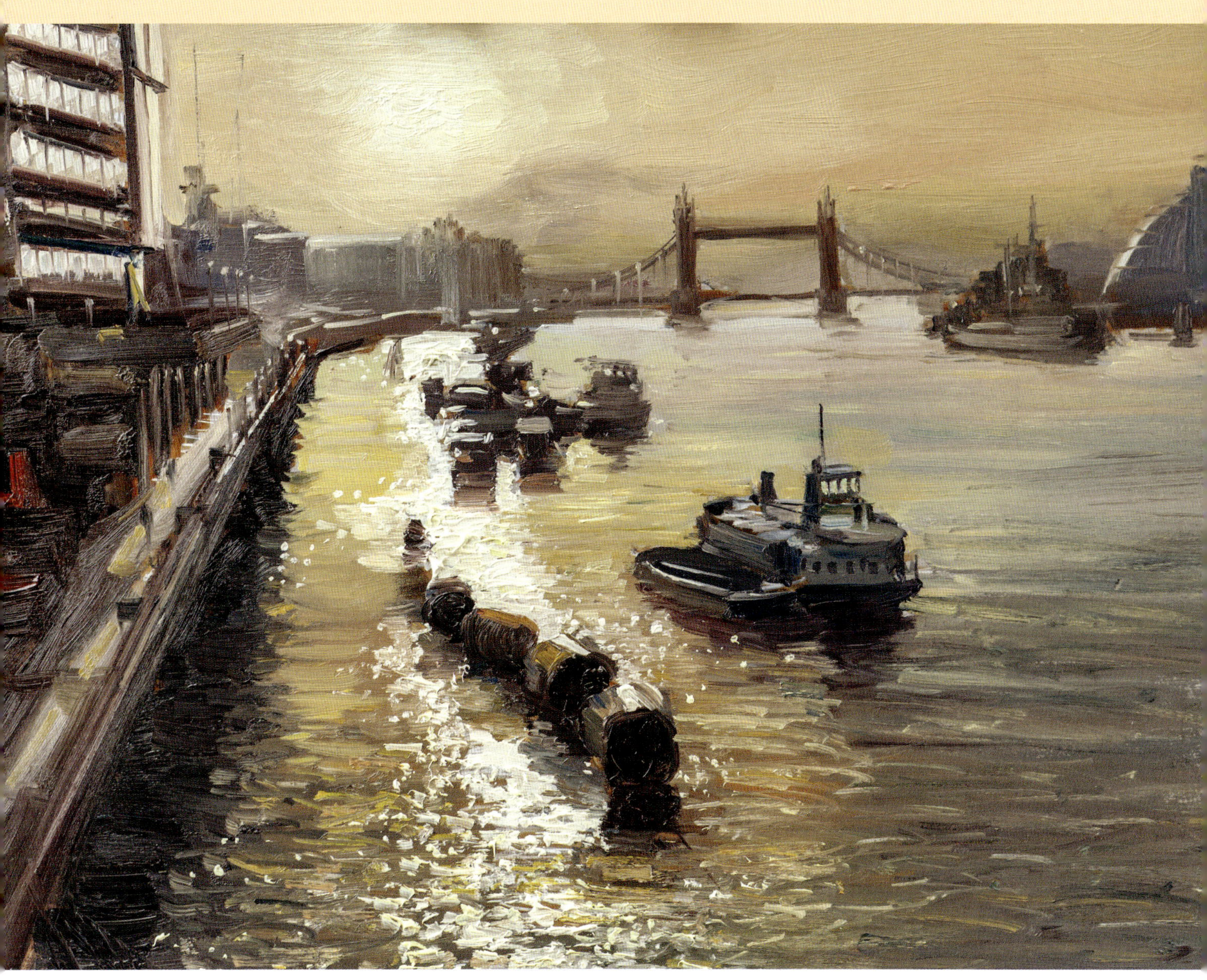

The finished painting

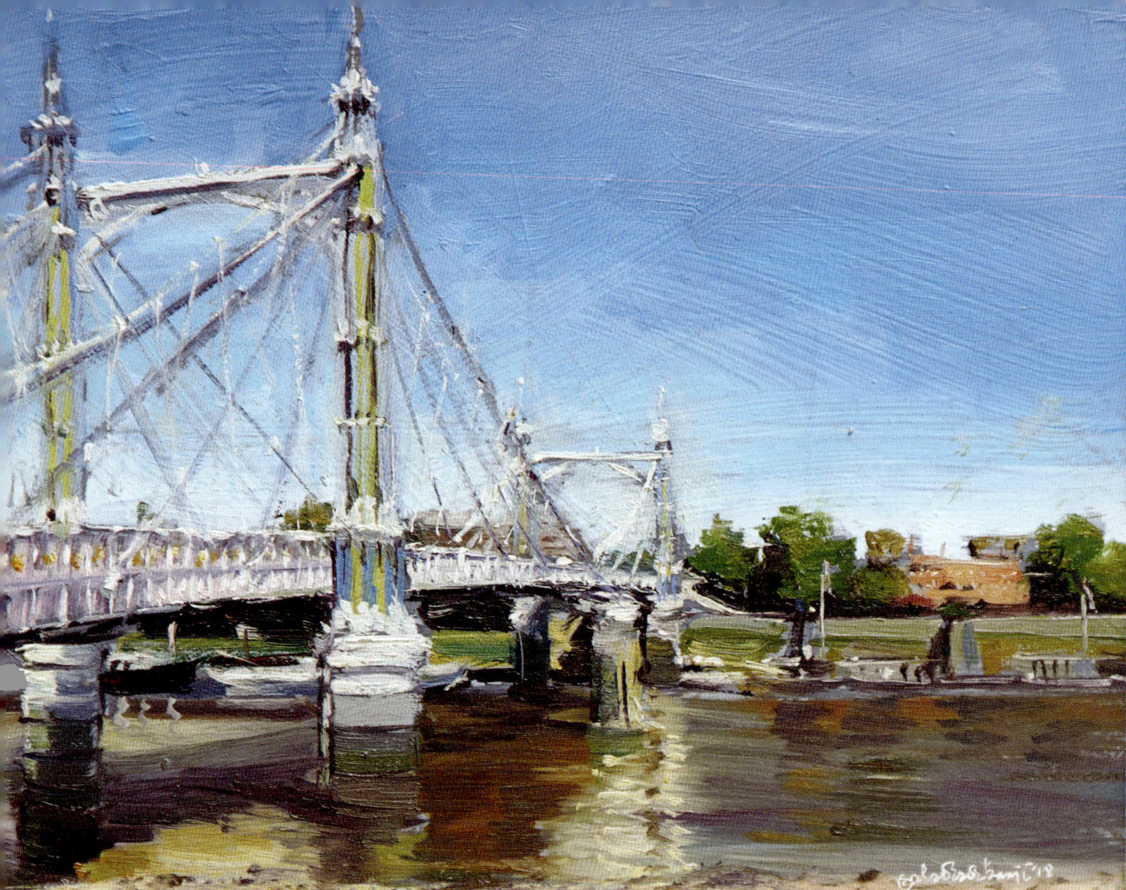

Placing the horizon

Placing the horizon is so important in any painting, but particularly so for seascapes. You should decide very early on whether you want more sky or more water in the painting, as knowing what you want to emphasize in a painting like this can change the whole dynamic. The placement of the horizon fundamentally changes the composition, so give it plenty of thought.

For seascapes, it's more common to place the horizon higher up the painting, giving more weight and emphasis to the water. When I decide to have more sky, it's usually because the water is not that interesting to paint, or I have a particular idea in mind – as in *Albert Bridge*, above. Here, the focus is the bridge itself, so I placed the horizon lower down to avoid drawing the viewer's eye from it. Placing the bridge against clear sky, rather than complex ripples and waves, helps the complex shape to read out, too.

It's unusual to have the horizon exactly halfway across a landscape painting, as it splits the composition into parts of equal weight – the eye doesn't know which to go for. For seascapes, however, it can work well, as the difference in brushstrokes and energy makes for striking contrast. In *Morning Light Reflections, Battersea Power Station*, opposite, it simply means sky and land are of equal importance – but note how your eye is drawn back and forth between the building and its reflection.

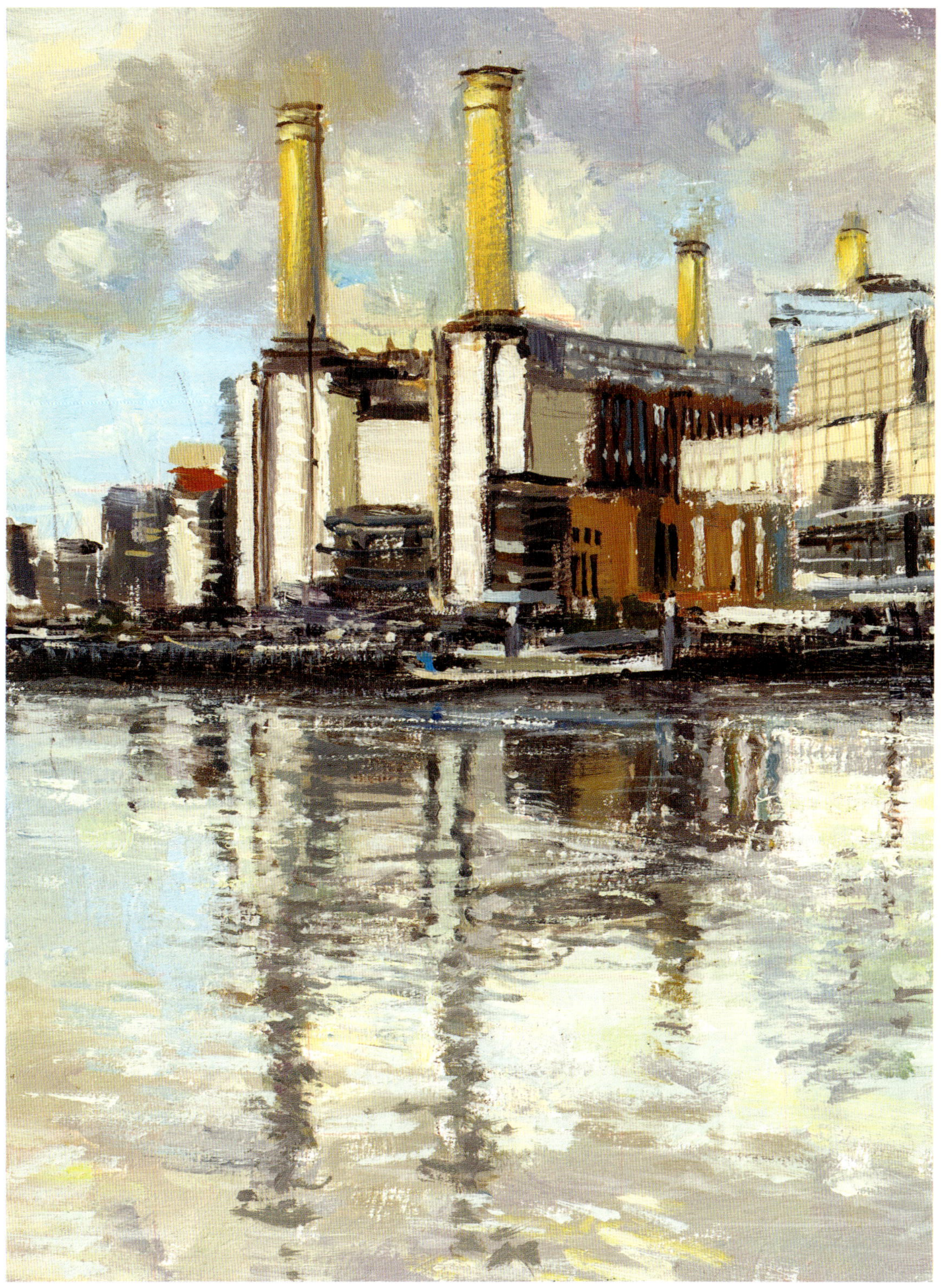

Morning Light Reflections, Battersea Power Station

15 × 20cm (6 × 8in)

Painted from a photograph I took some years back, this painting of Battersea Power Station is really more about the reflections of the station on the water than anything else. I wanted to emphasize the reflections, so they were worked to ensure they looked a bit more interesting than in real life.

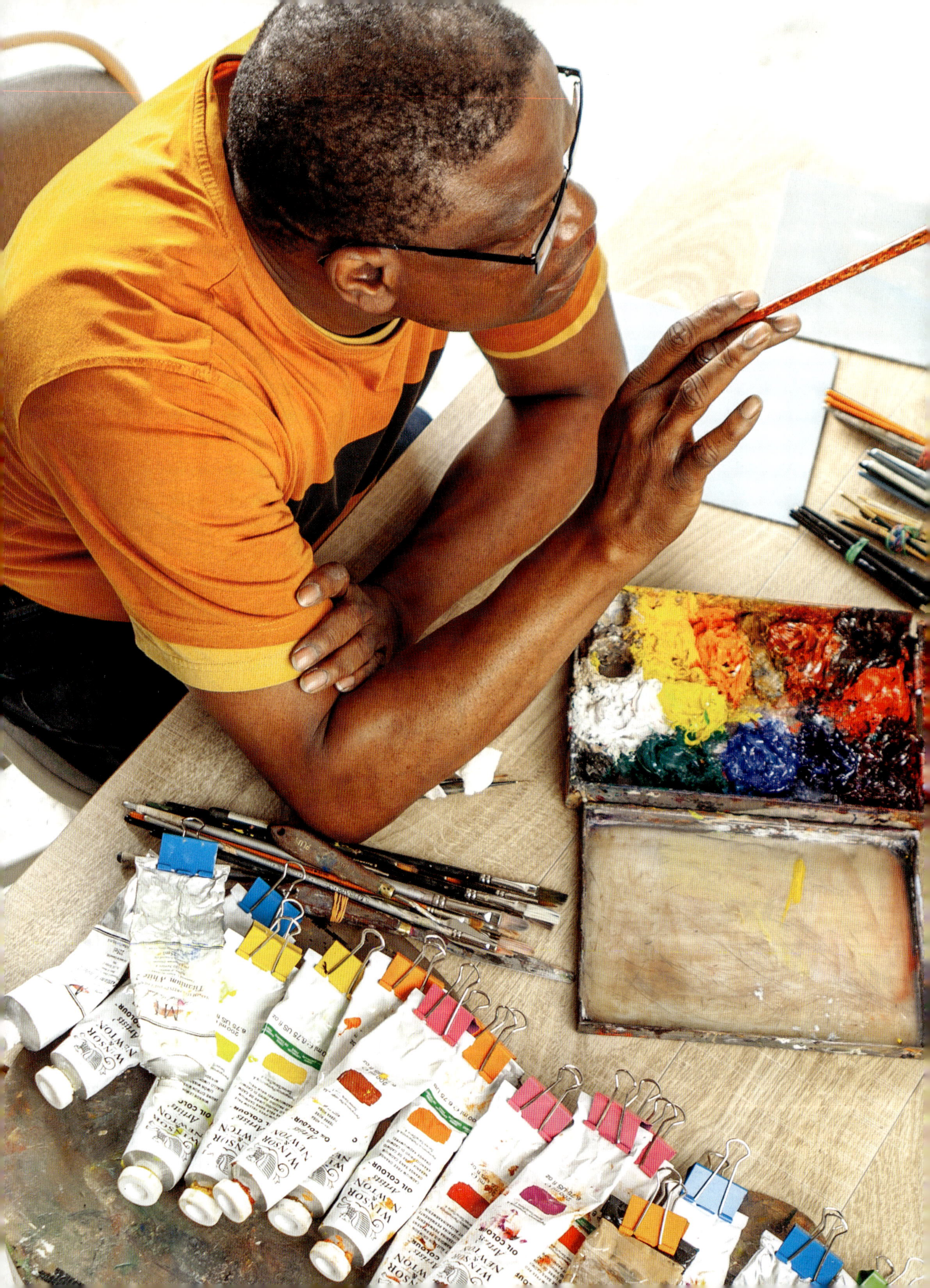

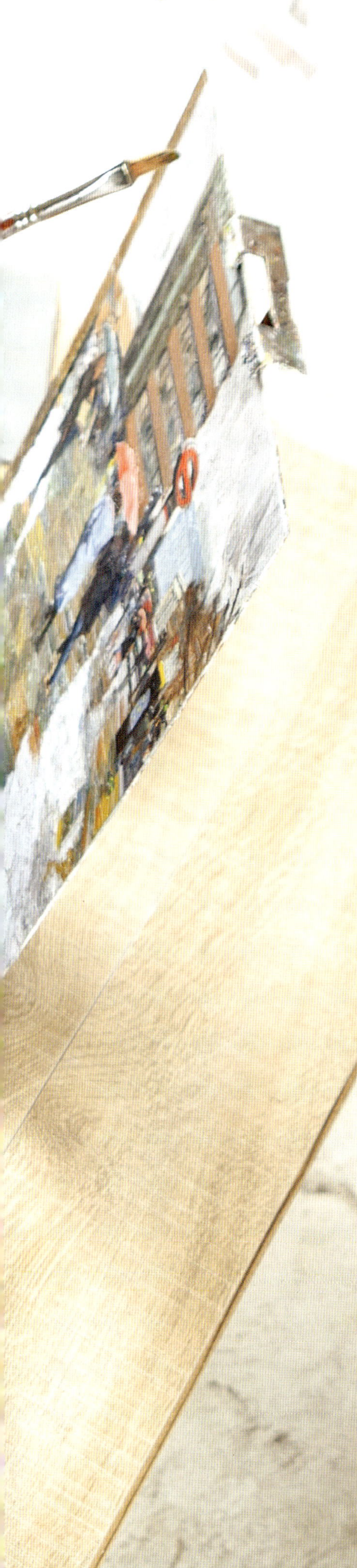

Afterword

I HOPE YOU HAVE ENJOYED THIS BOOK and that it has inspired you to consider people and places in a new light. Every artist has their own unique way of expressing their ideas and working out their techniques to make their paintings sing. If you have read my first two books, you will already have known how sketching forms the bedrock of everything I do. Making the foundation of your work – the sketch – really solid will ensure that painting will just happen naturally, and you won't have to think too much about drawing as you paint. This method might be totally new to you, in which case I hope it helps you explore further, and leads you to discover your own new techniques and strategies. I also hope this book serves as a springboard to keep you painting people and places for as long as you can while here on planet earth.

Another point I'd like to raise here, which is a common concern for many artists, is the question of whether it is right to paint from photographs or not. That discussion will go on for as long as we live. For myself, I simply say that while the debate goes on, painters like me are just getting more work done – and that's just what I want you to do, too. Just keep painting, just keep creating, just keep bringing those ideas into fruition. Whether you paint from life or from photographs, the fact that you are painting will bring you rewards and an artistic advantage. And if you were born to do this, you will know no peace and fulfilment unless you constantly – and consistently – do what you were born to do.

I'll end by saying that the world needs to see what you see when you encounter people and places; the world needs to celebrate what you find fascinating; the world is waiting for your version of the beauty that surrounds you, and the only way you can achieve this is to show them through your works. Don't tell them – *SHOWDEMMMM*!

Index